# Praise for PETER MATTHIESSEN

"Mr. Matthiessen has three indispensable qualities for an all-around writer: a sense of style, a sense of humor, and an ungovernable curiosity."
                                        —*The New York Times*

"Peter Matthiessen is beyond dispute the best nature writer working today."
            —Peter Farb, author of *Man's Rise to Civilization*

"The best nature writer since John Burroughs."
                                        —William Styron

"Matthiessen has a strong claim to being the most distinguished all-around writer of our post-war years. The breadth and quality of his achievements in fiction and social history, in ethnography and travel writing, in biography and environmental writing, is simply stunning."
            —Frederick Turner, author of *Beyond Geography*

"There is, to my mind, no writing life more vital and of greater distinction in the second half of our century."
            —Howard Norman, author of *The Bird Artist*

# THE PETER MATTHIESSEN READER

## NONFICTION 1959–1991

Peter Matthiessen was born in New York City in 1927 and had already begun his writing career by the time he graduated from Yale University in 1950. The following year, he was a founder of *The Paris Review*. His career as a naturalist and explorer has resulted in numerous widely acclaimed books of nonfiction, among them *The Tree Where Man Was Born*, which was nominated for the National Book Award, and *The Snow Leopard*, which won it. Mr. Matthiessen is also an acclaimed novelist, whose works include *At Play in the Fields of the Lord*, which was nominated for the National Book Award, and eight other works of fiction.

A former staff writer for *The Atlanta Constitution*, McKay Jenkins has a master's degree in journalism from Columbia and a Ph.D. in English from Princeton. He currently teaches literature and nonfiction writing at the University of Delaware. He is the author of *The White Death*, a book about avalanches, and *The South in Black and White*, a book about race and literature in the 1940s. He lives in Philadelphia.

## Books by Peter Matthiessen

### Nonfiction
Wildlife in America
The Cloud Forest
Under the Mountain Wall
Sal Si Puedes
The Wind Birds
Blue Meridian
The Tree Where Man Was Born
The Snow Leopard
Sand Rivers
In the Spirit of Crazy Horse
Indian Country
Nine-Headed Dragon River
Men's Lives
African Silences
East of Lo Monthang

### Fiction
Race Rock
Partisans
Raditzer
At Play in the Fields of the Lord
Far Tortuga
On the River Styx and Other Stories
Killing Mister Watson
Lost Man's River
Bone by Bone

# THE

# PETER
# MATTHIESSEN

## READER

NONFICTION 1959–1991

# THE

# PETER
# MATTHIESSEN

## READER

NONFICTION 1959–1991

Edited with an Introduction by **McKay Jenkins**

**VINTAGE BOOKS**
A Division of Random House, Inc.
New York

For Brian and Denny

—M.J.

Library of Congress Cataloging-in-Publication Data
Matthiessen, Peter.
The Peter Matthiessen reader / edited with an introduction by
McKay Jenkins.
p.    cm.
ISBN 0-375-70272-5
I. Jenkins, McKay, 1963–    .  II. Title.
PS3563.A8584A6   2000
813'.54—dc21        99-35246
CIP

www.vintagebooks.com

# Editor's Acknowledgments

Thanks to William Howarth, for setting an example, and to Neil Olson, for his patience and skill. At Vintage, thanks to Dawn Davis, Adam Pringle, Susan Brown, and Mark Maguire. Most of all, thanks to Peter Matthiessen, for his lifetime of good work and good spirit.

# Contents

## x | Contents

# Introduction

## McKay Jenkins

**The opening passages of** Peter Matthiessen's first nonfiction book, *Wildlife in America*, tell the story of the great auk, a species of North Atlantic bird wiped out in the mid-nineteenth century. These first pages describe a group of hunters on the island of Eldey, off the coast of Iceland, looking for the great auk, which, having been "slaughtered indiscriminately" for its flesh, feathers, and oil, was nearing extinction, with no protection in sight. The hunters, Matthiessen writes, smashed the solitary egg they found and killed two birds for their skins—"a fact all the more saddening when one considers that, on all the long coasts of the northern ocean, no auk was ever seen alive again.

> One imagines with misgiving the last scene on desolate Eldey. Offshore, the longboat wallows in a surge of seas, then slices forward in the lull, its stern grinding hard on the rock ledge. The hunters hurl the two dead birds aboard and, cursing, tumble after, as the boat falls away into the wash. . . . The finality of extinction is awesome, and not unrelated to the finality of eternity. Man, striving to imagine what might lie beyond the long light years of stars, beyond the universe, beyond the void, feels lost in space; confronted with the death of species, enacted on earth so many times before he came, and certain to continue when his own breed is gone, he is forced to face another void, and feels alone in time. Species appear and, left behind by a changing earth, they disappear forever, and there is a certain solace in the inexorable. But until man, the highest predator, evolved, the process of extinction was a slow one. No species but man, so far as is known, unaided by circumstance or climatic

change, has ever extinguished another, and certainly no species has ever devoured itself, an accomplishment of which man appears quite capable.

*Wildlife in America* did much to cultivate Matthiessen's image as a kind of Thoreau-on-the-Road; as legend has it, his research included driving a convertible around the country equipped with only a stack of books, a sleeping bag, and a shotgun. Over the years that image has stuck, sometimes to Matthiessen's dismay. His many readers like to think of him as a kind of literary Indiana Jones, searching the wilds of New Guinea or Africa or Nepal and bringing stories back alive. Certainly this hard-traveling reputation has been earned; no writer of his time has logged more miles, in more remote places, than Peter Matthiessen. But lost in the romantic image is the recognition of a remarkable literary voice, characterized mostly by a deep mourning for the natural magic the world has lost, and is losing. Matthiessen's work is marked above all by an unblinking gaze at the world's subtle beauty, and at its fragility when set against humankind's blundering self-interest. In a passage from a book about Africa, *Sand Rivers*, Matthiessen considers the black rhino, nearly obliterated by poachers: "Its rough prong of compacted hair would be hacked off with a panga and shoved into a gunny sack as the triumphant voice of man moved onward, leaving behind in the African silence the dead weight of the carcass, the end-product of millions of browsing, sun-filled mornings, as the dependent calf emerges from the thicket and stands by dumbly to await the lion."

Matthiessen's body of nonfiction can be seen as a sharp and consistent critique of half a century of capitalist expansion, resource exploitation, and political hubris, in America and abroad. In the late 1950s, when he began his work, postwar markers of environmental degradation like atomic explosions, urban decay, and chemically sanitized American suburbs began to darken much of the period's literature, particularly that concerned with the natural world. In *Silent Spring*, published first in a 1962 edition of *The New Yorker*—a magazine that has also published much of Matthiessen's work—Rachel Carson warned about the human capacity to "alter the nature" of our world. The intensity of Carson's rhetoric matches that of the early Matthiessen, who from the beginning developed an acute distaste for the by-products of American capitalism. His books about native American history, *Indian Country* and *In the Spirit of Crazy Horse*, are powerful critiques of twentieth-century versions of Manifest Destiny; his book about Long Island fishermen, *Men's Lives*, was widely praised for its ability to capture both the dwindling landscape and the depressed working conditions under which the few remaining local fishermen labored. "Matthiessen's portrayal of a disappearing way of life has a biting eloquence no outside reporter could command," *Newsweek* declared. "The fishermen's voices—humorous, bitter, bewildered, resigned—are as clear as the technical procedures of their work and the threatened beauty of their once quiet shore."

Throughout his writings Matthiessen relies on scientific accuracy and his own extensive fieldwork to bolster the political and artistic integrity of his work. He painstakingly credits those from whom he has drawn inspiration, among them scientists, historians, and archivists at museums and universities; naturalists and "field men" at the U.S. Fish and Wildlife Service; and conservationists and rangers working at national parks and wildlife refuges. But if his research is scrupulous in its attention to science, it is only so because it offers his writing an additional stance from which to explore the ineffable. Another book that grew from the landscape of his home on Long Island, *The Shorebirds of North America* (later reprinted as *The Wind Birds*), provides not only elegiac descriptions but an intricate catalog of threatened species. "The sense of beauty and mystery is indelible," Jim Harrison has written of Matthiessen's work. "Not that you retain the specific information on natural history, but that you have had your brain, and perhaps the soul, prodded, urged, moved into a new dimension." Writing in *The Washington Post Book World*, Terrence Des Pres called Matthiessen "a visionary, but he is very hard-minded as well, and his attention is wholly with abrupt detail. This allows him to render strangeness familiar, and much that is menial becomes strange, lustrous, otherworldly."

The handful of pieces collected here, arranged chronologically to give a sense of Matthiessen's growth as an artist, were culled from a body of work matched in its literary polish and sheer volume by very few writers this century. Not included, of course, is the equally impressive catalog of Matthiessen's fiction, which especially since the completion of the Watson trilogy (*Killing Mister Watson, Lost Man's River,* and *Bone by Bone*) in 1999 has cemented his reputation as a narrative stylist of the highest order.

Some of the selections found here were made in consultation with Matthiessen during a visit to his home on Long Island. Others, like the selections from *Sal Si Puedes* and *Sand Rivers,* were chosen because they have gone out of print or fallen from view. Countless additional pieces had to be left out for lack of space: Matthiessen's book *Baikal,* for example—about a journey to the great, endangered Russian sea—and innumerable pieces of journalism he has written for *Audubon* and *The New Yorker,* some of which he promises to gather himself in future books about cranes, tigers, and Asian travels.

The guiding idea in this collection was to present both Matthiessen's stylistic eloquence and his considerable political energies in all their beauty and power; at his best Matthiessen is able to create images that leave a reader doubly shaken. In the last paragraph of *The Tree Where Man Was Born,* he describes a quiet moment of tribal people in their native Africa: "From a grove off in the western light, an arrow rises, piercing the sun poised on the dark massif of the Sipunga; the shaft glints, balances, and drops to earth. Soon the young hunters, returning homeward, come in single file between the trees, skins black against black silhouetted thorn. One has an mbira, and in wistful monotony, in hesitation step, the naked forms pass one by one with their small bows in a slow dance of childhood, the figures winding in and out among black thorn and tawny twilight grass, and vanishing once more as in a dream, like a band of the Old People, the small Gumba, who long ago went into hiding in the earth."

Here and elsewhere Matthiessen has the eyes of a tracker. Like the native people and field biologists who so often accompany his travels, he cocks his head, sniffs the air, puts palm to ground. So full of details is his writing, so luminous his prose, that after just a few pages a reader grants him the kind of trust a voyager gives a well-weathered guide; his choice of sonorous native words only enhances the sensuous pleasure of the expedition. In all his travels Matthiessen promises more than excitement; he promises subtlety, the unexpected, the delightful surprise. Writing elsewhere of Africa, he remarks that "in the Selous, one can sip rain with impunity from pools and puddles and even from big footprints in the mud."

The vibrancy of Matthiessen's work comes from his unequaled powers of observation and the remarkable clarity with which he transmits this to the page. In a passage of his book *Nine-Headed Dragon River*, a collection of journals about his Zen training, he tells of his admiration for the writings of the thirteenth-century Zen patriarch Dogen: "Like all born writers, he wrote for the sheer exuberance of the writing, in a manner unmistakably fresh and poetic, reckless and profound. Though the risks he takes make the prose difficult, one is struck at once by an intense love of language, a mastery of paradox and repetition, meticulous nuance and startling image, swept along by a strong lyric sensibility in a mighty effort to express the inexpressible, the universal or absolute, that is manifest in the simplest objects and events of everyday life." Appropriate to a man who has spent nearly half a century writing and half a lifetime practicing Zen—his greatest literary expression of this spiritual journey appears in *The Snow Leopard*, excerpted here—Matthiessen's own pursuit of the inexpressible has made him one of our most celebrated, versatile, and influential writers. His prose too is difficult and nuanced, and, like good poetry, serves as a pond mirroring the stars. His language is full of vivid nouns and verbs rather than overwrought adjectives; his work is marked by movement rather than ornamentation. Matthiessen is remarkably attentive to sights and sounds, and relies almost not at all on human conversation; he avoids long swatches of empty dialogue, which for many nonfiction writers serves as a kind of crutch. One gets the sense that he relies more on his own intuitive reading of people and landscapes than he does on received wisdom from anyone else. Talking, he writes, almost invariably detracts from the real pleasure of walking.

Given his lifelong fascination with wild nature, Matthiessen has often faced one of writing's most difficult challenges: giving literary life to the nonhuman world. "On the old shore there is no sign of life, no bird, only gray shell and dusty rock and small concretions that hold fossils. All is dead but for a solitary toothbrush bush, msawki, drawing a magic green from the spent stone. Then out of the emptiness flies a hare with a gaunt jackal in pursuit. The animals whisk back and forth, they circle rises; the hare dives into the lone bush, the jackal close behind. A rigid silence is pierced by a small shriek. Soon the jackal reappears, hare in its jaws, and reverting to its furtive gait, makes off with its quarry down a gully. The rocks are still." [*The Tree Where Man Was Born*]

Such writing is devoid of sentimentality, but more than that, it is acutely attentive, not just to the drama of the moment but to the vast quiet that then hangs in the air like the resonance of a brass gong. How many writers would have bothered to note the stillness of the rocks? Matthiessen lingers a moment longer than he might have, aware that the rocks, which existed before and will exist after the death scene, offer a blank stare to the drama that goes on around them. His scrupulous attention to the sensuous world is one of his defining traits; the capacity to notice the particular and infer the universal is for him a poetic as well as a spiritual practice. "The only way to be *truly* universal is to be very particular, moment by moment, detail by detail," one of Matthiessen's Zen teachers told him. "If you are merely 'universal,' you lose the feel of life, you become abstract, facile. . . . But if the emphasis on everyday detail is too rigid, our existence loses the religious power of the universal."

Matthiessen's own paragraphs manifest this point. They are vivid impressions of life as it occurs, tragic or sweet, registered by wide-open eyes. As an observer he takes everything in with an innocent amazement, as did the younger Rachel Carson, or Annie Dillard. But beyond the sense of wonder, his work is always touched with an abiding sadness, filled with wistful, resonant notes about the evanescence of life. "The rain forest communities are the oldest on earth, with hundreds of insect species specific to each of the many species of its trees," he writes in *African Silences*. "Almost half of the earth's living things, many as yet undiscovered, live in this green world that is shrinking fast to a small patch on the earth's surface. Man has already destroyed half of the rain forests, which disappear at an ever-increasing speed, and a mostly unknown flora and fauna disappear with them. Therefore, at every opportunity, we explore the forest, and often I go out alone, for walking in solitude through the dim glades, immersed in silence, one learns a lot that cannot be learned in any other way."

Throughout his work Matthiessen remains steadfast but heartbroken when confronted by our inexorable drive to subdue wilderness, assimilate native peoples, and wring the mystery from life. As a result he has continued to build a body of work that aspires both to high art and to deep political activism. In a period of American literature when many writers consider their inner torments to be their source of greatest mystery, Matthiessen has relentlessly focused his gaze outward, beyond suburban landscapes, toward wilderness, its threatened human inhabitants, and their punishment at the hand of civilization's wallowing greed and rapacity. In so doing he has inspired an entire generation of writers who have collectively helped make "nature writing" one of the most vibrant fields in contemporary American literature.

Matthiessen also has had a fine time of it. In the author's note to *The Tree Where Man Was Born,* he writes that "I lived mostly at Seronera, where I was very hospitably received by the parks staff and the scientists of the Serengeti Research Institute, set up in 1966 for the crucial ecological studies that will certainly affect the future of man and animal in Africa. Often these men—wardens and scientists alike—took me along on air surveys, field trips, and safaris, and gave me invaluable instruction in African ecology; meanwhile, I had my own Land Rover, with four-wheel drive, and the chance to investigate all and everything, as I pleased."

That desire "to investigate all and everything" is evident in Matthiessen's early work, and his desire to set out from a comfortable upbringing has defined his work in interesting and sometimes complex ways. His dedication to both literature and hard travel, writes William Dowie, a Matthiessen biographer, "is the same duality that is mirrored in the Matthiessen ancestry, with its direct line to the legendary seventeenth-century whaling captain Matthias the Fortunate (who took an astonishing 373 whales in his lifetime), and with literary forebears such as a nineteenth-century novelist Charlotte Matthiessen and twentieth-century critic F. O. Matthiessen, a first cousin of Peter's father."

Peter Matthiessen was born in New York City on May 22, 1927 (hours after Charles Lindbergh landed in Paris), to Erard A. and Elizabeth Carey Matthiessen. His older sister was Mary Seymour, and his younger brother, George Carey. His father was a successful architect who, after the Second World War, became a fund-raiser, spokesman, and trustee for conservation groups such as the Audubon Society and the Nature Conservancy. From Peter's earliest years his schooling was private: St. Bernard's School in New York City, Greenwich Country Day, Hotchkiss, and Yale, from which he graduated in 1950 after spending his junior year at the Sorbonne.

Matthiessen's early years were sheltered from much of the human suffering and ecological degradation he would later devote his life to writing about. "The Depression had no serious effect on our well-insulated family, which maintained a summer house on Fisher's Island, a country house with a fine view of the Hudson, and a comfortable apartment around the corner from St. Bernard's at 1165 Fifth Avenue," Matthiessen wrote in an article published in *Architectural Digest* in 1989. "I admit to a lot of rich-boy fun, brushing past the street poor with the cool callousness one must cultivate to avoid the discomforts of guilt, pity, or distress."

In the piece, Matthiessen recalls a time when, as a teenager, his

formerly uproarious and heedless nature turned dark and moody. Brooding, lonely, aching with romantic longings for unfettered "real life," I had developed a small drinking problem, and one morning during my great-aunt's absence on a voyage, I was accosted by the elevator man while lugging in a bag of booze. This kind tough man had noticed my erratic comings and goings, which did not seem to include shopping for food, and he stopped his elevator between floors to bawl me out. . . .

One bitter night early that winter, passing a dark alley off Twelfth Street, not far from University Place, I made out a still form deep in the shadows. Entering the alley, I shook the man hard, offering hot soup or coffee, for fear he might catch his death of cold. Alas, he had already perished; the stiff middle-aged corpus had no pulse. Too late to be of use to him, and late for class at The New School for Social Research, I abandoned him to municipal attentions. At the mouth of the alley, I looked back at the first dead human I had ever touched—even the poor clothes he wore, the broken shoes, looked done for—and went on about my sheltered life more uneasy than ever.

Matthiessen's impressions of New York City—and America generally—bear the mark of a deep alienation born out of such experience: "A city that I once found exhilarating now seems oppressive in its noise and filth, and the homeless and hopeless on the stoops and benches, the humans lying in sharp-smelling crannies of the railway stations, as that dead man lay in that back alley years ago, reawaken the old anger and disappointment that history's richest (and at times most generous) nation should produce a leadership so shortsighted and greedy. Suppressed rage seeps through these city cracks like hardweeds through a broken sidewalk."

Matthiessen served in the Navy toward the end of World War II, and it was in the Navy that he got his first journalism experience, writing about sports for the *Honolulu Advertiser* while stationed at Pearl Harbor in 1945–46. Matthiessen has said he wanted to be a writer early on and "can't remember even considering doing anything else after I was about fifteen or sixteen." While still at Yale, Matthiessen published a short story titled "Sadie" (collected in *On the River Styx*) that won the Atlantic Prize from the *Atlantic Monthly*. When the *Atlantic* took a second story, Matthiessen got an agent and set out upon a career in fiction. "I started my first novel and sent off about four chapters and waited by the post office for praise to roll in, calls from Hollywood, everything," he told the interviewer Kay Bonetti. "Finally my agent sent me a letter that said, 'Dear Peter: James Fenimore Cooper wrote this a hundred and fifty years ago, only he wrote it better. Yours, Bernice.'"

After Yale, Matthiessen went to Paris, where, with Harold Humes, he founded *The Paris Review*. Matthiessen invited his childhood friend George Plimpton to be editor, and he credits Plimpton with holding the influential magazine together. From the outset the review published a number of notable pieces, including Samuel Beckett's first appearance in an English-speaking magazine and some of the earliest work by Jack Kerouac, Terry Southern, and Philip Roth.

While in Paris he and Ben Bradlee, who would go on to become the legendary editor of *The Washington Post* during the Watergate era and beyond, wrote an "Annals of Crime" piece for *The New Yorker* about Yvonne Chevalier, on trial for the murder of her husband. It was during an editing flap over this piece that Matthiessen first met *The New Yorker* editor William Shawn, whose magazine would subsequently finance much of Matthiessen's world travel writing, beginning with *The Cloud Forest* (1961).

In a wry piece entitled "Looking for Hemingway," published in *Esquire* in 1963, Gay Talese wrote that "*The Paris Review* Crowd" had, ten years earlier, made Matthiessen's Paris apartment "as much a meeting place for the young American literati as was Gertrude Stein's apartment in the Twenties." Unimpressed, Talese sniffed at the literary pretension of "the witty, irreverent sons of a conquering nation [who] though they came mostly from wealthy parents and had been graduated from Harvard or Yale, seemed endlessly delighted in posing as paupers and dodging the bill collectors. . . . They are obsessed, so many of them, by the wish to know how the other half lives. And so they befriend the more interesting of the odd, avoid the dullards on Wall Street, and dip into the world of the junkie, the pederast, the prizefighter, and the adventurer in pursuit of kicks and literature, being influenced perhaps by that glorious generation of ambulance drivers that preceded them to Paris at the age of twenty-six."

To be sure, Matthiessen has long been fascinated by rough characters, but they tend to be trackers of grizzly bears and great white sharks, not urban junkies and pederasts. Because of his ambivalence about his social background, it is perhaps not surprising that Matthiessen has never chosen to write about his place of birth, despite its opportunities for commentary about racial and class-based inequities. But he has written about Eastern Long Island, where he has lived since 1950. In his twenties, to help supplement his writing income, he worked as a bayman and ocean haul-seiner, and ran a deep-sea-fishing charter boat out of Montauk. By 1956, as he later wrote in *Men's Lives,* a book excerpted here, "my days as a commercial fisherman were over. My marriage had disintegrated, my old fishing partners were scattering, and my friend Jackson [Pollock], driving drunk, had destroyed himself and a young woman passenger when he lost control on the Springs-Fireplace Road. . . . [But] three years spent with the commercial men were among the most rewarding of my life, and those hard seasons on the water had not been wasted."

Matthiessen's imagination has long been stirred by men who make their living working outdoors. He has traveled with and written about such celebrated field biologists as George Schaller, David Western, and George Archibald, as well as Doug Peacock, the charismatic Montana grizzly bear advocate. Elsewhere Matthiessen's guides have been less illustrious, if equally colorful. In *The Cloud Forest,* an account of his travels in South America excerpted here, Matthiessen describes a man named Picquet; sounding like Matthiessen himself during his research for *Wildlife in America,* Picquet "arrived on this continent three years ago, traveling alone and on foot, with a shotgun and two compasses, down through the trackless jungles between the Canal Zone and central Colombia . . . since then he has walked, worked, and hitchhiked his way through every country but Paraguay."

*The Cloud Forest* marked the first of many trips Matthiessen would make to the wild regions of the world, and the stories he found in these places would dictate much of the writing—both fiction and nonfiction—that he would produce over the next four decades. Four years after *The Cloud Forest* came a novel about missionaries in the Amazon jungle, *At Play in the Fields of the Lord,* which would be nominated for a National Book Award. In 1961 he set off for New Guinea with a Harvard-Peabody museum expedition to work on *Under the Mountain Wall,* which, together with *The Cloud Forest,* would win an Award of Merit from the National Institute of Arts and Letters in 1963. On the way to New Guinea, he traveled in Sudan, East Africa, India, Nepal, and Southeast Asia, regions he would return to and write about later in his career. In 1964 Matthiessen joined an expedition to the Bering Sea to capture calves of the endangered musk ox for domestic breeding in Alaska; the journey was described in *The New Yorker*, then in a short book, *Oomingmak* (1967). That same year he convinced *The New Yorker* to send him to the Cayman Islands to research the voyage of an ancient schooner sailing to Nicaragua to fish green turtles, a trip that again produced both a nonfiction piece and material for what would become the critically acclaimed novel *Far Tortuga* (1975). "I'd always been drawn to the simplicity, the spareness of sailors. These were expert seamen whose lives were stripped down to nothing. This was true right down to the paint on their boats—you could see through to the wood. That was what struck me. I had just finished *At Play*, and it was full of metaphors; but I wanted this novel to be absolutely spare. I wanted the thing itself, as is said in Zen. I came back to Mr. Shawn and said, 'Mr. Shawn, I'm very embarrassed about this, but I'm going to hold back the best material for a novel. If you don't want the article, I'll return all the expenses and that will be the end of it.' But Mr. Shawn said, 'Mr. Matthiessen, do what's best for your work.'"

Indeed, Matthiessen's career as a nonfiction writer has always been colored by his desire to be thought of first and foremost as a novelist. "For me nonfiction is like making a cabinet," he says. "You can make an absolutely beautiful cabinet with no seams and no glue showing, but it is still a utilitarian object. A fiction writer is like a sculptor. He has no idea where he's going, no idea how it will turn out." Matthiessen is a tireless writer, routinely working on several books—and in several genres—at once; at this writing he has just published the third novel in his Watson trilogy and is completing work on a book about tigers. Remarkably for someone who has published so many books, he maintains exceedingly high standards for the shine of his prose. "I'm a terrific rewriter. I polish and polish and polish and polish," he says. "The last chapter, the descent of the river, in *At Play in the Fields of the Lord*—I'm sure I rewrote that thirty times. Even then I didn't get it the way I wanted it. I had started to wreck it, as one tends to do—you go stale, and become stiff and literary and useless. That's when you have to quit. That's the only reason I quit with *Far Tortuga*. I started to do it damage. If you find yourself coming back the next day and erasing more of the so-called improvements than you keep, you'd better get the hell out of that book."

Despite his preference for fiction, Matthiessen's career in journalism has provided him with enough assignments to stretch any writer's energies. In 1968 he visited Cesar Chavez in California for the book *Sal Si Puedes* (*Escape if You Can*), then spent seven months in Africa researching what would become *The Tree Where Man Was Born*, nominated for a National Book Award and considered by many to be one of his finest books. In 1970 he embarked with the diver Peter Gimbel on a voyage in search of the great white shark, a trip that produced both Gimbel's film *Blue Water, White Death* and Matthiessen's book *Blue Meridian*. A two-hundred-fifty mile trek through the Himalayas in 1973 with the biologist George Schaller produced *The Snow Leopard*, and Matthiessen's first National Book Award after three nominations. All of these works are excerpted in this volume.

During the 1980s Matthiessen turned his attentions to his own continent, publishing a collection of magazine pieces about Indian people in *Indian Country* in 1984 and *Men's Lives*, a book about the commercial fishermen he worked with, in 1986. His renewed interest in American places was also reflected in his fiction: *Killing Mister Watson*, situated mostly in the Florida Everglades, was published to broad critical acclaim in 1990. There was also a sharpening of Matthiessen's attention to domestic political affairs, particularly those related to native people. Matthiessen often mentions the 1957 Nobel Prize acceptance speech given by Albert Camus, in which Camus urged writers to speak for those who cannot speak for themselves: "Whatever our personal weaknesses may be, the nobility of our craft will always be rooted in two commitments, difficult to maintain: the refusal to lie about what one knows and the resistance to oppression."

With his deepening involvement in Indian affairs, Matthiessen's prose began to show a political pitch that in his previous work had been rendered more subtly. His harshest protest is undoubtedly *In the Spirit of Crazy Horse* (1983, 1991), the landmark story of an incident on the Pine Ridge Reservation in South Dakota as a result of which an Ojibwa Lakota activist named Leonard Peltier was imprisoned for two life terms after a shoot-out that killed two FBI agents. Matthiessen used the case to attack existing policy toward the country's native people. "With the near-destruction of the American Indian Movement, the Indians realized that the real enemy in the new Indian wars was not the federal and state bureaucracies and their hostile agents; what threatened them most was 'the corporate state,' that coalition of industry and government that was seeking to exploit the last large Indian reservations in the West."

In addition to stirring up political waters as none of his books had done before, *In the Spirit of Crazy Horse* prompted the longest libel lawsuit in U.S. history. William Janklow, the former (and subsequently reelected) governor of South Dakota, and a former FBI agent sued Matthiessen and his publisher, Viking, for a combined $49 million, and although the courts ultimately saw no merit in either case, it took nine years and $3 million from Matthiessen and his publisher for the appeals to run their course. The book also opened Matthiessen to his most bitter criticism. A lengthy 1995 article in *Outside* magazine—a publication to which he had frequently contributed—took Matthiessen and other "white outsiders" to task for using Peltier for their own political purposes, a charge that disgusted Matthiessen and prompted a long rebuttal in a subsequent issue.

Beyond the epic legal and rhetorical skirmishes surrounding *In the Spirit of Crazy Horse*, the book represents the maturation of a career spent discovering and then championing the plight of native people around the globe. *The Cloud Forest*, his earliest work engaging other cultures, at times seemed to look past the local people in favor of the incredible wildlife he discovered: "Buenos Aires at its best resembles Paris at its worst, reminding one—despite the noisy Latin jangle of its sidewalks—of the lugubrious bourgeois citadels in the neighborhood of the Parc Monceau. But then, I was stranded for two long weeks in Buenos Aires, and I may very well be prejudiced. To anyone who should find himself in that position I can recommend a first-rate zoo and botanical garden and the famous Natural History Museum in nearby La Plata."

As he traveled and matured, however, Matthiessen's perspective shifted. In *The Tree Where Man Was Born* he notes that "much has been written of the colorful decades when the Kenya Colony could be spoken of as 'white man's country,' and there seems no point in adding to it here. I wasn't there, and anyway, the patterns of colonialism do not differ very much from one place to another. For me, the least fascinating aspect of East Africa is the period of technocracy and politics that began under white rule, which lasted little more than half a century among the millenniums that man has been in Africa."

In this book, published little over a decade after *The Cloud Forest*, Matthiessen draws far more complex portraits of local people and digs deeper into their political struggles. Rather than make the generalizations of *The Cloud Forest*, in *Tree* Matthiessen does what he has always done so well with his natural history writing: he pushes for specificity, in both his reporting and his historical research into the upwelling of political conflict. "Four-fifths of this best land in Kenya was now the province of perhaps four thousand whites; a million Kikuyu were to make do with the one-fifth set aside as the Kikuyu Reserves," he writes. "The tribe's exposure to missions and clinics had led to a fatal population increase, and their growing poverty and frustration were all the more onerous for the education that numerous Kikuyu had struggled to obtain. . . . Whites are needed but not wanted—hence the undercurrent of rudeness beneath the precarious civilities. . . . For the new African, such confrontation is a way of forcing the white to look at him at last, to perceive him as a man, an individual, on equal terms and face to face. Or so I assume, without much confidence; after several stays in Africa, having read much and heard more, I knew less than ever about the essential nature of the African."

Despite his long-standing political engagement, Matthiessen considers his political books to have come at something of a cost to his artistic standards. Written for causes, books like *Crazy Horse, Indian Country, Men's Lives,* and *Nine-Headed Dragon River* lack some of the polish of his more refined work. These books "were all written to help out certain groups," he told Kay Bonetti. "I don't regret it, but I don't have any illusions about the literary quality of those books. They are not as good as *The Snow Leopard,* or *The Tree Where Man Was Born.* They're not. And they could have been. I knew how to make them good. But I couldn't make them good from a literary point of view and accomplish my purposes of social justice. It's very difficult to do."

If Matthiessen feels ambivalent about the "literary quality of those books," many of his readers consider the impulse to write them at all a mark of his character. "For what other Zen-minded patriarch can claim to be a founding editor of *The Paris Review?*" wrote Pico Iyer in *Time* magazine in 1993. "How many other American novelists have written whole books in Caribbean patois that were influenced by the principles of classical Japanese art? How many other *New Yorker* writers have taken part-Cheyenne mercenaries for their alter-egos? And which other scion of America's Eastern ruling class has devoted 628 pages and seven years of libel suits to defending the name of a young Native American charged with murder? While others pursue careers, Matthiessen has forged a path, and often it seems a high, chill path through what he calls 'some night country on the dark side of the earth that all of us have to go to all alone.'"

Matthiessen's spiritual and political "path" has done much to define his more recent public image, in some degree to his own dismay. A dedicated student of Zen, he received "transmission" as an ordained master in 1990 and certification (also through his teacher) as a senior teacher, or roshi, in 1998. Although he is among the more well-known Buddhists in the United States, Matthiessen has commented that his commitment to the practice evolved only because it formed an organic fit with his own particular journey. "If I had found an American Indian teacher willing to work with me—not some media medicine man but a true teacher—I might well have chosen a North American tradition over an Asian one," he writes in *Nine-Headed Dragon River*.

Indeed, Matthiessen's dedication to Buddhism deepened, rather than altered, his understanding of the world and humankind's place in it. A defining moment of transformation came upon his return from the Africa trip that led to the writing of *The Tree Where Man Was Born*. Upon pulling into his driveway, Matthiessen was surprised to find "three inscrutable small men"—Japanese Zen masters, he later discovered—visiting his second wife, Deborah Love. Soon after this auspicious meeting, Matthiessen began joining his wife for weeklong *sesshin,* or meditation retreats, and it was through her that he met his first Zen teacher, Soen Nakagawa-roshi. Just a few months later, in November 1971, Matthiessen and Deborah attended a weekend retreat at the New York Zendo. "For two months Deborah had been suffering from pains that seemed to resist all diagnosis, and she decided to limit herself to the Sunday sittings," Matthiessen writes in *Nine-Headed Dragon River.* "On Saturday evening, meeting me at the door of our apartment, she stood there, smiling, in a new brown dress, but it was not the strange, transparent beauty in her face that took my breath away. I had been in zazen since before daybreak, and my mind was clear. And I saw Death gazing out at me from those wide, dark eyes. There was no mistaking it, and the certainty was so immediate and shocking that I could not greet her. In what she took as observance of sesshin silence, I pushed past quietly into the bathroom, to collect myself in order that I might speak."

Twenty months after Deborah's death, Matthiessen set out for Nepal with the field biologist George Schaller to study blue sheep, and perhaps to catch a glimpse of the elusive snow leopard. For Matthiessen, the journey was also something more. He hoped to visit the remote Crystal Monastery, and perhaps secure an audience with the Lama of Shey, one of the most revered masters in the Tibetan tradition. Beyond this, of course, he hoped to navigate a mourning period and learn something of life, death, impermanence. The Buddha, Matthiessen writes, looks with the same unchanging smile upon rape and resurrection.

From the beginning Matthiessen was aware of the power of the mountains to humble the ego and transform the spirit. "The secret of the mountains is that the mountains simply exist, as I do myself: the mountains exist simply, which I do not. The mountains have no 'meaning,' they *are* meaning; the mountains *are.* The sun is round. I ring with life, and the mountains ring, and when I can hear it, there is a ringing that we share. I understand all this, not in my mind but in my heart, knowing how meaningless it is to try to capture what cannot be expressed, knowing that mere words will remain when I read it all again, another day."

After Deborah's death Matthiessen continued a rigorous dedication to Zen training that includes regular extended retreats and, since his formal appointment as a Zen priest in 1990, the teaching of other students.

In the context of his spiritual training, Matthiessen can be humble to the point of self-negation about his writing; he even puts quotation marks around references to his work. "Finally, there is the consequential matter of my 'literary endeavors' of nearly forty years," he writes in *Nine-Headed Dragon River*, "which place me at once in the most hopeless category of Zen student, according to the Rinzai master Muso Soseki (1275–1351): Muso names three grades of disciples, then concludes: 'Those who befuddle their minds in non-Buddhist works and devote their efforts to literary endeavors are nothing but shaven-headed laymen and are not fit to be classed even with those of the lowest grade.'" In an interview with *Publishers Weekly*, Matthiessen went further: "One is always appalled by the idea of wearing one's so-called religion on one's sleeve," he said. "I never talk about Zen much. . . . If people come along and want to talk about Zen, that's wonderful, but I don't want to brandish it. It's just a quiet little practice, not a religion . . . just a way of seeing the world . . . and I find myself very comfortable with it."

In a chapter heading of his book of Zen journals, he quotes Zen master Dogen's comment that intensive meditation will help the practitioner to "wander freely outside ordinary thinking, enriched with great enlightenment. If you do this, how can those who are concerned with the fish trap or hunting net of words and letters be compared with you?" As someone who has been caught up in words and letters—to say nothing of fish traps and hunting nets—Matthiessen has had to negotiate a creative life that somehow fits with a spiritual practice that considers writing to be dust on the clear mirror of reality. Perhaps this is why much of his writing is in journal form. Even when polished, journal entries aspire to an immediacy of response not far different in spirit from the "automatic writing" of the Beats; Gary Snyder, Jack Kerouac, and Allen Ginsberg were all devoted students of Zen. Matthiessen's language often takes on the shimmering affectlessness of a Zen koan; his mind struggles not to distort the received images with metaphor or judgment. "A shard of rose quartz, a candy-colored pierid butterfly, white with red trim, and the gleam of a scarlet-chested sunbird in the black lace of an acacia," he writes in *The Tree Where Man Was Born*. "Set against the sun at dawn or evening, its hanging weaver nests like sun-scorched fruit, its myriad points etched on the sky, there is nothing so black in Africa as the thorn tree."

What Matthiessen seems to have concluded, after a life spent writing in the presence of great beauty and great peril, is that the two are inextricably bound; his is an eloquent call for curiosity, awareness, and respect for one's intimate relationships with people and the natural world. Watching a lion die in *The Tree Where Man Was Born*, he writes: "I was swept by a wave of feeling, then a pang so sharp that, for a moment, I felt sick, as if all the waste and loss in life, the harm one brings to oneself and others, had been drawn to a point in this lonely passage between light and darkness." It is this fierce, unwavering awareness of impermanence, this courageous confrontation of quiet beauty and vast extinctions, that gives Matthiessen's work its sustaining power.

# THE
# PETER
# MATTHIESSEN
### READER

NONFICTION 1959–1991

# *from* Wildlife in America

1959

In the late 1890s the United States established an organization known as the Division of Biological Survey to help chart the country's rich biological diversity; report on the fish, birds, and mammals that faced extinction because of excessive fishing and hunting; and chronicle the countless "exotic" creatures that had been imported from other countries and wreaked havoc on native species. In 1956 a twenty-nine-year-old Peter Matthiessen set out in a Ford convertible with some natural histories, a shotgun, and a sleeping bag to conduct his own exploration of the country's wildlife refuges and to assess the state of America's natural environment. The result of this trip was Wildlife in America, a narrative report that, along with Rachel Carson's landmark Silent Spring, published three years later, marked the rebirth of the American environmental movement. Carson's book, written for general readers but with scientifically compelling evidence, explained the concept of the ecological web, in which DDT sprayed on suburban trees might sicken people and kill birds hundreds of miles away. Wildlife in America provided a political and biological history of the American landscape; organized by faunal region, from eastern shorelines through midwestern prairie to western mountains, it showed how inextricably connected all natural systems are, and how irrelevant political boundaries are to our environment. The writing is filled with wonder at the country's magnificent diversity and despair over the rapid decline of so many species. The book contains a complete appendix of "Rare, Declining, and Extinct Species of North America North of the Mexican Boundary Protected by the Endangered Species Act." A much-imitated classic in the field,

Wildlife in America *was updated and reissued in 1989 and remains in the permanent collection of the White House.*

*Beginning with the ominous story of the killing of the last great auks—the first creatures native to North America thought to have been extinguished by humankind—the book's opening selection presents an overview of human impact on North American natural history. "Man is invariably a new factor of the most dangerous potential," Matthiessen writes. "The fiercest animal of all, he is especially destructive when he introduces, in addition to himself, such rapacious mammal relatives as the rat, the mongoose, and the cat, all of them beasts superbly equipped to make short work of birds, eggs, and other edible life escaping the attention of their large ally."*

## The Outlying Rocks

**In early June of 1844,** a longboat crewed by fourteen men hove to off the skerry called Eldey, a stark, volcanic mass rising out of the gray wastes of the North Atlantic some ten miles west of Cape Reykjanes, Iceland. On the islets of these uneasy seas, the forebears of the boatmen had always hunted the swarming seabirds as a food, but on this day they were seeking, for collectors, the eggs and skins of the garefowl or great auk, a penguinlike flightless bird once common on the ocean rocks of northern Europe, Iceland, Greenland, and the Maritime Provinces of Canada. The great auk, slaughtered indiscriminately across the centuries for its flesh, feathers, and oil, was vanishing, and the last birds, appearing now and then on lonely shores, were granted no protection. On the contrary, they were pursued more intensively than ever for their value as scientific specimens.

At the north end of Eldey, a wide ledge descends to the water, and, though a sea was running, the boat managed to land three men, Jon Brandsson, Sigourour Isleffson, and Ketil Ketilsson. Two auks, blinking, waddled foolishly across the ledge. Isleffson and Brandsson each killed a bird, and Ketilsson, discovering a solitary egg, found a crack in it and smashed it. Later, one Christian Hansen paid nine pounds for the skins, and sold them in turn to a

Reykjavik taxidermist named Möller. It is not known what became of them thereafter, a fact all the more saddening when one considers that, on all the long coasts of the northern ocean, no auk was ever seen alive again.

The great auk is one of the few creatures whose final hours can be documented with such certainty. Ordinarily, the last members of a species die in solitude, the time and place of their passage from earth unknown. One year they are present, striving instinctively to maintain an existence many thousands of years old. The next year they are gone. Perhaps stray auks persisted a few years longer, to die at last through accident or age, but we must assume that the ultimate pair fell victim to this heedless act of man.

One imagines with misgiving the last scene on desolate Eldey. Offshore, the longboat wallows in a surge of seas, then slides forward in the lull, its stern grinding hard on the rock ledge. The hunters hurl the two dead birds aboard and, cursing, tumble after, as the boat falls away into the wash. Gaining the open water, it moves off to the eastward, the rough voices and the hollow thump of oars against wood tholepins unreal in the prevailing fogs of June. The dank mist, rank with marine smells, cloaks the dark mass, white-topped with guano, and the fierce-eyed gannets, which had not left the crest, settle once more on their crude nests, hissing peevishly and jabbing sharp blue bills at their near neighbors. The few gulls, mewing aimlessly, circle in, alighting. One banks, checks its flight, bends swiftly down upon the ledge, where the last, pathetic generation of great auks gleams raw and unborn on the rock. A second follows and, squalling, they yank at the loose embryo, scattering the black, brown, and green shell segments. After a time they return to the crest, and the ledge is still. The shell remnants lie at the edge of tideline, and the last sea of the flood, perhaps, or a rain days later, washes the last piece into the water. Slowly it drifts down across the sea-curled weeds, the anchored life of the marine world. A rock minnow, drawn to the strange scent, snaps at a minute shred of auk albumen; the shell fragment spins upward, descends once more. Farther down, it settles briefly near a *littorina*, and surrounding mollusks stir dully toward the stimulus. The periwinkle scours it, spits the calcified bits away. The current takes the particles, so small as to be all but invisible, and they are borne outward, drifting down at last to the deeps of the sea out of which, across slow eons of the Cenozoic era, the species first evolved.

For most of us, its passing is unimportant. The auk, from a practical point of view, was doubtless a dim-witted inhabitant of Godforsaken places, a primitive and freakish thing, ill-favored and ungainly. From a second and a more enlightened viewpoint, the great auk was the mightiest of its family, a highly evolved fisherman and swimmer, an ornament to the monotony of northern seas, and for centuries a crucial food source for the natives of the Atlantic coasts. More important, it was a living creature which died needlessly, the first species native to North America to become extinct by the hand of man. It was to be followed into oblivion by other creatures, many of them of an aesthetic and economic significance apparent to us all. Even today, despite protection, the scattered individuals of species too long persecuted are hovering at the abyss of extinction, and will vanish in our lifetimes.

The slaughter, for want of fodder, has subsided in this century, but the fishes, amphibians, reptiles, birds, and mammals—the vertebrate animals as a group—are obscured by man's dark shadow. Such protection as is extended them too rarely includes the natural habitats they require, and their remnants skulk in a lean and shrinking wilderness. The true wilderness—the great woods and clear rivers, the wild swamps and grassy plains which once were the wonder of the world—has been largely despoiled, and today's voyager, approaching our shores through the oiled waters of the coast, is greeted by smoke and the glint of industry on our fouled seaboard, and an inland prospect of second growth, scarred landscapes, and sterile, often stinking, rivers of pollution and raw mud, the whole bedecked with billboards, neon lights, and other decorative evidence of mankind's triumph over chaos. In many regions the greenwood not converted to black stumps no longer breathes with sound and movement, but is become a cathedral of still trees; the plains are plowed under and the prairies ravaged by overgrazing and the winds of drought. Where great, wild creatures ranged, the vermin prosper.

The concept of conservation is a far truer sign of civilization than that spoliation of a continent which we once confused with progress. Today, very late, we are coming to accept the fact that the harvest of renewable resources must be controlled. Forests, soil, water, and wildlife are mutually interdependent, and the ruin of one element will mean, in the end, the ruin of them all. Not surprisingly, land management which benefits mankind will benefit the lesser beasts as well. Creatures like quail and the white-tailed deer, adjusting to man, have already shown recovery. For others, like the black-footed ferret and the California condor, it is probably much too late, and the grizzly bear dies slowly with the wilderness.

This book is a history of North American wildlife, of the great auk and other creatures present and missing, of how they vanished, where, and why; and of what is presently being done that North America may not become a wasteland of man's creation, in which no wild thing can live.

"Everybody knows," one naturalist [Aldo Leopold] has written, "that the autumn landscape in the north woods is the land, plus a red maple, plus a ruffed grouse. In terms of conventional physics, the grouse represents only a millionth of either the mass or the energy of an acre. Yet subtract the grouse and the whole thing is dead."

The finality of extinction is awesome, and not unrelated to the finality of eternity. Man, striving to imagine what might lie beyond the long light years of stars, beyond the universe, beyond the void, feels lost in space; confronted with the death of species, enacted on earth so many times before he came, and certain to continue when his own breed is gone, he is forced to face another void, and feels alone in time. Species appear and, left behind by a changing earth, they disappear forever, and there is a certain solace in the inexorable. But until man, the highest predator, evolved, the process of extinction was a slow one. No species but man, so far as is known, unaided by circumstance or climatic change, has ever extinguished another, and certainly no species has ever devoured itself, an accomplishment of which man appears quite capable. There is some comfort in the notion that, however *Homo sapiens* contrives his own destruction, a few creatures will survive in that ultimate wilderness he will leave behind, going on about their ancient business in the mindless confidence that their own much older and more tolerant species will prevail.

The *Terra Incognita*, as cartographers of the Renaissance referred to North America, had been known to less educated Eurasians for more than ten thousand years. Charred animal bones found here and there in the West, and submitted to the radiocarbon test, have been ascribed to human campfires laid at least twenty-five thousand years ago. Thus one might say that the effect of man on the fauna of North America commenced with the waning of the glaciers, when bands of wild Mongoloid peoples migrated eastward across a land bridge now submerged by the shoal seas of the Bering Strait. In this period—the time of transition between the Pleistocene and Recent epochs—the mastodons, mammoths, saber-toothed tigers, dire wolves, and other huge beasts which had flourished in the Ice Age disappeared forever from the face of the earth, and the genera which compose our modern wildlife gained ascendancy.

Man was perhaps the last of the large mammals to find the way from Asia to North America. In any case, many species had preceded him. The members of the deer family—the deer, elk, moose, and caribou—had made the journey long before, as had the bison, or buffalo, and the mountain sheep. Among all modern North American hoofed mammals, in fact, only the pronghorn antelope emerged originally on this continent. The gray wolf, lynx, beaver, and many other animals also have close relations in the Old World, so close that even today a number of them—the wolverine and the Eurasian glutton, for example, and the grizzly and Siberian brown bear—are widely considered to be identical species. Similarly, many bird species are common to both continents, including the herring gull, golden plover, mallard, and peregrine falcon. The larger groupings—the genera and families which contain those species and many others—are widespread throughout the Northern Hemisphere. Even among the songbirds, which are quite dissimilar on the two continents in terms of individual species, the only large American family which has no counterpart in Eurasia is that of the colorful wood warblers, *Parulidae*.

Since the American continents are connected overland, it seems rather strange that the faunas of North America and Eurasia are more closely allied than the faunas of North and South America. One must remember, however, that the Americas were separated for fifty million years or more in the course of the present geologic era, and during this time their creatures had evolved quite differently. It is only in recent times, in geological terms—two million years ago, perhaps—that the formation of the huge icecaps, lowering the oceans of the world, permitted the reappearance of the Panama bridge between Americas.

The animals moved north and south across this land bridge, just as they had moved east and west across the dry strait in the Arctic. But the South American forms, become senile and overspecialized in their long period of isolation, were unable to compete with the younger species which were flourishing throughout the Northern Hemisphere. Many archaic monkeys, marsupials, and other forms were rapidly exterminated by the invaders. Though a certain interchange took place across the land bridge, the northern mammalian genera came to dominate both continents, and their descendants comprise virtually all the large South American animals of today, including the cougar, jaguar, deer, peccaries, and guanacos.

The armadillo, opossum, and porcupine, on the other hand, are among the primitive creatures which arrived safely from the opposite direction and are still extending their range. A large relation of the armadillo, *Boreostracon*, and a mighty ground sloth, *Megatherium*, also made their way to North America. These slow-witted beasts penetrated the continent as far as Pennsylvania, only to succumb to the changes in climate which accompanied the passing of the Ice Age.

The mass extermination of great mammals at this time occurred everywhere except in Africa and southern Asia. Alteration of environment brought about by climatic change is usually held accountable, but the precise reasons are as mysterious as those offered for the mass extinction of the dinosaurs some seventy million years before. Even among large animals the extinctions were by no means uniform: in North America the moose and bison were able to make the necessary adaptations, while the camel and horse were not. The camel family survived in South America in the wild guanaco and vicuña, but the horse was absent from the Western Hemisphere until recent centuries, when it returned with the Spaniards as a domestic animal.

Large creatures of the other classes were apparently less affected than the mammals. Great Pleistocene birds such as the whooping crane and the California condor prevail in remnant populations to this day, and many more primitive vertebrates, of which the sharks, sturgeons, sea turtles, and crocodilians are only the most spectacular examples, have persisted in their present form over many millions of years. For these, the slow wax and wane of the glacial epoch, which witnessed the emergence of mankind, was no more than a short season in the long history of their existence on the earth.

The last mastodons and mammoths were presumably hunted by man, who may have been hunted in his turn by *Smilodon*, the unsmiling saber-toothed tiger. Possibly the demise of these creatures at the dawn of the Recent epoch was significantly hastened by nomadic hunters whose numerous tribes were wandering east and south across the continent. The red men were always few in number and, the Pueblo peoples of the Southwest excepted, left little sign of their existence. They moved softly through the wilderness like woodland birds, rarely remaining long enough in one locality to mar it.

The visits by Vikings, few records of which have come down from the Dark Ages, were transient also, and the forest green soon covered their crude settlements, leaving only a few much-disputed traces. These fierce warriors, whose sea-dragon galleys were the most exotic craft ever to pierce the North Atlantic fogs, had colonized Greenland by the tenth century and were thus the earliest white discoverers of the Western Hemisphere. That they also discovered North America by the year 1000 seems hardly to be doubted, and the Norse colonists of an ill-defined stretch of northeast coast were the first to record the resources of the new continent. In addition to the wild grapes for which the country was called Vinland, "there was no lack of salmon there either in the river or in the lake, and larger salmon than they had ever seen before," according to the chronicle of Eric the Red. But they concerned themselves chiefly with the export of timber and fur, and in their murderous dealings with the Skrellings, as they called the red men, established a precedent firmly adhered to in later centuries by more pious invaders from France, England, Spain, and Holland. The last Vinland colony, in 1011, was beset less by Skrellings than by civil strife; in the following spring, the survivors sailed away to Greenland, and the history of Vinland, brief and bloody, came to an end.

The modern exploitation of North American wildlife, then, commenced with Breton fishermen who, piloting shallops smaller still than the very small *Santa María*, were probably appearing annually on the Grand Banks off Newfoundland before the voyage of Columbus, and certainly no later than 1497, the year that Americus Vespucius and the Cabots explored Vinland's dark, quiet coasts. "The soil is barren in some places," Sebastian Cabot wrote of Labrador or Newfoundland, "and yields little fruit, but it is full of white bears, and stags far greater than ours. It yields plenty of fish, and those very great, as seals, and those which commonly we call salmons: there are soles also above a yard in length: but especially there is great abundance of that kind of fish which the savages call baccalaos." The baccalao, or cod, abounding in the cold offshore waters of the continental shelf, formed the first major commerce of what Vespucius, in a letter to Lorenzo de' Medici, would term the New World; in its incidental persecution of seabirds, this primitive fishery was to initiate the long decline of North American fauna.

Though the Breton fishermen left no records, it must be assumed that they located almost immediately the great bird colonies in the Magdalen Islands and at Funk Island, a flat rock islet thirty-odd miles off Newfoundland. Since many seabirds, and especially those of the alcid family—the auks, puffins, guillemots, and murres—are of general distribution on both sides of the North Atlantic and nest on the rock islands of Brittany even today, these sailors were quick to recognize their countrymen. A concept of the plenty they came upon may still be had at Bonaventure Island, off the Gaspé Peninsula of Quebec, where the four-hundred-foot cliffs off the seaward face form one vast hive of alcids. The birds swarm ceaselessly in spring and summer, drifting in from the ocean in flocks like long wisps of smoke and whirring upward from the water to careen clumsily along the ledges. Above, on the crest, the magnificent white gannets nest, and the kittiwakes and larger gulls patrol the face, their sad cries added to a chittering and shrieking which pierce the booming of the surf in the black sea caves below. At the base of the cliff the visitor, small in a primeval emptiness of ocean, rock, and sky, feels simultaneously exalted and diminished; the bleak bird rocks of the northern oceans will perhaps be the final outposts of the natural profusion known to early voyagers, and we moderns, used to remnant populations of creatures taught to know their place, find this wild din, this wilderness of life, bewildering.

The largest alcid, and the one easiest to kill, was the great auk. Flightless, it was forced to nest on low, accessible ledges, and with the white man's coming its colonies were soon exterminated except on remote rocks far out at sea. The size of a goose, it furnished not only edible eggs but meat, down and feathers, oil, and even codfish bait, and the Micmac Indians were said to have valued its gullet as a quiver for their arrows. The greatest colony of garefowl was probably at Funk Island, where Jacques Cartier, as early as 1534, salted down five or six barrels of these hapless birds for each ship in his expedition. In 1536 an Englishman named Robert Hore improved upon old-fashioned ways by spreading a sail bridge from ship to shore and marching a complement of auks into his hold. Later voyagers, sailing in increasing numbers to the new continent, learned quickly to augment their wretched stores in similar fashion, not only at Funk Island but at Bird Rocks in the Magdalens and elsewhere. The great auk is thought to have nested as far south as the coast of Maine, with a wintering population in Massachusetts Bay, but the southern colonies were probably destroyed quite early.

As a group, the alcids have always been extraordinarily plentiful—the Brünnich's murre and the dovekie, which may be the most numerous of northern seabirds, each boast colonies in Greenland of two million individuals or more—and the great auk was no exception. The relative inaccessibility of its North Atlantic rookeries deferred its extinction for three centuries, but by 1785, when the frenzy of colonization had subsided, George Cartwright of Labrador, describing the Funks, was obliged to take note of the bird's decline: "it has been customary of late years, for several crews of men to live all summer on that island, for the sole purpose of killing birds for the sake of their feathers, the destruction which they have made is incredible. If a stop is not soon put to that practice, the whole breed will be diminished to almost nothing, particularly the penguins: for this is now the only island they have left to breed upon." Cartwright does not mention the complementary industry of boiling the birds in huge try-pots for their oil, an enterprise made feasible on the treeless Funks by the use of still more auks as fuel.

The naturalists of the period, unhappily, did not share Cartwright's alarm. Thomas Pennant, writing in the previous year, makes no mention of auk scarcity, and Thomas Nuttall, as late as 1834, is more concerned with the bird's demeanor than with its destruction. "Deprived of the use of wings," he mourns, "degraded as it were from the feathered ranks, and almost numbered with the amphibious monsters of the deep, the Auk seems condemned to dwell alone in those desolate and forsaken regions of the earth. . . . In the Ferröe isles, Iceland, Greenland and Newfoundland, they dwell and breed in great numbers." Though Nuttall pointed out, somewhat paradoxically, that recent navigators had failed to observe them, his contemporary, Mr. Audubon, was persuaded of their abundance off Newfoundland and of their continued use as a source of fish bait. In 1840, the year after Audubon's account, the auk is thought to have become extinct off Newfoundland, and two decades later Dr. Spencer F. Baird was of the opinion that, as a species, the bird was rather rare. His remark may well have been the first of a long series of troubled observations by American naturalists in regard to the scarcity of a creature which was, in fact, already extinct.

"All night," wrote Columbus, in his journal for October 9, 1492, "they heard birds passing." He was already wandering the eastern reaches of the Caribbean, seeking in every sign of life a harbinger of land. The night flyers mentioned were probably hosts of migratory birds, traversing the Caribbean from North to South America, rather than native species of the Greater Antilles or Hispaniola. Columbus could not have known this, of course, nor did he suspect that the birds seen by day which raised false hopes throughout the crossing were not even coastal species, but shearwaters and petrels, which visit land but once a year to breed.

Certain shearwaters, storm petrels, and alcids are still very common in season off the Atlantic coasts, but it is no coincidence that the great auk and two species of petrel were the first North American creatures to suffer a drastic decline. The Atlantic islands, rising out of the endless fetch of the wide, westward horizon, were much frequented by ships, and often provided new ship's stores for the last leg of the voyage. Fresh meat was usually supplied by seabirds, incredibly plentiful on their crowded island nesting grounds; in temperate seas, the shearwaters and petrels, like the great auks farther north, were conscripted commonly as a supplementary diet.

In spite of local plenty, the bird communities of islands around the world are often early victims of extermination. The breeding range of island species is small and therefore vulnerable, and the species themselves may be quite primitive. Some are relict populations of forms which, on the mainland, have long since succumbed in the struggle for survival. Other species, freed from competition and mammalian predation, grow overspecialized, diminished in vitality, and thus are ill equipped to deal with new factors in their environment.

Man is invariably a new factor of the most dangerous potential. The fiercest animal of all, he is especially destructive when he introduces, in addition to himself, such rapacious mammal relatives as the rat, the mongoose, and the cat, all of them beasts superbly equipped to make short work of birds, eggs, and other edible life escaping the attention of their large ally.

The ship rat may have explored Bermuda as early as 1603. That year a Spanish crew under Diego Ramírez, frightened at first by the unearthly gabblings of myriad nocturnal spirits, discovered upon closer inspection that these evil things were birds, and highly palatable birds at that. The good impression of the Spaniards was confirmed six years later by a Mr. W. Strachey, shipwrecked in those parts with Sir George Somers on the *Sea Venture*,* who wrote as follows:

> A kind of webbe-footed Fowle there is, of the bigness of an English greene Plover, or Sea-Meawe, which all the Summer we saw not, and in the darkest nights of November and December . . . they would come forth, but not flye farre from home, and hovering in the ayre, and over the Sea, made a strange hollow and harsh howling. They call it of the cry which it maketh, a cohow. . . . There are thousands of these Birds, and two or three Islands full of their Burrows, whether at any time . . . we could send our Cockboat and bring home as many as would serve the whole Company.

Strachey's implication that the nesting burrows were confined to a few islands—or more properly, islets—is significant, for the cahow, or Bermuda petrel, was the first New World example of a creature endangered by its narrow habitat. The cahow's original nesting range throughout the islands was doubtless restricted to the offshore rocks not long after the first sail broke the ocean horizons. In addition to man and his faithful rats, a number of hogs were turned loose in the Bermudas about 1593, and these are thought to have rooted out the colonies on the larger islands. Nevertheless, the cahow and the "pimlico," known today as Audubon's shearwater, remained abundant on the islets of Castle Roads and elsewhere, and it may have been the famine in the winter of 1614–15 which brought about the final decline of the former. The following year, a proclamation was issued "against the spoyle and havock of the Cahowes, and other birds, which already wer almost all of them killed and scared away very improvidently by fire, diggeing, stoneing, and all kinds of murtherings." A law protecting the nesting birds was passed in 1621 which, to judge from its results, was unavailing. About 1629, scarcely a quarter-century after the first accounts of it, the cahow disappeared entirely.

*The accounts of this shipwreck are said to have inspired Shakespeare's *The Tempest*.

In the ordinary course of events, the cahow would have thus become the first North American species to die by the hand of man. (Bermuda is here considered an extension of North America, since it cannot be geographically allied to any other land mass and since, in this period, it was part of the Virginia Colony. For the purposes of this book, North America may be taken to include the continent north of the Mexican border, with its offshore islands and the oceanic islands of Bermuda, although the border is not a continental line, and is somewhat north of the vague faunal "boundary" which roughly separates the representative animals of the two Americas.) But the species was marvelously resurrected in 1906, when an unknown petrel was discovered in a Castle Island crevice. The bird at first was considered a new species, but three other specimens located in subsequent years closely fitted a description of the historic cahow constructed from antique remains. In 1951, some nesting burrows, occupied, were found in islets near Castle Roads. Carefully guarded, these burrows are nonetheless subject to the whims of rats as well as to confiscation by the yellow-billed tropic birds, and there is small hope that the cahow's stamina can maintain it another century. Less than one hundred individuals are now thought to exist, but the fact remains that the species managed to survive nearly three hundred years of supposed extinction. Its status as a "living fossil" cannot compare with that of the coelacanth which, first captured off South Africa in 1938, is a five-foot specimen of an order of fossil fishes thought to have vanished from the earth, not three hundred but three hundred million years ago. Nevertheless, the cahow's story is remarkable, and one must admire the persistence of the survivors. Scattered out across the great Atlantic, they have homed to their rock islets every autumn, year after year after year, to perpetuate their kind beneath the very shadows of the planes which fly man in and out of Bermuda's airfield.

Though remains have been found in the Bahamas, the former occurrence of the cahow off the coasts of the Atlantic states can only be presumed. Similarly, the Guadalupe petrel, first noted on Guadalupe Island off Baja California in 1887, has never been recorded elsewhere, though probably it ranged to California before cats left behind by transient fishermen apparently overpowered it.

Little is known of its original distribution, and it is not likely that we will learn much more, the species having disappeared after 1912. The short-tailed albatross of the western Pacific, on the other hand, was sighted offshore commonly, from Alaska to California, until an Oriental market for its feathers all but finished it, and is therefore a member *in absentia* of our fauna.

The diablotin, or black-capped petrel, not only has visited our coasts but has journeyed far inland. This oceanic wanderer makes its nest in West Indian mountain burrows, and has turned up, usually after storms, in such unlikely haunts as Kentucky, Ohio, New Hampshire, Ontario, and Central Park, in New York City. As a significant food source for mankind, however, it has a history almost as dark and brief as that of its near-relative, the cahow. An account dating from 1696 refers probably to the diablotin in observing that "the difficulty of hunting these birds preserves the species, which would have been entirely exterminated years ago, according to the bad custom of the French, did they not retire to localities which are not accessible to everyone." Localities inaccessible to man, however, were readily accessible to mongooses and opossums imported to its islands, and as a consequence the species has all but disappeared. Its last nesting grounds are unknown, and the few sightings of this large black-and-white petrel in recent decades are largely of random individuals glimpsed on Columbus's western ocean. Columbus himself may well have seen it, and the ultimate record will doubtless be made from aboard ship. One imagines with a sense of foreboding this strange, solitary bird passing astern, its dark, sharp wing rising and vanishing like a fin as it banks stiffly among the crests until, scarcely discernible, it fades into eternities of sea.

# *from* The Cloud Forest

## A Chronicle of the South American Wilderness

### 1961

In the fall of 1959 Matthiessen boarded a freighter in Brooklyn bound for South America. In an extended series of journal entries and short narratives, he chronicles a journey that took him through the Sargasso Sea to Haiti and the islands of the Caribbean, and sixteen hundred miles up the Amazon River to Iquitos in Peru, where his six-month journey began in earnest. Before returning to the U.S. in May 1960, he had traversed the continent, from the mountains of Peru to the jungles of Bolivia, to Patagonia and Tierra del Fuego. Each wilderness resonated with centuries of myth and legend, which Matthiessen hoped to investigate on his own. In Brazil he wrote that "in places the land behind the river banks is unexplored, and lost cities, lost tribes, and strange animals may be discovered. This much is true, and exciting enough too, but even so, an immense store of legends has been propagated throughout the centuries, ever since Francisco de Orellana, in 1541, first reported the existence of fierce female warriors in the region of Obidos. The legends are augmented at every opportunity, not only by the Indians and the settlers, but by the adventurers of all nations who drift in and out of the towns on this huge frontier, and by incautious writers like myself who venture within hearing distance."

The following excerpt is taken from the book's final chapter, entitled "Beyond Black Drunken River." With a jungle veteran named Andrés Porras, a local rancher named César Cruz, and a group of Machiguenga Indians, Matthiessen goes in search of a lost Inca city called Picha and a monstrous fossil jaw, rumored to have been left by some huge protean beast somewhere in the upper reaches of a tributary of Peru's Urubamba River. Matthiessen also meets Wayne Snell, *who runs a series of linguistic research stations in the jungle and translates native languages into written form. Snell had learned of the existence of the Picha ruins from stories told by local Indians. Matthiessen's writing here is as moody and evocative as the landscape it describes, and it represents a literary nod to Joseph Conrad, whom he has cited as a stylistic forebear.*

## Beyond Black Drunken River

**With its mud streets,** thatch roofs, and raffish waterfront, and its barefoot Shipibos with their nose ornaments and bright clothing, the Peruvian river town of Pucallpa is as colorful as it is hideous. The trading post for thousands of square miles of wilderness, it attracts a motley fleet of cargo craft and long canoes; these swarm like a hatch of flies on the broad brown Ucayali, drawn out of the water courses of the vast *selva* or Amazon jungle, which, lying there in steaming silence across the river, stretches away for twenty-five hundred miles to the Atlantic coast.

The cultural center of Pucallpa is the bar of the Gran Hotel Mercedes, which serves coffee and liquor and *gaseosas*, or soft drinks, from dawn until after midnight. From its open doors and windows a splendid view may be obtained of the hogs and vultures which pick over the orange quagmire of the street. Here, in January of 1960, I had first encountered Vargaray, an intense dark man with that South American badge of white blood, the mustache, and the man who first told me of the monstrous fossil jaw near the Mapuya River. The Mapuya does not appear on maps, but was identified as a tributary of the Inuya, which is in turn a tributary of the Urubamba; the latter joins the Tambo near Atalaya to form the Ucayali, which, flowing northward, joins the Marañon about five hundred miles downstream, forming the main body of the Amazon. The Mapuya is located in the flat rain forest, eastward toward the frontier of Brazil, and therefore seemed a most unlikely site for paleontological discovery; in fact, no man in the Mercedes had ever heard of fossil bones found in the open selva. Flood, humidity, and voracious ants were among the numerous factors presented to poor Vargaray to assure him that his fossil could not exist. But Vargaray became very angry when he was doubted, and his passion about the huge *mandíbula* was impressive.

The plot thickened with the appearance in the bar of a man named César Cruz. Cruz was brought forward by our genial host, Señor Fausto Lopez, as just the man to conduct a search party to the bone. A rancher on the Urubamba, he possessed all the necessary *canoas*, outboard motors, *mosquiteros*, guns, and men. Furthermore, he knew of a mysterious ruin on a more distant tributary of the Urubamba, the Río Picha, which no white man had ever seen. Cruz suggested that an expedition—which by now was considered a foregone conclusion in the bar—attempt to locate both *mandíbula* and *ruinas*.

The legends of the lost cities, and especially of the Inca El Dorado known as Paititi, die very hard indeed, in part because lost cities are still being found. The most famous of these, of course, is the Inca mountain town of Machu Picchu, which was found in 1911. Since then several other important locations have come to light, and almost certainly there are more.

Nevertheless, the great majority of those one hears about never existed, or if they did exist, their discoverers have not lived to tell the tale. Jungle legends are, in the main, absurd, and Cruz's story of the lost city on the Picha put me on my guard, especially since there was not the slightest question in the mind of anyone in the room, myself included, as to who was expected to pay for the Picha expedition. I explained what was true, that my sponsors expected me to go to Africa directly from Buenos Aires, where I was to arrive the following month. But, as I have said, there is no world beyond the selva, and my excuse was scarcely heeded; it had already been determined, in fact, that my friend the local Army *comandante*, Juan Basurco, would accompany me in the discovery which was to make all of us famous. At a loss, I let an ironic smile play about my lips, in the manner of one willing to go along with a good joke, and peered cynically about the room through my own cigarette smoke. No one took any notice of this, however. Details of the trip were now discussed, and Cruz added fuel to the general excitement with the statement that a Machiguenga Indian working on his cattle farm had actually been to the Picha ruin and could guide us there.

Cruz is a graceful, quiet man of medium height, very dark, with wary eyes pinched close to the large hawk nose of an Indian and a sudden smile which reveals three teeth of gold in the very center of his upper *mandíbula*. He speaks gently and has an infrequent, appealing laugh, and I took to him immediately. In the following days I had a few whiskies with him, and by the time I left I had contracted the jungle fever. Tentative plans for an expedition had actually been set up, and the journey to Africa postponed. In the early spring, when the rains had abated and the upper rivers would be navigable, I was to meet Cruz and his men at the headwaters of the Urubamba.

In the clear air above the Andes, flying out, I wondered if I had not lost my mind, if I were not, indeed, the greatest gringo idiot that had ever fallen into that nest of thieves. At best, the existence of the monster jaw was most improbable, and that of the Picha ruin beneath serious discussion. I could only console myself with the certain prospect of seeing the jungle at close hand at last, and this had become important to me.

The fossil jaw is there or it is not: the death of precedence in the finding of large jungle fossils and my own lack of education in the matter make it hard to advance any theory of probabilities. The likelihood, such as it is, of the existence of the ruin is based on the theory that the Incas retreated from the Spanish down into the Urubamba Valley, to Machu Picchu and perhaps beyond: the Picha ruins, however, would be at least two hundred miles beyond, at a lower altitude by far than any ruin found to date on the eastern side of the Andean cordillera.

In Lima I called on Señor Rafael Larco Hoyle, one of Peru's leading archaeologists and the owner-curator of the country's finest collection of pre-Inca artifacts. Señor Hoyle assured me that no ruin, large or small, had ever been found in the region described or, in his opinion, ever would be. He cautioned me strongly against believing any such tale, on a theory of his own to the effect that even an honest man, after one week in the jungle, contracts strange fevers and becomes a liar. This is a charitable theory and may serve to excuse some of the jungle's wild-eyed chroniclers; it remains to be seen whether or not I come down with the disease itself.

On the other hand, a jungle veteran named Andrés Porras Cáceres, who worked on the Ucayali around 1944, had heard of a ruin in the Picha area. Before he could visit it, however, the river man who was to conduct him there, one Alejandro Angulo, was killed by the Machiguengas.

Andrés Porras is the brother of Alfredo Porras, a friend in Lima whose interest and kindness have been instrumental in setting up the journey. Andrés, in fact, decided to join me, which is a great stroke of luck, for he has all the experience that I lack and is a most agreeable man besides. During the winter, while I was traveling to Tierra del Fuego and Mato Grosso, he and Alfredo set up the details of the expedition. I returned to Lima in late March and in the first days of April left with Andrés for Cuzco, in the mountains, where our journey into the selva will begin.

I dearly wish that there were another word for "expedition," since I could scarcely apply that term to any trip sponsored by myself: one "mounts" a reputable jungle expedition and equips oneself with pith helmets, lean white hunters, inscrutable Indian scouts, and superstitious bearers who will go no farther. Furthermore, an expedition is backed by millionaires, museums, and foundations—either that, or the explorer (who in this case is invariably an author) sets off alone, or nearly so, and miserably equipped, into country from which, as he is told by old jungle hands in the early pages of the resultant book, he has not the slightest chance of returning alive. Since I am not an explorer, and since I have every intention of returning not only alive but sleek and well, none of these basic conditions can be said to apply to the outing I have in mind.

### April 8, Cuzco

Here is a rough outline of the journey: from Cuzco we proceed down the Urubamba—it is called the Vilcanota in these upper reaches—to Machu Picchu, and from there to Quillabamba. Beyond Quillabamba there is no scheduled transportation, but apparently there is a road of sorts to a point on the river at its conflu-

ence with the Río Yanatili, called El Encuentro. Here the Urubamba becomes navigable, and here we are to be met by César
Cruz and three of his men with a small river boat and canoe. We
descend the Urubamba, including a famous rapids called the
Pongo de Mainique, and eventually turn off westward up the Rio
Picha, in search of the ruin. We then return to the Urubamba and
descend to the settlement of Atalaya. There we pick up Vargaray
and head eastward again into the Inuya and the Mapuya, where we
hope to locate and retrieve the famed *mandibula*. We then return
to the Urubamba and to Atalaya, from where we descend the Ucayali to Pucallpa. Whether or not we locate bone or ruin, we will have
traveled close to a thousand miles on the jungle rivers.

This, as I have said, is the rude itinerary; we can't know more
about it until we have spoken with Cruz himself. The last word
from him was a cable from Atalaya to Lima which required four
days to arrive (in the United States a cable is sent or it is not, but this
system would offend every custom in South America, where ineffi-
ciency is an art nothing less than awe-inspiring) and signally failed
to take into account a cable of questions and instructions sent off
by Andrés a week before. This indicates that he failed to receive
Andrés's cable—or rather, one *hopes* that this is what it indicates,
the alternative being damaging to one's faith in the trusty Cruz.
César's cable stated that he would meet us at El Encuentro on April
10, which would leave him so little time for the journey up the
Urubamba that I wondered if he did not mean the *encuentro*, or
confluence, of the Tambo-Urubamba, near Atalaya. But Andrés
had been in Pucallpa two weeks before and had carefully established with Cruz's wife—Cruz himself was absent—that the
*encuentro* in question was the one near Quillabamba. He did not
feel there could be any honest confusion on the point.

In any case, Andrés and I will be at El Encuentro the day after
tomorrow. As for Cruz, only time will tell.

Because we have no idea, owing to communications failures, of
the completeness of Cruz's preparations, our three days in Cuzco
have been largely devoted to minor outfitting—*curarina*, or snake
medicine, malaria pills, meat sauce (for monkeys and other doubt-
ful provender), machetes, and so forth. Fortunately Andrés was

already well equipped with more basic material, including a pup tent, hunting knives, waterproof river sacks for our gear, a .44 Winchester carbine, and a portable radio. In addition, he has lent me a .38 revolver, as one is never certain what manner of unfriendly beast one may encounter in the selva.

While in Cuzco I had a look at several books of Peruvian exploration, through the kindness of Señor Benjamín de la Torre, and one of these, the *South American Adventures* of an Englishman, Mr. Stratford Jolly, directly concerned the Urubamba region. Mr. Jolly, in 1929, descended the Urubamba, though he was not the first Briton to do so: the previous year Mrs. Bertha Cox, an evangelist of sixty-five and "a courageous and very obstinate old lady," had made her way down the valley with an immense amount of luggage, after suffering incredible maltreatment at the hands of the settlers near the headwaters. Turning the other cheek, Mrs. Cox "gave the people who had treated her so abominably most of her chickens, in return for which they stole her dog, and followed the party for some hours down through the forests along the riverbank, in the hope that the canoe would upset and that they would be able to salve and steal the cargo." She survived her journey only through the assistance of "the rubber trader Peyrera, who was absolute king of the river below." Among the river people, this man had a very evil reputation—he was, among other things, a murderer—and Jolly himself was apprehensive. But he then received a message from the trader, who hoped to prove that "there were still decent people to be found, even in the inaccessible mountains of Peru." And in fact Jolly and his party were treated with utmost courtesy. With the help of Machiguenga Indians attached to Peyrera, both Mrs. Cox and Mr. Jolly were portaged past the Pongo de Mainique—an awesome place, to judge from his account—and arrived eventually at the settlements on the Ucayali.

The one other reference to this region I have come upon to date occurs in a work called *The Rivers Ran East* by an American, Leonard Clark: I came across this volume in La Paz. Mr. Clark, with a single Peruvian companion, descended the Andean rivers—the Perene and the Tambo, farther east—to Atalaya and Pucallpa, and his adventure, therefore, might be said to parallel closely the one which lies before us. (I hope, I must own, that all parallels have already been stated. In his very first hours in the wilds Clark is threatened by a huge rattlesnake, by a jaguar which approaches to a point fifty feet away, and by his own companion, who threatens to blow Clark's head off. From this point forward he is exposed almost constantly to assault by Indians, piranhas, crocodiles, vampire bats, and poisonous reptiles of "intense cunning," an "immense" specimen of which, in the climactic chapters, succeeds at last in burying its fangs in the author's throat. Since the wound adjoins the jugular, Mr. Clark is unable to bleed it, an irony which causes him to laugh; in a calm voice he informs his companion that he has four or five minutes to live, and it looks very much as if the constant prophecies of his certain doom are about to be borne out. But an Indian leaps into the jungle and gathers, prepares, and administers a potion unknown to science in the allotted time, thus sparing the author and his exciting story for the publishing firm of Funk & Wagnalls.) Despite the successful passage of Mrs. Cox and others two decades before the period of which he writes, Clark speaks of "the forbidden Urubamba" and the terrible savages who control it. Here, as elsewhere, he appears to have been the victim of considerable misinformation, a minor example of which is a report that in recent years a trader named Pereira was killed by Machiguenga slaves while attempting to establish a holding above the Pongo. The holding, of course, was established before 1920, and Pereira is still very much alive. He is said to be a most interesing man, and both Andrés and myself now hope to meet him.

Andrés once lived in Cuzco, and I have been here previously, which accounts for our failure to take advantage of its Inca splendors or the more vulgar monuments of the colonial Church. Also, Andrés has many relatives here, and these kind people, and especially his sister-in-law, Gloria Estelle Ladrón de Guevara León de Peralta, have seen to it that our every free moment was assigned to food and drink. Nevertheless, we took time to revisit the Inca fortress of Sacsahuaman above the city, and let the bare sun and distances of the sierra seep into our souls. Andrés, however, is bothered by the altitude, and the mountains themselves oppress him; he is anxious to get down into the jungle. I agree and am, in fact, nearly beside myself with anticipation.

We passed down the empty, raining river without undue incident, having to repair to the bank but twice before reaching the Coribene mission; a solitary bigua cormorant perched on the snag of a drowned tree was the only living creature I observed, though one of the crew glimpsed a large *shushupe*, as the dread bushmaster is known, on a steep bank by the water's edge. Just above Coribene a group of peons at a small *chacra*, apparently surprised to see us, had cheered our doughty craft, but at the first huts of the Machiguengas, where the Indians on the pouring banks stood like statues in the rain, we were greeted with dismal silence.

At Coribene, Father Giordia succored us with coffee. He is an intelligent-looking man with white hair standing straight up on his head, and he voyages frequently on the river although he does not know how to swim. But he assured us that the river farther down, and especially the Pongo, was not navigable at this season, and that Cruz could not possibly come upriver, even if we were foolish enough to try to go down. Furthermore, his radio was out of order, so that he was unable to transmit any messages; the suspense as to César's whereabouts and intentions would continue.

I digested this spate of good news with some difficulty staring out across the thatch huts of the Machiguengas on the river slope below the mission; in the rain, they seemed to grow up out of the mud. The valley of the Coribene, climbing away into the mountains across the river, was obviously a lovely one, but I was in no mood to appreciate it.

The padre said that there was a foot trail through the jungle, two and a half days from Sirialo to the Pongo de Mainique; there, perhaps, Machiguengas attached to the hacienda of the legendary Pereira could get us past the Pongo, and down to the next mission at Timpia, where Cruz might be waiting. But there was no trail of any sort from Timpia onward, and it was quite possible that Cruz had never come at all, or had come and gone. We asked again if we could not hire a few of the padre's expert Indians to take us on the river, and he said again that this would be impossible. At a loss for a solution, we rejoined Marquez and started off for Sirialo.

For, navigable or no, the river was navigated once again by Don Abraham Marquez and his merry men, this time with near-fatal consequences. The rough swirl at one of the final bends inspired some plain and fancy seamanship which left me gasping; even the indomitable Marquez exclaimed afterward, "That was an ugly one, hey, *señores?*" We careened to a landing in a canebrake, just short of a horrid pile of black rocks tumbled at the mouth of a thick, sulphurous stream; the black rocks formed the first real *mal paso* of the river and were therefore the point at which Marquez no longer considered the April river navigable. The canoe was hauled in among the rocks, and we forded the rush of yellow water, waist-deep, holding our gear on our shoulders. This was a bad moment, too, as my knees were still weak and shaking with cold and offered little or no control over my sneakered feet, which splayed wildly on the slippery rocks below; one false move, I thought, and I would slip beneath the yellow waves, to be swept onward to the Pongo and points north. I froze momentarily, and Andrés, who chatters at these nervous moments—I tend to remain silent and morbid—sensed my alarm. His own assurance and encouragement stung me forward like a goad, and I came plunging out at last on the far side.

The hacienda at Sirialo is typical of these small river holdings: an adobe house, thatch huts for the peons, mud, chickens, pigs, a donkey or two, coffee and cacao trees struggling up out of the choking flora, mud, insects, a damp heat of imminent rain, more mud. The jungle rises up behind, looming forward as if ever on the point of obliterating man's intrusion in a wild maelstrom of green. The adobe hut itself had been invaded by jungle weeds, and on this dark day its half-built shell littered with boards and burlap seemed particularly uninviting. We stood dully, our clothes soaked and muddy, with nothing dry to change into, while the hacienda manager expressed his conviction that the foot trail to the Pongo gave out entirely a few kilometers below Sirialo. Marquez himself, exhausted and nervous from the passage down the river, had taken to the manager's bed. Left to ourselves, Andrés and I contemplated the insects and the mud, which was steaming now that the rain had stopped; our state of mind was so abysmal that it is difficult to describe without inducing it all over again, right here and now.

As of this evening, this is our situation: we are less than a day's canoe travel downriver, but returning upstream by the trail is a matter of three days, and any further progress would only increase the discrepancy. We are faced with the choice of an expensive retreat of at least ten days, to Atalaya via Quillabamba, Cuzco, Lima, and Pucallpa, or a desperate plunge down a river said to be unnavigable at this season. *Canoas* and *balsas* are apparently unavailable, even if a crew could be found willing to man them; the extent of the foot trail is a matter of general ignorance and dispute, though everyone, from the smiling man at Lugarte's to Marquez's man at Sirialo, agrees that it is *bruto*—extremely tortuous. Even should we reach the Pongo and get past it, there is no assurance that Cruz will be waiting on the other side, or even at Timpia, some thirty miles beyond, and no means of advising him to do so. And in the hundreds of miles of wilderness between Timpia and Atalaya there is no trail of any kind.

The sensible course is to retreat. But the idea sticks painfully in our craws: the trip here has been made in such high hopes, and the return seems arduous and humiliating. We discussed alternatives this morning. We were spreading our dank gear and soaked sleeping bags on the muddy rocks and stumps when I suggested to Andrés that we might have to go back.

"I know," Andrés said almost gratefully. "I've been thinking the same thing."

He was grateful, not for the chance to retreat, of course, but because I'd finally voiced our mutual doubts; I was grateful in turn that he had not concealed his own misgivings under cover of mine. A smaller man might have said, Oh, do you think so? as if the possibility of turning back had never occurred to him. In any case, the moment the misgivings had been voiced, our morale rose again, and the idea of retreat appeared intolerable—as I have indicated elsewhere, both Andrés and myself tend to be pigheaded. This afternoon we made our way through the jungle to the neighboring hacienda, where a young man named Rosell heard us out with an indulgent smile: too many people had drowned just below his place, at Sirialo Falls—why, a bishop had died there only the year before—for him to consider a descent of the river at this season. Machiguengas might make it, he said, on a strong balsa: we should return to Coribene by the trail and prevail upon Padre Giordia to help us. As for the trail itself, it was impassable for mules beyond the Sirialo River, and human bearers were impossible to find.

But at supper Marquez was very discouraging about our chances at Coribene; he did not think that Giordia would risk his Machiguengas at this time of year, even if the Indians themselves were willing. It occurred to me in desperation that if I could prevail upon Andrés to dispense with some of his gear—thus dispensing with the need for mules, or for more than one or two peons—we could attempt a fast trip to the Pongo on foot, in the hope that we might obtain help from the Pereiras, or even pick up a balsa on the way. To my surprise (for he is over sixty, after all), Andrés immediately agreed: we would lay out our gear in the first light of the morning and pare our equipment to the bone. Whatever we left could return upriver with Marquez, to be sent eventually to Estelle León de Peralta in Cuzco. Far from being tempted to return ourselves, we were now repelled by the idea of wasting two more days in what would almost surely be a vain effort to get assistance from Padre Giordia; we planned to set off downriver on the trail as soon as we could get organized in the morning.

### April 14, Rodríguez

I slept happily last night on top of a bin of cacao beans, having first searched the shed with a flashlight for snakes, tarantulas, and scorpions. When I scrambled down at dawn, Andrés was already at work on his equipment but had managed to reduce his five large bags of gear by only one. He also planned to leave behind his sleeping bag, keeping only his poncho and a piece of canvas; by sacrificing the sleeping bag he felt justified in keeping with him such luxuries as a portable radio and a quart bottle of eau de cologne.

Andrés is in love with his equipment, which has seen him through many an adventure, but over the years he has accumulated quite a lot of it. The dates of his various expeditions are scrawled all over the stock of his carbine and the inner brim of his broad frontier hat, and in this sense he clings, through his equipment, to the past. He is unquestionably a jungle man of experience and courage, but he is nevertheless the only such man I have ever come across who is willing to burden himself unnecessarily. Had Cruz met us with canoes, as planned, his equipment would have been welcome, but it was now crucial that we travel light. I reduced my own gear to one sack, two-thirds full, and a small knapsack, and placed them next to his pile by way of contrast; I then suggested as gently as my irritation would permit that the refreshment to be gained from a heavy radio and a quart of eau de cologne would not begin to compensate for the possible loss of sleep he was risking by leaving his bedroll behind.

Andrés is a man who is not at home on the defensive and dislikes criticism almost as much as I do. Therefore he was soon irritable himself. Nevertheless, he sliced a little of the fat out of his sacks, and meanwhile Marquez had located for us a Quechua, one Zacharias, who for twenty *soles*, plus a twelve-*sole* bottle of *pisco* to be used en route as fuel (or a total salary of approximately one dollar and fifteen cents) contracted to bear a truly enormous weight for one whole day downriver. The enormity of his travail—two large rubber duffel bags full of heavy gear, plus a sack of canned goods and other emergency food—cannot be imagined unless one keeps in mind the steep, muddy trails full of slippery and sliding rocks, the stream crossings, the insects and clinging thorns, the fierce heat in the open swamps, and the promise of the long walk back over what, in any other part of the world, could only be called an obstacle course.

Nonetheless, Zacharias rolled the sacks up in his *qquepina*, the cloth sling of the mountain Indians, and we hoisted it onto his bent back. He set off cheerfully, the *pisco* bottle snug against his side, a wad of coca in his cheek, and his small mongrel, Tarzan, at his heels. Having thanked Don Abraham Marquez for his many kindnesses and said good-bye, we followed him. Andrés was truly a hard-looking character, with his broad hat and rawhide chin strap, his carbine slung on his shoulder, his machete and packs, and, on his belt, his canteen, drinking cup, sun glasses, bullet pouch, and two hunting knives; if I had not borrowed a third knife and the revolver, he would have worn these too. To Andrés's annoyance, I carried the revolver in my pack, not only because its holster would catch on thorns and bushes as we went along but because I felt like a damn fool wearing it.

By nine the day was already very hot. A short distance below the hacienda we had to ford the Sirialo River, just above its confluence with the Urubamba. Zacharias plunged across the current, barefoot on the boulders; Andrés and I struggled through with a little more difficulty. The packs upset our sense of balance, and Andrés once slipped and fell, though he recovered himself before water could reach his camera. Halfway across we came to a rock island; the water beyond was too deep to traverse with the gear. But there was a small hut across the way, and its owner swirled over in his canoe to fetch us.

The banks of the Urubamba, above the Pongo de Mainique, are a series of steep ridges broken by mountain valleys; there is no trail along the river banks, since these are too precipitous, and therefore one must climb the ridges, plunge down into the valleys, and climb all over again immediately. From the top of the first ridge, we glimpsed the dread *tumbos* of the Sirialo, which lie below the *encuentro*; perhaps because we were on foot, and far above, there seemed to be nothing very alarming about them.

On theory, we were bound for the hacienda of one Rodríguez, a man, so it was said, who might be helpful; he was supposed to live four or five miles below the Sirialo and to have some Machiguengas working for him. But as the day wore on and the miles moved slowly past, there was no sign of the good Rodríguez. Zacharias, *pisco*-crazed, got farther and farther ahead, while Andrés slowly fell behind. Whenever we stopped to rest, I could see that he was suffering. Once, offered a swig of the Quechua's white lightning, he accepted gladly, which was quite uncharacteristic. I felt a pang of conscience and began to worry.

The day had become frightfully hot: we were soaked beneath our packs. Andrés put up no resistance when, toward midday, I relieve him of his carbine. His pants were ripped and falling away at the knee, and though he did not complain, his face was gray. Shortly thereafter we came to the hut of a Rodríguez, though not the man we sought: an old woman there gave us lemon and water, and Andrés gulped at it like a man dying of thirst. He tried to pour some into his canteen, and his hand shook so that he slopped most of it onto the ground. His self-control was precarious, and for the first time since I had known him he actually looked his age.

By this time I was desperately concerned. I felt bad that I had taken him at his own estimate of his endurance, had encouraged him in his courageous decision not to let me continue by myself. He admitted now that he had felt a twinge of pain in his heart, and I got to the point where I had to consider what I would do should his heart give out. There would be no possibility of getting a body out of this valley to Quillabamba in this heat; he would have to be buried in the jungle.

But Andrés knew that we had gone too far now to turn back; retreating would mean a four-day walk, and he was not up to it. He felt that his trouble had stemmed from the straps on his pack which, in combination with the steep terrain, had made his breathing difficult. We decided that he was not to carry anything when walking, and that we would move more slowly. The woman gave us some fried eggs and bananas, and he felt better; afterward we rested in the hut until the heat had eased a little. A second peon was located who took over Andrés's gear and part of mine, and as it was only two hours to the right Rodríguez, we decided to move on, as we could accomplish nothing where we were.

At dusk we came out on the bank opposite the Rodríguez huts; their owner came across for us in his canoe. In this swift current the technique is to lead the canoe far upstream along the bank, make a break for the other side, and try to land as little below the target point as possible. Rodríguez and the boy in the bow were skillful, but even so they landed well below us and had to inch upstream along the bank.

Señor Rodríguez, a small dark suspicious man who later proved quite hospitable, denied any knowledge of available canoes or balsas with a vehemence suggesting that he felt himself falsely accused; he further denied that he harbored Machiguengas, much less the slightest inclination to take us anywhere on the river. Like everyone else, he spoke optimistically of hopeful prospects only a few miles farther down; if necessary, he swore, we could make it overland to the Pereira holdings in two days.

I have the impression that we make these people nervous, arriving armed as we do, on a mission so senseless as to make them suspect that it is actually something nefarious; they get our hopes up with their optimistic tales simply to get rid of us. It also appears that most of these people who have ventured down a short distance on the Urubamba are people of the sierra rather than the jungle. They fear the river, as Andrés points out, and know nothing about it, not even the actual distance to the next hacienda below. Beyond Rodríguez there are two or three small holdings; from the last of these to the Pongo de Mainique is a vast wilderness controlled by the Pereiras. Rodríguez could tell us this much, but he felt certain that we could obtain a balsa before we reached the Pereira country. He was not very convincing, and privately I felt that we faced the possibility of a three- or four-day march, with nothing we could count on at the end of it.

*April 15, Ardiles*
Last night I slept badly on a hard cane mat laid on the mud, beset by chicken lice, small flies, and mosquitoes: Andrés, who had no sleeping bag, was given a kind of mattress, an ironic reward, I thought, for his improvidence, but one which came at a fortunate time, as he needed all the rest he could get. I awoke this morning rather low in my mind and taped a growing boot chafe on my ankle.

Our faithful Zacharias and his valiant Tarzan had departed in the early hours, bearing with them, as it turned out, the greater part of our emergency rations. Tired before we started, we soon set off ourselves, accompanied by two fresh bearers lent us by Rodríguez, and bound for the hacienda of César Lugarte—no relation, it was said, of the César Lugarte upriver. This Lugarte lived "three hours away, *señores*, walking slowly."

We reached our destination early in the afternoon. The march had required five or six hours over a path infinitely more tortuous than that of the previous day; once we paused to fire the .44 in vain at a *pava*, or guan, of which we saw several during the morning.

Our feet were giving out, and we slumped exhausted on the bank while Lugarte peons on the opposite shore waved us back upstream; they were trying to indicate that they had no canoe and that we should cross at a point farther up where, an hour previously, we had been waved downstream. This latter intelligence, of course, was impossible to convey across the roar of the river, and so we simply slumped there, at a loss; we refused to retrace our steps over that terrible trail, for reasons which were becoming psychological as well as physical.

At last two young men came across the river on a small balsa to talk to us. One of them, called Ardiles, claimed to have a larger balsa farther downriver; to our surprise and pleasure, he agreed to take us down to the Pereiras'. He departed immediately on the trail upstream, to return in less than an hour with a *canoa*, in which he transported us to the Lugarte clearing across the way. One of our bearers, Alejandro, came along with us; he had decided to run away from Señor Rodríguez. In return for his services, we agreed to see to it that he got eventually to Lima.

Tomorrow we walk again, the usual *"cuatro o cinco kilometros, señores, nada más,"* but at the end of this walk, whatever its distance, there is at least a balsa. Ardiles claims that he is willing to take us into the jaws of the Pongo itself, and Andrés, who would now willingly risk his life rather than walk even one mile farther on this jungle trail, is all for it. (He may feel, of course, that walking is more dangerous for him, for his heart, than the Pongo could possibly be, and after yesterday I can scarcely blame him.) Though he feels better today, his legs are swelling badly, and he will soon reach the point where courage will not be enough.

We decided to put off our departure until morning. I returned to the hacienda, climbing up through large banana groves. There Andrés and Alejandro had arrived at last, and both of them were prostrate. I gathered that Andrés had had a bad time of it on the trail, and feel very guilty about it. Poor Andrés expected a calm journey by canoe, surrounded by all his beloved gear, and instead he has spent the last three days stumbling up and down these steep jungle valleys, with nothing certain at the end of it but another dirt floor and more yuca. His clothes are torn and his legs are swollen, and he carries with him a secret dread about his heart. But he scarcely complains, and, as the saying goes, I hope I am half the man he is when I reach his age.

We have now marched from above the Sirialo to well below the Casireni, a negligible distance on the river but a formidable route over land, burdened with gear. Actually we have walked little more than fifteen hours in the past three days, not counting delays and rests, but anyone willing to try this goat path in its present condition for five hours in the heat of a jungle day—anyone, that is, who is not of Quechua extraction and equipped with Quechua lungs, as all these mestizos appear to be—is welcome to do so, with my blessings. I can only say that Andrés Porras Cáceres, a very durable man, will not walk another step if he has to go through the Pongo de Mainique on a papaya rind.

It seems, at last, that our days on foot are over. I am tired myself, and my impressions of our route are blurred, for most of the time, trudging and clambering and sliding onward, I stared at the ground in order to find my footing. But there were some fine moments as well as painful ones—the cold water drunk face down in the white mountain streams, the mysterious cries and bird calls, the light-dappled forest stretched high above the roaring river, the scarlet macaws—*bolivars* or *papagayos*—which followed us with their raucous screeches, the long files of leaf-cutting ants swaying along with their burdens, like an endless thin green snake, the perched wood butterflies with the strange "eye" on the underside of their lifted wings, and the "eyes" themselves, staring owlishly from the jungle shadows. These details I shall remember longer than the muddy hillsides, the dry, rasping canebrakes, the palm thickets and thorns, the fierce humidity.

### April 17, *Pangoa*

In regard to weather, we have had bad luck on the river. Today it is raining hard again—it has rained hard at least once every day—and the brown river with its dark, dense green walls is cheerless. We shoved the raft into the current about 7:00 A.M., and at 7:02 were thrashing toward the bank again, perilously awash; we needed at least two more balsa poles, and Rudi and Julio went into the forest to cut and strip them.

By nine we were off again into the rain, and immediately the river seized us up and bore us remorselessly toward our first emergency, at a *mal paso* which the Machiguengas call Vacanique, or Cattle Drowning Place: we came over a shallow fall into a strong whirlpool, or *remolino*, and Ardiles's uncapsizable craft for a few horrid moments rode at a forty-five degree angle. In the process waves smashed across the raft and bore away the largest of our sacks. The sack floated, and we retrieved it farther down, only to note for the first time that it had two capacious holes in it, in addition to my sleeping bag.

Bacanique was the worst passage of the day, though several others were a little tight. Had the sun been shining, the whole business might have been quite exhilarating, but the rain poured down and a cold wind was blowing up the valley, and the wildlife which might have stimulated us consisted of one orange serpent, drowned and belly-up in the swollen river. We paddled furiously all morning, not only to avoid the falls, or *tumbos*, and the *remolinos*, but to keep warm, for as a safety measure we were near-naked in our underpants. The raft was permanently awash, to a point above the ankles in the smooth stretches and above the navel—we were sitting—in the rapids. At midday the rain stopped at last, and shortly thereafter, exhausted by a *mal paso* called Quirimotini, or Place of the River Demon, we beached the raft on a gravel island and rested. A *pisco* bottle was produced, and a little water-logged yuca, and Julio supplied us with a big jawful of coca, the juices of which, when swallowed, produce a numb, pleasant sensation, a relief from both cold and hunger, and even a vague serenity of mind—one sees immediately why this plant is carried everywhere by the Quechuas, whose bleak existence might otherwise be insupportable. Our Alejandro is a Quechua, and the coca and *pisco* had a strong effect on him: manning one of the bow paddles when we took to the river once again, he failed to squat when we plunged into a rapid, swaying fearlessly until a shout brought him to his senses.

Just below Señor Olarte's we had glimpsed two small haciendas:

from that point onward we had traveled in Machiguenga country controlled by the Pereiras, though we had seen no sign of human habitation. Even the animals kept their distance, though after the rain had stopped, the birds began to move a little—we saw a few parrots and parakeets and a single flock of macaws. I questioned Ardiles about the trees, and he pointed out a hardwood he called *sandematico*, which he said was used commonly for *canoas*. Julio said that monkeys were common in these valleys—as a matter of fact, we ate one last night at Olarte's, an experience I don't care to repeat soon again—but we saw none, though we heard everywhere the small white *chito*, which sounds like a full-throated bird.

In a few hours on the river we had covered twice the distance made in all the past three days on foot.

In the early afternoon the hacienda of Fidel Pereira came into view, high up on a bank at a bend of the river. We wished to stop, but Ardiles, plainly uneasy, stalled around until the swift current had swept us irretrievably past. He repeated an earlier claim that the old man had become extremely difficult and kept an armed guard of Machiguengas to waylay trespassers, and said that we would be far better off in the hands of one of his sons, his own good friend Epifanio. Some Indians attached to Fidel Pereira came to the bank and watched us in silence until we disappeared around the bend.

Epifanio Pereira, a round-faced young man with a permanent vague smile and an air so innocent as to be rather disconcerting, greeted us cheerfully enough farther down the river at Pangoa; Pangoa, the monkey demon associated with the frogs on a nearby peak, is the name of the old man's former *chacra*, now worked by Epifanio. At the moment the hacienda consists of one very large high shed, open on all sides, under the eaves of which is a small loft in which Epifanio has his bed; below, there are a rough table and some bins of drying coffee, and around the edges the Indian fires. Spears, bows and arrows, tom-toms, cane baskets, feather apparel, and other equipment of the Indians are strung from the cross beams, and there are, in addition, two small, low Indian palm-leaf huts. Two Indian women, an old squaw and a girl, were squatting over a fire before one of the huts, and two other girls were washing coffee beans in a long trough at the mouth of a small brook. Just after we arrived four men appeared out of the canebrake behind the hacienda and stood watching us with that implacable Indian silence; the women, on the other hand, would not look at us and kept their back to us whenever possible. All of the Indians were dressed in the poncholike *cushma*, a coarse cloth woven from wild cotton, with black, brown, and red stripes.

Ardiles had suggested that the friendship of Epifanio could be won by an offering of *pisco*, which is hard to come by in the jungle; we placed a half-bottle—we now have a single bottle left—at his disposal, and he drank it off, without apparent effect, almost immediately.

The sun came out in the middle of the afternoon, too late to dry anything; my poor saturated sleeping bag is all one man can carry, and I'm not quite sure where I'm going to lay my head. Not that I shall probably sleep very much in any case, for Andrés tells me I am subject to bodily harm. I have had a stupid dispute with Ardiles, at the end of which I told him that he was *sin vergüenza*: I should have known better, and I did, but I lost my temper. The expression, mild enough in translation—it means "without shame," or simply "shameless"—invariably produces an important reaction in Spanish countries, and especially, perhaps, in South America, in the wilder regions of which it is often more sensible to kill a man than to insult him. In any case, Ardiles feels mortally insulted and is openly plotting revenge.

Briefly, Ardiles, sensing our desperation, charged us a bandit's fee for his services; he excused it by saying that most of it would go toward paying two *bogas* for their dangerous work. If they did not receive very high salaries, they would not come. But there was only one *boga*—actually, we needed three—and Andrés, Alejandro, and I did the work of the other. Therefore I suggested to Ardiles that the fee was a little high. He demanded the full fee, however, and since he has us by the throats, I had to pay it. But I also told him what I thought of him, to the dismay of Andrés, who was standing just behind him. "You've made a hell of a mess now," Andrés said to me in English; I can't recall ever having heard him swear before. Andrés was already seizing the arm of Ardiles, who was on the point of hurling the money to the ground; Andrés signaled to me to go away and let him handle it, and I am watching them now from the table. For the past two hours Andrés has not once let go of Ardiles's arm, and he has now got him to sit down on a log, down by the river. The Machiguengas and Epifanio (who is three-fourths Indian himself) are observing the whole business with a kind of wary calm, like watchful animals, and Epifanio is still smiling, if that expression of his can really be called a smile.

Andrés's heroic efforts have now brought about an uneasy truce, though Andrés himself is most unhappy about the present state of affairs. Ardiles has a code and pride of sorts, and it may be that the reason he is so angry is that he does not feel entirely right about his own position. Nevertheless, he is still talking wildly of revenge—quite seriously, according to Andrés. Ardiles is a Quechua mestizo who feels he has always been cheated and insulted by gringos—and his insistence on the word *gringo* was a factor in the dispute which caused me to lose my temper, though Andrés now assures me that the term applies to all fair-skinned people, not just Americans, and is not insulting in itself. Ardiles is anxious that I pay the penalty for all the gringos in his past. I'm not anxious to pay, of course. Andrés has warned me to keep my revolver under my head tonight, and I think I'll accept this advice, though I believe the whole thing will blow over. Somehow, Andrés has gotten the money into Ardiles's proud pocket, which is a big step forward. Andrés's position with Ardiles is that I do not speak Spanish well enough to realize what I am saying, which is probably true enough; also, I have contributed an apology to the cause. The apology was neither gracefully delivered nor graciously received, but on theory, it permits Ardiles to have his pride and money too.

One reason Andrés is so worried is that the dispute occurred after Pereira had agreed to get us through the Pongo on a balsa. It now appears that Ardiles is Pereira's brother-in-law and could probably dissuade the latter from assisting us. Should Ardiles provoke a fight, we would be badly outnumbered; we cannot count on Alejandro, and our opponents, besides Pereira, Ardiles, and Julio, would include a number of Machiguengas, whose arrows, Mr. Jolly claims, can "bring down a hummingbird . . . at forty feet." But the alternative—Pereira's refusal, that is, to help us—wouldn't be much better, as we can go neither upriver nor down without his cooperation and, under the circumstances, would not be safe where we are even if we had enough to eat. Fortunately, however, Andrés has already suggested to Epifanio that he might be able to use his influence in Lima to help Epifanio obtain some sort of legitimate title to Pangoa, and as Epifanio already has the scent of our dwindling cash, he is, if anything, on our side, at least for the moment. We are all quite aware that he and his Indians could take our guns, money, and equipment by force, should they choose to do so, and possibly it is only the prospect of assistance with the land title which deters him. In any case, he is charging us the same high fee as Ardiles did, excusing this breach of his father's long tradition of hospitality with the confession that he owes so much money in Cuzco that he can no longer go there. We are taking the punishment lying down, and even smiling, for, as Andrés says, we have no choice in the matter and these people know it. Andrés is furious and swears that one day he will even the score.

Our dinner of banana soup went peacefully enough, and even Ardiles and myself managed to address each other in abrupt asides. Meanwhile, the Machiguengas have toasted my sleeping bag over their fire, a permanent installation centered between the burning ends of three large logs; the logs are inched forward as they dwindle. The Indians have relaxed somewhat, and some of them are giggling at our various eccentricities of dress and behavior; they are an open-faced and wide-mouthed lot, very appealing. One of their legends is that long ago their god took away their wisdom and cleverness because the child of this beneficent spirit, while entrusted to them, was swallowed by the river demon of the Pongo de Mainique. The wisdom was given to the whites, or gringos, who have put it to use in the manufacture of billboards and hydrogen bombs: one day, the Machiguengas hope, their god will relent, and their former cleverness will be restored to them, but for the moment they have resigned themselves to both ignorance and stupidity, a marvelous stroke of luck for the Pereiras and other *patrones* who have enslaved them.

Epifanio told us a number of Machiguenga legends and showed us a book of notes on the tribe that his father had compiled; a copy of these notes, which must be of great potential interest to ethnologists, is apparently in the hands of Padre Matamola in Quillabamba. Even Ardiles expressed interest, squatting next to Epifanio on a log bench, but the atmosphere is still strained. Later in the evening, when we lay down at last, Andrés had his carbine and his flashlight at his fingertips, and I kept the loaded revolver in my hand, beneath my head, though I took pains not to show it. There is a popular idea in South America that the British are frightened of cold steel, and in this regard I could easily be mistaken for an Englishman. I think that Andrés's idea of the difficulties is perhaps exaggerated, but I'd much, much rather be safe than sorry.

### April 18, Pongo de Mainique

The night passed without incident, and this morning the air had cleared to the extent that Epifanio took me on a guided tour of Pangoa; Ardiles came along, and so did Alejandro. We took one of the canoes downriver a short distance, to a point on the bank known as Sangianarinchi, or "painted stones"; there, on the smooth boulders by the river's edge, partly submerged at this time of year, are some extraordinary hieroglyphics and symbols of obscure origin, including a striking "dancing frog."*

Sangianarinchi is just below a former mission station of the *lingüísticos*, as the personnel of the Summer Institute of Linguistics are known throughout the jungles of Peru; this Protestant organization . . . specializes in the transcription of the many Indian tongues into the written word and the translation of the Bible into Indian. The Pangoa station was run by a man named Snell, according to

---

*These drawings are not dissimilar to those found on rocks at the mouth of the Rio Branco in Brazil by Richard Spruce, a botanist who worked in the Amazon Valley at the same time as H. W. Bates, and whose text, like Bates's, remains a standard reference work a century later.

Epifanio. It has been abandoned for some time, for reasons which he did not make clear, and the jungle has reclaimed the clearing. The thatch roofs of the buildings are falling in, and the two rude crosses which still rise out of the growing tangle are precariously aslant, about to tumble.

At the hacienda, meanwhile, the Indians were assembling a balsa, using some logs already cut and dried as well as some green poles cut this morning; we returned in time to see two braves come sailing down the bank, clinging to slippery fresh poles gathered at a point upriver. These were soon notched and spiked and lashed together, and it occurs to me with rather a start that we are actually on the brink of "risking our lives," as Andrés remarked, unfortunately, I thought, in the Pongo de Mainique. But between risking his life and making his way back upstream on foot, Andrés would infinitely prefer the former, and though I am filled with a growing dread as we wait here, I must say I agree. One is through the Pongo, it is said, in fifteen minutes, though ideas on it vary so much that I wonder at times if anybody has ever been through it at all. Ardiles speaks loosely of waves twenty feet high, whereas Pereira claims that, in certain respects, the passage of the Pongo in the rainy season is less dangerous than in the dry season, when people ordinarily try it: his theory is that some of the dangerous rocks are covered over. I hope he is right, but I would have more faith in what he says if he were going to accompany us.

Whatever the truth of the matter, we are casting off at midday. I'm not at all sure we know all we should, and would feel much happier with a life-preserver. I asked Epifanio if he thought we would make it to the mission at Timpia before nightfall. He and Ardiles grinned at each other in a way I disliked very much, and Pereira said, "Maybe, if you go directly." This sounded pretty sinister to me.

I do not trust Epifanio, but he is an appealing fellow and I bear him no grudge. Standing there on the bank as we clambered gingerly onto our new balsa—in a desperate attempt to amuse myself at this ominous moment, I have christened her the *Happy Days*—both he and the unkempt Ardiles seemed genuinely sorry to see us go. Between them, they had all our money in their pockets, and no doubt felt that, in letting us disappear into the Pongo, they were killing the goose that laid the golden egg.

The *Happy Days* is comprised of four large balsa poles, with two much smaller ones along each side, and the usual cargo frame mounted in the center. It strikes me that about twelve more large poles would be just the thing, but apparently there comes a point— it is said to come rather often in the Pongo—when maneuverability is more important than bulk. In all, our craft is about eighteen feet long by four and one-half feet wide, very little larger than its predecessor but infinitely better made. Though rude in appearance, it has a nice feeling of solidity about it, and in calm water its deck is actually above the surface.

Our *bogas* are three young Machiguengas, dressed in *cushmas*, with shorts beneath; they wear only the shorts while on the river. They have with them their hard black *chonta* bows and long cane arrows, to provide for them on the return trip through the jungle; they also have yuca, plantains, and a watery fruit called *limas*, in fiber bags. The three have been given Christian names—Toribio, Raul, and Agostino—but they do not speak Spanish. Our faithful Alejandro, a Quechua, manages to divine their intentions now and then, though when asked to interpret he only smiles gently, saying, "I don't know. Theirs is a different tongue." Alejandro is the fourth *boga*, kneeling clumsily behind the bow man, Toribio. He is dressed in his poor underwear, and he is a very ugly boy, with a head which could only look natural beneath the distracting head- gear of the *puno*; his skin, when cold, is the nameless color of an old bruise, blotched with old healed sores of purple. His shoulders are narrow and his joints knobby, while his feet are short and thick as clubs; he has none of the grace of the Machiguengas, who slide into place like fishes. He has a low brow and exceedingly long lashes over small discolored eyes, giving him a lidded look, and he is not alert. Yet he is strong and faithful and has natural gentleness and manners. He also has a little plastic comb, his sole belonging, and with this he goes each morning to the riverside and carefully draws flat his coarse black hair; this is the substance of his ablutions, and five minutes later his hair is awry once more, thus to remain for the next twenty-four hours. He was born in Cuzco, where he belongs, and wishes to seek his fortune in Lima, where he does not.

We had not gone very far downriver when we came upon a small *canoa* drawn into the bank; the Indians steered our balsa in beside it. Without a word, all three disappeared into the tangle. One reads of Indians being "swallowed up" by the jungle, and the phrase is a good one: one moment they were there, and a second later they were not.

Surprised, we sat stupidly where we were. In the silence that followed we listened to a *chito* monkey and to the ubiquitous *pustes*. Andrés was openly apprehensive; we were not beyond the reach of foul play or "revenge," one form of which would be to have the Indians remove us downstream, thus, and suddenly desert us. A balsa cannot be poled upstream, and the trail, if one existed, not only would be difficult to find but would lead us straight back to the difficulties at Pangoa. Our emergency food was all but gone—we had two cans of peaches, a bottle of *pisco*, and Celeste Allen's ceremonial Scotch—and starvation in this jungle, for anyone but a native Indian, is a simple matter. In effect, our one chance would be to risk the Pongo and try to reach the mission at Timpia; undermanned and inexperienced as we were, this course would be all but suicidal.

Within ten minutes, however, the Indians returned. They brought with them lengths of strong liana, and these they secured to the cross-pole forward, then led back to the stern. To Alejandro they managed to convey the idea that from now on we could expect to use these lianas as a safety measure and should hang on for all we were worth.

A few of the *mal pasos* above the Pongo de Mainique are alleged to be worse than the Pongo itself, and while this is not so, at least in the rainy season, they are worse by far than anything to be found farther above. And no two are alike: the *encuentros* of the Yavero and Mantaro Rivers are very different in the type of maelstrom they create, and besides these there are such places as Bongoni (waves-next-to-the-land), Maranquiato (ravine-of-vipers), Shintorini (place-of-pig-transformed-into-fish), Patirini (where a bishop—*patirini*—was drowned), and Mapirontoni (place of many stones). These are but seven of the sixteen *mal pasos* between Pangoa and the Pongo which are recognized by name, and of all of them Mapirontoni, where gray waves leaped up in a narrow channel and crashed down across the raft, was perhaps the most spectacular. But there was something for every taste—swift rapids and evil *remolinos*, and water climbing the canyon face, tilting the raft at an uneasy angle, and holes-in-the-water where a boulder did not quite protrude, and rushing white wakes where a boulder did, and the inevitable *tumbos*—each *mal paso* drenched us. We wore only shorts and shirts, in case we had to swim, though I can't believe swimming would have helped very much in the *mal pasos*; everything, in the end, depended on the stoutness of the *Happy Days* and the skill of the Machiguengas.

Both of these seemed in good order, for though the dangers were far more serious than any we had encountered with Marquez and Ardiles, the actual emergencies were probably less. For the most part the Indians, squatting on their heels, worked deftly and silently, without the desperate shouting and confusion which characterized the earlier journeys; they spoke to one another softly, in little whoops, like children, and only in three or four places prior to Megantoni, as they called the Pongo, did their alarm get the better of them. Then they would screech at one another to paddle harder—"*Shin-tse! shin-tse!*"—and, when paddling was of no avail, would set up an unearthly howling, especially Raul, who emitted sounds of terror and psychic pain which were extremely hard on the nerves. On the other hand, a certain amount of racket comes naturally to these Indians in tense moments, and they continued to do their work very well indeed. We were racing along into a driving rain and wind when suddenly we dropped over a shallow *tumbo*, at a bend, and there, two hundred yards ahead, rose the sheer portals of reddish granite which form the entrance of the Pongo de Mainique.

At this the Indians howled anew and struggled desperately to bring about an emergency crash landing at a small beach of black sand lying under the steep bank on the left side. The bow man, Toribio, leaped for the beach with a liana, but he sank from sight into the torrent, and the line pulled free: I was certain in that instant that we had seen the last of him. But he popped up, mouth wide, and, as the current swept him down, caught hold of the stern as the raft swung around, for his tug had pulled her in toward the bank. The timing was miraculous, but, though Toribio grinned uneasily, the Indians otherwise took no notice of it. They tied the balsa to a stiff, scraggy shrub which is common on the banks in this part of the river, and Agostino and Raul went downstream along the sharp rocks, barefoot, apparently to peer into the Pongo.

There had been some idea before we left Pangoa that we would not try the Pongo until morning, on the theory that, in case of accident, we would not have the oncoming darkness to contend with. Now I was not sure how I felt about it: I was afraid, I knew that much, and more so because of this dark, gloomy afternoon of rain and cold, and I kept asking myself what in the name of God I thought I was doing here in the first place. On the other hand, there was no turning back, we were already trapped in the outer canyon, between cliff and torrent, and the side of me already frozen stiff and scared longed to be put out of its misery as speedily as possible, one way or the other. Andrés was shaking so with cold that he could scarcely talk; I imagine he felt as I did. As for poor Alejandro and Toribio, they squatted and shivered on the rocks, arms wrapped around their knees, naked and resigned as a pair of apes; their dark skin looked nobbly and dead.

I had in my shirt a little coca, presented me as a last-minute love token by Ardiles: I took a little and almost immediately felt better. At least I stopped trembling sufficiently to walk. I offered some to Andrés, but he refused it, saying it made him dizzy.

Now the two scouts returned, moving swiftly, and without a word untied the raft. A few moments later, much too hastily for my taste—it seemed to me that I had a lot of important questions about the Pongo, though of course our *bogas* could not communicate the answers—we were aboard and bearing down upon the Pongo, and at a speed which, had we had even the slightest control over it, could only have been called insane.

The word *pongo* denotes a ravine or gorge where a river bursts through the mountains, and the Pongo de Mainique, to the Machiguengas, is known as the Place of the Bears: the legend is that a river monster or demon in the form of a bear lurks in its waters, rising up now and again to do some drowning. The single *mal paso* on the far side of the Pongo is called Tonkini, or Place of Bones, which may or may not be an indication of the bear's success.

"The Pongo de Mainique," wrote Mr. Jolly, "is the worst pass on the river. . . . The approach was a magnificent sight. Gaunt rocks rose sheer on either side, with great white waves dashing high against them. . . . The river thunders over huge boulders in a mass of foam and spray at a speed I estimated at forty miles an hour. The fall is from fifty to sixty feet."

My own impressions of the Pongo are less definite, owing to a certain nervous confusion; I can only say that if the conditions in the Pongo are as Mr. Jolly described them, then in portaging the rapids on foot—I insert this here with a certain calculating smugness—he and his party did the right and sensible thing. It is true that the approach is a magnificent sight, as the Gate of Hell must be, and the gaunt rocks and high waves at the entrance made a marked impression on me, to be sure, but after that I had but a tenuous grasp on my aesthetic vision. I don't say that everything went haywire, but my outlook was decidedly blurred, even when my head was not submerged.

Fear is very much like pain, in the sense that, in the intervals that one is free of it, one forgets how very disagreeable it is. I am not an authority on fear, avoiding the condition whenever possible, but I do know that its worst agony comes well beforehand, in the period of suspense; by the time the crucial moment arrives, a certain detachment—a fatalistic sense, a longing to finish the suspense, and finally a dull resignation—has replaced the quaking. Stupidly, one plods to meet one's fate. In any case—and the coca may have helped a bit—I found myself able to absorb the experience more or less objectively. Here are my impressions, written down the following morning. I shall check them later with Andrés, who, as a dedicated believer that the rapids of the good old days on the Huallaga are worse than anything we could possibly come upon in these puny times, is sure to cut away the excess fat.


The *Happy Days*, then, rushed down upon the entrance and struck a white swirl under the great monolith on the east side; the Indians screamed, and the balsa yawed down into a kind of hole, spun around twice, and bobbed free again. The waves came at us from all directions, and we took several large ones full in the face; the next moment, to my astonishment, we had surfaced again and were sweeping along in swift, calm water. I had expected a maelstrom from one end of the Pongo to the other (one alleged veteran had told us that the waves accumulated all the way, reaching a terrifying pinnacle at the far end), and this breathing space came as a very pleasant surprise. Not only that, but it gave me a chance to look around, though I had to jar myself out of an odd state of mental suspension—perhaps the dull resignation I referred to previously—in order to do so.

First of all, the Pongo must certainly be one of the most beautiful canyons in the world; on a late afternoon of rain, it must also be one of the darkest. The sheer cliffs rise several hundred feet on both sides of the narrow cut, and the higher walls are overgrown with rich mosses and ferns and other denizens of shade and shadow. The rocks near the water, however, as well as the numerous caverns, look black, and the water itself, where it runs clear, is as black as in a fairy tale. The current bore us along in soft, slow ominous swirls— we were actually moving swiftly—passing us from one vague *remolino* to another. All this time the rain and wind swept at us up the canyon, which stretched away like a long avenue of high, dark battlements.

On the raft there was now that utter silence of simple awe, awe of the *mal paso* traversed at the entrance, perhaps, and even of the majesty of this forlorn place, which might be the rock garden of a giant, but mostly of the fact that we were now in it, irretrievably, with no place to stop or even to pause. (In the dry season, apparently, one can catch one's breath, take photographs, and so forth, at several small beaches and footholds which appear in the canyon, but this was not true on April 18, 1960.) And I remember a small yellow bird, like a yellow warbler, flicking along from moss to dripping branch; the bird seemed so heedless and natural in that world, as we were not.

I was sitting in the fore part of the raft, behind Toribio and Alejandro. Then came the small cargo rack, and behind it Andrés; I turned to look at him, and he peered at me noncommittally, like a beaver. We were just hanging on now, psychically as well as physically. Behind Andrés, Raul and Agostino commenced to moan, and I faced forward again: the channel was narrowing, and ahead the water had turned white.

The Indians were yelling something, and Andrés called to me, his voice a little strained. "Look out, now," he said. "Hang on with all you've got." I got a death grip on the lianas. Alejandro was staring forward at the waves, and even the back of his head looked surprised. The waves had not looked very high at first, but this was because we had seen only the crests of them; the waterfall between the raft and the waves had not been apparent in the rain. "Alejandro," I said. "Be ready, now." He nodded rapidly and flashed a kind of smile in a quick half-turn of his head. This was all he had time for. The Machiguengas were yipping and grunting, and Raul was making a special sound of his own that came from somewhere in his pelvis, a sound a man might make when, having been confronted with the imminence of his own death, he was then punched in the stomach. The next moment, forsaking their paddles, they howled as one and sprang for the lianas, for there was nothing more they could do: we seemed to slide sideways down the waterfall, and then we were looking up from the bottom of a hole, with the waves caving in on us from impossible heights.

I say "impossible heights" because, from a raft, any wave looks very large, and these waves would have been beauties anywhere. But with all due respect to Ardiles, they were nothing like six meters; a better guess would be anywhere from eight to twelve feet. And they had little force: at one point, when one swept across us, I was washed violently to one side of the raft, but I recall shouting to myself with relief how weak they seemed for their size. And of course they are not true waves at all, but only the upflung boil or chop of a great rapid.

Nevertheless, when the first big one loomed above our heads, I said to myself quite clearly, with a kind of startled exasperation, "Oh, come on!"—as if waves of this dimension had no business in a river, Pongo or no Pongo. After that, for an endless period which may not have exceeded half a minute, the Pongo went totally berserk. The raft spun and tossed, dove down and popped up again, tilted, leaped, and backslid, and behaved generally in what Mr. John Brown, the imperturbable British author of *Two Against the Amazon*, might have described as an eccentric manner. At the same time, it behaved very well, for it remained intact and at no point reached that precarious angle on the point of overturning which the Ardiles craft had achieved at Bacanique.

While in this world of water, both Alejandro and Toribio, floundering together like a couple of dogfish on the ends of their lianas, were washed back against the young *caballero* riding first-class. We were all piled up like maggots, and there was a good deal of vulgar clutching before things got straightened out. Then the waters abated and the two resumed their stations, as did Agostino and the hysterical Raul, and a good thing too, because this particular *mal paso*, the worst on the Urubamba, is followed immediately by its near-equal, a very large whirlpool on the right side of the river. (I have since been told that in the dry season this particular *remolino* does not exist.) The Indians paddled furiously, but the clumsy balsa slid implacably across the *remolino*'s outer rim. Instantly it was spun around and sucked toward the neat hole at the vortex; there came a horrid gurgling as the bow was drawn beneath the surface.

This, for me, was almost the worst moment. Alejandro and Toribio scrambled up on the slope to a chorus of death cries from astern, and then the raft popped out, turned around, and tried it all over again, backward. Again the good old *Happy Days* surged free, and this time, having made the complete circuit of the *remolino*, it skated out to the rim again: the frantic skill of the Indians drove it onward, into the open current.

It is just below this spot, as I recall, that a lovely waterfall feathers down the cliff face on the east side. Rather coolly, I thought—

though, on reflection, I was probably trying to ease my nerves—I remarked on its elegance to Andrés. But Andrés only stared at me from behind the cargo as if I were some sort of madman. He had been calm throughout the passage, but later, when I asked him his opinion about the *remolino*, he said fervently, "I didn't like it."

Alejandro, squatting in front of me, could not get over his experience. He kept wringing one hand, eyes shining, as near vivacity as he may ever get. "*Ai-ee, qué rico!*" he repeated several times, rather inexplicably.

We went on down the black current, and in a little while Andrés called forward.

"I think they're saying that we're through the worst of it," he said.

"Good," I said. I was dying of relief and could say no more.

We went on in silence, through rapids and swirls that could only seem negligible by comparison to their predecessors, and in a few minutes approached the lower portals of the Pongo. These are less imposing than the entrance, but they are mighty all the same and contribute immensely to the drama of the place. The rocks toward this end are rectangular in shape, as if cut by some mighty hand, and the moss on them, the ferns, and the lavender-red flowers of a vine falling down the face of the portal to the left give the whole place the air of an ancient landscape in the romantic concept.

I turned and looked backward, up the canyon. The dark walls were merging in the distance, closing us off, and beyond, the mountains rose and disappeared into the mists of the cloud forest; there somewhere lay the dank realms of Pangoa. For the Pongo de Mainique is the entrance to the Andes, in a way more dramatic than can possibly be described: the jungle on the lower side is quite different jungle from that above, only a few miles away. The river emerging from the narrow Pongo, through a cut perhaps twenty yards across, broadens out into a river of the rain forest, with its sweeping forks and river islands of gravel. The mountain valleys and shadows have disappeared, replaced by the flat selva, which stretches away indefinitely behind red, eroding banks. The swift white streams plunging into the river are gone too; in their place are quiet creeks and shady leads. Even the wildlife has taken on a fresh aspect: within a mile of the Pongo, we saw a *maniro*, a pygmy deer not much larger than a hare, and a pair of black ducks or small geese rose out of the river, large white patches vivid on their wings.

There were several tricky places, one of which, presumably, was the Place of Bones, Tonkini. But we were veterans now, with full trust in the *Happy Days*. On we drifted in a kind of growing realization, exultation.

Behind me, at last, I heard a sigh. I turned to see a new Andrés, grinning from ear to ear. "Now I feel at home," he explained. "Isn't it beautiful here? Flat, flat, flat! We're out of the Andes, and I'm glad. The mountains make me gloomy, and I hate them." The change in his appearance was remarkable: for the past week he had looked old, and now he looked simply tired.

The Indians were grinning too, Raul with his black face tattoos and crude haircut, Toribio with his tight gas belly and thin legs of malnutrition, and Agostino, who in his way is beautiful. And Alejandro: Alejandro, in an excess of belated nerves, was devouring one *lima* after another.

And I was grinning, at least inwardly. We were through the Pongo and we were an important step forward on our way, and at Timpia, not far below, Cruz might be awaiting us; in any case, there would be a radio there with which to reach him. And I too had had enough of the mountain valleys, the lowering clouds, the wary, nervous people. The weather was clearing, and my spirits were clearing with it. I felt a terrific surge of joy and life and felt like singing.

It was late now, nearly five, and darkness was not far away. In a little while the Machiguengas eased the balsa toward the shallow *encuentro* of a small river. We wanted to reach Timpia this evening, for in the jungle the custom is that people wait eight days and then go on; this was the eighth day since the date that Cruz had planned to meet us. Andrés pointed downriver, saying, "Timpia," and the Indians nodded and smiled. They understood that we wanted to go on, but Indians do not have our own exaggerated sense of time's importance, and they could not take our haste too seriously. They were tired, understandably, and they meant to camp here; that was that. The Indians of the selva come and go much as they please, having little or no concept of duty, and as each *vuelta* of the river meant a longer trek for them, through a wild jungle without trails, we would be lucky if they did not slip off during the night.

They drew the balsa into the mouth of the small river, and we camped beneath a yellow-flowered tree. Removing our soaked clothes, we realized how deeply cold we were: the last bottle of *pisco* was hunted out, and all six of us took deep swallows of it. The Indians, who had only their wet *cushmas*, built a fire and kept near it; over the fire they constructed their precarious grill of sticks and placed yuca and plantains there to cook.

Andrés was exhausted. He made his bed quickly on some branches cut with the machete and did not bother to eat supper. By six o'clock, when darkness came, he had turned in. Relaxed a little by the *pisco*, he spoke bitterly of the people we had had to deal with. "They are not jungle people," he kept saying, "but people of the sierra who have come down into the jungle. And there is an old saying in Peru: 'Never trust the people of the sierra.' These people have lied to us and cheated us, but wait and see: everything comes around in life a second time, and I am going to revenge us, wait and see. They have taken a year of my life, these people, and especially that business with your friend Ardiles." He looked up and shook his head. "I just don't think you realize what a bad spot we were in."

This was true—and I still don't quite accept it. I was in fine spirits, and I went over to the Indians' fire, where Alejandro loitered hungrily. One never touches the belongings of the jungle Indian unless one wishes to risk trouble, nor does one request food from them, according to Andrés, without insuring their contempt. But Agostino, the most civilized of the three, was quite aware that we were without food. Neither Andrés nor myself had felt like begging from Epifanio, and Epifanio had not offered anything but a few *limas*: we had counted on getting some supplies at Timpia. Whether because we had shared our *pisco* with him, or because we had been through the Pongo together—probably it was neither of these reasons, for the Indian is not sentimental—Agostino rose suddenly and thrust some yuca and bananas at us, silent and unsmiling.

We ate our supper in the darkness. Alejandro is no conversationalist, and my Spanish is poor, but we talked anyway because we were happy. Across the mouth of the stream a strange animal voice resounded, very loud and fast, *"ock, ock, ock, ock, ock,"* and then slowed quickly, *"ock . . . ock . . . ock,"* and, after a few seconds' silence, a solitary *"ock."* The Machiguengas called this a *tarato,* and while Alejandro felt it was a monkey, I felt certain it must be a remarkable sort of frog or toad. We discussed this a little, and then it occurred to me—for the first time, I'm ashamed to say—to ask this uncomplaining boy if he could swim. He smiled sheepishly. *"Poco,"* he said. *"Muy poco, señor"*—as if he were somehow at fault.

We arrived at the *encuentro* of the Mapuya about three that afternoon. On the clay bank above the junction there was once an extensive rubber camp, which prospered in the days of the "black gold"; until last year a military garrison was maintained there, as a check on the wild Amahuacas farther upstream, but now the huts sink slowly beneath the jungle. These Amahuacas, the same mentioned by Cruz, live in a naked state on the upper Inuya and are said to be very treacherous; according to the *lingüísticos,* the Inuya station is presently the most precarious of their missions. The linguist there has a small band of loyal Indians, but other groups come in constantly on raiding parties, and he is unquestionably in serious danger. These same tribes, about 1910, put an end to rubber operations in this area by wiping out the camp at the Mapuya *encuentro.* More than sixty people died, according to Cruz, and only one solitary woman escaped. This was token revenge for the Indians, who had been shot down like rats throughout the selva of Peru, Brazil, and Bolivia. Someone has estimated that the number of Indians butchered in the few decades of the rubber boom exceeded all the lives lost in World War I—this figure entirely apart from the thousands who died in slavery. To this day the wild peoples of the interior rivers are considered by most South Americans as subhuman creatures, to be shot on sight—not, it should be said, that North Americans are in a very good position to bewail this matter.

The Mapuya is much smaller than the Inuya, but it is still deep enough at this season to permit good progress, and we arrived toward dark at the lumber camp of Victor Macedo, one of whose peons is the discoverer of the fossil. On the Mapuya, in late afternoon, we had seen a lovely pair of swallow-tailed kites, that most graceful of the hawks, swooping in gentle arcs over the shadowy slow stream; a few of these birds still survive in the wilderness swamps of the southern United States.

### April 26, Quebrada Grasa

Until the very last minute Andrés was skeptical about the existence of the giant bone. But there it was, sunk in the mud of the Mapuya bank, and it is almost everything Vargaray said it was: a *mandíbula* so large and heavy that it takes, if not six men, at least four strong men to lift it. Its great weight, which must exceed two hundred pounds, is less a consequence of its size than of its matter: beneath the smears of petrified clay which have adhered to it lies a solid block of petrified marblelike stone.

It appears to be the small upper jaw of an enormous animal, though of what age, and whether mammal or reptile, I am not equipped to say: we shall learn this, hopefully, in due time. It measures twenty-four inches across what was once the roof of the mouth—the corresponding distance in our own jaw might be an inch and a half—and twenty-eight inches in a line drawn from the front teeth sockets to a line drawn through the rearmost sockets on both sides. There were twenty-six teeth in all, though none remain, and the sockets are approximately round in shape, of a more or less equal size, somewhat larger than a silver dollar in diameter—in short, a formidable apparatus. On the upper side there appears to be, beneath the clay encrustations, at least one petrified nostril, as well as a large cavity behind the snout, as if the creature had ended its own life by lowering its head and charging headlong into a boulder.

Otherwise I am at a loss to describe it, so protean and amorphous is it; I have taken a photograph of César seated in the mouth, for want of any finer inspiration. César and I had a mild celebration, on *pisco* and a Peruvian vermouth called Gancia, I believe, both of which tasted excellent. We sat up very late by jungle standards, before bunking in with the peons of Macedo's camp—Macedo himself is absent—including the proud Juan Pablo, who described at some length how he found the jaw. César was attired in a handsome pair of white pajamas, surely the sole pair of pajamas which has ever found its way into the Mapuya. Really, he is a man of parts and continues to surprise me.

This morning at six I set off with Juan Pablo, another peon named Luis, and my friend Guillermo Tejo, of César's crew, to visit the original site of the *mandibula* and determine if the rest of the animal is still visible. Andrés has given up walking for life—his ankles are still swollen from our trek in the jungle valleys—and he felt, in any case, that he would only slow us down. Though genuinely surprised and impressed by the jaw, he has no real interest in it and is most anxious that we leave here quickly, to insure his arrival in Lima five days hence. As for César, he did not pretend to an interest he did not feel, but elected to stay and savor his breakfast.

Andrés's decision turned out to be the right one, for it took us nearly an hour and a half to reach the place, and the going wasn't easy. The first half-hour or so we poled up a side creek or *quebrada* in a small canoe—the stream is nameless (the Mapuya itself cannot be located on available maps, since its region lies in those great blanks of jungle cartography which are generally labeled "unexplored") but, because of the shiny oil slicks which ooze from the mud of the bank, is called by the peons Quebrada Grasa, or Grease Creek. The slippery banks of deep mud were enough in themselves to give the place its name, and we had to ford the stream a number of times, sometimes over our waists in water.

About two miles above the Mapuya, Juan Pablo stopped at a rocky place in the stream bed. At this exact spot, he announced, he had found himself one day standing on a submerged rock and, happening to look down, discovered that he stood in something's mouth. He called out to Victor Macedo, who was nearby. Macedo was at first impatient, but came over at last and had a look. Together they managed to lever the thing to the shore.

This occurred last November, Vargaray, who lives near Atalaya, must have heard the story shortly thereafter, and he bore it with him downriver to Pucallpa, where he told it to me in the early days of January. The story was still too young to have grown very much, and was thus one of the few cases where a barroom rumor on the Amazon turned out substantially as advertised. Since November, Juan Pablo has discovered two more fossil sites, one of which contains, embedded in a rock, the petrified shell of a giant turtle, and the other a variety of enormous bones.

We located a few more bones this morning in the river bed, but whether these belonged to the possessor of the jaw would be hard to say; in any case, the great bulk of that animal was buried or missing. Since the bones were too heavy to carry back with us, I encouraged the men to leave them exactly where they were, on the theory that any horsing around we might do would only make things harder for the properly equipped expedition which might come after; I asked them to take the same precautions with the other sites as well.

We found also the skull of a modern *sajino*. Like the fossils, this was petrified, though the ivory of the tusks was still fresh and white, and it would be interesting to know what geological characteristic of this region permitted petrifaction millions of years ago as well as now; perhaps it is the oil. Finally, we found a living fossil, a sleepy baby crocodile, representing a family many millions of years old and slowly disappearing from the earth; Guillermo claims it is of the dangerous black species, and its color, unlike that of the young animals seen here and there along the rivers, is certainly black rather than bamboo. Guillermo lashed its mouth with fronds of palm, and we are taking it back with us as a mascot.

From Juan Pablo's information I was able to construct a crude diagram of the other bone sites. They are some distance from the first, more than a day's round trip, and I now very much regret having encouraged Andrés to accompany us to the Mapuya, since he is most anxious to get back for his anniversary, and we will not be able to stay here long enough to make even a cursory investigation of what may prove to be an important paleontological discovery. (It now seems to me, too, that I want very much to visit the wild Amahuaca tribes upstream; it's a pity, and infinitely frustrating, that I wasn't more decisive about this while we still had a chance to drop Andrés off at Atalaya.)

I haven't said that I've had a magnificent morning. I have. And curiously, the magnificence did not consist of finding what we were after—more poor old bones, and thus a certain scientific confirmation of the site—but lay instead in the purity of this jungle stream. Only a few woodcutters like Juan Pablo, seeking the isolated *cedro* and *coaba* trees, may ever have ascended this *quebrada*, and there is no mark of the white man's heavy hand upon it. Its still banks are laced with the tracks of tapir, capybara, and other creatures, and its clear water, running quietly on sandy shoals, sparkles with the flash of the pretty *sabalo*. In the bends the water runs beneath stone banks and is a pure, limpid green, and the trees which lend their leaf color to the water soar away in great white columns. The queer and clumsy hoatzin huffs everywhere in the lower branches, and hidden birds of unknown shape and color whistle and answer down the cool silences, in counterpoint and incredible clear harmonies. The tree frogs loose their prodigious croaks, and from a mile away resounds one of the mightiest sounds in nature, like nothing so much as an ominous moan of wind, the community howl of the *mono colorado*—the red howler monkey. In the stream itself lie the striking shells of a variety of mollusks, including a gastropod so large—the size of a very large pear—that it is difficult to believe it is not a marine creature. (Louis Agassiz, a century ago, pointed out the marine character of the dolphins, fishes, and other aquatic fauna of the Amazon basin.) We paused to breakfast on a kind of nut, the Indian name for which has now escaped me, and I wondered why the stream itself was so much more exciting than the bones we had found in it—more exciting than the first sight of the great jaw itself the night before. And it occurred to me that, aside from its beauty—for it is precisely this inner, mysterious quality of the jungle, represented so well by this lost stream, that I have been searching for and feel I have found at last—there was an adventure here, an exploration, however timid.

It is adventure I have missed a little in the past few days, and which a visit to the wild Amahuaca tribes would restore. These days have been fun, they have even been exciting—I note here with surprise that one of the original aims of the expedition is practically accomplished—but they have lacked that element of the unknown, the unpredictable, that the ordeal of the mountain river had in abundance. We know now where we will be from one day to the next, and that we will have enough to eat: we carry our food with us, and there is plenty of it. Everything is organized, everything taken care of, and I think back on the first days of the journey with a faint regret. As so often happens, we did not comprehend, did not evaluate our experience until it was all over and gone forever from our days.

## *May 2, Pucallpa*

On Saturday morning, just as Andrés was about to board the plane for Lima, Cruz came running up. A telegram had arrived for the police chief of Pucallpa from his confrere in Atalaya.

"Please detain a Señor César Cruz," it read—for I saw it myself later, and am paraphrasing only a little—"who appears to have removed a fossil mandible from property on the Mapuya River without consulting the owner, Victor Macedo."

Cruz's worst fears had been realized, for clearly Macedo, upon learning from Juan Pablo what had happened, had raced downriver to Atalaya and registered—despite the nice wording of the radiogram—a charge of theft. Macedo feels entitled to a share of the loot, for there was a fast-spreading and troubling rumor in Atalaya and now in Pucallpa that the fossil is worth a fortune. Having heard Juan Pablo's account, I don't feel Macedo has any claim—though Macedo and the luckless Vargaray might well argue that they had at least as much right to a fee as César Cruz. In any case, the bone has now been confiscated by the police "until the matter is clarified." In South America this phrase can usually be translated "until a satisfactory amount of money has changed hands, or more powerful influences are brought to bear." Before boarding the plane, Andrés promised to arrange for those influences in Lima, in the form of a cable from a cabinet minister which would release the local police from further responsibility and direct them to return the bone to me, but so far there has been no word. I am scheduled to fly out tomorrow, to Tingo María in the montaña, but it looks very much as if I shall have to stay.

Yesterday Macedo himself turned up in Pucallpa. Cruz ran into him on the street, and they greeted each other with their relentless Peruvian civilities, but Macedo walked off coldly without mentioning the small matter of the bone. This afternoon the three of us convened in the office of the chief of police, who was duly informed by Macedo that the poor unsuspecting Juan Pablo had delivered up a very valuable stone belonging to Macedo for the equivalent of eighty cents, having been brought previously to a state of total intoxication. Either Juan Pablo gave this story to Macedo to avoid handing over a share of the spoils, or Macedo gave this story to the police to strengthen his own claim. It doesn't much matter, though I am inclined to believe the latter. As it happens, Juan Pablo received five hundred and thirty *soles* from my own hand before touching the single draft of *pisco* handed around by Cruz to celebrate the transaction, and he had not touched a drop in the previous four hours, all of which had been spent with me in Quebrada Grasa.

But Macedo's claim as the owner of the stone was supported by the circumstance that in March he had been offered one thousand *soles* for it by the defendant, César Cruz, a point which Cruz had not seen fit to tell me until this afternoon: this shot a terrific hole in our position that Juan Pablo had always been recognized by all parties as the lawful owner, though I still believe this to be the case. Cruz now claims that he had dealt with Macedo only as the employer of Juan Pablo, not as the jaw's owner (though where this maneuver would have left poor Juan Pablo is difficult to say, unless it was up Grease Creek), and that anyway, he had informed Andrés of the offer of *mil soles*. (Andrés subsequently denied this.) César is the very picture of a man unjustly accused and complains bitterly of his plight, though in fact he is the only person to make anything out of the whole business. Macedo is also embittered. He tells me that if we had awaited his return that day everything would have worked out, but that now he is so angry with the thieving Cruz that he will not give up the bone for any price. He has a great many unkind things to say about Cruz, and Cruz, who says that everything would have been dandy if Andrés had not made us hurry, has a great many unkind things to say about Macedo. As for myself, I am mired indefinitely in the heat and mud of Pucallpa, and I have a great many unkind things to say about them both.

*May 6, Pucallpa*

I have now passed a week in Pucallpa, attempting to deal with an aroused populace. The bone has become the talk of the town, almost every inhabitant of which has come to the yard outside the police station to stare at it. The misinformation heaped up by the excited reports of Pucallpa's radio station has caused me to be recognized by one and all as I stalk the streets, and I am frequently stopped and asked my opinion as to the identity of the monster. The truthful answer, that I have no idea, is entirely unsatisfactory, and I now say that it appears to be some sort of long-extinct herbivorous mammal. Depending on the alertness of my audience, this answer brings about either a blank stare or a furious nodding of the head, as if to say, Of course, of course, it's just what I suspected.

After six days of suspense a radiogram has at last arrived from Andrés, saying everything is OK, whatever that means. Things are not OK here, for the police have still heard nothing, and Macedo, who also stalks the streets, is open to neither bribe nor logic. The question of ownership is hopelessly lost in a mountain of lies and accusations, and the only hope of a change in this situation appears to be a wire from Lima stating that the bone belongs to neither Macedo nor myself but has been confiscated by the state. Meanwhile it stands mutely in its crate beneath this vulture sky, of no use to anybody.

My original plan was to take the fossil to the American Museum of Natural History in New York, since there is nobody in Peru equipped to make an exact identification. But an expert is not required to state that our unwieldy find is of considerable scientific value, and it seems unlikely that the Government of Peru, should they once claim it, will ever let it go: this is especially true since Peruvians, resenting the number of Inca and pre-Inca artifacts which have been taken from the country, are more than sensitive about "national treasures." The law on national treasures does not embrace paleontological finds, but doubtless it can be construed to do so.

I have taken photographs of the bone from every angle, but there seems to be nothing else that I can do here, if indeed there ever was: I am flying out to Tingo María tomorrow, minus the object of the expedition, with only the faint hope that matters can be straightened out in Lima. The week has passed in a sort of dream, a kind of miasma of unreality which only a jungle town could induce. Aside from the interview with Wayne Snell, the only noteworthy experience was an evening when César and myself took a jungle potion prepared by an old Indian of the town. This bitter stuff, which in color alone resembles opaque apple cider, is called variously *ayahuasca*, which is Quechua for "dead man's vine," or *soga de muerte*, which is Spanish for "vine of death." It produces hallucinations of faraway music and arrested time, a sense of several simultaneous worlds, which is quite remarkable; there is also the vague giddiness of being drunk, without the exhilaration. Toward the end a distinctly morbid state occurs, quite disagreeable. I have since identified the plant as *Banisteriopsis caapi*, a flowering liana of the Malpighiad family first described by Richard Spruce in 1853 and used as a narcotic by the Indian tribes throughout the Amazon: it is the narcotic known to the American writer William Burroughs and other admirers of its use as "yage." (In Lima I turned over a large draft of *ayahuasca* to the wandering beat poet Allen Ginsberg, who subsequently visited Pucallpa and saw the "excellent monstrous fossil." Of *ayahuasca* he wrote me fervently, "No wonder it's called *soga de muerte*.")

I have talked many times to César on the subject of the Picha ruins. He is sincerely convinced that they exist, on the basis of what he has been told by the Machiguenga at his *ganadería*. His description corresponds with that of Basagoitia, except that, according to Cruz, the ruin lies four days upriver rather than fifteen, plus a trek of several days into the jungle. Last year, he says, two Englishmen tried to reach it but had to give up when their guide refused to go any farther.

Another man who believes completely in these ruins is Wayne Snell. Snell, incidentally, lent four of his Pangoa Indians to the Tennant expedition which discovered the ruin on the Mantaro: he says that the party would not have gotten through had Fidel Pereira not approved it and passed word of his approval from tribe to wild tribe of the savage Machiguengas who inhabit the interior tributaries. Apparently there are also Machiguengas on the upper Camisea who kill on sight, and one gets the impression that civilization has reached only the outposts of some of these peoples; in many areas of Peru there remain wild rivers up which, past a certain point, no traveler dares to go. The Mantaro ruin lies about fifteen days, by canoe and foot, from the Urubamba.

Like César Cruz, Snell knows a Machiguenga who claims to have visited the Picha ruin. There is also another boy, a Machiguenga-Campa now at Yarina Cocha, who he thought might have been there too, and he talked to this boy the afternoon I was there. The boy had indeed been to the ruin, as had his father. He and Snell talked for a while in Machiguenga, and, adding this new information to what he already had heard, Snell was able to supply the following description, by far the most complete I have obtained to date.

The ruins lie at a journey of two days up a small tributary of the Picha, followed by four days on foot: this more or less corresponds to the distance estimated by Cruz's man. The Machiguengas do not like strangers prowling around in the region and avoid going there themselves, as their legend is that the place was cursed and deserted by its original chief: this may account, Snell feels, for the reluctance of the Machiguengas at the Dominican mission at the mouth of the Picha to admit any knowledge of the place.

The site itself is not a ruin in the usual sense, but a high cliff with a huge cavern: in former times a waterfall ran over the cliff and down across the cave mouth, making a natural fortress which was almost impregnable. The watercourse has now changed, and the cave has become accessible. A low wall surrounds the entire place, which is known to the Indians today as Shankivirintsi.

Snell hopes to reach the ruin this summer and, if he succeeds, will be the first white man ever to see Shankivirintsi. I wish him luck, but I must confess to a deep regret that Cruz was not there awaiting us at Timpia. For on the basis of all the evidence, pro and con, that I have heard, I now believe that the Picha ruin exists.

But if it served once as an excuse to enter the jungle, it can serve again. At this point I am suffering from a certain sense of failure, for not only did we miss our chance of locating Shankivirintsi but, after all this time and risk, we are also unable to leave the jungle with the bone. Still, I am leaving Pucallpa willingly, in the certainty I will be here again another time, for I have caught Andrés's jungle fever, the strong sense that something mysterious exists here which, even if located, can never quite be found.

And Alejandro. Alejandro, bowing and tugging his forelock to the last. Alejandro Condoris, beloved son, one hopes, of people named Condoris in Cuzco, though Alejandro, wandering away with us from the Rodríguez hacienda and now anxious to try his luck in Lima, gives the impression of being alone. Alejandro spent most of his meager pay on a great shining clumping pair of black shoes, for he had arrived in Pucallpa barefoot. (At one point he possessed a rude pair of sandals hewn from the defunct tire of a large truck, but these met an obscure fate somewhere on the rivers.) Besides his salary, he has been given his fare and food money and a little extra for his own diversion, should he care to make a distinction between diversion and food, and the promise from Andrés of a job in Lima. He left on a lumber truck this afternoon.

I feel bad about Alejandro, though he himself is as happy as his mountain melancholy will ever let him be. I feel bad because, in a very trying moment on the Ucayali—Cruz lost his hold on the rope by which I was swinging myself from the canoe to a steep mud bank, and I fell ignominiously into the river, camera and all; I managed to hold the camera high, but in doing so smashed that hand hard on the snout of the great fossil—I became exasperated by his weak grasp of the situation, and I showed it. Afterward he brooded and seemed sullen. I bought some fresh bananas from the Chamas (he loves bananas and has a way of lying down next to a large bunch and quietly absorbing the lot, without ever appearing to take one up and peel it) and presented these, repentant, but still he looked distraught.

Alejandro had been longing to shoot the pistol or the rifle, and on the Inuya I had suggested to Andrés permitting him to do so, but both Andrés and César had dismissed any such idea as unheard of, and no more was said about it. On that afternoon on the Ucayali, however, I gave him the pistol to console him; he fired wildly at one crocodile, turned pale, and handed the gun back, sinking immediately into an even more impenetrable gloom. And I kept thinking how very much we had taken this slow, shambling boy for granted, as a kind of ungainly presence, as faceless and heavy and patient as one of the big duffels—this is the way such peons are treated here, and, having always had liberal pretensions, I disliked very much how easily I had fallen into this custom and become hardened to it.

At a loss, I tried to talk to him. This is not a rewarding occupation, especially when a certain language barrier is compounded by a Quechua accent, and probably I have avoided it more than I should. But anyway, we talked haltingly, reminiscing about our trip together, and immediately he came alive. I had been mistaken: the poor fellow had not been resentful of me but only despondent because he had angered me. Now it was clear to him that we were friends again, and he could scarcely contain himself, hunching forward over the rubber duffels until he was perched at my shoulder. With a frantic smile, eyes shining, he began to wring one of his hands, just as he had that afternoon in the Pongo de Mainique.

He cried out, "And the Pongo! Do you remember that time we went through the Pongo together, *señor*, do you remember how terrible it was!"

"*Si, si,*" I said as eagerly as I could. "*Si, si,* Alejandro." But I felt heavy-hearted and very small. I thought of all the interest and credit Andrés and I had received for having gone through the Pongo de Mainique in *el tiempo de agua*: Alejandro Condoris had been with us on the *Happy Days* and had received no credit whatsoever. As a peon, he was presumably not supposed to know what had befallen him, much less give himself airs.

Well, he's off to Lima, our good and faithful Alejandro, to match his wits with his loud *vivo* compatriots of the city streets. I'll remember him with fondness, and I wish him well.

## *Epilogue*

Since returning to the United States, I have looked at a number of journals of South American exploration in attempts to find further information about the Urubamba and the Pongo de Mainique. Mr. Leonard Clark, as we have seen, has referred to the river as "forbidden," and while this is scarcely the case, there are few references to it in the literature of the jungle. Mr. Stratford Jolly and Mr. Julian Tennant, already mentioned, are the only writers known to me who speak about the Pongo.

The first descent of the Urubamba of which I have found record was made in the summer of 1846 by a party under the direction of a noted French naturalist, Francis de Castelnau: an account of its hardships appears in *The Valley of the Amazon,* by William Herndon and Lardner Gibbon, published in 1854. The account makes no reference to the Pongo de Mainique by this name, but an extract quoted from Castelnau's journals describes the loss of one of the party in an attempt to cross the river and portage around a dangerous waterfall — quite possibly that which lies at the head of the main rapid of the Pongo.

> We found the current of exceeding rapidity; and the second cataract roared and foamed only one hundred metres below us. The Indians at every instant cast anxious glances over the distance that separated them from the danger. . . . At this moment we heard the cries behind us, and an Indian pointed with his finger to the canoe of M. Carrasco, within a few yards of us. It was struggling desperately with the violence of the current; at one instant we thought it safe, but at the next we saw that all hope was lost, and that it was hurried toward the gulf with the rapidity of an arrow. The Peruvians and the Indians threw themselves into the water; the old priest alone remained in the canoe, and we could distinctly hear him reciting the prayer for the dying until his voice was lost in the roar of the cataract. We were chilled with horror; and we hastened to the bank, where we met our companions successively struggling to the shore from the lost canoe. . . . We deeply regretted the loss of our companion, whose death was as saint-like as his life.

The photographs of the giant *mandibula* I took to the American Museum of Natural History in New York. Dr. Charles Mook, the museum's senior authority on fossil reptiles, inspected the prints with a magnifying glass and tentatively identified the former owner of the jaw as a very large fossil crocodilian. Dr. Edwin Colbert of the museum agreed with this opinion; he estimated that the giant animal must have attained a length of at least thirty-five feet. According to Dr. Mook, it inhabited the earth at some period between five million and twenty-five million years ago. He was much interested in the discovery of this fossil, which represents a species heretofore unknown to him; he said that the museum would very much like to see it and would pay for its shipment from Peru if I could obtain permission for its export.

I have written a number of inquiries to Peru, where César Cruz has since become the defendant in a suit brought by his former friend Victor Macedo, and the ownership of the bone itself obscured for good by the mass of documents and memoranda: but for the written testimony of Mr. Allen Ginsberg, who saw it in its last known resting place, in Pucallpa, I might almost believe that the whole adventure of the jaw was the very sort of jungle hallucination against which I had been warned. "Between the outer world and the secrets of ancient South America," as Colonel Fawcett once lamented, "a veil has descended," and it now appears that the giant *mandibula* will remain behind it, sinking slowly beneath man's detritus on the steaming banks of the Ucayali.

# *from* Under the Mountain Wall

## A Chronicle of Two Seasons in the Stone Age

1962

*In the spring and summer of 1961 Matthiessen joined a Harvard-Peabody Museum expedition to a valley in western New Guinea (now Irian Jaya) to study the remote and little-known Kurelu tribe, whose one encounter with the outside world had resulted in the shooting of a Kurelu warrior. Among the group were anthropologists, botanists, sound technicians, and photographers, including Michael Rockefeller, a son of the New York governor, whose mysterious disappearance before the project was completed has become a legend in its own right. As elsewhere in his writing, Matthiessen's tone here is frequently elegiac; even as he revels in the wonder of his experience, there is no mistaking the melancholy of his narrative. "The Kurelu offered a unique chance, perhaps the last, to describe a lost culture in the terrible beauty of its pure estate," he writes. "The armed patrols and missionaries invaded their land on the heels of the expedition, and by the time this account of them is published, the proud and warlike Kurelu will be no more than another backward people, crouched in the long shadow of the white man."*

*The following excerpt, which Matthiessen calls "The Death of Weake," shows a violent side of the tribe's life; in it a man and three young boys are ambushed when they go to the river for water. The brutality inflicted on the young victim is mirrored in this piece by the graphically described slaughter of pigs for ceremonial feasting at victory celebrations and at funerals, of which there were many. The letting of blood is a relentless theme throughout the narrative, men and animals alike living and dying with shocking immediacy.*

# The Death of Weake

**High in the dark cloud forests** of the upper Elokera stands a huge beech, and high in this tree hangs a ponderous nest of the great black hawk. Weaklekek wished to obtain this hawk, the feathers of which are valuable, and he set off with his bow and arrow to investigate the nest, the news of which had spread down to the valley. With him he took Asukwan, the young warrior of his *pilai*,* who is credited with a sense of birds and a keen eye. They were accompanied by Tukum, who is credited with almost nothing.

The three went up the valley along the stream bed of a tributary, wading the quiet pools under the banks and leaping from rock to mossy rock; honey eaters and birds of paradise shrieked at their passing, and mountain pigeons, veering off, broke the humid airs with the sharp clap of pigeon wings. Farther on, they took to high ground, crossing abandoned fields; in the hillside woods small flocks of parakeets, red under wing, crisscrossed the treetops in loud senseless consternation.

At a place along the trail the grass was crushed and flattened; Auskwan laughed. He poked the forefinger of one hand back and forth between the second and third fingers of the other, and Weaklekek grinned. Tukum, embarrassed, grinned as well.

In the forest of the upper slopes, with its black mud and thorned rattan, its hanging shapes and gloom, the pale clear boles of the canopy trees soared to crests which closed away the sky; the trail crossed sagging pig fences, and hidden animals grunted hollowly from the shadows of these dark pastures. The trail skirted dismal wells where the limestone had caved in; one well was a hundred feet or more in depth, and strongly fenced around, though the fence was water-logged and rotten. Asukwan tossed a stone into the well, and the three exclaimed at the time which passed before the splash resounded. Lagging behind, Tukum tossed another stone, but this time a sound came back immediately, for Tukum's stone, barely

*Men's round house.

clearing the edge, had fallen on a ledge inside the rim. Tukum glared balefully at the well and trotted onward.

Farther still, in a steep clearing, lay a new pig village, perched on a ledge of mud. Here miniature blue butterflies fluttered like gentian petals, alighting as one on the mud's black gleam and all but vanishing, for with closed wings they were nothing more than small scraps of drab gray. Then the blue color would explode again as the butterflies danced in their odd motion. Tukum laughed, pronouncing their apt name—sigisigit.

At the village a man joined them, and the four went on to the high forest above. A black hawk soared in the gray cloud which hung upon the forest, and Weaklekek whispered at it, making gestures, in order that it circle lower. But the hawk slid off and disappeared, and its nest, when they came to the base of the tree, had no bird at its edge. Weaklekek crept higher on the slope but could not attain the nest level. After a while he came down again and, on the way home, out of frustration, wasted an old arrow in a shot at one of the green parakeets.


The season turned, and the night was clear and cold. The *akuni**
kept to their warm huts until the morning was well started, and out in the crisp air built high brush fires. The brush was of dead sticks and dry brown leaves, and around a large fire built under the pines the air sparkled with autumn; light filtered down in long delicate columns onto the fallen needles. But in the undergrowth just at the wood edge the sun was hot, and the bushes flowered into the rich green of the valley's ceaseless spring.

Once or twice a year, depending on its current fortunes, a clan will hold a ceremony which renews the power of the holy stones and invigorates and protects in battle the warriors of the clan that holds the stones: the cleaning of the stones with grease of ceremonial pig, *wam wisa*, is the most sacred of all rituals practiced by the akuni.

In early June a stone ceremony was held by the *pilai*, in the sun.

---

*"The people," i.e., the Kurelu.

Aloro held the first pig by the head, and Woknabin held it by the haunches, and U-mue shot it through the lungs; the process was repeated with the others. U-mue bit his lower lip as his arms strained at the bow; he smiled briefly upon the release of every arrow, as if in response to some private satisfaction.

A large sow was wheedled toward its doom by Tegearek and Apeore; U-mue awaited them, posed on one knee. But the sow broke free repeatedly and had finally to be seized and overpowered by eight strong warriors. They struggled forward, and the men laughed. A lath was held under the pig's chin to support its head, and the pig bellowed, shuddering all over. U-mue shot it gingerly, and it wrenched free, scattering the people in its path. The grunts and laughter of the men made him look cross. More small pigs were brought and killed; they ran bleeding down the yard, in flight from death, and kept on running even after they had fallen.

The big sow was cornered once again and thrown to earth. Tegearek pumped at its lungs with his foot, but it had been shot badly, and Aloro brought a spear to finish it. It was carried up the yard at last, big dewlaps quaking, its bloodied bristles stiffening in the sun. There were nine pigs in all. Each pig was earmarked, and each man in the company of more than fifty knew not only who had brought them but exactly which was which; they had a very good idea, as well, as to which piece of which pig each man would receive, for the akuni world is a world of protocol and gesture, and those details not preordained by time are painstakingly determined at the slow small fires.

The sow was a long time at the fire, hoisted and kicked and rolled and scraped by Apeore and Tegearek. The dressing of the eight small pigs was already in progress, with two or three men working on each. U-mue stood regally above his people as they bent over their work, the new clay like yellow gold on his black shoulders.

While the pig-dressing proceeded, the sili* became quiet once again. Voices drifted from the shadows, to the fitful chopping of stone adze on bone. Behind the pilai, in the yard, a large fire was

---

*A compound, one or more of which makes up a village.

constructed, like a pyre: here the cooking stones were piled and heated. From the steep hill above the sili men rolled more rocks down the hill; the rocks rumbled through the woods.

Behind the fire, under a pandanus, a small fencing guards the spirits of the dead. The fencing was replaced now with new laths, and its earth weeded and tamped down, to show the spirits that they are not neglected. In the center of the fencing stands a pole of cane with dried ferns attached; this is a warning sign, to indicate that the place must not be violated.

On a rack by the pilai Aloro and Tegearek hung bloody slabs of meat. The hands of both warriors were crimson, and when they were through they drank water from a gourd and wiped their hands with ferns.

Apeore stood in the cooking pit, covering its earthen sides with long fresh grass; the strands of grass fanned outward several feet from the edge, until the pit looked like a gigantic blossom. Wet leaves were placed around the rim, like a bright green heart of the grass flower; nearby lay purple *hiperi*.* The rock fire popped loudly as a stone exploded; the stones were seized and borne away in tongs to line the pit, mounting the sides until an igneous center had been formed. The stones were covered with wet grass, and the big hiperi laid in the steam. U-mue appeared and shouted orders, but in the general exhilaration everyone else was shouting orders too. The voices meant nothing; everyone worked hard and willingly, with swift efficiency. The hiperi were brought, and more wet grass; the rock fire rose above the ground. More stones were laid into the core, while Polik and others wove the grass sides tight: Polik does not hesitate to work side by side with the warriors, or even the *yegerek*,† though he is an older and a greater *kain*‡ than U-mue. The tong men came and went, grunting like penitents; they moved mechanically from pit to fire, fire to pit, their six-foot implements clacking dismally on the rocks. On the pit's edge Apeore sprang about, demonic in the steam.

---

*Sweet potato.
†Youth between infancy and puberty.
‡Leader.

More stones, more leaves, and a large packet of ceremonial pig, wrapped in banana leaf. And still more stones. The stones exploded and a fragment burned hard-faced Huonke, who cried out. More grass, and now a heap of fern, brought forward in huge bundles and sprinkled with water from a sunlit gourd. Tegearek ran forward with the raw sow hide, heaving it flesh down onto the ferns. More pig meat was arranged around it, in fern packets. More stones, more ferns, more silver water, sparkling in the sunlight—and a cry passed on from a distant *kaio.** *Kaio, kaio,* a man shouted, and there was a brief stir, but no one left the feast: today the other clans must take care of the enemy.

The grass extending outward from the pit was folded upward, enveloping the whole, and the entire edifice, like a small haystack, was bound around with a long coil of rattan. The finished job was handsome and compact, the product of uncounted years of practice; the voices had been profligate, but scarcely a gesture had been wasted.

Aloro removed the spare meat from the rack and hung it in the pilai; it would be eaten in the ceremonies of the second day. Nilik came, walking quietly up the yard: the name Nilik derives from this man's lifelong knack for finding himself in the vicinity of pig-eating. There is something ominous in Nilik's hungry presence, and his arrival seemed foreshadowed by the clouding-over of the sun. The west wind freshened, and the skeletal fronds rising above the roofs stirred in hollow, ruined apprehension. He greeted, unsmiling, Asikanalek and other men who passed him in the yard; they were taking advantage of the cooking time to go and investigate what had happened at the kaios.

The rock fire was stripped in the late afternoon, and the browned ferns spread out in a great mat before the pilai. More than one hundred men had now assembled, and most of them sat in a circle around the ferns. Many of the ferns were eaten, and on the rest the pig meat was arranged. The fatty skin of the large sow was hoisted up, and U-mue sliced it in thin strips: these were passed to the individuals and groups deserving them, and there was no sign of quar-

*Lookout tower.

reling, for each knew and received his share. The warriors ate the meat with gusto but without haste or greed, saving some of the hot lard next to the hide to rub on their own skins. The grease of the ceremonial pig is beneficial in every way, providing both strength and good appearance; by the end of the afternoon the dark skins were gleaming.

The sow rump and other special cuts had been taken into the pilai, where U-mue and the old kains had disappeared; there a bundle of new fiber strings, worn at the throat to protect the men in war, were rubbed in *wisa** grease. The fibers were dispensed to warriors like Yeke Asuk, whose recent wound, a serious one, indicated his need of new protection; Yeke Asuk handed some spare strings through the door, and the men outside grasped at them eagerly.

In the rear of the pilai the holy stones, still wrapped, lay in a line on the banana leaf. The following morning, the cleansing of the stones was to take place. Noisily, in the near-darkness of the hut, the old men ate, while behind them, slung from the rafters, the raw meat dripped cold blood, turning slowly against the chinks of light.

For several days the Wittaia, unable to effect a death in battle or in their field raids from the Tokolik, had attempted a raid near the river, coming across early in the morning from the Turaba. The akuni were aware of this, and Weaklekek's kaio had been strengthened by Aloro, Husuk, and other warriors, who attempted to ambush the raiders; despite several alarms, no real battle had occurred.

This morning the men did not go to the kaio, for the feast of the Wilil was taking place. Aloro was an important Wilil, Weaklekek an important guest, and Husuk went off to war on the north frontier. No women were permitted in Weaklekek's fields, and the kaio was abandoned for the day. The Aike frontier, with the looming Turaba, had always been a dangerous place, and as Weaklekek's absence, like all other important matters, was common knowledge, no trouble was expected.

*Infused with supernatural power.

But the day was hot, and in the afternoon the solitary Woluklek went to the river to drink water. The people tire of the stale, silted waters of the ditches—they have no drink but water—and in dry weather will often go a long way to the river, where they squat on the bank and drink slowly and steadily for minutes. Woluklek took with him three little boys who were playing near Mapiatma.

One of the boys was Weake, whose father had been killed the year before on the Waraba. His mother had since run off to the Wittaia, and Weake was now the ward of his uncle, the warrior Huonke. He was a small yegerek, a friend of Tukum, with the large eyes and thick eyebrows which make many of the children beautiful. His name meant "Bad Path," and recently he had hurt his leg. For this reason, on this day, he was slower than his friends.

Near the Aike, on a little rise just short of the side path to Weaklekek's kaio, Woluklek and the three boys were ambushed by a party of Wittaia; the raiders sprang from the low reeds and bushes. Afterward Woluklek was not sure about their numbers, but a raiding party is usually comprised of about thirty men. There was nothing to be done. He dropped his spear and fled, the boys behind him.

All his life Weake had been taught to hate and fear the enemy, and when he saw the strange men with their spears he turned with the rest and ran. But he was not fast enough and was almost immediately run down. He screamed for help, but the others were running for their lives and did not turn. The face of a man, of several men, loomed above him on the bright blue sky, with harsh, loud breathing. The men rammed their spears through him over and over, pinning him to the ground, and then they were gone, and Weake was carried home.

The cry of *Kaio, kaio* carried swiftly past Homuak and to the pig feast: the hot stone fragment that had burned Huonke must have struck him close to the same instant that his nephew had been pierced by the long spears. While the rock fire was still steaming, word came from Abulopak about the boy. The two villages almost adjoin, and the pilai where Weake lived was scarcely a hundred yards across the fences from the Wilil fire. Huonke and Tamugi, his brother-in-law, ran toward Abulopak, where the women's wailing had already started.

In the long yard of the sili two women were kneeling, facing the mute pilai. The sili lies under the mountain, at the north end of the great grove of araucaria, and the pilai at its southern end is shaded by the tall pines against the hill. Inside the pilai were a few old men, and then Asikanalek arrived, and Tamugi and Huonke, and Siloba.

Weake lay on a banana frond beside the fire. He was still alive, and his clear childish voice seemed out of place in the brown solemnity of the men's round house: it cut through the decrepit snuffling of the old men as the shaft of daylight in the doorway cut through the motes of dust. Weake spoke of his own *etai-eken*, his seed-of-singing, the life he clung to with all his strength, as if the mourning he could hear must be some dark mistake. *An etai-eken werek!* But I'm alive! Though he not once screamed or whined, his voice was broken as he spoke by little calls of pain, and the blood flowed steadily onto the frond beneath him.

Huonke tried to quiet him, repeating the same terse phrase over and over, like a chant: *Hat nahalok loguluk! Hat nahalok logu-luk!* — But you're not going to die! Huonke's voice was the only firm one in the pilai. Tamugi, a large-muscled man whose ready smile is bolder than his nature, sobbed as loudly as he could, while Asikanalek cried silently. The boy's voice answered Huonke obedi-ently — *Oh, oh*, he repeated gently. Yes, yes. But now and then pain or terror overcame him, and he cried out and fought to escape the death that he felt in their hands. Huonke held his left arm and Siloba his right, while Tamugi and Asikanalek held down his legs. Siloba neither talked nor cried, but breathed earnestly and cease-lessly into the boy's ear, oo-Phuh, oo-Phuh: this ritual breathing, which brought health, would be used in the next hour on the wisa pig meat in the pilai of the Wilil.

Weake twisted in their grasp, his back arching; his legs were released and he drew his knees up to his chin, covering the gleam of the neat spear holes at his navel and lower belly. The old cut on the boy's leg still had its green patch of leaf dressing, but the spear holes, like small mouths in his chest and sides, his arm and leg and stomach, had not been tended. Some fresh leaf was brought at last, and the two stomach wounds were bound up hastily, almost carelessly, as if the true purpose of the leaf was to protect the pilai floor from blood; in their distress the men handled him ineptly, and he cried out. The figures hunched over him in the near-darkness, with the old men's snuffling and the steady oo-Phuh, oo-Phuh, and the harsh tearing of the leaf.

Behind Huonke, in the shadows, a woman sat as rigid as a stone. The custom excluding women from the pilai had been waived while the child lived, but nevertheless she maintained silence: when she spoke, but once, out of the darkness, her voice came clear and tragic, like a song. The woman was Huonke's sister, married to Tamugi; she has a wild sad quality in her face and is one of the handsomest women in the Kurelu. She counseled the men to take the boy down to the stream.

Weake clung to life and would not die. His writhings had covered him with blood, and he lay in a pool of darkness. When the woman finished speaking, the men agreed to take him to the water, which, entering his wounds, would leach out the dark blood of illness. He was picked up and carried outside, Siloba holding his head up by the hair. The women in the yard began an outcry, but the men did not pass through the yard. They took Weake through a hole in the back fencing, across a pig pasture, over a stile, down through a small garden to a ditch. There they laid him in the muddy water, so that it lapped up to his chest.

Tamugi did not come. After leaving the pilai with the other men, he kept on going, for the Wilil fire was now open, and he wished some pig. The others accompanied Huonke to the ditch. Soon they too left, for there was nothing to be done. Only Siloba remained, and his friend Yonokma. Yonokma sat in water up to his waist, holding the legs, while Huonke and Siloba, their own lower legs submerged, held the child's arms: Weake's head rested on Huonke's right thigh.

Fitfully Weake talked and now and then cried out: the voice rang though the silent garden, against the soft background of lament and the low hum of the men's voices at the pig feast. Once he cried, *Tege! Tege!* in terror of the spears, and Huonke shouted him down: *Hat ninom werek! Hat ninom werek!*—over and over and over: You are here with us, you are here with us! He said this dully every time Weake called out. You are here with us. Then Weake would resume his own meek, rhythmic *Oh, oh, oh,* of assent. *Hat ninom werek—oh. Hat ninom werek—oh.* His eyes closed, opened wide, and closed again; he seemed to doze. In the muddy ditch, with its water spiders, round black beetles, and detritus of old leaves, his blood drifted peacefully away. Against the firmament above soared the great arches of the banana trees, and the hill crest in a softening light, and the blue sky. Taro and hiperi grew about him, and the blue-flowered spiderwort lined the steep banks. Swiftlets coursed the garden, hunting insects, and the mosquitoes came; the men slapped one another.

Huonke sighed and leaned his head against the bank. In grief Huonke's face had lost its hard, furtive quality and become handsome. Yonokma, sitting in the water, yawned with cold. Okal, who had gone with Weake to the river, came and stared down at his friend; he looked restless and unhappy and soon went away again.

In his last sleep Weake cried, a small, pure sound which came with every breath. When pain awakened him, he tried to talk, but his voice was faint and drowsy. Siloba breathed fitfully into his ear, but his efforts were disheartened: he only did it, guiltily, when the little boy called out. The small slim body had more than twenty wounds, and the wonder was that the boy had lived so long. But Weake would live until the twilight, asleep in the healing water, while the men attending him grew tired and cold. They coughed and slapped themselves and stared into the water, and the little boy's chest twitched up and down, up and down. Sometimes Siloba poured water on the wounds above the surface, and more blood was drawn forth, flowing down his side. Huonke said, You will stay with us, You will stay with us, and the child said Yes, yes, yes, and did not speak again.

Siba came and stared at the little boy. He broke off the stem of a taro leaf and with it probed the wound on the left side. The belly leaf was floating, and the small *horim:*\* Siba attempted to push back a trace of white intestine which protruded near the navel as

\*Gourd penis sheath.

if, by concealing the evidence of hurt, he might somehow be of help. Weake was failing rapidly and did not cry out; his mouth was open, and his lips had puffed and dried. In the attack he had received a heavy blow, for the side of his face had grown swollen and distorted.

Yonokma leaned forward and removed a bit of straw from the dry lips.

Siba ran across the garden and sprang onto the roof of the pig shed by the fence. There, with a great cracking sound like anger, he broke off a banana frond and hurled it down into the sili yard: this leaf would be the little boy's last bed. Returning, he picked Weake up out of the water and carried him homeward through the garden. Huonke and the two *elege** trailed Siba through the dusk, shaking with cold.

The small body was limp, with one foot lying on the other, and arms hanging: the blood dripped very slowly on the weeds. His breathing had silenced, and his eyes, half closed, had glazed, like those of a fresh-killed animal. Nilik, Wereklowe, and Polik had come to look at him in his pilai, but it was evening now and he was dead.

The next morning, in the middle of the yard, Huonke and Tamugi built the chair. Four women emerged from the cooking shed and kneeled before it, and more women were already climbing the stile which separated the small sili from the main yard of Wereklowe. The wailing had commenced, and the Alua clan was coming through the fields from all across the southern Kurelu.

In the pilai crouched Asikanalek, twisted by grief. Against the wall, where sunlight filtered through the chinks, sat Weake's small silhouette, already arranged in the position he would be given in the chair. Asikanalek went to him and carried him outside into the day. Still holding the boy, he kneeled in the bright sun before the pilai and, staring upward at the sky, lamented. The men about him looked disheveled and distraught, and Asikanalek's shoulders were smeared with yellow clay. Weake's appearance in the yard had

*Youths.

caused a stir among the women; the long day of fierce wailing had begun.

Weake was draped with two large shell bibs, which covered not only his mutilated chest but his torn stomach; the wife of Tamugi kneeled before him, binding up his legs. A man adjusted a new funeral horim to replace the one which had floated off in the brown ditch. Beside the chair Huonke and Tamugi cried out and rubbed their legs. Now and then Huonke would rub his hands together in a strange, stiff-fingered way, and glance about him, as if uneasy in the light of day.

Weake was carried to his chair. His bound legs were hung over the cross piece, and his head was held up by a strip of leaf passed by Tamugi beneath his chin. At the foot of the chair, wailing, Tamugi's wife crouched upon the ground and mopped at it with torn-up grass; she made a circular motion with her hand, scarring the earth. Other women, with girls and small children, filed steadily into the yard and arranged themselves upon the ground before lending their voices to the waves of sound.

A lizard darted from the fence to seize an insect. It gulped busily, its small head switching back and forth, and moved in quick fits and starts back to the shadows. Above, a honey eater bounded to the limb of an albizzia. It too cocked its head, unsettled by the wailing, but calmed before it fled, and sat there preening. In the blue sky over the hill the kites harassed one another, screeching.

The men draped shell belts on Weake, binding his brow with the bright colors and building the belts into a kind of crown. But his head was small, and most of the belts were laid along his sides and down the chair arms. While his attendants scratched and shuffled and thought thoughts, in the warm doldrums of their existence, the child sat alone in cold serenity. He seemed to grieve, nevertheless, as if oppressed by all his trappings; when the women came and draped their nets, they almost hid him in the shadows. Huonke came and smeared him with fresh pig grease, and his shins, still in the sun, took on a gleam: Tukum, himself gleaming from the pig grease of the day before, perched by the fence on a small stone and watched Weake. Tukum was one of the few children who seemed upset, though, like all his companions, he had seen many funerals and would see many more.

A group led by Polik sang wheezily and long the ancient chants of mourning, working the ground with gnarled old toes and rubbing spavined thighs. One of them, his wrinkled skin reptilian, felt peevishly for the tobacco roll buried in the pouch strung on his back. At the same time he contributed his mourning, a frail *woo, woo, woo,* and his long nose ran tumultuously with all the rest: the hole for boars' tusks in his septum had stretched wide with old age, so that the light shone through it.

Some of the men brought belts, and Huonke called out to them in greeting, a loud *wah-h, wah-h,* somehow impertinent, and at the same time self-ingratiating. He and his brother-in-law stood at the chair and haggled covertly about the placement of the belts. While haggling, Tamugi contrived to sob, rolling his eyes in the frank, open face of cant.

Four pigs came forth, and the pilai's owner destroyed them with a kind of sad authority. All four died speedily, snouting the ground, legs kicking, as if they were trying to bore into the earth. They were dressed swiftly, and the yegerek brought logs. Weake's friend Okal was among them: he wore the yellow clay of mourning and a pad of leaves to protect his shoulder from the wood. Like all the other boys, he played a large part in the funeral of his friend.

Nilik, with his affinity for pig, had come in time to finger the bloody pieces, which were hung on a rack behind the chair. Before the chair an old woman beat her breast with stumpy hands: *Aulk, aulk, aulk, aulk,* she cried—*Loo, loo, loo, loo.* The yellow clay was crusted in the skin folds of old breasts, of fallen hips. On the far side of the yard a giant butterfly, dead white and black, danced out of the shadows of the woods and, passing through the akuni, danced back again.

Huonke and Tamugi cried loud and long, mouths trembling and eyes alert. They watched the entrance of Weaklekek, his people behind him carrying three large flat *ye* stones decorated around the middle with fur and cowries. The ye stones are valuable but not sacred, though they may later become so; they are used, like cowrie belts, as a medium of exchange. *Wah! Wah!* cried Huonke. *Wah! Wah!* cried Tamugi. The party stopped before the chair to grieve, and then the men went onward toward the pilai, while the women and small children remained in the upper yard.

Weaklekek sat down quietly and stared into the earth. He was one of Weake's *namis,* and plainly he blamed himself for the boy's death, since it was his kaio that had been abandoned. But the raid and death were part of akuni existence, and neither Weaklekek nor Woluklek was blamed by any of the others. Even so, Woluklek, who had been unwise enough to lead the three boys to the river, did not come to the funeral at all.

U-mue's wives had come, and with them the children of his sili. Aku and Holake joined the little girls of the village, who were going about on small self-conscious errands; the girls smiled modestly at everyone, in the pretty illusion that all eyes were upon them. Nylare, who is very young, had a poor grasp of the situation, but she took up the wail of mourning, humming it contentedly to her own rhythms. Natorek, escaping his mother repeatedly, played in the narrow path through the massed women; like most akuni children, he accepted his mother's cuffs and cries in great good spirits and smiled expansively at all and everything even when late-comers stepped upon him. He was finally placed under the care of his brother Uwar, who took him to a corner of the yard and picked his lice.

While the food cooked, more men arrived; they overflowed into the woods behind the fencing. The mourning faltered in the midday pall, and nothing stirred. Only the stinging bees, black and yellow, toiled remorselessly on a small open hive, hanging upside down from a pandanus leaf beyond the fence; they hung in the air below the hive, hair legs dangling, or clasped one another in dry, delicate embrace.

Near the main entrance of Abulopak the tips of the long grasses had been tied together in three places in the weeds: the tied grass forbids trespassing. The signs were a warning to the women, who were nearly two hundred strong, and whose use of the near weeds to urinate had become an offense to Wereklowe.

The rock fire was dismantled, and pig distributed among the

men: a few bits were borne to certain women. Asikanalek's daughter Namilike walked around with her small net stuffed with hiperi, passing it out; Weake's little sister Iki Abusake was also there, as pretty in a baby way as Namilike herself. Iki Abusake's curious name means "Hand That Could Not Help Itself," the expression used by the akuni to account for the phenomenon of pig-stealing.

During the eating, soft waves of mourning rose and fell. The sun, sliding down into the west, burned hotly on Weake, and women tried to shield him with their nets. But now the men came forward and stripped him of his belts: the meal was over, and the day's business must begin. The belts were stretched on a frond before the pilai, with the kains seated in a line along each side. When the belts had been admired for a time, and their destiny decided, Wereklowe stood up to dispense them.

Until this time Wereklowe had remained out of the way, ceding the administration of the funeral to Asikanalek: Asikanalek was not only a sub-kain of the Alua but a fine warrior who had killed two, and a close relative of the dead boy. But the exchange of goods was an end purpose of the funeral, and the greatest leader of the clan usually directs it. With a weighty pause between the names, Wereklowe gave out the belts; he was attended by respectful silence. One belt was awarded to Weaklekek, but Weaklekek was still morose and waved it off; in his despair, and despite all his rich gifts, he felt he did not deserve it. Lakaloklek, more practical, came forth and took it in her husband's name.

Despite the great amount of grieving there seemed small hint of outrage. Huonke complained that the *pavi** should not have done it, but then, Huonke has killed once himself, a harmless woman found near the frontier who had run away from the Siep-Elortak. Revenge there would be, inevitably, but without moral judgments. Nevertheless, for the funeral of a small boy, well over two hundred people had pushed into the small sili: more presents were brought, and more pigs killed, than for the funeral of Ekitamalek, a kain's son and a warrior. Only a few could have come there in real sorrow, and only a few for the exchange of goods. The rest had come

*A species of tree (slang: *enemy* or *excrement*).

because the killing of a child, despite its ancient sanctions, had made them unhappy and uneasy.

His back to Wereklowe, the child sat naked in the chair. The women came to remove the nets, and Weake stirred; his head dropped slowly to his breast, for his chin strap had been loosened from behind. Then suddenly a man began to shout and a complete silence fell. The speaker was Polik, and he was warning the people that they might be in danger.

In the fortnight previous Amoli, the violent kain of the Haiman, had killed the young brother of a man with whom he was having a dispute: taking the life of a relative of one's antagonist, or even that of his small child, is not unusual, being not only a more subtle punishment but a less dangerous one. The man had fled to the Siep-Kosi but had sworn revenge, and Polik, on behalf of Amoli, warned any of the latter's friends or kinsmen to be on guard. The fugitive's wife was ordered to come to him the next morning in Abulopak, so that he and Wereklowe might have a full explanation of the affair: it is one of the duties of the great kains to settle feuds within the tribe, not infrequently at the expense of their own pigs. When Polik had finished speaking, the guests fidgeted uneasily, but after a while the voices mounted once again, and the women returned to remove Weake's nets.

People were already departing from the sili. The thongs were loosened, and Weake was carried back to the banana leaves where the shell belts had lain. The yegerek, grim, brought timber for the pyre: Tukum looked frightened and was openly upset. The mourning quickened. Huonke greased the body a last time and, when he was finished, took up the bow and arrow. Another man held up the great thatch bundle. The arrow was shot into it, releasing the spirit from the body, and the man ran with the bundle up the yard; he laid the bundle on the sili fence.

The fire had been assembled quickly, and a loud outcry erupted with the flames: the body was hurried to its pyre. Weake was laid upon his side, in the way that small boys sleep, with a rough timber pillowing his head. The flames came up beside him, and more wood was laid on top of him, and he disappeared.

The mourning died after a time, and the sili emptied quickly. Huonke brought out a red parrot feather and performed the purification ceremony on the men who had handled the boy's body. The men, seated in a circle, held out both their hands, and Huonke passed the parrot feather through the air above the outstretched fingers. Afterward, as much was done for him.

The last of Weake was a sweet choking smell, carried upward by an acrid smoke from the crackling pyre, and diffusing itself at last against the pine trees, the high crest of the mountain wall, the sky.

# *from* The Shorebirds of North America

## 1967

*In his training and fieldwork in natural history, Matthiessen has become particularly adept as a bird-watcher, and among all bird families the Charadriidae and Scolopacidae (plovers and sandpipers), abundant on Long Island, have long been his favorites. "To the margins and vicinity of Sagaponack Pond come more than half of the shorebird species in North America," he writes, "not only because of the pond's location on the Atlantic flyway but because of the range of habitats in a small vicinity." Although a revised edition of this book appeared under the title* The Wind Birds, *the original large format* Shorebirds *contains beautiful paintings and pencil drawings by Robert Verity Clem and a compendious appendix by Dr. Ralph S. Palmer, which describes the physical features and habitat range of every species. Just as Matthiessen's later work* Men's Lives *honored the commercial haul-seiners of his native Long Island, with whom he worked from 1954 to 1956, this book stands as something of an ode to the wild residents closest to his home. "The restlessness of shorebirds," he writes, "their kinship with the distance and swift seasons, the wistful signal of their voices down the long coastlines of the world make them, for me, the most affecting of wild creatures." The following is taken from the early pages of the first chapter and several passages in the final chapter.*

**The pond at Sagaponack,** where I live, has its source in the small woodland stream which drains Poxabogue Pond and Little Poxabogue, further inland. From the west windows of my house, a fringe of trees parting the fields winds into view; here Sagg Pond, like a wide meadow river, curls down through miles of warm potato country to the sea. The Long Island farmland fills the landscape to the north and west and spreads toward the southward; Sagg Pond appears again, turned back upon itself by the hard white of the dunes, by the hard blue of the sea horizon. The pond bends like the shank of a great hook; it is now a mile across. But seasonally, in storm or flood, the pond is open to the sea. Then this lower reach is salt, a place of tidal creek and shallow flat which is today, as it has always been, a haunt of shorebirds.

On the fourth of July 1870, a Boston gentleman, George H. Mackay, killed twenty-seven woodcock at "Poxybang Pond"; a few days later, thirty-nine "dowitch" were gently slain at Sagaponack. The woodcock still comes to Poxabogue and the dowitcher to Sagaponack, though the dowitcher—its odd name may derive from "Deutscher snipe," due to its popularity, in Revolutionary times, among the Hessians—is now protected legally from guns, a circumstance which Mr. Mackay, one of the rare naturalist-sportsmen in an epoch of mighty game hogs, would doubtless find astonishing. Mackay and his contemporaries pursued the shorebirds with such vigor that when he died, in 1928, the hosts that flew down the long seacoasts of his youth had been reduced to fugitive small bands.

On September 28, 1964, after a day and night of onshore winds, a flock of sixty-eight golden plover pitched into the potato field between my house and Sagaponack Pond; in that small flock at Sagaponack there flew more golden plover than the total I had seen in twenty years. Yet Audubon once reported a flight of "millions" of golden plover near New Orleans, of which some forty-eight thousand were killed in a single day: the golden plover is thought to have been even more numerous than the Eskimo curlew, whose multitudes have been compared to the great flights of the passenger pigeon. From colonial times, plover and curlew had been hunted in spring and fall, but they suffered no fatal diminishment until the last part of the nineteenth century when, with the fading of the wild pigeon, the market guns were turned upon shorebirds and waterfowl. Even the least sandpiper met a violent end when the larger species were in short supply, though its minuscule roast would scarcely make a mouthful, bones and all: in one account, ninety-seven of these "ox-eyes" were cut down with a single shot.

But the plover and curlew were the favorite birds, not only because of their great numbers and fine taste but because they were unsuspicious to a fault. The Eskimo curlew would circle back over the guns, calling out to its fallen companions, a habit it shared with the dunlin, dowitcher, and many others. That the dunlin was called the "simpleton" on Long Island indicates the low esteem in which its brain was held (the piping plover was known as the "feeble" and the willet as the "humility," but the plover's name is derived from its call, and that of the willet from a family trait of feeding in the "humble mud"), and the buff-breasted and solitary sandpipers were celebrated far and wide for stubborn innocence. (Dr. Elliott Coues, taking advantage of a rare convention of solitary sandpipers, once collected seven of this species, shooting one at a time, before the eighth and last, suspecting that something was amiss, took leave—"I will add in justice to his wits," wrote Dr. Coues, "in a great hurry."

Under the circumstances, one wonders that any shorebirds survived into the present century. Not only were they trapped and shot, but great numbers of knots and other species were taken by "fire-lighting," a nocturnal practice much in favor on Long Island's Great South Bay and elsewhere, in which the resting flocks, blinded but undismayed by a bright beam, stood by patiently while market men stepped forth from punts and wrung their necks. Night hunting took such a toll of a then common source of public nourishment that Massachusetts in 1835 passed a law forbidding the taking of "Plover, Curlew, Dough-bird, and Chicken-bird" after dark: the Dough-bird was the Eskimo curlew, and the Chicken-bird was the ruddy turnstone.

A decade later, Rhode Island passed a law forbidding spring shooting of woodcock and snipe, but this admirable and precocious measure on behalf of the two species which least needed it was repealed in the face of public outrage, and for the next seventy years almost nothing was done to slow the destruction of the shorebirds, whose narrow migration paths, close-flocking habits, and chronic foolishness contributed heavily to their own decline.

By the turn of the century, George Mackay was growing concerned about the shorebirds, which were rapidly disappearing from his hunting circuit. Mackay's notes on the fall migrations of the Eskimo curlew and golden plover for the four years 1896–1899 are among the first warnings we have of the curlew's rapid disappearance, even though a "fute" at Montauk in 1891 was the last of this species ever seen on Long Island (four were reported at Montauk in September of 1932, but the sighting is not generally accepted), and in New England, after 1897, no more than three were seen again in a single flock. In that same year, Mackay inquired publicly: "Are we not approaching the beginning of the end?" though his private journal reveals that he was still blazing away at shorebirds of all descriptions and was out before dawn in vain pursuit of the very bird whose passing he so lamented. "Although hopeless," he writes, "I was driving over the western plover ground at daylight, hoping to find a few tired birds." In this period, "fire-lighted" knots still sold in Boston for ten cents a dozen.

Whether uneasy or discouraged at the meager sport, Mackay did little hunting after 1897, and later he was to lead campaigns against spring shooting. But in 1916, at a time when the golden plover was fast following the Eskimo curlew toward oblivion, Mackay and his party "succeeded in shooting" one forlorn specimen at Nantucket where, a half-century before, both curlew and plover had appeared in such waves as to "almost darken the sun." And he was still at it in October of 1921, flanked now by younger generations of Mackays. "We saw in all eight Black-breast plovers, young birds, and I shot four. On picking them up, one proved to be a young Golden plover (pale-belly). If I could have a little practice I feel I could come back to my old shooting form fairly well." One can't help but feel affection for this doughty old gentleman—he was then very close to eighty—who led in the public fight for the protection of the shorebirds without once questioning his private right to kill them.

George Mackay's last shorebird, a ruddy turnstone, was shot illegally in 1922; the species had come under the protection of the Federal Migratory Bird Treaty Act four years earlier. Within the decade, all shorebirds except the snipe and woodcock had been removed from the list of game birds. But the Eskimo curlew had already passed the point of no return (though it has made a miraculous reappearance every time it has been mourned and buried; two Eskimo curlews were reported at Galveston Island, Texas, as recently as 1963, and a solitary specimen, in September of the same year, was shot by a hunter in Barbados), and the Hudsonian godwit and buff-breasted sandpiper, the long-billed curlew and golden plover are still dangerously reduced. Probably these species will remain uncommon, for their breeding and wintering grounds in both Americas are ever more threatened by man, but they are no longer fluttering at the edge of the abyss. Even the stilt sandpiper, never abundant, was recently reported in Saskatchewan in a flight estimated at four thousand.

The Eskimo curlew excepted, the Hudsonian godwit is the one North American shorebird whose future is precarious at present. In 1926 hope for the species had been all but abandoned. ("The passing of this bird must be a cause for regret among sportsmen and nature lovers alike.") A decade later, the godwit had almost vanished. In recent years it has recuperated and is even common here and there in spring in the Mississippi Valley, but the flock of twenty-four that I watched (with Robert Clem) one misty August afternoon of 1963 on the salt flats of Monomoy Island, south of Cape Cod, represented a large percentage of the Hudsonian godwits that still occur on the coasts of the Atlantic in the fall: except for a solitary bird that came one Indian summer to Sagaponack, they were the only Hudsonian godwits I have even seen.

The last entry of Mackay's *Shooting Journal*, for August 16, 1922, concludes as follows:

At noon we picked up and went up to the house on Third Point, where we had dinner, Bunt having dug a bucket of clams. As usual we had a strong S.W. breeze to return with. They day was fine but very hot.

And we close the book with the warm breath of summer tide flats in our nostrils and a vague longing for those blue-and-golden days of vanished Augusts when the great bird companies that no man will see again disappeared southward into the ocean mists.

. . .

The restlessness of shorebirds, their kinship with the distance and swift seasons, the wistful signal of their voices down the long coastlines of the world make them, for me, the most affecting of wild creatures. I think of them as birds of wind, as "wind birds." To the traveler confounded by exotic birds, not to speak of exotic specimens of his own kind, the voice of the wind birds may be the lone familiar note in a strange land, and I have many times been glad to find them; meeting a whimbrel one fine summer day of February in Tierra del Fuego, I wondered if I had not seen this very bird a half year earlier, at home. The spotted and white-rumped sandpipers, the black-bellied and golden plovers are birds of Sagaponack, but the spotted sandpiper has cheered me with its jaunty teeter on the Amazon and high up in the Andes (and so has its seesawing Eurasian counterpart, the common sandpiper, on the White Nile and in Galway and in the far-off mountains of New Guinea); one bright noon at the Strait of Magellan, the white-rump passed along the shore in flocks. I have seen golden plover on Alaskan tundra and in the canefields of Hawaii, and heard the black-belly's wild call on wind-bright seacoast afternoons from Yucatan to the Great Barrier Reef.

The voice of the black-bellied plover carries far, a stirring *toor-a-lee* or *pee-ur-ee* like a sea bluebird, often heard before the bird is seen. In time of storm, it sometimes seems to be the only bird aloft; one day this plover flew across the first winds of a September hurricane, wings stroking fiercely through gray murk and tumult, before that fluting melancholy cry was whirled away downwind, a forlorn note of life high in the maelstrom.

With its wing span of two feet or more, the black-bellied plover is a strong flier; circumpolar and almost cosmopolitan, it migrates down across the world from breeding grounds within the Arctic Circle. Yet as a wanderer it is rivaled by several shorebirds, not least of all the sanderling of the Sagaponack beach, which ranks with the great skua and the Arctic tern as one of the most far-flung birds on earth.

The sanderling is the white sandpiper or "peep" of summer

beaches, the tireless toy bird that runs before the surf. Because of the bold role it plays in its immense surroundings, it is the one sandpiper that most people have noticed. Yet how few notice it at all, and few of the fewer still who recognize it will ever ask themselves why it is there or where it might be going. We stand there heedless of an extraordinary accomplishment: the diminutive creature making way for us along the beaches of July may be returning from an annual spring voyage which took it from central Chile to nesting grounds in northeast Greenland, a distance of eight thousand miles. One has only to consider the life force packed tight into that puff of feathers to lay the mind wide open to the mysteries—the order of things, the why and the beginning. As we contemplate that sanderling, there by the shining sea, one question leads inevitably to another, and all questions come full circle to the questioner, paused momentarily in his own journey under the sun and sky.

Most shorebirds leave the breeding grounds before the adverse days round to the fore, and those that do not are rarely driven southward by cold weather. Surfbirds, rock sandpipers, and black turnstones, waiting for low tides at Wrangell Inlet, keep company all winter on the docks and warehouse roofs of Petersburg, Alaska; other surfbirds winter on hot tropic coasts. So long as there is food, in other words, a remarkable range of temperature can be sustained, and food may still be plentiful when the wind birds rise from the moon rim of the northern waters and fly toward the southern stars. While not as strong as the spring impulse, the migratory urge of fall causes several species to leave behind the rich crowberry crops and intertidal zones of the maritime North Atlantic summer for the high winds and hungry sea of a long transoceanic crossing.

Favorable winds are less crucial than was once assumed. Strong gales may discourage the flocks from setting out, but once the migrants are aloft and underway, streaming across the stars of wild night skies, they will fly into the teeth of adverse winds. There is much evidence that head winds are preferred to windlessness, and even to tail or beam winds when the winds are strong: it is the head winds that provide the lift that carries the birds for hours over land and sea.

The frequency with which the wind birds rest at sea is still debated. While many species have been seen to alight and swim on sheltered water, good sight records of shorebirds alighted on the ocean—always excepting the red and northern phalaropes—are virtually nonexistent. Nevertheless, in May of 1907, an experienced naturalist saw a migration of "near a thousand" willets resting on the open sea of the Grand Bank; since the birds were so close that they had to flutter up from the path of the ship, it is hard to believe that this well-marked species could have been mistaken for anything else. (The size of the willet flock and its location southeast of Newfoundland is almost as astonishing as the mass settlement upon the sea; that the flock had gone astray in fog and passed east of Nova Scotia before it tired is my own unsatisfactory explanation.)

Present opinion is that while many species can and will rest on the surface if necessary, they do not often do so out of choice, nor can they survive long if the sea is rough. (Basking sea turtles, before their great numbers were reduced by commercial slaughter, may have provided resting points throughout the tropic seas; the red phalarope, at least, has been seen to use a turtle in this manner.) Thus the gale winds that sometimes carry shorebirds far off course and scatter the immature and inexperienced among them to strange coasts must also drown them in considerable numbers. Winds have carried ocean birds so far inland and southbound birds so far into the north that, tired and disoriented, the impulse toward migration spent, they linger where they find themselves: in a great storm of November 1888 this fate befell large flocks of killdeer, few of which managed to survive the long Massachusetts winter.

But true invasions—in which meaningful numbers of a certain species, strayed or storm-borne, establish a breeding population far beyond their usual range—are very rare: the only bird species which have invaded the North American land mass within the memory of man are the fieldfare, a European thrush blown to Greenland in a 1937 storm and now resident at the island's southwestern tip, and the cattle egret, an Afro-Asian species which, after millennia in its natural range, now seems intent on populating the whole world.

Among shorebirds, the closest thing to a North American invasion occurred in 1927. Large flocks of lapwings known to have left England for Ireland on the night of December 18–19 were overtaken by fog and violent winds, and by December 20 appeared in thousands throughout the Maritime Provinces of Canada, from Baffin Island to New Brunswick. Had they arrived at a benign time of year, a few might have established themselves, but in a very few days the last of them died of cold and hunger.

Ruffs and curlew sandpipers appear regularly on our North Atlantic coast (the first ruff was recorded before the Civil War, on Long Island; since then it has turned up at least once in every state from Maine to North Carolina), although the prevailing winds are set against them; redshanks and other European birds come also. But the obstacles against westward wandering across the Atlantic are great, and it may be that some of the accidental visitors do not come direct from Europe but from southward points on their migration route, riding the east winds of the Canary Current or the tropical storms that build off the coast of Africa. This possibility might help explain why that great wanderer, the curlew sandpiper, which breeds in central and eastern Siberia (a first North American nesting was reported in 1962, from the vicinity of Point Barrow) but winters as far west as Africa, turns up not on the Pacific coast, as one might expect, but on the Atlantic seaboard. It is also possible "that a few individuals may migrate in fall from their Siberian nesting grounds east by way of Alaska and Canada to the Atlantic seaboard—a route used by certain shorebirds breeding in tundra country."

North American birds, conversely, have no trouble getting lost, riding rapidly to Europe on the strong westerlies of the North Atlantic; the jet streams of high altitudes would blow them there in a matter of hours. New World visitors, especially in Great Britain, are comparatively abundant (bird-watchers are also abundant in Britain, but this does not entirely account for the high incidence of accidentals), and the most frequent visitors by far are the *Charadrii*. Yellowlegs of both species go regularly to Europe, as do the long-billed dowitcher and solitary sandpiper. But the commonest wanderer, with sixty-two recorded sightings, is the pectoral sandpiper, which goes too far in so many other directions as well.

A more surprising chronic stray is the buff-breasted sandpiper. Like the stilt sandpiper, the buff-breast has very narrow migration lanes, clinging close to the hundredth meridian, and it ventures even more rarely than its kinsman as far east as the Atlantic coast: in the spring, it is so faithful to its route that the majority of buff-breast migrants cross the Gulf of Mexico and alight in certain fields near Rockport, Texas, then make a second long-distance flight to certain fields near Edmonton, Alberta, to the virtual exclusion of all stopping points in between. But while the prudent stilt sandpiper has remained a homebody, daring but one recorded visit across the Atlantic, the far-flung buff-breast of the fall has delighted and surprised new friends not only in England but in France, Switzerland, Heligoland, and Egypt; it has been said that the autumn buff-breast is more likely to turn up in England than in "any area of similar size in eastern North America."

Other anomalies have been noted among transatlantic vagrants. Species of predominantly coastal distribution (cf. semipalmated sandpiper) and also those which make long transoceanic migrations (cf. lesser golden plover) cross the Atlantic far *less* often than several species of more inland distribution (buff-breasted and upland sandpipers), whereas species which breed in the western Nearctic (cf. long-billed dowitcher) wander *more* commonly to Europe than those breeding farther east (cf. short-billed dowitcher): the pectoral sandpiper of Siberia and Alaska is eight times as common in England as the Baird's sandpiper, even though the Baird's nests as close as Greenland. The theory is that the western nesters, which mainly strike eastward before heading south, are more apt to carry on to England than species which set out on a more southerly course at the beginning of migration: the same tendency, in reverse, may in part account for the 1927 invasion of lapwings, populations of which migrate west to Ireland in the autumn. (Spring records in Britain of the buff-breasted and Baird's sandpipers and the northern phalarope, which in this season are extremely rare on the Atlantic coast of North America, may represent individuals which strayed from South America to Africa, then proceeded north. The killdeer, unlike all other species, visits Britain most commonly in *winter*, perhaps in consequence of its luckless habit of being blown back north by winter storms.)

Shorebird wanderers have not been limited to European travel. The Hudsonian godwit has flown at least twelve times to New Zealand, a place so removed from its natural haunts that one must suppose that it followed the bar-tailed godwits which belong there. (The Hudsonian godwit and several other North American shorebirds recorded in New Zealand have never been recorded in Australia, but a few hundred miles away; whether this is a tribute to the bird-watchers of New Zealand or a phenomenon of zoogeography is not yet known.) In 1953 the sharp-tailed sandpiper of Siberia, which occurs in migration in northwest Alaska and winters in the southwest Pacific, turned up at Tristan da Cunha, a small volcanic peak of a submerged mountain range in the ocean wastes between Africa and South America. The red phalarope has found itself as far inland as Kansas and Colorado, while a jaçana has alighted on a ship forty miles at sea, off the coast of Surinam. Young long-billed dowitchers, Wilson's phalaropes, and western willets straggle eastward in late summer as far as the Atlantic seaboard (fall willets at Sagaponack are more likely to be westerns than not), a form of juvenile wandering analogous to the northward explorations of young summer egrets. Postjuvenile dispersion, as it is called, cannot be accounted for on the basis of food alone; in many creatures besides man, the young are more adventurous and less set in their ways, and thus prone to disorganized behavior.

The westerly winds of the northern land mass that account for a general west-east drift of autumn migrants may also explain this curious characteristic of shorebird distribution—that almost none of them winter west or even southwest of their breeding grounds. Even those long-billed dowitchers and pectoral sandpipers that breed in Siberia return east to North America before migrating southward, and the European ringed plover that breeds in Baffin Island goes east again to Europe before moving on to its winter latitudes.

The exceptions to the rule are three, and two of these, the marbled godwit and the avocet, migrate to both ocean coasts, then southward, wintering east as well as west of their summer range. The third exception is the mountain plover. In one of the most rigid and least explicable of all migrations, this plover travels southwest six hundred miles from its breeding grounds on the Great Plains, across the Rockies and the Coast Range to California; many of the arrivals in California then proceed south into northern Mexico, a region reached easily from the Great Plains without the trouble of negotiating two north-south ranges of high mountains. (Despite its name, which was given it only because the first specimen was taken in the Rocky Mountain foothills, this bird is not partial to mountains: it is a bird of short-grass country and would be better named the plains plover.) So fixed is it in its habits that though it breeds in Montana and Wyoming, it has never been recorded in the adjoining state of Idaho, nor in Nevada, nor in Oregon.

Except for those species like the surfbird, wandering tattler, and black turnstone which rarely or never leave the Pacific perimeter, the great majority of the Alaskan nesters travel a kind of transcontinental migration, flying southeast to Hudson Bay or the Atlantic Ocean before proceeding southward. This is markedly true of the western sandpiper, which breeds in northern and western Alaska and the Chukchi Peninsula of Siberia and winters chiefly in the Carolinas, and of the Eskimo curlew, Hudsonian godwit, and white-rumped sandpiper, which commonly perform the ocean flight from the Canadian Maritimes to South America.

Similarly, a number of buff-breasted sandpipers move east to Hudson Bay and onward, much less commonly, to the coast. From the coast the buff-breast apparently heads southwest again, across the Appalachians (it is not known to migrate through the South Atlantic states) to Central America, then southeast again to the Argentine. This odd zigzag route may be shared by the scattering of Baird's sandpipers that come east in the fall migrations, for their movements are also obscure once they leave the North Atlantic. There are few records of the Baird's sandpiper in the southeastern states and the West Indies.

Not all migrants, in other words, select the shortest route, much less the easiest. The Baird's sandpiper, quite apart from its zigzag course, migrates commonly along mountain chains in both the Andes and Rockies which would serve as barriers to ordinary birds; it has been seen flying busily along in the rarefied air at thirteen thousand feet. Similarly, the pectoral sandpiper has been recorded at thirteen thousand feet in Colorado and twelve thousand feet in Argentina. The Mongolian plover which, like the rufous-necked sandpiper, crosses occasionally from Asia to breed on Alaska's Seward Peninsula, may nest at three miles above sea level in the Himalayas. (Godwits and curlews have been sighted at close to twenty thousand feet in the same range, but these birds were presumably crossing the north-south barrier.)

While it may be that only the Baird's and pectoral sandpipers use the great cordilleras as a migration route, many wind birds migrate at high altitudes when conditions favor them. This would seem particularly logical for those that migrate after dark. The moon illumines coasts and rivers that serve as guide lines even in the night, and when the clouds close over, the night fliers may rise to high clear altitudes, their course oriented to the stars.

The sun is also used as a point of orientation—and certain shorebirds travel in the day as well as at night—but the majority of the smaller migrants prefer darkness. In daylight, when the sun consumes the precious energies needed for flight, it is more economical to feed and rest; at night, the air is apt to be more stable, and fewer predators are abroad. (Migrating birds, in the intensity of their journey, are notably unwary and may view with detachment small reductions of their number by hawk or prowling coon. But shorebirds can usually outmaneuver hawks in the rare instances when they cannot outfly them; on the several occasions that I have watched a peregrine falcon in pursuit of shorebirds, a shorebird was overtaken only once. The victim was a lone yellowlegs, caught low over the Sagaponack flats, and it was knocked spinning to the ground like an old feathered pinwheel. But the falcon, out of apathy or inexperience, did not turn fast enough to pin it down, nor did it pursue the wind bird very far when the latter pulled itself together and took off again with an impressive turn of speed.)

The night fliers rest well into the twilight, and most are aloft a short time after dark. Just before midnight, the migration reaches its peak; then a telescope trained on the moon can watch the steady stream across the sky. Before dawn, the tired birds have dropped onto other margins, hundreds of miles south. There they may rest a day, a fortnight, or a month, depending on food, weather, and the skies remaining between this point and their destination.

How birds orient themselves during migration remains the greatest of the unsolved questions in all avian studies. The young of the great distance fliers, starting southward without guidance on journeys of thousands of miles, must have at least an innate sense of primary direction. (A distinction should be made between directional sense, in which the bird, transplanted five hundred miles west of its intended route, will theoretically arrive five hundred miles west of its destination, and true homing ability, possessed by a few species, which would permit them to compensate for this displacement by the time they had arrived at their home latitudes. Most migrants do not seem to allow for wind displacement after their course is set; but they can apparently adjust the course, once arrived at a resting point, and have been observed to return east or west again before proceeding southward.) Sense of direction, in adult birds, is probably supplemented by high-altitude search and by acute visual memory, which permits them to return to a given point once they arrive within a wide radius of the area. It is also supplemented by an internal timing mechanism, not yet understood, which gives the migrant some kind of azimuth bearing, using the sun or stars.

For reasons of food and prevailing winds, the golden plover which came up from the Argentine in spring by way of Peru and Yucatan, perhaps, or flew from Peru to the Gulf Coast and proceeded up the Mississippi Valley, does not return by the same route. Most though not all will complete an elliptical migration, the southbound arc of which takes them from their nesting grounds southeast across the continent to western New England and Delaware—a few go as far east as Nova Scotia and even Labrador—and on out across the open sea to South America; those that are seen at Sagaponack and else-where on the North Atlantic coast are probably deflected there by fog or storm.

The Eskimo curlew also made an elliptical or "loop" migration, and the Hudsonian godwit and white-rumped sandpiper make one still. But these three species may rest at Bermuda and in the Antilles, where the golden plover is quite rare: the first place that the plover turns up commonly is the Guianas. (The Eskimo curlew, on the other hand, was uncommon in Guiana, and it has been suggested that this species flew a kind of "great circle" course, making its first landfall south of Cape San Roque in easternmost Brazil and possi-bly flying on southwest to the interior savannas without alighting.)

Yet even assuming an advanced navigational ability, how does one explain why many young golden plover, as if in defiance of the directional sense inherited from their parents, fail to follow the southeastward path that the adult birds have taken a few weeks ear-lier, choosing instead to take, in reverse, the path that brought the adults north? The choice of the interior route spares the young birds the awesome transoceanic flight of the adults, so that they may live to make that flight another year, but no known theory of migra-tion can explain this choice except one so startling that to recognize it would be acknowledgment of an historic and continuing failure to comprehend the life dimensions: a few authorities, dissatisfied with all other explanations, have wondered if the young migratory bird *inherits* a topographic knowledge of the globe (an inherited knowledge of the constellations has already been established), or at least of that segment of it that the bird must span each spring and autumn.

The great overseas flights add the question of ocean navigation to the problem of orientation. Assuming that migrants use topo-graphic features to refine a course based primarily on an inherited sense of direction, what landmarks prevent the wind bird which spans the gray trackless reaches of the sea from being carried far off course, or otherwise losing itself so irremediably that it must inevitably burn its strength and drop into the water, to flutter and blink and float a little before drifting down like a dead leaf into the void?

The ocean itself gives its mute signs—the cloud lines, for example, registering a change in air temperature and humidity in the region, say, of the Equatorial Current; or the long lines of sargassum weed and spindrift that betray the wind patterns; or the high cumulus which, looming over island outposts beyond the horizon, are visible to high-flying birds a hundred miles away. But all these signs presume fair weather and prevailing winds; if the voyager depends on them, then should it be caught at sea by heavy fog or overcast or even windlessness, it may be doomed. Considering the mixed conditions that the wind birds meet successfully in annual journeys of fifteen thousand miles or more, one should not underestimate their chances; yet good as a bird's orientation is, it cannot spare a large percentage of each species that one fatal mistake of navigation. Mere sense of direction seems inadequate. Without visual aids to correct its compass, a gale might cause the unlucky bird to miss or overshoot its target, as in the case of the ill-fated lapwings that flew to Canada.

And so there remains a mystery, and one pores anew over refuted theories based on bird sensitivity to the atmosphere's electric waves or to the guide lines of the earth's magnetic fields. Birds have been carried to far places in revolving cages or sent aloft with magnets fastened to their heads, without noticeable impairment of their homing ability. No experiment has ever proved that a bird can orient itself magnetically, but neither can the possibility be discarded, for the talent has been demonstrated in the otherwise ungifted common mud snail of our own Atlantic coast.

The combination of abilities and experience doubtless differs from species to species. Certain sedentary birds have no homing ability whatsoever, while certain seabirds perform feats of navigation which confound the theorists, especially those who have left no place for metaphysics. None of the theories or combinations of theories presently considered reasonable provides an explanation of how a shearwater released in Venice, on a sea that none of its species ever visits, could and did return on an unfamiliar east-west bearing, across the European land mass in all likelihood, to its nesting ledge on a skerry in the Irish Sea, not in the season following but in twelve and a half days. There is no reason to suppose that a shorebird, put to an equivalent test, could not perform as well; and in regard to such a mystery the exact scientists must do much better than they have done in the way of rigorous explanation if the rest of us, the awe-struck individuals who still glimpse fine strange happenings through the screen of words and facts, are not to continue calling mystery by its proper name.

The departure of curlew from a given place often occurs just prior to a storm, and in ancient days, in England, the curlew's cry, the plover's whistle boded no man any good. Of the golden plover it was said in Lancashire that its sad whistle was the plaint of errant souls—not any old souls but the souls of those Jews who had lent a hand at the Crucifixion. In North England, curlews and whimbrels were called "Gabriel's hounds"; the name whimbrel comes from "whimpernel," which, in the Durham Household Book of 1530, refers to a habit attributed to it of houndlike whimperings. Both birds were known as harbingers of death, and in the sense that they are birds of passage, that in the wild melodies of their calls, in the breath of vast distance and bare regions that attends them, we sense intimations of our own mortality, there is justice in the legend. Yet it is not the death sign that the curlews bring, but only the memory of life, of a high beauty passing swiftly, as the curlew passes, leaving us in solitude on an empty beach, with summer gone, and a wind blowing.

# *from* Sal Si Puedes

## Cesar Chavez and the New American Revolution

**1969**

Sal Si Puedes (Escape if You Can), *named for the barrio in San Jose, California, where Cesar Chavez was born, describes Chavez's crusade to reform the relationships between corporate farms and migrant farm workers. But it is also a hard look at the way the United States has historically mistreated its laborers and immigrants: crowded, polluted ghettos; exploitative working conditions and poor pay; the utter absence of political power. Matthiessen's admiration for Chavez, a man of humble origins who stood up to the states' powerful agribusiness, can be detected even in his first impression of the labor leader: "He is five feet six inches tall, and since his twenty-five-day fast the previous winter, has weighed no more than one hundred and fifty pounds,"* he writes. *"Yet the word* slight *does not properly describe him. There is an effect of being centered in himself so that no energy is wasted, an effect of* density; *at the same time, he walks as lightly as a fox." In* Sal Si Puedes, *Matthiessen ventures into the political activism on the part of oppressed people that would reach a rhetorical peak with* In the Spirit of Crazy Horse, *published fourteen years later. Both books take charismatic activists—Chavez here, Leonard Peltier later—as their centerpieces, then wrap them in the political and economic history against which they are struggling. When* Sal Si Puedes *was published, the author and cultural critic Nat Hentoff wrote that reading the book "becomes an act of self-confrontation, for Peter Matthiessen has made it clear that Cesar Chavez's battle is not only for the agricultural workers but for the redemption of the country."*

*The following selection is taken largely from the opening chapter, with short excerpts added from the book's final pages.*

**One Sunday of August 1968,** I knocked on the door of a small frame house on Kensington Street in Delano, California. It was just before seven in the morning, and the response to the knock was the tense, suspenseful silence of a household which, in recent months, had installed an unlisted telephone, not as a convenience, but to call the outside world in case of trouble. After a moment the house breathed again, as if I had been identified through the drawn shutters, but no one came to the door, and so I sat down on the stoop and tuned in to a mockingbird. The stoop is shaded by squat trees, which distinguish Kensington Street from the other straight lines of one-story bungalows that comprise residential Delano, but at seven, the air was already hot and still, as it is almost every day of summer in the San Joaquin Valley.

Cesar Chavez's house—or rather, the house inhabited by Cesar Chavez, whose worldly possessions, scraped together, would scarcely be worth the fifty dollars that his farm workers' union pays for him in monthly rent—has been threatened so often by his enemies that it would be foolish to set down its street number. But on Kensington Street, a quiet stronghold of the American Way of Life, the house draws attention to itself by its very lack of material aspiration. On such a street the worn brown paint, the forgotten yard (relict plantings by a former tenant die off one by one, and a patch of lawn between stoop and sidewalk had been turned to mud by a leaky hose trailing away into the weeds), the uncompetitive car which, lacking an engine, is not so much parked as abandoned, are far more subversive than the strike signs (DON'T BUY CALIFORNIA GRAPES) that are plastered on the car, or the Kennedy stickers, fading now, that are still stuck to the old posts of the stoop, or the STOP REAGAN sign that decorates the shuttered windows.

Behind those drawn shutters, the house—two bedrooms, bath, kitchen, and an L-shaped living room where some of the Chavez children sleep—is neat and cheerful, brought to life by a white cabinet of bright flowers and religious objects, a stuffed bookcase, and over the sofa bed, a painting in Mexican mural style of surging strikers, but from the outside it might seem that this drab place has been abandoned, like an old store rented temporarily for some fleeting campaign and then gutted again of everything but tattered signs. The signs suggest that the dwelling is utilitarian, not domestic, that the Chavez family live here because when they came, in 1962, this house on the middle-class east side was the cheapest then available in Delano, and that their commitment is somewhere else.

Chavez's simple commitment is to win for farm workers the right to organize in their own behalf that is enjoyed by all other large labor groups in the United States; if it survives, his United Farm Workers Organizing Committee will be the first effective farm workers' union in American history. Until Chavez appeared, union leaders had considered it impossible to organize seasonal farm labor, which is in large part illiterate and indigent, and for which even mild protest may mean virtual starvation. The migrant labor force rarely remains in one place long enough to form an effective unit and is mostly composed of minority groups which invite more hostility than support, since the local communities fear an extra municipal burden with no significant increase in the tax base. In consequence, strikes, protests, and abortive unions organized ever since 1903 have been broken with monotonous efficiency by the growers, a task made easier since the Depression years by the specific exclusion of farm workers from the protection of the National Labor Relations Act of 1935 (the Wagner Act), which authorizes and regulates collective bargaining between management and labor, and protects new unionists from reprisal. In a state where cheap labor, since Indian days, has been taken for granted, like the sun, the reprisals have been swift and sometimes fatal, as the history of farm labor movements attests.

The provision of the NLRA which excludes farm workers was excused by the bloody farm strikes of 1934, when the Communist label was firmly attached to "agrarian reformers"; its continued existence three decades later is a reflection of the power of the growers, whose might and right have been dutifully affirmed by church and state. But since 1965, America's last bastion of uninhibited free enterprise has been shaken so hard by national publicity that both church and state are searching for safer positions. And this new hope for the farm workers has been brought not by the Communist agent that his enemies have conjured up, nor even by a demagogue, but by a small, soft-spoken Mexican-American migrant laborer who could never leave the fields long enough to get past the seventh grade.

In no more time than it would take to pull his pants on and splash water on his face, the back door creaked and Cesar Chavez appeared around the corner of the house. "Good morning." He smiled, raising his eyebrows, as if surprised to see me there. "How are you?" He had not had much sleep—it was already morning when I dropped him off the night before—but in that early light he looked as rested as a child. Though he shook my hand, he did not stop moving; we walked south down Kensington Street and turned west at the corner.

The man who has threatened California has an Indian's bow nose and lank black hair, with sad eyes and an open smile that is shy and friendly; at moments he is beautiful, like a dark seraph. He is five feet six inches tall, and since his twenty-five-day fast the previous winter, has weighed no more than one hundred and fifty pounds. Yet the word *slight* does not properly describe him. There is an effect of being centered in himself so that no energy is wasted, an effect of *density*; at the same time, he walks as lightly as a fox. One feels immediately that this man does not stumble, and that to get where he is going he will walk all day.

In Delano (pronounced "De-*lay*-no"), the north-south streets are named alphabetically, from Albany Street on the far west side to Xenia on the east; the cross streets are called avenues and are numbered. On Eleventh Avenue, between Kensington and Jefferson, a police car moved out of an empty lot and settled heavily on its springs across the sidewalk. There it idled while its occupant enjoyed the view. Small-town policemen are apt to be as fat and sedentary as the status quo they are hired to defend, and this one was no exception; he appeared to be part of his machine, overflowing out of his front window like a growth. Having feasted his eyes on the public library and the National Bank of Agriculture, he permitted his gaze to come to rest on the only two citizens in sight. His cap, shading his eyes from the early sun, was much too small for him, and in the middle of his mouth, pointed straight at us, was a dead cigar.

At seven on a Sunday morning in Delano, a long-haired stranger wearing sunglasses and sneakers, in the company of a Mexican, would qualify automatically as a troublemaker; consorting with a *known* troublemaker like Chavez, I became a mere undesirable. The cop looked me over long enough to let me know he had his eye on me, then eased his wheels into gear again and humped on his soft springs onto the street. Chavez raised his eyebrows in a characteristic gesture of mock wonderment, but in answer to my unspoken question—for in this tense town it could not be assumed that this confrontation was an accident—he pointed at the back of a crud-colored building fronting on Jefferson Street. "That's our station house," he said, in the manner of a man who is pointing out, with pardonable pride, the main sights of his city.

A walk across town on Eleventh Avenue, from the vineyards in the east to the cotton fields in the west, will teach one a good deal about Delano, which lies in Kern County, just south of the Tulare County line. Opposite the National Bank of Agriculture is a snack stand, La Cocina—PEPSI, BURGERS, TACOS, BURRITOS—as well as the Angelos Dry Goods shop and the Sierra Theatre, which features Mexican films; from here to Main Street and beyond, Eleventh Avenue is lined with jewelry shops and department stores. Main Street, interrupting the alphabetical sequence between Jefferson and High, is a naked treeless stretch of signs and commercial enterprises, mostly one-story; today it was empty of all life, like an open city.

Toward High Street, Empire Ford Sales rules both sides of Eleventh, and the far corners of High Street are the properties of OK USED TRUCKS and KERN COUNTY EQUIPMENT: TRUCKS AND TRACTORS. The farm-equipment warehouses and garages continue west across High Street to the tracks of the Southern Pacific Railroad; the loading platforms of the farm-produce packing sheds and cold-storage houses front the far side of the tracks, with their offices facing west on Glenwood Street. Opposite these buildings are some small cafés and poker parlors frequented by the workers—Monte Carlo Card Room, Divina's Four Deuces, Lindo Michoacan—and beyond Glenwood, the workers' neighborhoods begin. Fremont Street, relatively undeveloped, overlooks U.S. Highway 99, which bores through the town below ground level like an abandoned subway trench. An overpass across the freeway links Fremont with Ellington Street, which is littered with small cafés and markets. The wrong side of the tracks, a community of small houses, mostly Mexican-American, spreads west to Albany Street and the cotton, food, and flower factories of the San Joaquin Valley.

Toward Dover Street, a car coming up behind us slowed too suddenly. Chavez, like a feeding deer, gave sign of awareness with a sidelong flick of his brown eyes, but he did not turn or stop talking. When a voice called out in Spanish, asking him if he would like a lift, he smiled and waved, then pointed at the church two streets away. "¡No, gracias! Yo voy a la misa."

Irregularly, Chavez attends this pretty stucco church at the corner of Eleventh Avenue and Clinton Street. The church sign, OUR LADY OF GUADALUPE, is garish and utilitarian, in the spirit of Delano, and the churchyard is a parking lot enclosed by a chain-link fence. But the place has been planted with cypress, pines, and yew, which, in this early light, threw cool fresh shadows on the white stucco. In the flat angularities of their surroundings, the evergreens and red tile roof give the building a graceful Old World air that is pointed up by twin white crosses, outlined against the hot blue of the sky.

Chavez hurried on the concrete path, in the bare sun. He was wearing his invariable costume—plaid shirt, work pants, dark suede shoes—but he was clean and neatly pressed, and though he had said nothing about church, it appeared that he had been bound here all along. "Let's just go in for a little while," he murmured. He was hurrying now as if a little late, though in fact the mass was near its end. From the church door came the soft drone of liturgy, of late footsteps and a baby's cry, the hollow ring of heels on church stone, and cavernous mumbling. A cough resounded.

Slipping through the door, he moved into the shadows on the left, where he crossed himself with water dipped from a font in the rear wall. At the same time he subsided onto his knees behind the rear-most pew. In the church hush, the people had begun to sing "Ben-dito." All were standing, but Chavez remained there on his knees behind them until the hymn was finished. Alone in the shadows of the pew, the small Indian head bent on his chest and the toes of the small shoes tucked inward, he looked from behind like a boy of another time, at his prayers beside his bed.

When the hymn ended, Chavez rose and followed the people forward to receive the blessing. A Franciscan priest in green cassock and white surplice loomed above him under the glowing windows. Then he turned left, passing an American flag that stood furled in the far corner, and returned down the outside aisle. Touching the water, he crossed himself again and followed the people out the door into the growing day. To the side of the door, under the ever-greens, he waited to talk to friends; meanwhile others in the con-gregation came forward to greet him.

"¡Cesar, cómo está?" . . .

"¡Oh," Chavez answered, "batallando con la vida!"—"I am still struggling with life." He grinned.

A Filipino in his sixties came up with a fine wordless smile and pumped Chavez's hand in both his own. "That's one of the broth-ers," Chavez explained when the old man had gone; the term "brother" or "sister" is used to describe a Union member, but it also has the connotation of "soul brother," and is so used by Chavez when addressing strangers. . . . With Chavez, it is sometimes hard to tell when he is joking and when he is serious, because he is so often both at the same time.

More people greeted him, "¿Va bien?" "¡Está bien!" Most of the people are jocular with Chavez, who has a warm, humorous smile that makes them laugh, but after the joking, a few stood apart and stared at him with honest joy.

A worker in a soiled white shirt with a fighting cock in bright col-ors on the pocket stood waiting for a hearing. Though Chavez is available to his people day and night, it is on Sunday that they usu-ally come to see him, and his Sundays are all devoted to this pur-pose. "Buscando trabajo," I heard the worker say when he had Chavez's ear: he was looking for work. He had just come in from

Mexico, and the visa, or "green card," that he carried in his pocket is the symbol of the most serious obstacle that Chavez's strike effort must face: the century-old effort of California farmers to depress wages and undercut resistance by pitting one group of poor people against another.

By the 1860s the local Indians used as near-slaves in Spanish California had been decimated; they were largely replaced, after the Gold Rush, by Chinese labor made available by the completion of the Southern Pacific railroad. But the thrifty Chinese were resented and persecuted by the crowds of jobless whites for whom the Gold Rush had not panned out, and also by small farmers, who could not compete with the cheap labor force, and when their immigration was ended by the Exclusion Act of 1882, the big farmers hired other immigrants, notably Japanese. The Japanese undercut all other labor, but soon they too were bitterly resented for attempting to defend their interests. Even worse, they were better farmers than the Americans, and they bought and cultivated poor ground that nobody else had bothered with; this impertinence was dealt with by the Alien Land Law of 1913, which permitted simple confiscation of their land. (The land was subsequently restored, then confiscated again after Pearl Harbor.)

The next wave of farm laborers in California contained Hindus (Sikhs), Armenians, and Europeans; they slowly replaced the Japanese, who by 1917 were referred to as the "yellow peril," and after the war, for patriotic reasons, were kicked out of their jobs to make room for red-blooded Americans. Meanwhile, the European and Armenian immigrants, less beset than the Asiatics by the race hatred that has advanced the economy of California from the start, were gaining a strong foothold; many were the parents of the Valley farmers of today.

Throughout the nineteenth century, Mexican peasants had crossed the border more or less at will. After the Mexican Revolution of 1910, the starving refugees presented the growers with a new source of cheap labor which, because it was there illegally, had the additional advantage of being defenseless. Cheap Mexican labor was pitted against cheap Filipino labor; the Filipinos were brought in numbers in the twenties. Many of the Mexicans were deported after 1931, when the Okies, Arkies, and up-country Texans swarmed into California from the dust bowls; the Depression had caused a labor surplus beyond the wildest dreams of the employers, and an effort was made to keep the border closed.

Still, Mexicans were predominant in the farm labor force from 1914 until 1934. In these years, because of their illegal status, they tended to be more tractable than other groups; the famous farm strikes of the thirties occurred more often among Anglos and Filipinos. Despite their quiet nature, the Filipinos refused to scab on other workers or underbid them. "The Filipino is a real fighter," Cary McWilliams wrote in *Factories in the Fields*, "and his strikes have been dangerous." Few Filipino women had immigrated, and the ratio of men to women was fourteen to one; predictably, the growers dismissed the Filipinos as "homosexuals." McWilliams quotes the *Pacific Rural Press* for May 9, 1936, which called the Filipino "the most worthless, unscrupulous, shiftless, diseased semibarbarian that has ever come to our shores." After the Philippine independence act of 1934, further importation of the spirited Filipinos came to an end, and their numbers have been dwindling ever since.

By 1942 the Chinese were long since in the cities, the Japanese-Americans had been shut up in concentration camps, the Europeans had graduated from the labor force and become farmers, and the Anglos had mostly drifted into the booming war economy of factories and shipyards; the minority groups that remained were not numerous enough to harvest the enormous produce that the war demanded.

The farm labor emergency was met by a series of agreements with the Mexican government known collectively as the *bracero* program, under the terms of which large numbers of day laborers, or *braceros*, were brought into California and the Southwest at harvest time and trucked out again when the harvest was over. The *bracero* program was so popular with the growers that it was extended when the war was over. In Washington the lobbyists for the growers argued successfully that Americans would not do the hard stoop labor required in harvesting cotton, sugar beets, and other crops; hence the need for the extension of the *bracero* program. Everyone conveniently forgot that the white fruit tramps of the thirties had done plenty of stoop labor and that domestic workers of all colors would be available to the farms if working conditions were improved. But the Mexicans, whose poverty was desperate, worked hard long days for pay as low as sixty cents an hour, and were used to undermine all efforts by domestic workers to hold out for better treatment; by 1959 an estimated four hundred thousand foreign workers (including small numbers of Canadians in the potato fields of Maine, and British West Indians in the Florida citrus groves) were obtaining work in an America where millions were unemployed.

Already the churches and citizens' groups were protesting the lot of the farm workers, and the domestic migrant laborers especially, and at the end of 1964 Public Law 78, the last and most notorious of the *bracero* programs, was allowed to lapse. (This was the year in which a long-accumulating sense of national guilt had permitted the passage of significant poverty and civil rights legislation, and it would be pleasant to assume that P.L. 78 was a casualty of the new humanism, but congressional concern about the outflow of gold was probably more important.)

The death of P.L. 78 was the birth of serious hope for a farm union, but by 1965, when the grape strike began, the growers had found another means to obtain the same cheap labor. Under Public Law 414 (the Immigration and Nationality Act of 1952, also called the McCarran-Walter Act), large numbers of foreigners were permitted to enter the United States as "permanent resident aliens" on a special green visa card. "Green-carders" could become citizens after five years' residence (and hold social security, pay taxes, and be drafted while they waited), but since the Mexican may earn fifteen times as much for a day's work in the United States (thirty dollars versus twenty-five pesos, or about two dollars), most have declined this opportunity in favor of "commuting," i.e., they cluster around the border towns and take their high harvest wages—an estimated fifteen million dollars' worth in 1967—back to Mexico.

Today almost half the membership of Chavez's union hold green cards; they are welcome so long as they do not work as scabs. The law specifies that no green-carders may work in a field where a labor dispute has been certified, or where a minimum wage (now $1.40 an hour) has not been offered first to domestic workers, but enforcement of this law has been desultory, to say the least. Many Mexicans, with the active encouragement of the growers and the passive encouragement of the Border Patrol of the U.S. Immigration Service, have joined the numerous "wetbacks" (that is, the illegal immigrants) as strikebreakers. As long as they are excluded from legislation that guarantees collective bargaining, the farm workers have no formal means to force employers to negotiate. When their strike against the grape growers was subverted by imported scabs and antipicketing injunctions, they were driven to what the growers call an "illegal and immoral" boycott. Originally this boycott was directed against one company, the Joseph Giumarra Vineyards, Inc., but Giumarra began selling its products under the labels of other companies, and in January 1968 the present consumers' boycott against all growers of California table grapes was begun.

In the autumn of 1968, according to the Fresno *Bee* of November 3, an estimated twenty to thirty thousand wetbacks were working in the Valley; though their presence is illegal, there is no penalty for hiring them, and since they are both economical and defenseless, the growers replace their domestic force with *alambristas* (fence jumpers) at every opportunity. "When the *alambrista* comes into a job," one of them is quoted as saying, "the regular workers are out, just like that." The Immigration Service picked up five hundred and ten wetbacks in the Delano area in August alone—about one-fortieth of the lowest estimated number.

Loosely enforced, P.L. 414 is no improvement over P.L. 78, and it poses a moral problem as well as an economic one: Mexican-Americans, most of whom have parents or grandparents south of the border, have deep sympathy with Mexican poverty and do not wish to get Mexicans into trouble by reporting them to *la Migra*, as the Border Patrol is known. Besides, many green-carders are innocent, having been hired without being told, as P.L. 414 requires, that their employer was the object of a strike; some of these people, poor though they are, have walked off the job in a strange country when they learned the truth, but most are in debt for transport and lodging before they ever reach the fields, and their need—and that of their families at home—is too great to permit so brave a gesture.

The man with the fighting cock on his shirt was a Union green-carder who did not wish to cross the picket lines. But at that time there were more Union workers than Union jobs—only three growers in the Delano area had signed contracts with the United Farm Workers Organizing Committee—and Chavez encouraged the man to take a job wherever he could find it. He did not have to encourage the green-carder to help the Union on the job by organizing work slowdowns; the man was already complaining that social security payments had been deducted from his last pay checks, even though no one had asked for his social security number.

Workers who cannot read, like this man, feel that they are chronic victims of petty pay-check chiseling on the part of both labor contractors and growers, not only on illusory social security but on unpaid overtime and promised bonuses. (In the first six months of 1967, the Department of Labor discovered that nearly two hundred thousand American laborers were being cheated by their employers, mostly on unpaid overtime and evasion of the minimum wage; this figure is probably only a fraction of the actual number of victims.) Chavez feels that the labor contractor, who sells his own people in job lots to the growers, is the worst evil in an evil system that is very close to peonage; the contractor would be eliminated if the growers agreed to get their labor through a union hiring hall.

"Those people make a lot of money that way," Chavez said. "A lot." At this moment, he looked ugly. "In the Union, the workers get an honest day's pay, because both sides understand the arrangement and accept it. Without a union, the people are always cheated, and they are so innocent." In silence, we walked on up Eleventh Avenue to Albany and turned south along the cotton fields. It was eight o'clock now, and the morning was hot. The flat farmland stretched away unbroken into dull mists of agricultural dust, nitrates, and insecticides, still unsettled from the day before, that hid the round brown mountains of the Coast Range.

Chavez said that many of the green-carders—and especially those who would return to Mexico—felt they could beat the Union wage scale by working furiously on a piece-rate basis; others did not join the Union out of ignorance—they had never heard of a union—or fear of reprisal. "It's the whole system of fear, you know. The ones we've converted—well, out at Schenley we have a contract, and P. L. Vargas, on his ranch committee—there was a guy named Danny. Danny was so anti-Union that he went to the management at Schenley and said, 'Give me a gun; I'll go out and kill some of those strikers.' He just hated us, and he didn't know why. Today he's a real good Unionist; he has a lot of guts and does a lot of work, but he still doesn't know why. He was working inside when we came with the picket line, and he wouldn't walk out, and I guess he felt guilty so he went too far the other way. And also, he told me later, 'I didn't know what a union was, I never heard of a union; I had no idea what it was or how it worked. I came from a small village down in Mexico!' You see? It's the old story. He was making more money than he had ever seen in Mexico, and the Union was a threat.

"Anyway, we won there, and got a union shop, and all the guys who went out on strike got their jobs back. And, man, they wanted to clean house, they wanted to get Danny, and I said no. 'Well, he doesn't want to join the Union! And the contract says if he doesn't join the Union, he can't work there!' So I challenged them. I said, 'One man threatens you? And you've got a contract? Do you know what the real challenge is? Not to get him out, but to get him *in*. If you were good organizers you'd get him, but you're not—you're lazy!' So they went after Danny, and the pressure began to build against him. He was mad as hell, he held out for three months, and he was encouraged by the Anglos, the white guys—they had the best jobs, mechanics and all, and they didn't want to join the Union either. But finally Danny saw the light, and they did too. That contract took about six months to negotiate, so by the time we got around to setting up a negotiating committee, Danny had not only been converted but had been elected to the committee. So when the committee walked in there, P. L. was one of them and Danny was another, and the employers stared at him: 'What are you doing here, Danny?'" Chavez laughed. "And now he's a real St. Paul; he'll never turn against the Union because he knows both sides. People who don't know, and come on so enthusiastic and all at first, they may be turncoats one day, but not the ones like Danny. That's why the converted ones are our best men.

"You know how we make enemies? A guy gets out of high school, and his parents have been farm workers, so he gets a job, say, as a clerk at the Bank of America. This way, you know, he gets into the climate, into the atmosphere"—Chavez shook his head in bafflement—"and I'll be damned if in two years they haven't done a terrific job on him, not by telling him, but just by . . . by *immersion*, and before you know it the guy is actually saying there's no discrimination! 'Hell, there's no poverty!' See? He knows his place. Or he gets a job at a retail store and then feels threatened because our people are making more than he does. 'Look,' he says, 'I went to high school for four years, so how come these farm workers are making more than I do?' That *really* hurts. Either way he is threatened by the Union."

On the left as we walked south on Albany were the small houses of large families, mostly Mexican. Though these houses are simple, their neatness reflects a dignity that was not possible in the labor camps, which have always been the ugliest symbol of the migrant workers' plight. "Besides being so bad, they divide the families," Chavez said. "We don't want people living out there, we want them in their own houses. As long as they're living in the camps, they're under the thumb of the employer." He nodded toward the small houses. "In Delano the need for housing is being met, even for the migrants. I mean, if we won the whole thing tomorrow, signed contracts with all the growers, we'd have to use some of the camps for a little while, but right now the people in the camps are strikebreakers." I kicked a stone, and he watched it skid into the field. "We're going to get rid of those camps," he said, as if making himself a promise.

A car passed us, bursting with cries, and rattled to a halt a short way beyond. Two workers were driving a third to the Forty Acres, the site of the proposed new Union headquarters, and to my surprise—we had been headed for the Union offices at the corner of Albany and Asti Streets—Chavez suggested that we ride out there. The car turned west at Garces Highway and rolled two miles through the cotton and alfalfa to a barren area of mud, shacks, and unfinished construction on the north side of the road. Here the car left us and went back to town, and the third man, a solitary Anglo tramp, a renegade from the thirties who helps the farm workers whenever he comes to town, shouted cheerily at Chavez and marched off to water some scattered saplings that shriveled slowly in the August heat.

"We've planted a lot of trees. Elms, mostly, and Modesto ash— only the cheapest kinds." Chavez stood with his back to the road, hands in hip pockets, gazing with pleasure at the desolation. The Forty Acres lies between the state road and the city dump. Useless for farming in its present condition, the property was obtained in 1966 from a widow who could not afford to pay the taxes on it. "Don't get me started on my plans," he said. To Chavez, who envisions the first migrant workers' center, the place is already beautiful; he comes here regularly to walk around and let his plans take shape. "There's alkali in this land," he said. "We're trying to get something growing here, to cut down the dust."

At the Forty Acres, near the highway, an adobe building which will house gas pumps, auto repair shop, and a cooperative store had recently been completed, though it was not yet in use: the shop was heaped high with food stores for the strikers, donated by individuals and agencies all over the United States. Just across from it is the windowless small room in which Chavez lived during the twenty-five-day fast that he undertook in February and March 1968. Behind this building was a temporary aggregation of shacks and trailers which included the workers' clinic and the Union newspaper, *El Malcriado* (the "rebellious child," the "nonconformist," the "protester"—there is no simple translation), which issues both English and Spanish editions every fortnight. Originally *El Malcriado* was a propaganda organ, shrill and simplistic: it saw Lyndon Johnson as a "Texas grower" careless of the lives of the Vietnamese "farm workers." Today it is slanted but not irresponsible, and it is well-edited.

One green trailer at the Forty Acres, bearing the legend MOBILE HEALTH CENTER, was the contribution of the International Ladies' Garment Workers Union; its medical staff, like that of *El Malcriado* and most of the rest of the UFWOC operation, is made up entirely of volunteers. So is the intermittent labor being done on the head-quarters building, a gray shell in the northwest corner of the property. The work was supervised by Chavez's brother Richard, who had been sent off a few days before to help out with the boycott in New York. "The strike is the important thing," Chavez said, moving toward this building. "We work on the Forty Acres when we get a little money, or some volunteers." The day before, six carpenters from a local in Bakersfield had given their Saturday to putting up gray fiberboard interior walls, and Chavez, entering the building, was delighted with the progress. "Look at that!" he kept saying. "Those guys really went to town!" The plumbing had been done by a teacher at Berkeley, and two weeks before, forty-seven electricians from Los Angeles, donating materials as well as labor, had wired the whole building in six hours. "I've never seen forty-seven electricians," I admitted, trying not to laugh, and Chavez grinned. "You should have seen it," he assured me. "I could hardly get into the building. Everywhere I went, I was in somebody's way, so I just went out through the window." . . .

Outside again, we walked around the grounds, in the hot empti-ness of Sunday. "Over there"—he pointed—"will be another build-ing, a little training center there, kind of a . . . a study center for nonviolence, mostly for people in the Union, the organizers and ranch committees. Nonviolent tactics, you know—to be nonvio-lent in a monastery is one thing, but being nonviolent in a struggle for justice is another. And we'll stress honesty. Some of these guys will be getting a lot of power as the Union develops, and some will be very good and some won't know how to handle it. If someone in the hiring hall is willing to take a bribe to put one guy ahead of another on a job, he may also be willing to steal a hundred dollars from the Union, or accept a hundred dollars for an act of violence. There's all kinds of chances for corruption, and things can go to hell fast—we've seen that in other unions. So the best way to teach them is by example."

His glance asked that I take what he was about to say as nothing boastful. Chavez is a plain-spoken man who does not waste his own time or his listener's with false humility, yet he is uncomfortable when the necessity arises to speak about himself, and may even emit a gentle groan. "I mean, you can write a million pamphlets on honesty, you can write books on it, and manuals, and it doesn't work—it only works by example. I have to give up a lot of things, because I can't ask people to sacrifice if I won't sacrifice myself." He was glad to change the subject. "We have some great guys in this Union, some really great guys. We've put together farm workers and volunteers, people who just wanted to do something for the cause. We have so many volunteers that we save only the best; they come and go, but the good ones never go. You don't say 'Stay!' They stay of their own accord!

"In a way we're all volunteers; even the ones—the lawyers and everybody—whose salaries are paid by outside people; they're not making money. You start paying the strikers for what they should do for themselves, then everything is done for money, and you'll never be able to build anything. It's not just a question of spending money, and anyway, we haven't got it. But the farm workers stand to benefit directly from the Union; it's their union, and we've been able to get that across to them—really, you know, it's working beautifully. Most of us work for five dollars a week. Outside people, the Teamsters and everybody, thought we were crazy, but it's the only way we can stay in business. It's a long, long haul, and there isn't any money, and if we start paying wages, then it means that only a *few* can be hired, and a few can't do as much as many.

"It has to be done this way. I've been in this fight too long, almost twenty years, learning and learning, one defeat after another, always frustration. And then of course, raising a family—you have to get your family to suffer along with you, otherwise you can't do it. But finally we're beginning to see daylight, and that's a great reward. And then, you see, these farm workers will never be the same. If they destroyed our union today, these people would never go back to where they were. They'd get up and fight. That's the *real* change."

Under the eaves of the garage, in the shade of the north wall, a blue wooden bench stood against the adobe. We sat there for an hour or more, cut off by the cool clay walls from the howl of the highway. To the west was a marginal dark farm—all dying farms look dark—with a lone black-and-white cow in the barnyard, and a sign, itself in need of repair, that advertised the repair of auto radiators.

Across the property to the north, dead cars glittered on the crown of the city dump; heaped high like a bright monument to progress, the cars form the only rise in the depressed landscape of Delano.

The adobe walls and red tile roofs of the Forty Acres were Chavez's own wish, to be repeated in the other buildings as they take shape: the idea comes from the old Franciscan missions, and from an adobe farmhouse of his childhood. "The people wanted something more modern—you know, kind of flashy—to show that they had a terrific union going here, but I wanted something that would not go out of fashion, something that would last." Eventually the entire Forty Acres will be surrounded by a high adobe wall, which will mercifully shut out its grim surroundings. The flat hard sky will be broken by trees, and he dreams of a fountain in a sunken garden, and a central plaza where no cars will be permitted.

Chavez drew his hopes in the old dust with a dead stick. Inside the walls, paths will lead everywhere, and "places for the workers to rest. There will be little hollows in the walls—you know, niches—where people can put little statues if they want, or birds and things. We'll have frescoes. Siqueiros is interested in doing that, I think. This place is for the people, it has to grow naturally out of their needs." He smiled. "It will be kind of a religious place, very restful, quiet. It's going to be nice here." He gazed about him. "I love doing this—just letting it grow by itself. Trees. We'll have a little woods." Arizona cypress had already been planted along the property lines, but in the August heat many of Chavez's seedling trees had yellowed and died. . . .

Because he is such an unpublic man, Chavez is one of the few public figures that I would go ten steps out of my way to meet. Besides, I feel that the farm workers' plight is related to all of America's most serious afflictions: racism, poverty, environmental pollution, and urban crowding and decay—all of these compounded by the waste of war.

In a damaged human habitat, all problems merge. For example, noise, crowding, and smog poisoning are notorious causes of human irritability; that crowded ghettos explode first in the worst smog areas of America is no coincidence at all. And although no connection has been established between overcrowding and the atmosphere of assassination, rat experiments leave little doubt that a connection could exist: even when ample food and shelter are provided, rats (which exhibit behavioral patterns disconcertingly similar to those of man) respond to crowding in strange and morbid ways, including neuter behavior, increased incidence of homosexuality, gang rape, killing, and consumption by the mothers of their young. But because the symptoms of a damaged habitat are social, a very serious problem of ecology (it seems fatuous to say "the most serious problem the world has ever known," not because it is untrue but because it is so obvious) will be dealt with by politicians, the compromisers and consensus men who do not lead but merely exploit the status quo. The apparatus of the status quo—the System is a partisan term but must do here for want of a better—not to speak of System ethics, is not going to be good enough when food, oxygen, and water become scarce. Although it seems likely, in purely material needs, that the optimisms of the new technologies will be borne out, most men in 1985 will have to live by bread alone, and not very good bread, either. Famine is already as close as Kentucky and the Mississippi Delta, and apart from that, there is hard evidence of environmental stress—noise, traffic, waiting lines, sick cities, crime, lost countrysides, psychosis. Meanwhile, the waste of resources continues, and the contamination of the biosphere by bomb and blight.

Before this century is done, there will be an evolution in our values and the values of human society, not because man has become more civilized but because, on a blighted earth, he will have no choice. This evolution—actually a revolution whose violence will depend on the violence with which it is met—must aim at an order of things that treats man and his habitat with respect; the new order, grounded in human ecology, will have humanity as its purpose and the economy as its tool, thus reversing the present order of the System. Such hope as there is of orderly change depends on men like Cesar Chavez, who, of all leaders now in sight, best represents the rising generations. He is an idealist unhampered by ideology, an activist with a near-mystic vision, a militant with a dedication to nonviolence, and he stands free of the political machinery that the election year 1968 made not only disreputable but irrelevant.

. . .

In the heavy Sunday silence of the Valley we rose from the bench, stretched, grinned, and went back out into the sun. Ten o'clock had come and gone, and the blue sky had paled to a blue-white. We walked toward town in silence. In the corner of Forty Acres, just off the highway, was a heavy wooden cross with ten-foot arms, made of old telephone poles, which had been consecrated at the time of the February fast; after Senator Kennedy's assassination it had been covered with a shroud. In late June, following two attempts to burn it, local vigilantes sawed it down. The charred remnants were left there in the mesquite desert dust so that no one on either side would forget the event. Chavez glanced at the despoiled cross but made no comment.

Our shoes scuffed along the highway shoulder, over the slag of broken stone, tar bits, glass, and flattened beer cans—Hamm's, Olympia, Coors. In the still heat, tar stink and exhaust fumes hung heavy in the air. Exhaust filters were first required by law in California, where air pollution is so pervasive that the whole state seems threatened by a dull gray-yellow pall; it is appropriate that Chavez's fight for a new ethic should have begun in California, which free enterprise has reduced from the most majestic of the states to the most despoiled.

Of all California's blighted regions, the one that man has altered most is this great Central Valley, which extends north and south for almost four hundred miles. The Sacramento Valley, in the northern half, was once a sea of grass parted by rivers; the San Joaquin Valley, in the south, was a region of shallow lakes and tule marshes. Both parts of what is commonly known as the Valley supported innumerable animals and birds, among which the waterfowl, antelope, and tule elk were only the most dominant; there were also wolves, grizzlies, cougar, deer, and beaver. To the Spanish, centered in the great mission holdings along the south-central coast, the grasslands of the interior were scarcely known, and their destruction was accomplished almost entirely by the wave of Americans that followed hard upon the Gold Rush. Game slaughter became an industry, and the carnivores were poisoned; by 1875 the myriad elk and antelope were almost gone. Meanwhile, unre-stricted grazing by huge livestock herds destroyed the perennial grasses. Oat grass, June grass, and wild rye gave way to tarweed, cheat grass, and thistle, which in turn were crowded by rank annual weeds escaped from imported food crops of the settlers. In land-scape after landscape, the poppies, lupines, larkspurs, and mariposa lilies were no more.

From the start, California land monopolies were so enormous that the big "farms" were not farms at all, but industrial plantations. (To this day, the Kern County Land Company owns 350,000 acres in Kern County alone.) In the latter part of the nineteenth century, the huge corporate ranches were challenged for the dying range by huge corporate farms; the first big factory crop was wheat, the sec-ond sugar beets. One by one the tule marshes were burned over and drained; by the end of the century, the lakes and creeks, like the wild creatures, had subsided without a trace. As the whole Valley dried, the water table that once had lain just below the surface sank away; in places, the competitive search for water made it necessary to resort to oil-drilling equipment, tapping Ice Age aquifers hun-dreds of feet down. To replace the once plentiful water, the rivers were dammed and rechanneled in the Bureau of Reclamation's Central Valley Project, begun in the thirties: Shasta Dam destroyed the Sacramento, and Friant Dam choked off the San Joaquin. Today there are no wild rivers in the Valley, and very few in all of California; the streams of the Coast range and the Sierra Nevada have been turned to irrigation, seeping across the Valley floor in concrete ditches.

Hard-edged and monotonous as parking lots, the green fields are without life. The road we walked across the Valley floor was straight and rigid as a gun barrel, without rise or curve. Passing cars buffeted with hot wind the cornflowers that had gained a foothold between the asphalt and the dull man-poisoned crop, and pressed toads as dry as leaves gave evidence in death that a few wild things still clung to life in this realm of organophosphates and chlorinated hydrocar-bons.

As the sun rose the sky turned white; the white merged with the atmospheric dust. The dry heat is tolerable, yet the soul shrivels;

this world without horizons is surreal. Out here on the flat Valley floor there is nothing left of nature; even the mountains have retreated, east and west. On all sides looms the wilderness of wires and weird towers of man's progress, including a skeletal installation of the Voice of America, speeding glad news of democracy and freedom to brown peoples all over the world.

A winter sun spun through the mist, but all the highway lights were lit, and other lights shone from the railway sidings, tanks, and anonymous towers of light industry, on the far side of metal fences that run down both sides of U.S. 99. Below McFarland the highway crosses the Friant-Kern Canal, a steep-sided concrete trench perhaps fifty feet across that bores across the Valley like a giant gutter; in the canal the water was low and in the old Kern River bed, just north of Bakersfield, there was no water at all.

The fog thinned and high billboards became visible, looming over the sunken trenches of the freeway. Where the freeway was at ground level, the signs were smaller: AUTO SUPPLY and THE BEST CEMENT PIPE CO. and a sign for car wreckers, off the road to Oildale (2 MI.). On either side of the highway, utility wires wandered in the mist; the low winter sun took shape and then withdrew. Stalled by the fog, strange yellow machines squatted on their mounds of heaped raw earth, and the few weed trees that straggled skyward did less to offset than to set off the desolation. Otherwise, all lines were straight: the six lanes and their center lines, the concrete island down the highway spine, the steel barriers flanking the concrete, the railroad tracks and ties, the vine rows in the rectangles of the uniform flat fields. Here and there a strip of planting had been jammed into the concrete of the "median divider"—a last rigid line in the pattern of progress laid down like an iron grid upon the land.

At the south end of the Valley the road climbed quickly to the sky. Northward the mist lay banked, like a brown cloud on the Valley floor. To the south, closing off the whole horizon, was the great gray-yellow contamination that hangs over the spreading megalopolis.

. . .

"But you know what I—what I really think? You know what I really think? I really think that one day the world will be great. I really believe the world gonna be great one day."

The man who said that was a migrant farm worker, and a black man. Cesar Chavez shares this astonishing hope of an evolution in human values, and I do too; it is the only hope we have.

I think often of the visit to the archdiocese on that summer day in San Francisco, and the way Cesar vanished into the cold modern house of God, so unlike the simple missions he prefers. An elevator must have rushed him to the top, because moments later there came a rapping from on high, and Cesar appeared in silhouette behind the panes, waving and beckoning from the silences of sun and glass like a man trapped against his will in Heaven. His dance of woe was a pantomime of man's fate, and this transcendental clowning, this impossible gaiety, which illuminates even his most desperate moments, in his most moving trait. Months later I could still see that human figure in the glittering high windows of the twentieth century. The hands, the dance, cried to the world: Wait! Have faith! Look, look! Let's go! Good-bye! Hello! I love you!

# from **Blue Meridian**

## The Search for the Great White Shark

1971

*In 1968 Matthiessen was invited by the filmmaker Peter Gimbel to join an expedition in search of the most dangerous fish in the sea, the great white shark. When Matthiessen asked how the voyage would differ from those of the famous French diver Jacques Cousteau, Gimbel replied, "Those films are fine, but I didn't see a shark over nine feet. The sharks we want will be dangerous to divers, and the shark we want most is the great white shark—in fact, the film is a search for the great white shark, whether we find him or not." Gimbel's film, called* Blue Water, White Death, *includes some of the most arresting wildlife footage ever shot; it appeared three years before Peter Benchley's novel* Jaws *described a great white shark terrorizing a New England summer resort town.*

*Matthiessen's account of the expedition,* Blue Meridian, *contains vivid descriptions of the mysterious realm beneath the surface of the ocean, off the coasts of South Africa, the Caribbean, and Australia. The following excerpt finds the expedition near Dangerous Reef, off South Australia, where the film crew made a final, desperate try for underwater footage of the sharks.*

**At daybreak on Wednesday** the *Saori* sailed for the Gambier Islands, on the Antarctic horizon south of the mouth of Spencer Gulf. A big ocean swell rose out of the southwest, from the far reaches of the roaring forties, but there was a lee of sorts east of Wedge Island. The Gambiers are remote and no gill netting is done there, and white sharks had been seen often in the past; occasionally the sharks would seize a horse when the animals raised here in other days were swum out to the ships. Now the old farm was a sheep station, visited infrequently by man. With Ron, Valerie, and Stan, I went ashore, exploring. Gaunt black machinery, stranded by disuse, looked out to sea from the dry golden hills, and the sheep, many of them dead, had brought a plague of flies; only at the island's crest, in the southwest wind, could one be free of them.

Wedge Island is a beautiful silent place, a great monument like a pyramid in the Southern Ocean. That night, white-faced storm petrels fluttered like moths at the masthead light. Some fell to the deck, and I put them in a box; once the deck lights were out, they flitted off toward the island. These hardy little birds come in off the windy wastes of sea just once a year to nest in burrows in the cliffs.

Overhead, shined by the wind, the austral sky was luminous. With the stem of his pipe, Ben Ranford pointed at the universe: "Canis Major," he pronounced with satisfaction. "The brightest star in all the heavens." In World War II Ben was captain of a destroyer in the Australian Navy, and is still the compleat seaman, clumping here and there about his ship in white coveralls and big black shoes without one wasted motion; he could have stripped the *Saori* from stem to stern and reassembled her in the dark. No man could do his job better than he, and yet Ben knew that this ship might be his last.

At dawn the day was already hot and still, the baits untouched, the ocean empty. Only a solitary eagle, white head shimmering in the rising sun, flapped and sailed over the sea, bound for the outermost islands.

Two weeks had passed, and there was no underwater footage, and running from place to place was not the answer. A decision was made to increase the volume of bait and chum and concentrate it at Dangerous Reef. The two sharks raised there were the only two that had been seen, the resident sea lions were an asset, and the Reef was only three hours from the abattoirs and fish companies at Port Lincoln. The ship sailed north again into Spencer Gulf, rounding the west end of the Reef and anchoring off its northern shore at noon; a southwest blow was expected that afternoon, backing around to the southeast by evening.

White shark number three came after dark on January 27, seizing the floating bait with a heavy thrash that brought a bellow of excitement from Gimbel, working on deck. No sooner had a light been rigged than the fish reappeared, making a slow turn at the perimeter of green night water. Then it rifled straight and fast for a carcass hanging at the ship's side, which it gobbled at and shook apart, oblivious of the lights and shouting men. Though not enormous, this aggressive brute was the one we wanted; by the look of it, it would not be deterred by cages or anything else. Then it was gone, and a cuttlefish rippled in the eerie light, and the sea thickened with a bloom of red crustaceans.

All baits were hauled in but a small flayed sheep, left out to stay the shark until the morning. At dawn, the unraveled bait line lay on deck. Taking the sheep, the shark had put such strain upon the line that, parting, it had snapped back clean out of the water. But there was no sign of the shark, and it never returned.

That morning the *Sea Raider* came out from Port Lincoln with big drums full of butchered horse; the quarters hung from the stern of the *Saori*, which was reeking like a charnel house. Buckets of horse blood, whale oil, and a foul chum of ground tuna guts made a broad slick that spread northeast toward Spilsby Island. The cages, cameras lashed to their floors, were already overboard, floating astern. The sky was somber, with high mackerel clouds and a bank of ocean grays creeping up out of the south, and a hard wind; petrels dipped and fluttered in the wake. The ship was silent.

Vodka in hand, Gimbel came and went, glaring astounded at the empty slick that spread majestically to the horizon. About 5:30 I forsook my post on the deckhouse roof and went below. Peter was lying in a berth, face tight. I said, "I'm taking a shower even though there's still light enough to shoot; there'll be a shark here before I'm finished." He laughed politely. I had just returned to the cabin, still half dry, wrapped in a towel, when a voice yelled "Shark!" down the companionway.

By the time we reached the deck, bound for the wet-suits, the sun had parted the clouds; with luck, there would be underwater light for at least an hour. Already a second shark had joined the first, and both were big. I went into the sea with Peter, and Stan and Ron soon joined us in the other cage. Almost immediately a great pale shape took form in the blue mist.

The bolder of the sharks, perhaps twelve feet long, was a heavy male, identifiable by paired claspers at the vent; a second male, slightly smaller, stayed in the background. The first shark had vivid scars about the head and an oval scar under the dorsal, and in the molten water of late afternoon it was a creature very different from the one seen from the surface. The hard rust of its hide had dissolved in pale transparent tones that shimmered in the ocean light on its satin skin. From the dorsal fin an evanescent bronze shaded down to luminous dark metallic gray along the lateral line, a color as delicate as that bronze tint on a mushroom which points up the whiteness of the flesh beneath. From snout to keel, the underside was a deathly white, all but the black undertips of the broad pectorals.

The shark passed slowly, first the slack jaw with the triangular splayed teeth, then the dark eye, impenetrable and empty as the eye of God, next the gill slits like knife slashes in paper, then the pale slab of the flank, aflow with silver ripplings of light, and finally the thick short twitch of its hard tail. Its aspect was less savage than implacable, a silent thing of merciless serenity.

Only when the light had dimmed did the smaller shark drift in from the blue shadows, but never did it come to the hanging baits. The larger shark barged past the cages and banged against the hull to swipe and gulp at the chunks of meat; on the way out, it repeatedly bit the propeller of the outboard, swallowing the whole shaft and shaking the motor. Then it would swing and glide straight in again, its broad pectorals, like a manta's wings, held in an upward curve. Gills rippling, it would swerve enough to miss the cage, and once the smiling head had passed I could reach out and take hold of the rubber pectoral, or trail my fingers down the length of cold dead flank, as if stroking a corpse: the skin felt as smooth as the skin of a swordfish or tuna. Then the pale apparition sank under the copper-red hull of the *Saori* and vanished in the gloom, only to reappear from another angle, relentless, moving always at the same deceptive speed, mouth gasping as in thirst. This time it came straight to the cage and seized one of the flotation cylinders of the cage roof; there came a nasty screeching sound, like the grating of fingernails on slate, before the shark turned off, shaking its head.

The sharks off Durban had probed the cages and scraped past, but never once, in hundreds of encounters, did one attack them open-mouthed. The white sharks were to attack the cages over and over. This first one arched its back, gills wrinkling, coming on mouth wide; fortunately it came at cruising speed and struck the least vulnerable part of the cage. The silver tanks, awash at the surface, may have resembled crippled fish, for they were hit far more often than anything else. When their teeth struck metal, the sharks usually turned away, but often the bite was hard enough to break the teeth out. Sometimes as it approached the cage, one would flare its mouth wide, then close it again, in what looked very much like the threat display of higher animals.

To escape the rough chop at the surface, the cage descended to fifteen feet, where Gimbel opened the roof hatch and climbed partway out to film; he was driven back each time. At one point, falling back in haste, Peter got his tank hung up on the hatch, and was still partly exposed when the shark passed overhead, a black shade in the golden ether made by the sinking sun. From below, the brute's girth was dramatically apparent: it blotted out the light.

The shark paid the cages such close attention that Gimbel burned up a ten-minute magazine in fifteen minutes. When he went to the surface to reload, Valerie Taylor and Peter Lake took over the cage. "Listen!" Gimbel yelled at them, still excited. "Now watch it! They're nothing like those Durban sharks, so don't take chances!" Then Stan came out of the second cage, and by the time he was reloaded, Ron was ready to come out; this gave me a chance to go down a second time.

For a while the atmosphere was quiet as both sharks kept their distance from the ship; they came and went like spirits in the mist. But emergencies are usually sudden, and now there came a series of near-emergencies. First the bigger shark, mouth open, ran afoul of one of the lines; the length of rope slipped past the teeth and hung in the corners of its mouth, trailing back like reins. So many lines were crisscrossed in the water—skiff lines, bait lines, hydrophone cable, and tethers to keep the cages near the bait—that at first one could not tell what was going to happen, and I felt a clutch of fear. Swimming away, the shark was shaking its head in irritation, and then I saw that the line was the tether of the other cage, where Gimbel had been joined by Peter Lake. The line was very nearly taut when the shark shook free. Lake was using a camera with a hundred-and-eighty-degree "fish-eye" lens, and was getting remarkable shots, but the close call rattled him considerably. At the surface, he yelled all the obscenities. "To hell with *that* shit," he concluded. "I'm going below to hide under my berth!" But Lake's trials were not over. A few days later, when the *Saori* returned to Dangerous Reef for continuity shots and supporting footage, a shark, tangled in a bait line, bent the whole cage with its slow thrashing; it actually *stretched* five of the bars, shaking the whole cage like a dice cup before Lake could get his leg knife out and cut it free. At the surface, he had difficulty joking: "When I saw those bars starting to go I felt like I had jumped at twelve thousand feet with my parachute eaten by rats."

Often the larger shark would appear from below, its ragged smile rising straight up past the cage; already its head was scarred with streaks of red lead from the *Saori*'s hull. On one of these ascents it seized a piece of meat hung from the taffrail just as the current swung the cage in toward the ship, so that the whole expanse of its ghostly belly, racked by spasms of huge gulping, was perpendicular against the bars. I scratched the belly with a kind of morbid sympathy, but at that instant we were jarred by a thrash of the tail; the cage had pinned the shark upright against the rudder of the *Saori*. While Waterman filmed at point-blank range, it lashed the water white. "I wasn't really worried about you guys," Gimbel said later. "I just knew it would knock hell out of you." The cage was swiftly heaved aside, and the shark glided for the bottom with that ineffable silent calm, moving no more rapidly than before. Except for size, it is often difficult to estimate shark age, and watching it go, it was easy to believe that this beast might swim for centuries.

I turned to congratulate Waterman on the greatest footage of a feeding white shark ever taken, but bald eyes rolled in woe behind his mask, and he made a throat-slitting gesture with his finger and smote his rubber brow, then shook his fist at his camera, which had jammed. Gimbel got the sequence from the other cage, thirty feet away, and Lipscomb caught one angle of it from the surface, but Stan was inconsolable.

Gimbel was still trying to film from the roof hatch, and now he ducked down neatly at a shark's approach, only to find himself staring straight into his face. The main cage door had opened outward, and the shark was so near that he could not reach out to close it. Badly frightened, he feinted with his camera at the shark, which cruised on past, oblivious.

Between bites the sharks patrolled the cages, the Saori, and the skiff, biting indiscriminately; there was no sense of viciousness or savagery in what they did, but something worse, an implacable need. They bit the skiff and they bit the cages, and one pushed past the meat to bite the propeller of the Saori; it was as if they smelled the food but could not distinguish it by sight, and therefore attacked everything in the vicinity. Often they mouthed the cage metal with such violence that teeth went spinning from their jaws. One such tooth found on the bottom had its serrated edge scraped smooth. It seemed to me that here was the explanation for the reports of white-shark attacks on boats; they do not attack boats, they attack *anything*.

When I left the water, there was a slight delay in getting the skiff alongside, and Rodney warned me not to loiter on top of the cage. "They've been climbing all over it!" he called. At one point Valerie, having handed up her exhausted tank, had to retreat into the cage, holding her breath as a shark thrashed across its roof over and over.

We had entered the water about six, and the last diver left it at seven-thirty, by which time every one of us was shaking hard with cold. In the skiff, transferring from the cages to the ship, people were shouting. The excitement far exceeded any I had seen in the footage of the greatest day off Durban; as Gimbel said, "Christ, man! These sharks are just a hell of a lot more exciting!"

The next morning, a sparkling wild day, the two sharks were still with us, and they had been joined by a third still larger. Even Ron estimated the new shark at fourteen feet, and Gimbel one or two feet more; it was the biggest man-eating shark that anyone aboard had ever seen. Surging out of the sea to fasten on a horse shank hung from a davit, it stood upright beside the ship, head and gills clear of the water, tail vibrating, the glistening triangles of its teeth red-rimmed with blood. In the effort of shearing, the black eye went white as the eyeball was rolled inward; then the whole horse quarter disappeared in a scarlet billow. "I've watched sharks all my life," Ben Ranford said, "but I've never seen anything as terrifying as that." Plainly no shark victim with the misfortune to get hold of a raft or boat would ever survive the shaking of that head.

Last night in the galley, Ron had suggested to Peter that swimming with one white might be possible, and Peter agreed. But this morning there were three, and the visibility was so limited that one could never tell where or when the other two might appear. The talk of swimming in the open water ended, and a good thing, too. In its seeming contempt for the great white shark, such a dangerous stunt could only make an anticlimax of the film's climax.

The cage will sink a foot or so beneath the surface under a man's weight—a situation to be avoided in the presence of white sharks—and the next morning, entering it, I performed with ease what I had heretofore done clumsily, flipping directly out of the skiff and down through the narrow roof hatch head first. Even before I straightened up, the largest of the sharks loomed alongside, filling the blue silence with its smile. I felt naked in my flimsy cell until Stan joined me. This shark was two or three feet longer than the next in size, but it looked half again as big, between eighteen hundred pounds and a fat ton. In white sharks over ten feet long, the increase in girth and weight per foot of length is massive; the white shark that I saw dead at Montauk, only two or three feet longer than this one, had weighed at least twice as much.

The new shark was fearless, crashing past skiff and cage alike to reach the meat, and often attacking both on the way out. Like its companions, which scooted aside when it came close, it attacked the flotation tanks over and over, refusing to learn that they were not edible. Even the smallest shark came in to sample the flotation tanks when the others were not around. I had seen one of its companions chase it, so probably its shyness had little to do with the *Saori*: unlike the sharks in the Indian Ocean the whites gave one another a wide berth. Occasionally one would go for the air tank in the corner, bumping the whole cage through the water with its snout, and once one struck the naked bars when I waved a dead salmon as it approached. Clumsily it missed the proffered fish, glancing off the bars as I yanked my arm back. Had the sharks attacked the bars, they would have splayed them. "He could bite that cage to bits if he wanted to," Valerie had said of yesterday's shark, and got no argument; for the big shark today, the destruction of the cage would be the work of moments. From below, we watched it wrestle free an enormous slab of horse, two hundred pounds or more; as it gobbled and shook, its great pale body quaked, the tail shuddering with the effort of keeping its head high out of the water. Then, back arched, it dove with its prize toward the bottom, its mouth trailing bubbles from the air gulped down with its last bite. Only one pilot fish was ever seen at Dangerous Reef; we wondered if the white shark's relentless pace made it difficult for a small fish to keep up.

Numbers of fish had come to the debris exploded into the water by the feeding, and the windstorm of the night before had stirred pale algae from the bottom. Visibility was poor, yet the sharks worked so close to the cages that the morning's filming was even better than the day before, and the cameramen worked from nine until one-thirty. By then, the ten months of suspense were over.

We were scarcely out of the water when the wind freshened, with the threat of rain. The cages were taken aboard and battened down while a party went ashore to film the *Saori* from the Reef. Then, in a cold twilight, drinking rum in the galley-fo'c's'le, we rolled downwind across Spencer Gulf, bound for Port Lincoln. Though the sea was rough, the fo'c's'le was warm and bright, filled with rock music. Valerie saw to it that the supper was cooked properly, and wine soon banished the slightest doubt that we all liked one another very much. "Is there anything more splendid," Waterman cried, "than the fellowship of good shipmates in the fo'c's'le after a bracing day before the mast?" After three weeks in the fo'c's'le, Stan had embraced the nineteenth century with all his heart.

Peter Gimbel, sweetly drunk, swung back and forth from fits of shouting to a kind of stunned suffused relief and quiet happiness. He looked ten years younger. What was surely the most exciting film ever taken underwater had been obtained without serious injury to anybody. The triumph was a vindication of his own faith in himself, and because he had earned it the hard way and deserved it, it was a pleasure simply to sit and drink and watch the rare joy in his face.

At the end of that week all the Americans returned home but myself and Cody. Stuart went into the Outback to try opal mining with Ian McKechnie, and I flew westward to East Africa. A month later, when I reached New York, Peter told me that the white-shark sequence was beyond all expectations, that the film studio was ecstatic, and that a financial success now seemed assured. How sad, I said, that his father wasn't here to see it. He grinned, shaking his head. "It is," he said. "He would have been delighted."

Already Peter was concerned about where he would go from here. Meanwhile, he had planned a violent dieting which he didn't need, and when asked why, he shrugged. "I just want to see if I can get down to a hundred seventy," he said. Perhaps I read too much into that diet, but it bothered me: the search for the great white shark was at an end, but the search was not. I recalled a passage in the letter Peter had written after the thirty-hour marathon off Durban, and when I got home I dug it out.

"I felt none of the dazed sense of awe," he wrote, "that had filled me ten days before during our first night dive. I remember wondering sadly how it could be that a sight this incredible could have lost its shattering impact so quickly for me—why it should be that the sights and sensations should have to accelerate so hellishly simply to hold their own with my adaptation to them. . . . Only a week or so after having come out of the water one night to say over and over, 'No four people in all the world have ever laid eyes on a scene so wild and infernal as that,' I wasn't even particularly excited."

And he continues, "I was filled with a terrible sadness that we had indeed determined precisely the limits we sought, that the mystery was at least partly gone because we knew that we could get away with anything, that the story—and such a story!—had an end."

## *from* The Tree Where Man Was Born

1972

*While on his way to join the expedition in New Guinea that would lead to his book* Under the Mountain Wall, *Matthiessen traveled for a time in Africa, where he got his first look at a leopard and became entranced by the beauty of that continent's wildlife and native people. "The wild creatures I had come to Africa to see are exhilarating in their multitude and colors," Matthiessen writes in a prefatory note, "and I imagined for a time that this glimpse of the earth's morning might account for the anticipation I felt, the sense of origins, of innocence and mystery, like a marvelous childhood faculty restored. Perhaps it is the consciousness that here in Africa, south of the Sahara, our kind was born. But there was also something else that, years ago, under the sky of the Sudan, had made me restless, the stillness of this ancient continent, the echo of so much that has died away, the imminence of so much as yet unknown. Something has happened here, is happening, will happen—whole landscapes seem alert."*

*Two selections from this book are included here. The first, from the chapters "Rites of Passage" and "Elephant Kingdoms," tells of a winter in the Serengeti, in which predators are pressed by diminished food supplies and poachers. Matthiessen's lyrical descriptions capture small moments and gritty detail. "All winter in the Serengeti damp scrawny calves and afterbirths are everywhere, and old or diseased animals fall in the night," he writes. "Fat hyenas, having slaked their thirst, squat in the rain puddles, and gaping lions lie belly to the sun." The second selection, "At Gidabembe," weaves together natural history and travels with a band of the traditional "small peoples" of Eastern Africa, the Hadza, or Wa-Tindiga. As elsewhere in his work*

*Matthiessen pays close attention to the intricate details of his sur-roundings, finding color and depth in the gestures of the people and the silences of the landscape.*

## Rites of Passage

**At Lemai on the Mara River,** eighty miles north of Seronera near the Kenya border, the Ikuria Bantu were displeased because part of their lands north of the Mara had been appropriated for the Serengeti park; they were harassing the Lemai guard post at night with threats and stones. Myles Turner flew an extra ranger to Lemai to strengthen the garrison, and I went along. We circled a concentration of six hundred buffalo near the Banagi River, then flew onward, passing east of the old Ikoma fort, built by the Germans in 1905 as a defense against rebellious Ikoma. Beyond Ikoma was another great herd of buffalo, black igneous lumps in the tsetse-ridden land. Zebra shone in the morning woods, but a rhino was as dull as stone in the early light.

To the north and west, over Lake Victoria, the cloud masses were a deepening gray-black; at times the plane flew through black rain. These lake basin storms are the worst in East Africa, building all day and coming to a boil in late afternoon. But the clouds were pierced by shafts of sun, and the plane cast a hard shadow on thatch roofs, bomas, and patchwork gardens scattered along the boundary of the park. Half-naked people stood outside the huts; they did not wave. "*Wa-Ikoma,*" Myles said. "Poachers." Poaching has always been a problem on park borders, all the more so because no park in East Africa is a natural ecological unit that shelters all its game animals all year around. To contain the natural wanderings of its herds, the Serengeti park, five thousand square miles in extent, would have to be doubled in size, expanding east to the Crater Highlands and northward into Kenya, through the Maasai Mara to the Mau Range. Human population increase and a lack of protein in lands which suffer from advanced protein deficiency in the poor have made the poaching of wild game a widespread industry, and an estimated twenty thousand animals are killed each year in the

Serengeti area alone. Poisoned arrows, which are silent, are still preferred to rifles, but traps and steel wire snares have replaced the traditional snares woven of the bayonet aloe or bowstring hemp that
gave its Maasai name to Olduvai Gorge.

The parks are the last refuge of large animals, which in most of
East Africa are all but gone. The game departments are chronically
bereft of funds, staff, and the technical training to protect the game,
and most of their resources are devoted to destroying animals worth
far more in meat and tusks and hides than the shamba being protected in the name of game control. Where animals are not shot
out, poached, or harried to extinction, they are eliminated by
human settlements at the only water points for miles around, or
their habitat vanishes in the fires lit to bring forth new grass. Thus
the survival of the animals depends on the survival of the parks,
among which the Serengeti has no peer.

For purposes of efficiency when dealing with poachers and to
inspire the African judiciary to impose meaningful sentences, all
poachers are classed together as brutal hirelings of unscrupulous
Asian interests in Nairobi or Dar es Salaam; traps, snares, and poisoned arrows maim and torture many more animals than are actually retrieved, and of late the gangs have become motorized, crossing
park boundaries at will. In this official picture of the matter there is
considerable truth, but it is also true that the majority of "poachers"
are people of the region who are seeking to eke out a subsistence
diet as they have always done. The parks for which their lands have
been appropriated, and which they themselves have no means to
visit even if they were interested, give sanctuary to marauding animals that are a threat to domestic stock and crops, not to speak of
human life, and their resentment is natural and just. It is no good
telling a shamba dweller that tourist revenues are crucial to the
nation when his own meager existence remains unaffected, or
affected for the worse. "The nation," the concept of national consciousness, has not penetrated very far into the bush; as in the
Sudan, there are many tribesmen who have no idea that they are
Kenyan or Tanzanian and would care little if they knew. Even the
urban African benefits little from a tourist economy, not to speak of
the revenues of the parks, which are resented as the private pre-

serves of white foreigners and the few blacks at the top. Not long ago it was estimated that only one East African in twelve had ever seen a lion, though lions are common in the park at the very outskirts of Nairobi, but one is not allowed into the parks without a car, and very few Africans have access to a car, far less own one. The average citizen has more fear of than interest in wild animals, which most Africans regard as evidence of backwardness, a view in which they were long encouraged by European farmers and administrators. Far from being proud of the "priceless heritage" so dear to conservation literature, they are ashamed of it.

Nor is poaching a simple matter of free meat. Rural Africans in the vicinity of game reserves and parks quite naturally believe that the numbers of wild animals are inexhaustible, and see no reason why they should not be harvested as they have always been. Hunting, with its prestige for the good hunter, is a ceremony and sport as it is for westerners; its place in his economy as well as its risk to the poorly armed native hunter make it considerably less decadent. And no one can explain why killing animals is permitted to foreigners in search of trophies but not to citizens in search of food. Yet to permit random poaching by local hunters would encourage ever bolder operations directed by outsiders and carried out by professionals who do not hesitate to turn their poisoned arrows on African game rangers; arrow poisons are obtained from several plants (two Apocynaceae, an amaryllis, and two lilies), but the one used most commonly in this region comes from a shrubby dogbane (*Acokanthera*) which has no antidote, and can kill in a matter of minutes. Still, bows are no match for rifles, and ordinarily, the poacher dies instead.

Last year four poachers died in the Serengeti. One was shot down by the rangers after firing his fourth poisoned arrow. Two corpses were found under a tree, caught by a fire probably set by themselves, for grasslands near a watercourse are often burned to give the hunters a better view and to make sure that their poisoned arrows are not lost; also, the use of bangi (the marijuana hemp, *Cannabis*, brought to the east coast in the earliest trade with Asia) and homemade spirits is popular in the poachers' camps, and perhaps the two were taken by surprise. The fourth was mangled and decapitated by a maimed buffalo caught in his wire snare. Myles was anxious to display the poacher's head as cautionary evidence in the small museum at Seronera, but was dissuaded by John Owen, who felt that the public display of an African head might be taken amiss. The head is on view in Turner's office, over the legend (from an Italian graveyard)

> *I have been where you are now,*
> *And you will be where I have gone.*

Myles Turner is sympathetic with the Ikuria, who are one of the peoples he admires. "The land is all they have," he says. But he is a traditionalist in his dealings with the Africans, and though he joked with the ranger in the plane, the jokes were firm. When his plane appeared over Lemai, a half-dozen of his "Field Force" rushed to the airstrip, where they were lined up more or less smartly by their corporal. In green drill shorts, shirts, berets, and black puttees, they made a fine-looking line, and when Turner stepped down from the plane, they sprang backward to attention, slapping rifles. "Jambo, Corporal," Turner said, by way of greeting and approval, then put the rangers at their ease. Plainly the men enjoyed these formalities as much as Myles did, and at the same time were amused. Myles gave them letters and news of their families, and they gave him messages to send back. Then we marched down to the Mara in a military manner to inspect the hippos.

Hippos can weigh twice as much as buffalo, or two or three tons each. Like whales, they are born in the water, but ordinarily they feed on land, and their copious manure, supporting rich growths of blue-green algae, is a great boon to fish. Here they had piled up in the river rapids, where the lateritic silt had turned them the same red as the broad-backed boulders. On land, the hippopotamus exudes a red secretion, perhaps to protect its skin against the sun, and Africans say that it is sweating its own blood. With their flayed skin, cavernous raw mouths, and bulging eyes, their tuba voices splitting the wash of the Mara on its banks seemed like the uproar of the damned, as if, in the cold rain and purgatorial din, just at this moment, the great water pigs had been cast into perdition, their downfall heralded by the scream of the fish eagle that circled overhead.

East of Soit Naado Murt, on the Girtasho Plain, a burrow had been taken over and enlarged by wild hunting dogs, which differ from true dogs in having a four-toed foot. In the Girtasho pack were eleven dogs and three bitches, black with patches of dirty white and brindle, and the invariable white tip to the tattered tail. Wild dogs are mangy and bad-smelling, with bat ears and gaunt bodies, yet they are appealing creatures, pirouetting in almost constant play, and rolling and flopping about in piles. Perhaps distemper keeps their numbers low, for they are faithful in the raising of their young, and the most efficient killers on the plain.

Wild dogs are nomadic most of the year, attending the migrations of the herds, but when a bitch whelps, they remain with her and bring her food. Ordinarily one dog—not necessarily the mother—remains with the pups when the pack goes out to hunt, and five dogs have been known to raise nine pups after their mother—the pack's only bitch—had died. At the den one afternoon four pups were frolicking from dog to dog, and one of the dogs dutifully disgorged some undigested chunks of meat, but the pups were bothered by bursts of thunder, looking up from their food to whine at the far, silent lightning. A mile to the westward, zebra herds moved steadily along the skyline. When the rain thickened, the pups tumbled down into their den, and the adults gathered in a pile of matted black and brindle hair to shed the huge tropical downpour. Toward twilight, the rain eased and the dog pile broke apart, white tail tips twirling; the animals frisked about the soggy plain, greeting anew by inserting the muzzle into the corner of another's mouth, as the pups do when begging food. When they are old enough to follow the hunt, the pups will be given first place at the kill.

Four dogs led by a brindle male moved off a little toward the west; they stood stiff-legged, straining forward, round black ears cocked toward the zebra herds which, agitated by the storm, were moving along at a steady gallop. Then the four set off at a steady trot, and the others broke their play to watch them go. Three more moved out, though not so swiftly, and George Schaller followed the seven at a little distance. Soon the remaining animals were coming, all but one that remained to guard the den. Only the first four were intent; the rest stopping repeatedly to romp and crouch or greet the stragglers. Then these nine would run to catch the four, loping along on both sides of the moving vehicle, casting a brief look at us as they passed. Ahead, the leaders trotted steadily, and the nine stragglers, overtaking them, would again break off to romp and play.

The four lead dogs, nearing the herds, broke into an easy run; the zebras spurted. Perhaps the dogs had singled out a victim—an old or diseased horse, a pregnant mare, a foal—for now they were streaming over the wet grass. Rain swept the plain, and gray sheets blurred the swirling stripes, which burst apart to scatter in all directions. The dogs wheeled hard, intent now on a quarry, but lost it as the horses veered, then milled together in a solid phalanx. A stallion charged the dogs, ears back, and they gave way.

The chase of a mile or more had failed; the wild dogs frisked and played. But now all thirteen were intent, and in moments they were loping back past the waiting vehicle, headed west. The leaders were already in their hunting run, bounding along in silence through the growing dark like hounds of hell, and the others, close behind, made sweet puppylike call notes, strangely audible over the motor of the car, which swerved violently to miss half-hidden burrows. All thirteen stretched cadaverous shapes in long easy leaps over the plain. In their run, the dogs are beautiful and swift, and came up with the herds in not more than a mile. Then the dark shapes were whisking in and out among the zebra, and a foal still brown with a foal's guard hairs quit the mare's side when a dog bit at it, and was surrounded.

A six-month zebra foal, weighing perhaps three hundred pounds, is too big to be downed easily by thin animals of forty pounds apiece. The dogs chivvied it round and round. One dog had sunk its teeth into the foal's black muzzle, tugging backward to keep the victim's head low—this is a habit of the dogs, to compensate for their light weight—and the dog was swung free of the ground as the foal reared, lost its balance, and went down. Now the mare charged, scattering the pack, and when the foal jumped up as if unhurt, the two fled for the herd. But the dogs overtook the foal again, snapping at its hams, and braying softly, it stopped short of its own accord. Again a dog seized its muzzle, legs braced, dragging the head forward, as the rest tore into it from behind and below. At the yanking of its nose, the foal's mouth fell open, and it made a last small sound. Once more the mare rushed at the dogs, and once again, but already she seemed resigned to what was happening, and did not follow up her own attacks. The foal sank to its knees, neck still stretched by the backing dog, its entrails a dim gleam in the rain. Then the dog at its nose let go and joined the rest, and the foal raised its head, ears high, gazing in silence at the mare, which stood over it, motionless. Between her legs, her foal was being eaten alive, and mercifully, she did nothing. Then the foal sank down, and the dogs surged at the belly, all but one that snapped an eye out as the head flopped on the grass.

Unmarked, the mare turned and walked away. Intent on her foal, the dogs had not once snapped at her. Noticing the car twenty yards off, she gave a snort and a jump sideways, then walked on. Flanks pressed together, ears alert, her band awaited her; nearby, other zebra clans were grazing. Soon the foal's family, carrying the mare with it, moved away, snatching at the grass as they ambled westward.

The foal's spread legs stuck up like sticks from the twisting black and brindle; the dogs drove into the belly, hind legs straining. They snatched a mouthful, gulped it, and tore in again, climbing the carcass, tails erect, as if every lion and hyena on the plain were coming fast to drive them from the kill. All thirteen heads snapped at the meat, so close together that inevitably one yelped, but even when two would worry the same shred, there was never a snarl, only a wet steady sound of meat-eating. When the first dog moved off, licking its chops, the foal's rib cage was already bare; not ten minutes had passed since it had died. Then the hyenas came. First there were two, rising up out of the raining grass like mud lumps given life. They shambled forward without haste, neither numerous nor hungry enough to drive away the dogs. Then there were five in a semi-circle, feinting a little. A dog ran out to chase away the boldest, and then two of the five, with the strange speed that makes them deadly hunters on their own, chased off a sixth hyena—not a clan member, apparently—that had come in from the north through the twilight rain.

Six of the dogs, their feeding finished, wagged long tails as they romped and greeted; there was just enough light left to illumine the red on their white patches. The rest fed steadily, eyes turned to the hyenas as they swallowed, and as each dog got its fill and forsook the carcass, the half-circle of hyenas tightened. The last dog gave way to them without a snarl. The forequarters were left, and the head and neck, and all the bones. For the powerful jaws of the hyena, the bones of the plains animals present no problem. Hoofs, bones, and skin of what had been, ten minutes before, the fat hindquarters of a swift skittish young horse lay twisted up in a torn muddy bag; the teeth of its skull and the white eye sockets were luminous. At dark, as the tail tips of the dogs danced away eastward, the hyena shapes drew together at the remains, one great night beast sinking slowly down into the mud.

I once watched a hyena gaining on a gnu that only saved itself by plunging into the heart of a panicked herd; the hyena lost track of its quarry when the herd stampeded. The cringing bearlike lope of these strange cat relatives is deceptive: A hyena can run forty miles an hour, which is considered the top speed of the swift wild dog. Cheetah are said to attain sixty but have small endurance; I have seen one spring at a Thomson's gazelle, its usual prey, and quit within the first one hundred yards. Hyenas, on the other hand, will run their prey into the ground; there is no escape. And in darkness they are bold—a man alone on the night roads of Africa has less to fear from lions than hyenas. In the Ngorongoro Crater the roles ordinarily assigned to lions and hyenas are reversed. It is the hyenas, hunting at night, that make most of the kills, and the lions seen on the carcasses in daytime are the scavengers. Hans Kruuk has discovered that the crater's hyenas are divided in great clans, and that sometimes these hyena armies war at night, filling the crater with the din of the inferno.

The natural history of even the best-known African mammals is incomplete, and such hole dwellers as the ant-bear, the aard-wolf, and the pangolin have avoided the scrutiny of man almost entirely. It is not even known which species excavate the holes, which may also be occupied by hyenas, jackals, mongooses, bat-eared foxes, aard-wolves, porcupines, ratels or honey badgers, and, in whelping season, the wild hunting dog. Often the burrows are dug in the bases of old termite hills, which stand on the plain like strange red statues of a vanished civilization, worn to anonymity by time. The termites are ancient relatives of the cockroach, and in the wake of rains they leave the termitaria in nuptial flight; soon their wings break off, and new colonies are founded where they come to earth. Were man to destroy the many creatures that prey on them, the termite mounds would cover entire landscapes. The African past lies in the belly of the termite, which has eaten all trace of past tropical civilizations and will do as much for the greater part of what now stands. At the termitaria, one may look at dawn and evening for such nocturnal creatures as the striped hyena, with its long hair and gaunt body, but in my stays in the Serengeti I never saw this wolf-sized animal that lived in the ground beneath my feet.

One day I surprised a honey badger some distance from its earth, and followed it for a while over the plain. This dark squat animal has long hair and a thick skin to protect it from bee stings, and like most of the weasel tribe, it is volatile and ferocious, with a snarl more hideous than any sound I heard in Africa. The ratel moves quickly, low to the ground, and in its dealings with man is said to direct its attack straight at the crotch.

Another day, observing hyenas with Hans Kruuk, I was lucky enough to see a pangolin, which has overlapping armor on its back and legs and tail. The pangolin has been much reduced by a Maasai notion that its curious reptilian plates will bring the wearer luck in love. At our approach it ceased its rooting in the grass and, with an audible clack, rolled up into a ball to protect its vulnerable furred stomach. We contemplated it awhile, then left it where it lay, a strange mute sphere on the bare plain.

. . .

In March, renewal of the southeast monsoon brings the long rains. Rains vary from region to region, according to the winds, and since the winds are not dependable, seasons in East Africa have a general pattern but can seldom be closely predicted. The cyclical wet years and years of drought are a faint echo of the pluvials and interpluvials of the Pleistocene. In 1961 drought had destroyed thousands of animals; the next year floods killed thousands more. In the winter of 1969 rain fell in the Serengeti almost daily, and no one knew whether the short rains of late autumn had failed to end or the long rains of spring had begun too early. A somber light refracted from the water gleamed in the depressions, and the treeless distances with their animal silhouettes, the glow of bright flowers underfoot, recalled the tundras of the north to which the migrant plovers on the plain would soon return.

The animals had slowed, and some stood still. In this light those without movement looked enormous, the archetypal animal cast in stone. The ostrich, too, is huge on the horizon, and the kori bustard is the heaviest of all flying birds on earth. Everywhere the clouds were crossed by giant birds in their slow circles, like winged reptiles on an antediluvian sky.

One morning the dog pile broke apart before daylight and headed off toward the herds under Naabi Hill. Unlike lions, which often go hungry, the wild dogs rarely fail to make a kill, and this time they were followed from the start by three hyenas that had waited near the den. The three humped along behind the pack, and one of the dogs paused to sniff noses with a hyena by way of greeting. In the distance, zebras yelped like dogs, and the dogs chittered quietly like birds as they loped along. As the sun rose out of the Gol Mountains, they faked an attack on a string of wildebeest and moved on.

A mile and a half east of the den, the pack cut off a herd of zebra and ran it in tight circles. There were foals in this herd, but the dogs had singled out a pregnant mare. When the herd scattered, they closed in, streaming along in the early light, and almost immediately she fell behind and then gave up, standing motionless as one dog seized her nose and others ripped at her pregnant belly and others piled up under her tail to get at her entrails at the anus, surging at her with such force that the flesh of her uplifted quarters quaked in the striped skin. Perhaps in shock, their quarry shares the detachment of the dogs, which attack it peaceably, ears forward, with no slightest sign of snapping or snarling. The mare seemed entirely docile, unafraid, as if she had run as she had been hunted, out of instinct, and without emotion: only rarely will a herd animal attempt to defend itself with the hooves and teeth used so effectively in battles with its own kind, though such resistance might well spare its life. The zebra still stood a full half-minute after her guts had been snatched out, then sagged down dead. Her unborn colt was dragged into the clear and snapped apart off to one side.

The morning was silent but for the wet sound of eating; a Caspian plover and a band of sand grouse picked at the mute prairie. The three hyenas stood in wait, and two others appeared after the kill. One snatched a scrap and ran with it; the meat, black with blood and mud, dragged on the ground. Chased by the rest, the hyena made a shrill sound like a pig squeal. When their spirit is up, hyenas will take on a lion, and if they chose, could bite a wild dog in half, but in daylight, they seem ill at ease; they were scattered by one tawny eagle, which took over the first piece of meat abandoned by the dogs. The last dog to leave, having finished with the fetus, drove the hyenas off the carcass of the mare on its way past, then frisked on home. In a day and a night, when lions and hyenas, vultures and marabous, jackals, eagles, ants, and beetles have all finished, there will be no sign but the stained pressed grass that a death ever took place.

All winter in the Serengeti damp scrawny calves and afterbirths are everywhere, and old or diseased animals fall in the night. Fat hyenas, having slaked their thirst, squat in the rain puddles, and gaping lions lie belly to the sun. On Naabi Hill the requiem birds, digesting carrion, hunch on the canopies of low acacia. Down to the west, a young zebra wanders listlessly by itself. Unlike topi and kongoni, which are often seen alone, zebra and wildebeest stick to the herd; an animal by itself may be sick or wounded, and draws predators from all over the plain. This mare had a deep gash down her right flank, and a slash of claws across the stripings of her quarters; red meat gleamed on right foreleg and left fetlock. It seemed strange that an attacking lion close enough to maul so could have botched the job, but the zebra pattern makes it difficult to see at night, when it is most vulnerable to attack by lions, and zebra are strong animals; a thin lioness that I saw once at Ngorongoro had a broken incisor hanging from her jaw that must have been the work of a flying hoof.

Starvation is the greatest threat to lions, which are inefficient hunters and often fail to make a kill. Unlike wild dog packs, which sometimes overlap in their wide hunting range, lions will attack and even eat another lion that has entered their territory, snapping and snarling in the same antagonistic way with which they join their pride mates on a kill, whereas when hunting, they are silent and impassive. In winter when calves of gazelle and gnu litter the plain, the lions are well fed, but at other seasons they may be so hungry that their own cubs are driven from the kills: ordinarily, however, the lion will permit cubs to feed even when the lioness that made the kill is not permitted to approach. Until it is two, the cub is a dependent, and less than half of those born in the Serengeti survive the first year of life. In hard times, cubs may be eaten by hyenas, or by the leopard, which has a taste for other carnivores, including domestic cats and dogs.

A former warden of the Serengeti who feels that plains game should be killed to feed these starving cubs is opposed by George Schaller on the grounds that such artificial feeding would interfere with the balance of lion numbers as well as with the natural selection that maintains the vitality of the species. Dr. Schaller is correct, I think, and yet my sympathies are with the predator, not with the hunted, perhaps because a lion is perceived as an individual, whereas one member of a herd of thousands seems but a part of a compound organism, with little more identity than one termite in a swarm. Separated from the herd, it gains identity, like the zebra killed by the wild dogs, but even so I felt more pity for an injured lion that I saw near the Seronera River in the hungry months of summer, a walking husk of mane and bone, so weak that the dry weather wind threatened to knock it over.

The death of any predator is disturbing. I was startled one day to see a hawk in the talons of Verreaux's eagle-owl; perhaps it had been killed in the act of killing. Another day, by a korongo, I helped Schaller collect a dying lioness. She had emaciated hindquarters and the staggers, and at our approach, she reeled to her feet, then fell. In the interests of science as well as mercy, for he wished an autopsy, George shot her with an overdose of tranquilizer. Although she twitched when the needle struck, and did not rise, she got up after a few minutes and weaved a few feet more and fell again as if defeated by the obstacle of the korongo, where frogs trilled in oblivion of unfrogly things. I had the strong feeling that the lioness, sensing death, had risen to escape it, like the vultures I had heard of somewhere that flew up from the poisoned meat set out for lions, circling higher and higher into the sky, only to fall like stones as life forsook them. A moment later, her head rose up, then flopped for the last time, but she would not die. Sprinkled with hopping lion flies and the fat ticks that in lions are a sign of poor condition, she lay there in a light rain, her gaunt flanks twitching.

The episode taught me something about George Schaller, who is single-minded, not easy to know. George is a stern pragmatist, unable to muster up much grace in the face of unscientific attitudes; he takes a hard-eyed look at almost everything. Yet at his moment his boyish face was openly upset, more upset than I had ever thought to see him. The death of the lioness was painless, far better than being found by the hyenas, but it was going on too long; twice he returned to the Land Rover for additional dosage. We stood there in a kind of vigil, feeling more and more depressed, and the end, when it came at last, was shocking. The poor beast, her life going, began to twitch and tremble. With a little grunt, she turned onto her back and lifted her hind legs into the air. Still grunting, she licked passionately at the grass, and her haunches shuddered in long spasms, and this last abandon shattered the detachment I had felt until that moment. I was swept by a wave of feeling, then a pang so sharp that, for a moment, I felt sick, as if all the waste and loss in life, the harm one brings to oneself and others, had been drawn to a point in this lonely passage between light and darkness.

Mid-March when the long rains were due was a time of wind and dry days in the Serengeti, with black trees in iron silhouette on the hard sunsets and great birds turning forever on a silver sky. A full moon rose in a night rainbow, but the next day the sun was clear again, flat as a disc in the pale universe.

Two rhino and a herd of buffalo had brought up the rear of the eastward migration. Unlike the antelope, which blow with the wind and grasses, the dark animals stood earthbound on the plain. The antelope, all but a few, had drifted east under the Crater Highlands, whereas the zebra, in expectation of the rains, were turning west again toward the woods. Great herds had gathered at the Seronera River, where the local prides of lion were well fed. Twenty lions together, dozing in the golden grass, could sometimes be located by the wave of a black tail tuft or the black ear tips of a lifted head that gazed through the sun shimmer of the seed heads. Others gorged in uproar near the river crossings, tearing the fat striped flanks on fresh green beds—now daytime kills were common. Yet for all their prosperity, there was an air of doom about the lions. The males, especially, seemed too big, and they walked too slowly between feast and famine, as if in some dim intuition that the time of the great predators was running out.

Pairs of male lions, unattached to any pride, may hunt and live together in great harmony, with something like demonstrative affection. But when two strangers meet, there seems to be a waiting period, while fear settles. One sinks into the grass at a little distance, and for a long time they watch each other, and their sad eyes, unblinking, never move. The gaze is the warning, and it is the same gaze, wary but unwavering, with which lions confront man. The gold cat eyes shimmer with hidden lights, eyes that see everything and betray nothing. When the lion is satisfied that the threat is past, the head is turned, as if ignoring it might speed the departure of an unwelcome and evil-smelling presence. In its torpor and detachment, the lion sometimes seems the dullest beast in Africa, but one has only to watch a file of lions setting off on the evening hunt to be awed anew by the power of this animal.

One late afternoon of March, beyond Maasai Kopjes, eleven lionesses lay on a kill, and the upraised heads, in a setting sun, were red. With their grim visages and flat glazed eyes, these twilight beasts were ominous. Then the gory heads all turned as one, ear tips alert. No animal was in sight, and their bellies were full, yet they glared steadfastly away into the emptiness of plain, as if something that no man could sense was imminent.

Not far off there was a leopard; possibly they scented it. The leopard lay on an open rise, in the shadow of a wind-worn bush, and unlike the lions, it lay gracefully. Even stretched on a tree limb, all four feet hanging, as it is seen sometimes in the fever trees, the leopard has the grace of complete awareness, with all its tensions in its pointed eyes. The lion's gaze is merely baleful; that of the leopard is malevolent, a distillation of the trapped fear that is true savagery.

Under a whistling thorn the leopard lay, gold coat on fire in the sinking sun, as if imagining that so long as it lay still it was unseen. Behind it was a solitary thorn tree, black and bony in the sunset, and from a crotch in a high branch, turning gently, torn hide matted with caked blood, the hollow form of a gazelle hung by the neck. At the insistence of the wind, the delicate black shells of the turning hooves, on tiptoe, made a dry clicking in the silence of the plain.

## Elephant Kingdoms

To Game Warden
Sir,

I am compelled of notifying your Excellence the ecceptional an critical situation of my people at Tuso. Many times they called on my praing me of addressing to your Excellence a letter for obtain a remedy and so save they meadows from total devestation. I recused for I thought were a passing disease, but on the contrary the invasion took fearfully increasing so that the natives are now disturbed and in danger in their own huts for in the night the elephants ventured themselves amid abitation. All men are desolate and said me sadfully, "What shall we eat this year. We shall compelled to emigrate all."

> —With my best gratefully
> and respectful regards,
> Yours sincerely,
> a Mission Boy

We are the fire which burns the country.
The Calf of the Elephant is exposed on the plain.
        —*from the Bantu*

**One morning a great company** of elephants came from the woodlands, moving eastward toward the Togoro Plain. "It's like the old Africa, this," Myles Turner said, coming to fetch me. "It's one of the greatest sights a man can see."

We flew northward over the Orangi River. In the wake of the elephant herds, stinkbark acacia were scattered like sticks, the haze of yellow blossoms bright in the killed trees. Through the center of the destruction, west to east, ran a great muddied thoroughfare of the sort described by Selous in the nineteenth century. Here the center of the herd had passed. The plane turned eastward, coming up on the elephant armies from behind. More than four hundred animals were pushed together in one phalanx; a smaller group of one hundred and another of sixty were nearby. The four hundred moved in one slow-stepping swaying mass, with the largest cows along the outer ranks and big bulls scattered on both sides. "Seventy and eighty pounds, some of those bulls," Myles said. (Trophy elephants are described according to the weight of a single tusk; an eighty-pound elephant would carry about twice that weight in ivory. "Saw an eighty today." "*Did* you!")

Myles said that elephants herded up after heavy rains, but that this was an enormous congregation for the Serengeti. In 1913, when the first safari came here, the abounding lions and wild dogs were shot as vermin, but no elephants were seen at all. Even after

1925, when the plains were hunted regularly by such men as Philip Percival and the American, Martin Johnson, few elephants were reported. Not until after 1937, it is said, when the Serengeti was set aside as a game reserve (it was not made a national park until 1951), did harried elephants from the developing agricultural country of west Kenya move south into this region, but it seems more likely that they were always present in small numbers, and merely increased as a result of human pressures in suitable habitats outside the park.

Elephants, with their path-making and tree-splitting propensities, will alter the character of the densest bush in very short order; probably they rank with man and fire as the greatest force for habitat change in Africa. In the Serengeti, the herds are destroying many of the taller trees which are thought to have risen at the beginning of the century, in a long period without grass fires that followed plague, famine, and an absence of the Maasai. Dry season fires, often set purposely by poachers and pastoral peoples, encourage grassland by suppressing new woody growth; when accompanied by drought, and fed by a woodland tinder of elephant-killed trees, they do lasting damage to the soil and the whole environment. Fires waste the dry grass that is used by certain animals, and the regrowth exhausts the energy in the grass roots that is needed for good growth in the rainy season. In the Serengeti in recent years, fire and elephants together have converted miles and miles of acacia wood to grassland, and damaged the stands of yellow-bark acacia or fever tree along the watercourses. The range of the plains game has increased, but the much less numerous woodland species such as the roan antelope and oribi become ever more difficult to see.

Beneath the plane, the elephant mass moved like gray lava, leaving behind a ruined bog of mud and twisted trees. An elephant can eat as much as six hundred pounds of grass and browse each day, and it is a destructive feeder, breaking down many trees and shrubs along the way. The Serengeti is immense, and can absorb this damage, but one sees quickly how an elephant invasion might affect more vulnerable areas. Ordinarily the elephant herds are scattered and nomadic, but pressure from settlements, game control, and poachers sometimes confines huge herds to restricted habitats which they may destroy. Already three of Tanzania's new national parks—Serengeti, Manyara, and Ruaha—have more elephants than is good for them. The elephant problem, where and when and how to manage them, is a great controversy in East Africa, and its solution must affect the balance of animals and man throughout the continent.

Anxious to see the great herd from the ground, I picked up George Schaller at Seronera and drove northwest to Banagi, then westward on the Ikoma-Musoma track to the old northwest boundary of the park, where I headed across country. I had taken good bearings from the air, but elephants on the move can go a long way in an hour, and even for a vehicle with four-wheel drive, this rough bush of high grass, potholes, rocks, steep brushy streams, and swampy mud is very different from the hardpan of the plain. The low hot woods lacked rises or landmarks, and for a while it seemed that I had actually misplaced four hundred elephants.

Then six bulls loomed through the trees, lashing the air with their trunks, ears blowing, in a stiff-legged swinging stride; they forded a steep gully as the main herd, ahead of them, appeared on a wooded rise. Ranging up and down the gully, we found a place to lurch across, then took off eastward, hoping to find a point downwind of the herd where the elephants would pass. But their pace had slowed as the sun rose; we worked back to them, upwind. The elephants were destroying a low wood—this is not an exaggeration—with a terrible cracking of trees, but after a while they moved out onto open savanna. In a swampy stream they sprayed one another and rolled in the water and coated their hides with mud, filling the air with a thick sloughing sound like the wet meat sound made by predators on a kill. Even at rest the herd flowed in perpetual motion, the ears like delicate great petals, the ripple of the mud-caked flanks, the coiling trunks—a dream rhythm, a rhythm of wind and trees. "It's a nice life," Schaller said. "Long, and without fear." A young one could be killed by a lion, but only a desperate lion would venture near a herd of elephants, which are among the few creatures that reach old age in the wild.

There has been much testimony to the silence of the elephant, and all of it is true. At one point there came a cracking sound so small that had I not been alert for the stray elephants all around, I might never have seen the mighty bull that bore down on us from behind. A hundred yards away, it came through the scrub and deadwood like a cloud shadow, dwarfing the small trees of the open woodland. I raised binoculars to watch him turn when he got our scent, but the light wind had shifted and instead the bull was coming fast, looming higher and higher, filling the field of the binoculars, forehead, ears, and back agleam with wet mud dredged up from the donga. There was no time to reach the car, nothing to do but stand transfixed. A froggish voice said, "What do you think, George?" and got no answer.

Then the bull scented us—the hot wind was shifting every moment—and the dark wings flared, filling the sky, and the air was split wide by that ultimate scream that the elephant gives in alarm or agitation, that primordial warped horn note out of oldest Africa. It altered course without missing a stride, not in flight but wary, wide-eared, passing man by. Where first aware of us, the bull had been less than one hundred feet away—I walked it off—and he was somewhat nearer where he passed. "He was pretty close," I said finally to Schaller. George cleared his throat. "You don't want them any closer than that," he said. "Not when you're on foot." Schaller, who has no taste for exaggeration, had a very respectful look upon his face.

Stalking the elephants, we were soon a half-mile from my Land Rover. What little wind there was continued shifting, and one old cow, getting our scent, flared her ears and lifted her trunk, holding it upraised for a long time like a question mark. There were new calves with the herd, and we went no closer. Then the cow lost the scent, and the sloughing sound resumed, a sound that this same animal has made for four hundred thousand years. Occasionally there came a brief scream of agitation, or the crack of a killed tree back in the wood, and always the *thuck* of mud and water, and a rumbling of elephantine guts, the deepest sound made by an animal on earth except the whale.

Africa. Noon. The hot still waiting air. A hornbill, gnats, the green hills in the distance, wearing away west toward Lake Victoria.

## At Gidabembe

The Abatwa are very much smaller people than all small people;
they go under the grass and sleep in anthills; they go in the mist;
they live in the up country in the rocks. . . . Their village is
where they kill game; they consume the whole of it, and go away.
— *an anonymous Zulu*


*Hamana nale kui,*
*Nale kui.*
Here we go round,
Go round.
— *a Hadza dance*


**One winter day in 1969,** returning to Seronera from Arusha, Myles
Turner flew around the south side of the Crater Highlands, which
lay hidden in its black tumulus of clouds. The light plane skirted
Lake Manyara and the dusty flats of the witch-ridden Mbugwe,
then crossed Mbulu Land, on the Kainam Plateau. Soon it passed
over a great silent valley. "That's the Yaida," Turner told me. "That's
where those Bushman people are, the Watindiga." Down there in
that arid and inhospitable stillness, cut off from a changing Africa
by the ramparts of the Rift, last bands of the Old People turned their
heads toward the hard silver bird that crossed their sky. There was
no smoke, no village to be seen, nor any sign of man.

Later that winter, at Ndala, Douglas-Hamilton had suggested a
safari to Tindiga Land, where his friend Peter Enderlein had lived
alone for several years, and was in touch with wild Tindiga still living in the bush. But Iain was never able to get away, and a year had
passed before I crossed paths with Enderlein in Arusha, and
arranged to visit his Yaida Chini game post in the summer. In July
of 1970 I picked up Aaron Msindai, a young Isanzu from the
Mweka College of Wildlife Management at Moshi, who had been
assigned to Yaida Chini. We loaded Aaron's kit into the back of the

Land Rover—a rifle and an iron bed, clothes, lantern, fuel, food for a month—and headed west, spending that night at Manyara, and at seven the next morning climbing the Rift wall into the clouds of the Crater Highlands. In the dense mist, trees shifted evilly, and slow cowled figures with long staves, dark faces hidden in the gloom, moved past the ghostly fields of maize and wheat. These are the agricultural Mbulu of the so-called Irakw cluster, a group still unclassified in the ethnographic surveys, whose archaic language, related to Hamitic, suggests that they have been here in the highlands a very long time, perhaps well before the Iron Age. Like the Hamitic tribes, the Mbulu practice circumcision and clitoridectomy, but they lack the age-set system and other customs of modern Hamites such as the Galla. Doubtless they have mingled with the waves of Bantu and Nilotic peoples who came later, but many retain a Caucasoid cast of feature: the volatile narrow faces of the men, especially, are the faces that one sees in Ethiopia. The Mbulu live in pits dug into hillsides and covered over with roofs of mud and dung; in former days these pit dwellings or tembes, like low mounds in the tall grass, are said to have hidden the people from the Maasai. Today the tembes give way gradually to tin-roofed huts.

At Karatu, a track turns south onto the fertile Kainam Plateau that forms a southern spur of the Crater Highlands. Off the main road, the Mbulu are not used to cars—in the fifty miles between Karatu and Mbulu, I met no other vehicle—and the old run disjointedly along the red sides of the road, while the young jump behind the rocks and bushes. Today was Saba Saba (Seven Seven Day, commemorating the founding of TANU, the Tanganyika African National Union Party, on the seventh day of the seventh month, 1954), and near Mbulu, the track was filled with people streaming along toward the settlement. All were hooded against wind and rain, and from behind, in their blowing shrouds, they evoked the migration of those ancestors of many centuries ago who came down out of the north into a land of Stone Age hunters, the Twa, the Small People, most of whom, like the pit-dwelling Gumba found by the Kikuyu, have vanished into the earth.

. . .

From Mbulu a rough track heads west, dropping eventually off the Kainam Plateau into the Yaida Valley. It passes a fresh lake called Tlavi, edged by papyrus and typha, a rare pretty place of swallows and blowing reeds in a landscape of sloping grain fields, meadows, and soft sheltering hills that shut away the emptiness of Africa. The lake turned slowly in the lifting mists, a prism for the first rays of sun to pierce the morning clouds on the Crater Highlands. Beyond Tlavi the road rises into sun and sky and wanders along the westward scarp where highland clouds are parting; below lie the pale plains of a still valley, fifty miles long and ten across, like a world forgotten in the desert mountains. A rough rock track winding downhill is crossed by two klipspringer, yellow and gray; they bound away through low combretum woodland. Under the rim, out of the southeast wind, the air is hot. A horde of flies pours through the air vents, and Aaron strikes at them. He hisses, "Tsetse!"

In the wake of tsetse control programs that ended a few years ago, the Mbulu, already pressed for space due to population increase, overgrazing, and crude farming practices that have badly eroded the Kainam Plateau, began to move down into the Yaida Valley, while the Bantu Isanzu seeped in from the south. From the south also came fierce Barabaig herdsmen, and all of these people compete with the Tindiga and wild animals for the limited water. At the same time, the government, embarrassed that a Stone Age group should exist in the new Africa, has attempted to settle the hunters in two villages, one at Yaida Chini, the other farther west at an American Lutheran mission station called Munguli. Some three hundred now live in the settlements, and a few hundred more are still hiding in the bush.

Today, Tindiga, Mbulu, Isanzu, and Barabaig are all present at Yaida Chini, which may be the one place in East Africa where its four basic language families (Khoisan or click-speech, Hamitic, Bantu, and Nilotic) come together. Yaida Chini is a small dusty settlement strewn along under the line of giant figs by the Yaida River, and a group of Africans celebrating Saba Saba at the pombe bar milled out to greet the Land Rover as it rumbled down out of the hills. These people were mostly Isanzu, barefoot and ragtag in European shirts and pants, but to one side stood a dark thickset pygmoid girl, and Aaron said, "Tindiga." The girl had a large head with prognathous jaw and large antelope eyes in thick black skin, and by western standards she was very ugly. Unlike the yellow-eyed peasants, who offered shouts as evidence of sophistication, she came up softly and stared seriously, mouth closed, like a shy animal. "Tindiga have a very hard tongue," Aaron told me, ignoring his pombe-drunk people. "My tongue is not the same as theirs, but when I speak, they know." It is Aaron's tribe, the Isanzu, that has assimilated most of the southern Tindiga, and few are left who do not have an Isanzu parent; even "Tindiga" is an Isanzu name for a people whose true name is Hadza or Hadzapi.

Because of tsetse and the scarcity of water, the Hadza once had the Yaida to themselves, and scarcely anything was known of them before 1924, when a district officer of what had become, after World War One, the Tanganyika Territory, reported on a people who hid from Europeans and were even less affected than the Bushmen by the world beyond: "a wild man, a creature of the bush, and as far as I can see he is incapable of becoming anything else. Certainly he does not desire to become anything else, for nothing will tempt him to leave his wilderness or to abandon his mode of living. He asks nothing from the rest of us but to be left alone. He interferes with no one, and does his best to insure that no one shall interfere with him." A few years later, the Hadza were inspected by an authority on the Bushmen, who stated in the peremptory tones of colonial scholarship that "there must have been some connection between this black ape-like tribe and the small delicately built yellow man," whose habits, thoughts, and language structure seemed so similar.

This second authority, Miss Bleek, agrees with the first one, Mr. Bagshawe, that the typical tribesman was very black, short, thickset, ugly, and ill-smelling, with prognathous jaw and large splay feet. The blackness and the cast of jaw were most pronounced in the "purest" specimens, for even in Bleek's day, many Hadza in the south part of their range had an Isanzu parent. She does not comment on Bagshawe's contention that the Hadza is "intensely stupid and naturally deceitful" as well as "lazy," that he "does not understand why he should be investigated . . . it is more than probable that he will lie." Yet Bagshawe feels constrained to note that the Hadza "worries but little about the future and not at all about the past," that he is "happy and envies no man." Bagshawe's perplexed tone is echoed by Bleek, who observed that this unprepossessing people often danced in simple pleasure: *"Hamana nale kui,"* they sang. *"Nale kui."*

> *Here we go round,*
> *Go round.*

The early descriptions of the Hadza bring to mind the small men with large bows and strange speech who were driven high onto Mt. Kilimanjaro by the Chagga, and also the "people of small stature and hideous features," as L. S. B. Leakey describes the Gumba aborigines found by the Kikuyu in the Kenya Highlands. But in the years since they were first reported, the Hadza have mixed increasingly with the Isanzu, who may eventually absorb them as Bantu tribes have been absorbing hunter-gatherers for two millenniums. A recent student, Dr. James Woodburn, does not believe that a characteristic physical type is distinguishable any longer, nor does he accept Miss Bleek's assumption of a linguistic link between these people and the Bushmen (although the link between the click-speaking Sandawe, an acculturated tribe of south Tanzania, and the pastoral Bushman relatives known as the Hottentots is clearly established). On no evidence whatsoever, one is tempted to speculate that the Hadza may represent a relict group of pre-Bantu Negroids of the Stone Age, although there is no proof that the Hadza are a Stone Age remnant, or a remnant at all—very probably, they are as numerous as they ever were. They may even be regressive rather than primitive, a group cast out long ago from a more complex civilization, though their many affinities with the Bushmen make this unlikely. Probably we shall never come much closer to the truth than the people's own account of Hadza origins:

Man, say the Hadza, descended to earth on the neck of a giraffe, but more often they say that he climbed down from a baobab. The Hadza themselves came into being in this way: a giant ancestor named Hohole lived at Dungiko with his wife Tsikaio, in a great hall under the rocks where Haine, who is God, the Sun, was not able to follow. Hohole was a hunter of elephants, which were killed with one blow of his stick and stuck into his belt. Sometimes he walked one hundred miles and returned to the cave by evening with six elephants. One day while hunting, Hohole was bitten by a cobra in his little toe. The mighty Hohole died. Tsikaio, finding him, stayed there five days feeding on his leg, until she felt strong enough to carry the body to Masako. There she left it to be devoured by birds. Soon Tsikaio left the cave and went to live in a great baobab. After six days in the baobab, she gave birth to Konzere, and the children of Tsikaio and Konzere are the Hadza. "The Hadza," as the people say, "is us."

At the west end of the settlement, downriver, Peter Enderlein has built a house. At the sound of the motor, he came out on his veranda, a tall bare-legged man in shorts, boots wide apart, hands stuck in his hip pockets. We went immediately on an inspection of the ostrich pens, where he is raising an experimental flock for plumes and skins and meat. (In the wild, there is a heavy loss of eggs and chicks to predators of all descriptions, including lions, which are fond of playing with the eggs.) With their omnivorous habits and adaptations to arid country, ostrich could be domesticated in the Yaida, where tsetse and a shortage of surface water—the annual rainfall is less than twenty inches—are serious obstacles to agriculture and livestock. Enderlein, who is employed to investigate the valley's resources, would like to try game ranching here, but he has received little support for this scheme or any other, and for the moment must content himself with shooting the animals instead. Fresh meat is sold cheaply to the local people, or dried for sale elsewhere as biltong; the valuable common animal is zebra, and the sale of zebra hides to wholesalers is the game post's main source of income.

Pending approval of his projects, Enderlein spends most of his time supplying food for the impounded Hadza, who are not supposed to leave the settlement, much less revert to their old lives in the bush. But hunters have always made the transition to agriculture with the greatest reluctance (the Ik of the north Uganda hills are an exception), and as a rule, the people will consume immediately any livestock or maize seed that is given them, and beat their hoe blades into arrowheads. Neither the dry climate nor their temperament lends itself to tilling, and in consequence they do little but drink pombe. This enforced idleness and dependence will certainly lead to their utter disintegration. Until they can come to agriculture of their own accord, Enderlein is trying to persuade the government to establish the Yaida Valley as a game reserve in which Hadza would be hired as trackers, game scouts, and hunters in a game-cropping scheme like the one that gave work to the Ariangulo elephant hunters in the region of Tsavo. Meanwhile, settlement by outsiders would be concentrated instead of scattered at random over the landscape, destroying thousands of square miles of wildlife habitat for the sake of a few shambas that cut off the water points. The Yaida has the last important population of greater kudu in north Tanzania, in addition to all the usual trophy animals, and as a game reserve, would receive income from game cropping and hunting fees, which at present, due to lack of roads, are negligible. There are old rock paintings in the hills, many still doubtless undiscovered, and Eyasi Man, the Rhodesioid contemporary of the Neanderthalers, was dug up near Mangola in 1935 by a German named Kohl-Larsen, who also found an Australopithecine here in 1939, two decades before the better publicized *Australopithecus* was turned up by the Leakeys at Olduvai Gorge. All that is needed to encourage tourists is a good track into the north end of the valley from the main road across the Crater Highlands.

Although he has submitted to the government a careful analysis of game numbers and potential in the valley and an imaginative program of resource management, and although Tanzania's astute president Julius Nyerere is said to agree that the Hadza might come more readily to civilization through game-cropping than agriculture, Enderlein's plans have been regularly aborted by the district politicians, who have replaced European civil servants almost everywhere, and who take care not to approve or disapprove any project of a white man lest they expose themselves to the ambitions of their peers. As in other new African nations, the government endorses the principle of conservation, since conservation seems important to those western countries which are helping it in other ways. But most educated Africans care little about wild animals, which are vectors of the tsetse fly, a threat to crops and human life, and a competitor of livestock, and are also identified emotionally with the white man, white hunters, white tourists, and a primitive past which the new Africans wish to forget. As for the Hadzapi, they are the last tribe in Tanzania that is not administered and taxed, and the sooner they vanish the better. Like the Twa, Bushman, and Dorobo, the small hunters are looked down upon by their own countrymen, and most of those who come into the settlement soon flee back to their former life of dignity and independence.

Of the Maasai, President Nyerere has remarked quite rightly that the government cannot afford to keep part of its people as a human zoo for tourists, and the same could be said about the Hadza: the time of the hunter is past, and will never return. Yet to judge from wild peoples I have seen in South America and New Guinea, the Hadza would be better left alone until a choice that they can make naturally is provided, for this people is acknowledged by all who have met them to be healthy and happy, with no history of epidemic or famine, and able to satisfy all needs in a few hours of each day. Modern medicine, motor transport, radios, and even shoes may be crucial to the poor man, whose wants are endless, self-perpetuating, whose every acquisition means that he cannot afford something else. The wants of the primitive are few, since he does not envy what he knows nothing of. Poverty and the inferior status that await the acculturated Hadza is no alternative to bush life and the serenity of the old ways, and to take this from him by exposing him to a "progress" he cannot share is to abuse his innocence and do him harm.

But Enderlein is accused of wishing to keep this people in the Stone Age "as the Americans wish for the Maasai," and told not to give game work to idle Hadza, since the government is committed to a national program of agriculture. Tsetse control is to be resumed, and the people sent out to girdle and kill the "useless" tsetse-harboring acacias that keep the valley from turning to a desert, and ever more outsiders are encouraged to settle the Yaida even though two crops out of three are lost to drought, even though the land is blowing away under the sharp hooves of the cattle.

Enderlein showed me the hard bare flats in the grasslands that spread west to the hills called Giyeda Bárakh. "Ten years ago," he said, "the people walked a long way around the grove where my camp is now, there were so many rhino, and they still speak of the great herds of eland and elephant moving through. Ten years from now, this whole valley will be a desert." He spoke sadly of his abandoned projects, of all the potential of the Yaida, of the rock paintings and other mysteries of this region that is still so unexplored—he has never found time to go down into Isanzu Land, where there are caves containing great log drums too enormous to be moved. According to the Isanzu, the drums had been built in an older time, by an older people; one thinks of the oracle drums of the great Bantu kingdoms of the lake country. The Isanzu are superstitious about the drums and keep them hidden.

Enderlein is a handsome Swede with a young officer's mustache and a mouth broken on one side by a fist of long ago. Though tall and strong, his eyes are restless, he looks haunted and tired; the solitude and frustration of his work are wearing him down. Either he commits more time that will probably be wasted, or he abandons three years of hard lonely work and all hope, as he sees it, for the Yaida. "I think it's the loveliest place in Africa. And it's almost an ecological unit, too, much more so than the Serengeti—almost all its animals are nonmigratory, or would be if they'd let them get to water. I *hate* to give up, but I'm thirty-one now, and I'm getting nowhere; I just can't waste my life here."

The greatest present threat to the Yaida Valley is the cattle of the Barabaig, a pastoral people from the region of Mt. Hanang and the Barabaig Plain, fifty miles southeast. On Saba Saba, there were numbers of lean Barabaig in the settlement, drinking pombe with their traditional antagonists, the Isanzu. They are a tall, handsome people whose dress and customs resemble those of the Maasai, and on the basis of language, they are usually linked to the Nandi, who are thought to have displaced them from the region of Mt. Elgon, on the Kenya-Uganda border, about two hundred and fifty years ago. But little is known of the Barabaig, who appear to have a strong Hamitic mix; their own tradition is that they are related to the Mbulu, and that both groups came south from the shores of Lake Natron. Such names as Barabaig, Hanang, and Giyeda Barakh evoke the northern deserts, as do such habits as the cutting of trophies from the bodies of human enemies, a custom of the Danakil of Ethiopia. In any case, they display all the simplehearted ferocity of the desert nomads, and to the Maasai are known as Il-man'ati, "the Enemy," a name reserved for a worthy foe whose warriors, unlike those of the Bantu, are entitled to extend a handful of grass to the Maasai in a plea for mercy. The Mangati, as they are generally known, were once scattered by attacks of the Maasai, but more recently have withstood Maasai encroachment from the west of Lake Eyasi, and have matched them raid for raid; it is their faith that ten Barabaig will overwhelm twenty Maasai. Being farther from the reach of the authorities, their moran have retained the custom of killing a lion in sign of manhood, or a man, for that matter, and what are known as "Barabaig spear-blooding murders" have made them a great source of chagrin to government and neighbors alike. Those murdered are "enemies of the people"—the real or potential thieves of Barabaig cattle, a very broad category which includes all lions and strangers, as well as the mothers of thieves as yet unborn.

One night not long ago in Yaida Chini, a young Hadza girl was pierced through the lungs by a spear hurled from behind. Since the hard-drinking Mangati are the only ones with spears and the wish to use them, it is thought here that the girl was fleeing a Mangati admirer who was unable to resist a running target. The dying girl was discovered by Enderlein's cook who, interpreting her gasps as evidence of helpless drunkenness, took speedy advantage of his opportunity and raped her; it is hard to imagine the poor creature's last conclusions on the nature of her fellow man. The cook, himself drunk, got covered with blood, in which condition he was apprehended, and since no one has spoken up for him, he may stay in jail indefinitely, and perhaps be hanged, for a crime of which nobody thinks him guilty.

Last September a Yaida Chini game scout, accompanied by three unarmed companions, caught some Barabaig with a dead giraffe and was unwise enough to attempt an arrest. Outraged, the moran pursued the four for three miles or more, trapping them finally in a cave, where they laid siege all night. In the morning, as the game scout came to the end of his ammunition, the warriors departed. Shortly afterward they lost one of their number to an elephant that they had actually attacked with spears, but they were never arrested. This age-set of moran has stalked the Yaida for several years, passing through on poaching raids and raids into Maasai Land. "Their habit of killing people and cutting ears, nose, fingers, etc., off the bodies might sound exotic and interesting to somebody faraway from Mangati Land," Enderlein wrote in September 1969, in a plea for help from the Game Department, "but for my Game Scouts and myself who have to live here and move around where these people are to be found this habit is rather disturbing. Our number is quite small already, and before it is reduced any further we would like to ask for assistance to deal with this dangerous situation."

At sunset the hot wind died, and the dust settled in the stillness; the western hills above Lake Eyasi glowed in a dusty desert sun. In Enderlein's grove the yellow-wing bats hung from the thorns in silhouette, flitted off one by one to meet the dark, while to roosts in the fat figs by the river came companies of storks and vultures, sacred ibis, a solitary pelican, sailing onto the high branches with thick wing thumps, hollow bill clack, and guttural weird protest.

At dark, the yard filled with drunken people, come to invite the white man to a party. In rural villages of East Africa, pombe-drinking consumes half the people's time and money, and the less sophisticated they are, the more hopeless they become. In his concern for the Hadza, Enderlein is trying to get the Mbulu district council to restrict the sale of pombe in this settlement: "We have seven pombe parties at Yaida Chini every week, and the men do their very best to attend all of them." But he knows perfectly well that a restriction is of small value, since anyone can brew the stuff at home.

In an Isanzu hut, we squatted on stools in the dim light and drank from a communal calabash of pombe, which at its best has a woody astringent taste and at its worst beggars description. Y-supports held up the roof beams of the flat-topped hut, and the walls were made of grass and mud caked over with dried dung. The smoke and soft voices, the hunched dark forms catching the ember light on gleaming foreheads, the eyes, the warmth, the slow hands at the hearth protected all there against the emptiness and the cold stars, night sorcery and the hyena riders. Later, the Isanzu danced to four big drums of hide and wood played by swift hands and a tin disc beaten in two-stroke rhythm with a stick, while a chanting old man was answered by fierce chorus. Here, well east of the African lakes, was the echo of the Congo and West Africa. The pounding went on and on and on, and the dry valley quaked with sound like a beaten hide, and far away on the Giyeda Barakh the night sky glowed in a flame twenty miles long, as if the whole country would go up in fire.

Toward midnight, in a sudden silence of the drums, the yelling Africans cursed the white men, the Wazungu, who had gone to bed. One man threw something at the house that banged on the wall and fell to the veranda.


In the morning, Enderlein is exhausted. Lately he has had great trouble sleeping; his eyes twitch, and he does everything with violence. Carving a bird, he seizes the whole carcass in his hand and slings the pieces onto plates. Hunting on the plains, he yanks his car too hard, too fast, and he seems careless with his rifle though he is not. Catching himself, or realizing he has been perceived, he mutters sheepishly, "I haven't taken care of myself; I've let everything go. Perhaps I have bilharzia." He shrugs, indifferent. "When I came out here, I was so keen, but now I am not. The people I try to work with do not care, so I cannot care indefinitely. They let everything go." He nodded his head toward the kitchen. "Last night Mfupi was drunk, and didn't bother to close the gate to the duck pen, and a honey badger got all my birds but two. I ask him to set some rice aside for our safari, and he cooks my entire supply. We need two camp cots, but all twelve cots assigned to Yaida Chini are now missing. A cot that will last fifteen years is ruined in three months—the rest have been lost, or perhaps sold in Mbulu." He shrugged again. "It's the same with everything—the land, the animals. Nobody cares, and all of it is going to go." He went outside and stood on his veranda, boots spread, hands in hip pockets, glaring at an African sky shrouded in fire clouds of smoke and blowing dust. In this valley, the only land that goes unburned is land too overgrazed to carry fire.

We head north under the Yaida Escarpment. Like all mornings in the dry season, this day is born in a dusty sun and restless wind, a desert wind, or so it seems, so vast and empty is the plain from which it comes. There is an old safari track, grown over, but the Land Rover makes its own way through acacia savanna where a slender-tailed mongoose, dark and lustrous, slips like a swift fish through the fading grass. At midmorning the lower Udahaya is crossed, a slow stream dying in the plain. Slowly we wind toward the south Sipunga Hills.

Somewhere in the Sipunga, perhaps thirty miles north of Yaida Chini, small bands of Hadza hide from the resettlement program, living as they have always lived, by hunting and gathering, a people without pottery or gardens or domestic animals other than the random dog. Probably they will hide from us, as well, unless they see that we are with Hadza whom they trust. Magandula is a game scout and the prestige of his bunduki, or rifle, entitles him to two porters, Gimbe and Giga. Magandula is loud and opinionated; Gimbe and Giga are quiet. Magandula and Gimbe have Isanzu fathers, but Giga, smaller and older, is pure Hadza, black, with heavy jaw and swollen cheekbones and flat nose in a head too big for a small thick body which will never attain five feet in height. Until recently Giga has been living in the bush—he is one of a number of Hadza who drift back and forth between the old life and the new—and as if in sign of his transitional state he is wearing a sandal on his right foot but not on his left. Magandula, on the other hand, is an outspoken convert to the new Africa, and wears bright red socks in black street shoes with broken points.

In early afternoon, under Sipunga, Giga speaks. Off among black wrinkled trunks and silvered thorns he has glimpsed a shift of shadows, and now Magandula is speaking, too: "Tindiga!" he says in tones of triumph, choosing the Isanzu name.

There is more than one, it is a hunting party, crouching low in the golden grass to peer under the limbs; the black of their skin is the old black of acacia bark in shadow. Giga is smiling at them, and they do not run; they have seen Giga, and they have a fresh-killed zebra. Enderlein is grinning freely for the first time since I have known him. "Oh, we are *lucky!*" he says twice; he had not thought we would find the hunters this first day.

A striped hock shines in the fork of a tree; the rest rides on the hunters' shoulders. There are ten Hadza, seven with bows and three young boys, and all are smiling. Each boy has glistening raw meat slung over his shoulders and wrapped around him, and one wears the striped hide outward, in a vest. Except for beads at neck and waist, the boys are naked. The men wear loincloths faded to an olive-earth color that blends with the tawny grass; the rags are bound at the waist by a hide thong, and some have simple necklaces of red-and-yellow berry-colored beads. All wear crude sheath knives in the center of the back, and one has a guinea fowl feather in his hair.

Shy, they await in a half-circle, much less tall than their bows. "*Tsifiaqua!*" they murmur, and our people say, "*Tsifiaqua mtana,*" and then the hunters say, "M-*taa*-na!" for warm emphasis, smiling wholeheartedly. (*Tsifiaqua* is "afternoon" as in "good afternoon," and *mtana* is "nice" as in "nice day," and *tsifiaqua m-taa-na*, as the hunters say it, may mean, "Oh beautiful day!") I am smiling wholeheartedly too, and so is Enderlein; my smile seems to travel right around my head. The encounter in the sunny wood is much too simple, too beautiful to be real, yet it is more real than anything I have known in a long time. I feel a warm flood of relief, as if I had been away all my life and had come home again—I want to embrace them all. And so both groups stand face to face, admiring each other in the sunlight, and then hands are taken all around, each man being greeted separately by all the rest. They are happy we are to visit them and delighted to pile the zebra meat into the Land Rover, for the day is hot and dry and from here to where these Hadza live, behind the Sipunga Hills, is perhaps six miles of stony walking. The eldest, Mzee Dafi, rides, and others run ahead and alongside, and others stay behind to hunt again. The runners keep pace with the car as it barges across the stones and thorn scrub and on across the south end of Sipunga through the ancestral Hadza land called T'ua. Soon Giga kicks off his remaining sandal and runs barefoot with the rest, and then Magandula, in red socks and shiny shoes, is running, too. Gimbe, a young mission boy from Munguli, sits quietly; he is not yet home.

There is no track, only an intermittent path, and here and there Enderlein heaves rocks out of the way to let us pass. Peter is happy, and he works with exuberance, casting away his pent-up angers. So glad are the hunters of our coming that they hurl rocks, too, but since most of them, Giga included, have no idea what they accomplish, they struggle with rocks that are far off the route, out of pure goodwill. On the sky rise twin hills walled with soaring monoliths, quite unlike anything I have ever seen; the hills overlook the upper Udahaya Valley, between the Sipunga and the Mbulu Escarpment. Seeing the hills the hunters cry out, leaping rocks, and the swiftest is he with the guinea fowl feather, Salibogo.

Behind the twin portals, on a hillside, rise groves of monumental granites. Approaching this place across a meadow of pink baobabs, Dafi whispers, "Gidabembe." Still there is no sign of habitation. But bright green in the sun are two fresh gourds set out to dry on a rock shelf; the placement of the gourds gives man away. A yellow dog, the first and last such animal we saw in Hadza Land, walks stiff and silent from the bush under a tilted monolith, and from the shadows of the stone a thin smoke rises into the dry sunlight, and a crone the color of dry brush appears among the leaves. In the shadows she stands like a dead stick, observing.

At the next grove of rocks, a stone has toppled in such a way that its flat face, some fifteen feet by fifteen in dimension, is held clear of the ground by the debris of its own fall, forming an open-sided shelter five feet high; similar rock shelters at Magosi, in Uganda, have been inhabited since the Middle Stone Age. Small trees at the cave's twin mouths filter the sunlight, and at the hearth is a cracked gourd, a rag, a dik-dik skin, a bone, all now abandoned, for except in time of heaviest rains, the Hadza live beneath the sky. With hand brooms of grass and twigs, Gimbe and Magandula and the hunters brush loose dust from the cave floor, while squat Giga pushes three hearthstones together and with fingertips and breath draws grass wisps into a fire and places a black pot on the points of stone to boil. Outside, an old woman has appeared, bent under a morning's harvest of orange grewia berries, which are dry and sweet and taste like nuts; offering these, she is given a strip of the zebra meat spread out across a stone. Our people take meat for ourselves, and so do others who come quietly into the glade, for the Hadza have no agonies of ownership. Soon the wild horse is gone. On sharpened sticks Gimbe skewers the red meat, laying two sticks across the fire; the rest he places in the trees to dry for biltong. Our arrival at Gidabembe is celebrated with a feast of tea and zebra, ugali and the fire-colored berries.

Gidabembe, the Hadza say, has been one of their camps for a long time, longer than the oldest of them can remember. It is used mainly in the dry season, when large animals are more easily killed, and people gather into larger groups to be in the vicinity of the good hunters. The main encampment lies uphill from the cave, on a knoll overlooking the river, where four small hearths with thornbush walls are grouped among the stones. Two are backed by upright granite and a third by a fallen tree; no roofs are constructed in this season, for there is no rain. The people are invisible to the outside world, which at Gidabembe is no farther than the glint of a tin duka on the slope of the Kainam Plateau, high on the far side of the valley. Their fires are small and their voices quiet, and they are so circumspect in all their habits that no scent of human habitation is detectable, although they do not bother about the droppings of baboons, which appropriate these rocks when man is absent; the baobab seeds in the baboon droppings are sometimes gleaned for man's own use. Only a rare infant's cry betrays the presence of human beings, for the children play quietly, without squalling. One is among them very suddenly, a community of small people speaking prettily in soft click-speech in the light airs of afternoon. Far below the shelter of the rocks is green forest and the brown wind-sparkled river that in July is already running dry.

Soft voices in leaf-filtered sun, and a child humming, and a warm wind off the highlands that twitches the dry trees and blows color into the embers at the hearth. The earth behind the fire has been softened with a digging stick. Here, at dark, covered only with the thin rags worn in the day, the family lies down together on the small mat of kongoni hide or hay. From the thorn walls hang gourds and arrow packets and bird skins for arrow vanes, and by one hearth is an iron pot, black and thin as a leaf cinder. In these simple arrangements is a ceremonial sense of order in which everything is in place, for the ceremony here is life itself, yet these shelters last no longer than the whims of their inhabitants, who may move tomorrow to another place, nearby or far. In the rains, especially, they scatter, for game and water are widespread. Somewhere they draw a few sticks over their heads, with grass matted on top, though they are casual about the rain when food is plentiful. In the dry season, many will return to Gidabembe, by the river, for Gidabembe is permanent, although all but the oldest of its people come and go. The hunter, who must travel light, limits his family to parents and children, and the people move in ever-changing groups, with little sense of tribe. The Hadza have no chiefs, no villages, no political system; their independence is their very breath. Giga speaks of an old man who wandered off last year and was thought lost. Three months later he turned up again, well rested from the stress of human company.

In the day the men and boys remain separate from the women. The men carry a fire drill among their arrows, and wherever Hadza tarry for more than a few minutes, and tarrying occupies much of their life, a small fire will be built. One hearth overlooks the river. Here in the broken sunlight, in the odor of wood smoke, the men and boys squat on their heels, shoulder to shoulder in a warm circle around the fire. With Dafi is his son Kahunda, and Saidi the son of Chandalua, who is still hunting in the land called T'ua; both are beautiful children whose eyes are not yet red from fire smoke, nor their teeth broken and brown. Dafi and Ginawi butcher zebra with deft twists of their crude knives; at Dafi's side is an ancient sharpening stone, glinting with soft iron shavings and concave with many seasons of hard use. Knives and metal arrow points come mostly from other tribes, but sometimes they are hammered cold from soft iron acquired in trade for skins and honey. Sheaths are fashioned from two flat bits of wood bound round with hide and sinew. Until recently, a male Hadza wore the pelt of a genet cat, bound on by the hide thong that holds his knife, but now almost all wear small cloth skirts. Each carries a hide pouch with shoulder strap containing scraps of skin and tendon, tobacco leaves and hemp, a disc of baobab wood, lucocuko, used in gambling, a hunk of vine tuber which, when chewed, serves as a glue for binding arrow vanes, some rag-wrapped hornet larvae medicine or dawa, useful for chest pain, and snakebite dawa, of ingredients known only to a few, which is used in trade with the Mbulu and Mangati, spare arrowheads and scraps of metal, a chisel tool made from a nail, a pipe carved from a soft stone in the river. This pipe, one of the few Hadza objects that is not obtained in barter, is no more than a tube, and the tobacco or bangi will fall from it unless it is held vertical. Both men and women, staring at the sky, smoke the stone pipe with gusty sucks accompanied by harsh ritual coughing, which is followed in turn by a soft ecstatic sigh.

Dafi and Ginawi eat zebra skin after burning off the hair, and put aside strips of the thick hide to be used for the soles of sandals, which most though not all of the hunters have adopted. They are joined by a Hadza with oriental eyes, high cheekbones, and a light skin with a yellow cast, who brings to mind a legend—not entirely without evidence to support it—that long ago Indonesians penetrated inland from the coast; the Tatoga of this region say that their ancestors came originally from beyond the sea. This man has been to Yaida Chini, and is sorry that Enderlein does not recall his name. "Zali," he says. "It is bad of you to forget. I have told it to you at Yaida Chini."

Certain other sallow Hadza might be Bushmen but for the lack of wrinkles and steatopygous buttocks, and Enderlein says that in their attitudes and ways, the Hadza seem identical to the click-speakers of the Kalahari, whom he has read all about. Bushmanoid peoples once inhabited East Africa, and it is tempting to suppose that the two groups were related long ago. On the other hand, certain Negroid groups such as the Bergdama of southwest Africa have adopted the Bushman culture, and even the Zulu have adopted a click-speech from these Twa or Abatwa, whose old hunting lands they have appropriated. The Bushmen themselves have Negroid attributes that they may not have always possessed—it is not known what their ancestors looked like.

But the yellow-brown Hadza look not at all like Giga, and most of the tribe are of mixed appearance, despite the striking heavy-browed appearance of such individuals as Giga, and Andaranda who killed the zebra, and a man named Kargo who, in size, is a true pygmy, and the large-headed girl at Yaida Chini who was the first Hadza that I ever saw, and one identified on sight, it must be said, by my Isanzu passenger, who had never seen her in his life.

Already the hunters are tending to their arrows, long thin shafts cut from a grewia or dombeya and feathered with vanes of bustard, guinea fowl, or vulture. Bird arrows are tipped with sharpened wood, and each bundle has an arrow with a lance blade of honed iron that is used for small game like guinea fowl and dik-dik. All the rest have single or double-barbed metal points dipped in black resinous poison, made ordinarily from seeds of the black strocanthus fruit or sap of the desert rose. Both poisons are heart stimulants, consumed safely in meat but fatal when received into the blood-stream. Dafi wraps the poisoned barbs in thin strips of impala hide so that the poison will not dry out; the protection of the hunter is incidental. His long stiff bow of dombeya is also wrapped with circlets of impala, though this is maridadi—decoration. Ordinarily, Hadza bow strings are of zebra tendon, while split tendons of impala are the sinew that binds the arrow vanes onto the shaft.

When not out hunting roots and tubers with their digging sticks, Hadza women remain at their own hearths. Here their children, with their big bellies and small prominent behinds dusted gray with hearth ash, play a variety of games with the hard bright yellow fruits of nightshade known as Sodom apples. Gondoshabe sits with

Gindu, mother of Andaranda who killed the zebra, and lank-dugged Angate with a tobacco wad behind her ear, and Hanako, young wife of the swift hunter Salibogo, threading beads on long strands of fiber from the baobab, and Giga's daughter Kabaka, who with her baby has run away from the game scout Nangai at Yaida Chini. The women wear the same three garments as the women of the Bushmen: a genital cover, skirt, and carrying bag, formerly of hide, but now of cloth. They sit flat on the ground with legs straight out, toes upright, or squat on their haunches like the men. Though the nomadic Hadza do not burden themselves with metal bracelets, most women wear single headbands of white, red, and blue beads as well as bead armlets, anklets, and knee bands, and like the men, they may have three scars cut on the cheek in decoration. Small boys wear a simple strand of beads around the waist, small girls a rag and small bead apron, while infants may wear fetishes and charms as protection against the touch of menstruating women and the night cries of hurtful birds. Kabaka's baby is immobilized by strings of beads, but for all her wealth Kabaka looks disgruntled, and it is she who raises her voice against the mzungu's presence in the camp. The wild Hadza women pay her little mind; though shyer than the men, they soon disregard the visitors and go on about their business. They grind maize, gather firewood; they dry new gourds bartered from the Mbulu, for they have no pottery, and fetch water from the river in the old. The gourds of cool water stand at angles beside a calabash of bright fresh berries. In this dry place, the sparkle of precious water borne in gourds has a true splendor. Gourds and arrow shafts may be marked with cross-hatching incised between parallel lines, these pairs of lines being set at angles to each other, but otherwise the Hadza have no art besides the decoration of their persons and the simplicity of their lives.

The Gidabembe rocks fall to the river edge, two hundred feet below. On the far side of the river lies low heavy forest, and beyond the forest is acacia savanna with big trees. Mbulu people have come down off the escarpment to clear patches of savanna; their presence has brought the humble duka that glints against the hills. Already a few Mbulu have crossed the river and set up maize shambas in the region of Gidabembe, and meanwhile Mangati filter up into the Sipunga from the south. While as yet there is no sign of overgrazing, this will come. The Mbulu and Mangati have caused the wild animals to scatter, and large game has become scarce during the dry season, when the only water available, in the Udahaya, is cut off by man. Eventually the Mbulu will call upon the Game Department to destroy the last elephant and buffalo, and meanwhile the wild animals are poached relentlessly by tillers and herdsmen alike.

A very few strangers, scattered through this valley, threaten the wildlife on which the Hadza depend, yet the Hadza accept these strangers as openly and cheerfully as they accept us. They cannot know that their time is past, although hunting is much harder now, and soon may be beyond their skills. In the old days, in time of famine, people of other tribes would go into the bush to live with the hospitable Hadza, who have no memory of hunger—despite a passion for honey and meat, they depend on seeds, tubers, roots, wild cowpeas, ivy gourd, borage, and berries of toothbrush bush and grewia, in addition to certain fungi and such seasonal tree fruits as baobab, figs, desert dates (*Balanites*), and tamarind. Excess meat and honey, used formerly in trade for beads and iron and tobacco, is hard to come by, for log hives brought in by the Mbulu are attracting the wild bees, and game is scarce. When the hunting is gone, the Hadza may take to killing stock, as the Bushmen did. Already one Hadza has been speared to death near Mangola for the killing and consumption of a goat.

A few Mbulu and Mangati stroll through Gidabembe, tall and contemptuous; they grin coldly for the benefit of the white man by way of answer to the Hadza greetings. There are two Mbulu shambas within a mile of Gidabembe, and already the Hadza have adopted this Mbulu name for their ancestral place, which in their own tongue is Ugulu. Recently, a family of Mangati has built a typical figure-eight stockade close by; one of the loops of the stockade is used for cattle, and in the other is the rectangular Mangati hut, like a Mbulu tembe but built above the level of the ground. The Mbulu and the men of the Mangati wrap themselves in trade cloth, but Mangati women wear skirts of leather cured in human urine, as

Maasai women did in former days. Certain warm-breasted leather-skirted girls of the Mangati, carved northern faces softened by the south, are the loveliest women, black or brown or white, that I have seen in Africa.

At dark, we go with drink onto the rock over the cave and roll a smoke, and stare out over Hadza Land, and listen. Already Peter has relaxed, though he has not slept, and I find him an excellent companion, well informed, inquiring, with an open mind and a capacity for silence, and possessed of an ironic perception that has surely spared his sanity. People who knew him from his sprees on infrequent visits to Arusha had warned me that Enderlein was "bushed," as the saying goes here, from too much time alone out in the bush; they spoke of Peter's beautiful young wife who had found bush life unbearable and had fled two years before, not to return. But a letter sent me in Nairobi gave me confidence that we would get on all right: "I think if you allow yourself two weeks here," he wrote in part, "you would be able to get a fair insight into the valley and its mysteries; if you stay longer, you might well end up at my position, knowing nothing at all. It seems the longer one stays at a place, the less one has to say about it. . . ."

For this safari we had settled on two low camp cots, without tent, a few essentials such as rice and tea and rum, and whatever tinned goods might be rattling around in the rear of my old Land Rover. For the rest we would make do as we went along. Even so, our camp was infinitely more complex than the Hadza hearths, and soon seemed littered. Both of us have a passion for traveling light, deploring the ponderous caravansary which Anglo-Saxons in particular tend to conceive of as safaris—the table, camp chairs, ice chests, private toilet tents, truckloads of provender and swarming staff that permit them to lug the colonial amenities of the Hotel Norfolk "into the blue." Like myself, Peter has often been ashamed in front of Africans by the amount of equipment that his white friends required. Yet Africans admire wealth, and anyway, they do not make judgments in such matters, but accept a different culture as it is. The people at Gidabembe, who still trust, are neither subservient nor rude. Here was the gentleness, the loving attention to the moment, that is vanishing in East Africa, as it has vanished in the western world.

Exhilarated, happy, we lie flat out on the high rocks, still warm from the hot sun of afternoon. Peter draws his finger across the sky, starting to laugh. "Fake stars have five points, isn't it true?" he says. "Now I shall try to count how many points the *real* stars have. . . ." He laughs quietly for a long time. And later he shouts suddenly, "You see? You see that constellation veering? It's like a kite! It's like a kite in that one moment just before it falls. . . ." And I turn my head to watch him bellow at the universe.

Three months after our stay at Gidabembe, Peter would write as follows from hospital in Arusha:

It seems my time in Hadza Land has come to an end. I was recently called to a meeting in Mbulu to discuss my project but I found myself the witch in a medieval witchhunt where the bonfire was built and the match already lighted. It seemed I wanted to ruin their efforts of settling the Hadza—of course everybody knows that white men like to see Africans primitive and naked only—and turn them back to the bush. I also payed them money to strip nude so that my friends could photograph them in this state—all of course to discredit the development of the country. Somebody suggested that I shoot more zebras than I account for and keep the money myself. Somebody else knew that the Hadza despised me, etc., etc., etc. So here I am, having chosen to be hospitalized for a while—how can one choose jaundice?— looking for new horizons.

In a day the zebra is already gone, and Dafi and Salibogo will rejoin the hunters beyond Sipunga Hills. We go along to watch them hunt. A solitary elephant crosses a rise among great baobabs, and they cry out, but except at close range, it is hard to drive an arrow through the thick hide of an elephant. Their bows require a hundred-pound pull from a hunter who weighs little more than that himself, and the poison used here is not strong enough.

On the far side of Sipunga, down toward the Yaida Plain, there are impala, and Dafi and Salibogo run through the scattered trees, moving downwind before cutting back toward the animals. Both are very small and quick, as if in hunters, this small size, like the long legs of the nomadic herdsman, was a phenomenon of natural selection. In the case of the well-fed Hadza, it would be hard to argue that small size is the consequence of life in a hostile and stunted environment; like hunter-gatherers the world over, they tend to be better nourished than more settled peoples, who must struggle to subsist. Until recently there was no need to hunt hard to get all the meat they wanted, and probably the game will be all gone before they refine their skills. Enderlein once watched Ariangulo trackers brought here from the Tsavo country by white hunters. He says that the Hadza, who hunt alone except when encircling baboons, compare in neither tactics nor persistence with the Ariangulo, who have huge bows with arrows tipped in acokanthera and specialize in hunting elephants.

Magandula, grabbing a bow, trots after the hunters in his black shoes; the self-conscious leer upon his face fails to conceal an innocent excitement. Eventually Salibogo goes on by himself, running bent double over long stretches of open ground, rising and falling, crouching, peering, and snaking at last on his belly to the caper bush where he will lie. The animals drift away from Dafi, who, in the way of lions, drives them gently into ambush, but the wind shifts and the lead animal crosses Salibogo's scent. In the stillness comes the impala's blowing snort, and the bright-eyed ones are gone.

With the impala goes the last good opportunity of the day. Even when Enderlein decides to use his rifle, we come up with nothing. Zebra, impala, and wildebeest are all shy and scarce, and a wildebeest bull struck at long range fails to come down. The day is dry and very hot, and much of this landscape south and west of the Sipunga has been burned by the Mangati; on a black ground, Senegal bustards pick the burnt eggs of guinea fowl. Farther north, in a grassland with low suffocated thorn, there are no animals at all. Overhead passes a pelican, flapping and sailing on its way to distant water, but here the thorn wood and dense dusty grass is empty, and as the morning turns to afternoon, black man and white fall silent.

An African landscape full of animals, even dangerous ones, does not seem hostile; life is sustained here, and somewhere there is water. But without animals, the parched grass and bitter thorn, the hard-caked earth, the old sky shrouded by fire smoke through which a dull sun looms like a blind eye—all seems implacable. The sun god Haine, though worshipped by the Hadza, is remote and ill disposed toward man, and is not invoked. In the dark of the moon the hunters dance all night to insure good hunting and good health, for sometimes a hunter, crouched in night ambush at a waterhole, is taken by the lion, Sesemaya.

At home, hot, tired, and oppressed, we tramp down to the Udahaya. Careless of bilharzia, we lie in the cool flow, six inches deep, that streams over fine copper-colored sand. We wash, dry off on the green bank in a cool north wind, and climb back up to Gidabembe, feeling better. There Gondoshabe and Angate are singing on their knees, breasts swinging across big flat-topped tilted stones on which maize meal is refined by being scraped by a flat rock. The meal pours onto clean impala hide below the stone.

The boy Saidi, preparing his small arrows, sits alone at a fire above the river. All Hadza boys, developing their bow strength from an early age, have weapons suitable to their size that are in constant play and practice, and the glint of a bird arrow risen through the trees of a still landscape is a sign of Hadza presence. Though some men never hunt at all, content to accept charity in return for the loss of prestige, Saidi's intensity and bearing say that he will be a hunter. Squatting on his heels, he trims his vulture plumes and binds them to a shaft with neck ligament of the impala. Four vanes are trimmed and bound on tight in as many minutes, and the binding sealed over with the glue from a chewed tuber. He sights down his new arrow shafts, then gnaws at one to soften it for straightening before fitting his arrow tips into shaft sockets dug out with a bent nail. Then he rises and goes off after dik-dik and rock hyrax, which both abound here. The hyrax looks like a sharp-nosed marmot, but on the basis of certain anatomical similarities, notably the feet, it has been determined that its nearest living kin are elephants. Perhaps as a defense against the attack of eagles, the hyrax has the astonishing ability to stare straight upward into the equatorial sun.

Watching Saidi go, Enderlein says, "Do you know what will become of him?" He scowls. "First, when all the game is gone, and the trees, too, he will be forced to go to Yaida Chini. Untrained, he can do nothing, and because he is Hadza he will be treated as inferior everywhere he goes. If he is very lucky, he might become a thief in Dar es Salaam; otherwise he will be just another one of all those faces in the streets, hopeless and lost, with all the dignity that this life gives him gone." He got to his feet, disgusted, and we walked in silence toward the cave, through the beautiful rock monuments and wild still twilight orchards of commiphora like old apple trees and terminalia with red pods like fruit, and figs, and fruiting grewia bushes, and a small sweet-scented acacia with recurved spines that catch hold of the unwary—the wait-a-bit thorn, from the Swahili *ngoja kidogo*, which means wait-a-little.

At the cave is the game scout Nangai, come on foot from Yaida Chini to fetch back his young wife Kabaka, daughter of Giga. "Who knows why she ran away?" Nangai shrugs, smiling shyly at his sullen wife. Giga, holding his ornamented grandchild to his cheek, rolls his eyes and croons, a love all the more affecting for the great ugliness that, as one comes to perceive this man, turns to great beauty.

Tea is served by sad-faced discreet Gimbe, who says, "*Karibu chai*," welcome to tea, with the same sweet simplicity with which another African once said to me, "You are nicely welcomed to Samburu." With his wood ladle he stirs maize meal into boiling water to make the thick white paste called ugali that is subsistence in East Africa; ugali, eaten with the fingers, is rolled into a kind of concave ball used to mop up whatever is at hand in the way of meat, vegetables, and gravy. Soon he presents a bowl of water in which the right hand is to be dipped and rinsed prior to eating, because here in the cave our posho, or ration, is eaten from a common bowl. The

Moslem washing of one hand comes up from the coast by way of the part-Arab Swahili, once the agents of the trade in slaves and ivory; so does the mbira or "marimba," called irimbako by the Hadza, who have no musical instrument of their own. The mbira, or flat-bar zither, came to East Africa centuries ago from Indonesia. It is a hollow box faced with tuned strips of stiff metal that produces soft swift wistful rhythms of time passing, and the old one here at Gidabembe is passed from hand to hand. It is Giga who plays it by the fire as we dine on ugali and delicate doves shot in the hills.

At Gidabembe Hill, among the monoliths, baboons are raving, and there comes a sudden brief strange sound that brings Giga from his cave. "*Chui*," he whispers. Leopard. But the others shrug—how can one know? The Hadza never like to give opinions. A few days later, in this place, we find the vulture-gutted body of a young leopard on an open slope where no sick leopard would ever lie, and the grass all about has been bent and stamped by a convocation of baboons, as if the creature had been caught in the open by the huge baboon troupe, which had killed it. Yet there was no baboon fur in its mouth, nor any blood or sign of struggle in the grass.

The dark falls quiet once again. From Sipunga comes the night song of unknown birds, and the shrill ringing yip of a distant jackal, and inevitably the ululations of hyenas. The Hadza are comparatively unsuperstitious, and unfrightened of the dark: "We are ready for him," they say of Fisi, reaching out to touch their bows. "Hyena can be a bloody nuisance," Enderlein says, recalling an account, no doubt apocryphal, of a sleeping man who had his foot bitten clean off by a night hyena. He places a dim kerosene lantern near our bed rolls, for we are sleeping outside the cave. At my head is a white hyrax stain on the dark rock, and beside the stain are stacked the rifles. Mosquitoes are few and we sleep without a net, staring up through the black leaves at cruel bright stars. Gimbe is sleeping in the Land Rover, and the others sleep on hides inside the cave. Magandula curls up with his bunduki, and Giga is hooked close to the embers. They murmur in their soft deep voices, which drop away one by one. Soon Giga is asleep, and all night he breathes rapidly, like a wild creature stunned and felled while running.

. . .

The Hadza see no sense in hunting hard with bow and arrow when there is a rifle in the camp. In hope of meat, people are coming in out of the hills, and there are seven hearths where there were four. The Hadza here are now no less than thirty and a buffalo would feed everyone for days.

Many buffalo, as well as rhino and elephant, live in the forest below Gidabembe. When Peter asks me if I wish to hunt, I tell him I will think about it. Enderlein is a good shot who is shooting badly, who is sleeping badly, whose every action has a trace of rage in it; he is not the companion I would choose for the pursuit of dangerous animals, and especially buffalo, toward which he seems more disrespectful than any hunter I have ever met. "He's too damned careless about buffalo; he's going to catch it one of these days," says Douglas-Hamilton, who is not known for prudence. On the other hand, though I had no wish to shoot a big animal myself, hunting dangerous game is a part of the African mystique that I did not know. And this morning is a soft green morning when death, which never seems remote in Africa, but hangs about like something half-remembered, might come almost companionably . . . be that as it may, I leave my doubts behind.

We descend to the river at daybreak, accompanied by the game scouts Magandula and Nangai, and Mugunga, who is Nangai's young porter, and two wild Hadza, Yaida and Salibogo. Magandula carries Peter's .375, which few hunters consider powerful enough to stop a buffalo, and Nangai brings a .22 for small game. Yaida and Salibogo carry bow and arrows. We ford the river where it winds around the base of Gidabembe, and enter the dense forest single file. Salibogo is in the lead, then Enderlein, Nangai, Mugunga, who carries Peter's pouch of bullets, then Magandula, then myself, and finally Yaida, who looks like a young Bushman. For the first time Magandula is shirtless, and he has a porcupine quill stuck in his hair, but he clings to his red socks and pointed shoes.

Trees in this virgin place are huge—umbrella thorn and soaring fever trees, and here and there a mighty winterthorn (*A. albida*), the noblest of all acacias, these interspersed with fat sycamore figs and sausage trees. But along the animal trails and walling the small glades is head-high thicket, hollowed out, where rhino and buffalo may stand entirely hidden. Their spoor is everywhere, and Salibogo drops behind; there is no need for a tracker. We move carefully and quietly, bending each moment to peer into the grottoes. The trick is to sight any hidden beast before it feels crowded and decides to charge, but the cover is dense, and Enderlein offers a tense grin. "Bloody dangerous bush," he murmurs. "They can see you but you can't see them." In Peter's opinion, rhino are more dangerous than buffalo, being stupid and unpredictable, a "warm-blooded dinosaur," as he says, that has outlived its time; rhinos are apt to rush out blindly where a buffalo would slip away. But I share the more common dread of the low-browed buffalo, shifting its jaws sideways as it chews its cud, light glancing from its horn.

Oblivious birdsong in the early morning wind; warm butterflies spin sunlight through the glades. The Hadza pause every little while to wring dry berries from the grewia bushes, but my own mouth is too dry, I am not hungry. There is exhilaration in the hunt, and also the quick heart of the hunted. I feel strong and light and quick, and more than a match for the nearest tree that can be climbed in haste. These are damnably few: the big trees lack low branches and the small are shrouded with thorn vine and liana. Yaida and Salibogo, like myself, keep a close watch on the trees, and we grin nervously at one another.

In a circular glade, Enderlein crouches, stiffens, and steps back, holding out his hand. Magandula gives him his rifle. In the shadows ten yards to the left, the cave of leaves is filled with a massive shape, as still as stone. A little way back there was fresh rhino track, and Peter thinks this is the rhino. He circles out a little ways, just to make sure. A slight movement may bring on a rhino charge—its poor vision cannot make out what's moving, and its nerves cannot tolerate suspense—whereas a sudden movement may put it to flight. I am considering a sudden movement, such as flight of my own, when I see a tail in a thin shaft of light, and the tail tuft in fleeting silhouette, and grunt at Peter, "Buffalo."

A sun glint on the moisture at the nostril; the animal is facing us. The tail does not move again. We stand there for long seconds, at a loss. Enderlein cannot get a fair shot in the poor light, and at such close quarters, he does not want a wounded buffalo. He starts a wide circling stalk of the entire copse, signaling his game scouts to follow. But it is the boy Mugunga who jumps forward, and the game scouts shrug, content to let him go. We follow carefully, but soon the hunters vanish in the bushes. Heat and silence. Soon the silence is intensified by a shy birdsong, incomplete, like a child's question gone unanswered.

The bird sings again, waits, sings again. Bees come and go. Soon Mugunga reappears. The beast will not be chivvied out of hiding, and there is no hope of a clear shot with the rifle. But a poisoned arrow need not be precise. The hunter has only to wait a few hours before tracking, so as not to drive the dying animal too far away, and in this time he would return to camp to find help in cutting up the meat, or if the animal was big, to move the whole camp to the carcass.

Mugunga draws on Yaida's bow, then picks the stronger bow of Salibogo. The Hadza faces fill with joy; they respect the rifle but they trust the bow. Then Mugunga vanishes once more, and the silence deepens. Leaves stir and are still.

The birdsong ceases as the buffalo crashes free, but there is no shout, no rifle shot, only more silence. When the hunters reappear, Enderlein says, "I thought the arrow might bring him out where I could get a shot at him, but Mugunga waited a split second too long, and the bloody brute pushed off, out the far side." Even so we will track this buffalo; Peter keeps the gun. The Hadza move on, bush by bush, glade by glade, checking bent grass, earth, and twigs, darting through copses where one would have thought so large an animal could not have gone. To watch such tracking is a pleasure, but this is taut work, for the buffalo is listening, it has not taken flight. Somewhere in the silent trees, the dark animal is standing still, or circling to come up behind. Wherever it is, it is too close.

In the growing heat, our nerves go dead, and we are pushing stupidly ahead, inattentive, not alert, when the spoor dies, too, and we cut away from the river in search of another animal. But the sun is climbing, and the big animals will have taken to the shade. The chance of catching one still grazing in the open is now small.

In a swampy place the Hadza fall on a tomato bush. The small fruits are warm red, intensely flavored, and we eat what we can and tie the rest into a rag to bring back to Gidabembe. Not that the hunters feel obliged to do this: men and women seek and eat food separately and quickly, to avoid the bad manners of refusing it to others, and occasional sharing between the sexes is a matter of whim. Farther on, Yaida and Salibogo locate honey in a tree, and again the hunt for buffalo is abandoned. Usually a grass torch is stuck into the hole to smoke out the bees, but the Hadza are more casual than most Africans about bee stings, and Yaida is wringing one stung hand while feeding himself with the other. The honeycomb is eaten quickly, wax, larvae, and all. The Hadza also eat hyena, cats, and jackals, though they draw the line at frogs and reptiles, and not every man will eat a vulture.

Hyena prints, and spoor of waterbuck. Nangai kicks at buffalo manure to see its freshness, and it is plain that we have passed the dark silent animals close by. Mugunga, frustrated, shoots a lance arrow at a dik-dik half-hidden by low, intervening branches—he leans into the shot on his left foot as he shoots—and the arrow drives hard into a sapling by the dik-dik's neck. He turns to look at us, shaking his head. We circle slowly toward the Udahaya, striking it at midday far downriver. The hunt is over, and we walk barefoot in the water, shooting doves and hyrax with the .22 as we return upstream. Peter is brooding, but I am still excited by the hunt, and glad to be free of the dense bush, and so I celebrate this moment of my life, the sparkle of gold mica on my brown feet, a pair of pied kingfishers that racket from dead limb to limb, the sweet scent of the white-flowered vernonia, swarming with bees that make honey for the Hadza. And the Hadza seem happy, too: their time is now. Though there will not be nearly enough to go around, it awes them to see the doves fall to our gun. They are used to failure in the hunt, which these days occurs often, and in the future must occur more often still.


A visitor to Gidabembe comes from a small camp in the Sipunga Hills, where he helps take care of a young invalid, apparently an epileptic. Last year this boy was badly burned when he fell into a fire, and was led across the hills to the clinic in Mbulu, but after two days he ran away, back to Sipunga. This spring, left alone in camp, he fell again into the fire and was burned so drastically that he can no longer move.

Magandula has borrowed a wood comb from Giga; perched on a rock, he combs his head for a long time without discernible results. According to Magandula, it is only the influence of civilization that prevents the *Sipunganebe* from deserting the man burned, and the Hadza cheerfully agree: among nomadic hunter-gatherers, who cannot afford responsibility for others, such desertion is quite common. Only last year, Yaida says, a man in fever was abandoned in the mountains: "We left him his bow, but he could not live; surely he was eaten by lions." Magandula, scrubbing his shoes, becomes excited and speaks shrilly: "To live in the bush is bad! Hasn't the government taught us to live in houses? I want nothing to do with the bush!" In recent years the government has made of the Hadza a symbol of primitive apathy to their countrymen, who are exhorted to increase their numbers and work hard on their shambas—"Don't rot in the bush like the Watindiga!" And tillers from Mbulu come sometimes to Yaida Chini and jeer at them: "How can people be so primitive!"—just as the people of Arusha might speak of the poor peasants of Mbulu, or the people of Dar es Salaam of the provincial folk met in Arusha.

Four naked children have clambered up into a grewia bush and hunch there in the branches, knees under their chins, munching sweet berries while they watch us. Despite big bellies and thin legs, which are lost early, Hadza children are clear-eyed and energetic, and like their parents, they are cheerful. Somewhere it has been suggested that hunter-gatherers seem happier than farmers, and of necessity more versatile and alert than people who live mostly in a rut. But their good spirits may come also from their varied diet, which is far healthier than the ugali and pombe fare of the shamba dwellers they are told to emulate.

Magandula watches the white man watching the small dark naked bodies in the branches. "*Kama nyani,*" he jeers, with terrific ambivalence, for Magandula is in pain—"Just like baboons!" He searches our faces for the affirmation that he feared was there before he spoke. "Look at old Mutu, and that old woman!" he bursts out again, pointing. "Life is too hard here!" And the old woman herself, coming home one day with her rag sack, speaks of berries with disdain. "Ugali is better," she declares, to show her acquaintance with maize meal paste, although ugali is woefully poor in both taste and nutrition.

Magandula's emotion is disturbing because he is angry without provocation, therefore afraid, therefore fanatic. And what can Magandula be afraid of? Unless he fears that he has lost touch with his origins, his clans, the earth and the old ways, with no real hope or promise from the new.

As if to bear witness for Magandula, old Mutu comes tottering to his hearth and sinks down in a heap against a stone. He no longer bothers with his bow and arrows, which rot in the bush behind his head; the sad old broken arrows with their tattered vanes are the home of spiders. Mutu is back from begging maize at an Mbulu shamba, and complains as ever of his feet, which are leprously cracked and horned up to the ankle bone. To my touch, his afflicted flesh feels rubbery and dead. Once Mutu walked as far east as Mbulu, where he came by his disease. "Things like *this*"—and he flicks his ruined flesh, contemptuous, lip curling around a villainous old mouthful of snag teeth—"you don't find in the bush." In proof of his corruption by the world, Mutu begs cynically for two *shillingi*—the only Hadza that ever begged at all—and is happy to accept a dove instead. Despite his misery and decrepitude, he has no wish to visit the dispensary at Yaida Chini, and waves away the offer of a ride. Already he has his stone pipe lit, tucking a red cinder into it with his bare fingers, and now he lies back laughing at some ancient joke, coughing ecstatically after the custom of his people.

Twig-legged Mutu is big-bellied as a baby, lying there in the sunlight in his swaddling. He rails at life with unholy satisfaction, and so do the two old women whose hearths adjoin his own at the base of the great tilted rock with the rounded top that might be the gravestone of God. All three worn-out souls are of separate families, and fiercely maintain their family hearths as symbols of the independence which is so vital to the Hadza, although not one has relatives at Gidabembe who might look after him. Yet Mutu has maize and berries for his supper, and so do his two neighbors. And it was Mutu who explained the greatest mystery of life at Gidabembe: how it was, when times were hard, that a scorned people were able to beg maize and tobacco from the Mbulu, who were few and poor here, and living themselves at a subsistence level.

The Hadza claim to perform certain services for the Mbulu, helping them to dig their shambas, tend their stock, and cultivate during the wet season; also, the Mbulu come to them for honey and dawa. But these infrequent services cannot account for the munificence of the Mbulu, and it seems clear from the quantity of maize obtained that the Hadza are not begging, but go to the shambas with every expectation of reward.

For the Mbulu, death is a great disaster, and the evil effects or pollutions that they fear the most are those associated with dead bodies. In former days, bodies were left to the hyenas, as with the Maasai, but nowadays, according to Mutu, who is borne out in every particular by Giga and Nangai, the dead person is buried quickly, after which a Hadza is summoned who is of the same sex as the dead. The Hadza shaves the head of the bereaved, who then strips himself naked and presents to the Hadza his clothes and all belongings of the dead person except money, which is not thought of as polluted, and also four debes (the debe or four-gallon kerosene can is the standard container in the bush) of maize. He or she then copulates with the Hadza, who thereby inherits the disaster, and will die eventually of this act. "He may count his years," cries Magandula, who writhes at Mutu's words but does not deny them, "but it will catch him before long." Mutu is emphatic about his facts, pounding his old hand on the earth to simulate copulation. When he is finished he averts his gaze, shrugging his shoulders. Such was the penalty that his people paid for being poor; there was nothing to be done about it. But Nangai and Magandula say they would not perform such a service; it is only for these wild Hadza, who are so poor that they have no choice. (Perhaps the game scouts spread the word that there were wild Hadza at Gidabembe, for not long after our departure Enderlein sent evil news: "The people there were rounded up and taken to Yaida Chini, arriving in time for a measles epidemic in which nine Hadza children died.")

Listening politely to the shouts of Magandula, the hunters do not protest. They accept the scorn of their fellow man as a part of Hadza life. On the other hand, they prefer to remain in the bush. "I have got used to it," says Chandalua, who is Yaida's older brother and the father of the boy Saidi. With Dafi, he lives ordinarily in the Giyeda Barakh, on the far side of the Yaida, overlooking Lake Eyasi: Giyeda Barakh, known in their click-speech as *Hani'abi*, "the rocks," will be a last stronghold of the Hadza. Chandalua's gentle face has the transparence of infinity. Sitting on his warm stone notching an arrow shaft, he smiles approvingly on Magandula, who still scrubs fiercely at his shoes.

A stony path of rhino, man, and elephant leads up into Sipunga, and ascending it one morning, we met four lean Mangati entering the valley armed with spears and poisoned arrows. The arrows are illegal, since only the Hadza are permitted to hunt here without restraint, but rather than kill their scraggy beasts, the meat-eating Mangati poach wherever possible.

Both groups stop at a little distance, regarding each other without pleasure. The tall sandaled Mangati, cowled and scarified with half-circles of raised welts about the eyes, are handsome remote men with a hard cast to their gaze. They look like legendary desert bandits, and their spears have a honed shine. But our party is the stronger, with two white men and the armed game scout Nangai, as well as Salibogo, Andaranda, and Maduru; we have two rifles and three bows. When Nangai steps forward and takes hold of the poisoned arrows, the Mangati leader abandons his bad smile. He refuses to let go, and his companions, scowling, shift their feet. The youngest, a very beautiful cold-faced morani, not yet twenty, makes contemptuous remarks to Andaranda, who steps past him on his pigeon-toed bare feet and continues up the trail. To save face for both sides, it is decided that the shafts will not be taken, only the arrowheads, and the two groups part in silence, looking back over their shoulders until the others are out of sight.

The few Mangati in the region of Gidabembe are at peace with the Hadza, who have nothing worth taking away. "They do not kill us now," the Hadza say. But the hunters, who are small and peaceable and claim no territory, are neither defenseless nor lacking in courage, and their forbearance has its limits. Not long ago, near Tandusi, to the south, some Hadza caught two Mangati moran in a prized bee tree, and when the Mangati defied a request that they come down, shot them out of it with lance arrows, killing both.

The Mangati, too, pay careful attention to death. An elder's funeral may last nine months, while a monument of mud, dung, and poles some twelve feet high is erected in stages on the grave; at the end of the final ceremonies, as darkness falls, two ancient men crawl naked to the deserted mound and fasten a magic vine about its base, whispering, "Don't hurry, wait for us, we will join you soon." Most women and all children are left to the hyenas, but a female elder of good repute may also be given a small mound on which her wood spoon and clay cooking pot are placed. Toward the end of a brief mourning period, a hole is poked through the clay pot, to signify that her work on earth is done.


We climb steadily through the early morning, across dry open hillsides without flowers. In a broad pile of dik-dik droppings on the trail is a small hole six inches deep and six across. Though it moves in daylight with the shadows of rock and bush, the tiny antelope returns at night to these rabbity heaps out in the open; here it feels safe from stealing enemies, and waits out the long African dark. Dik-dik (so the Dorobo say) once tripped over the mighty dung pile of an elephant, and has tried ever since to reply in kind by collecting its tiny droppings in one place. Man takes advantage of the habit by concealing in a hole a ring of thorns with the points facing inward and down. The dik-dik—meaning "quick-quick" in Swahili—cannot extract its delicate leg, and is killed by the first predator to come along. Whoever is hunting here is not a Hadza, for the Hadza know nothing of traps or snares of any kind.

Rhinoceros, also sedentary in their habits, follow the same trails to water, dust wallow, and browse, and on a grand scale share this custom of adding to old piles of their own droppings, which are then booted all about, perhaps as a means of marking territory but more likely as an aid to orientation in a beast whose prodigious sniff must compensate for its poor eyesight. Rhino piles are common on this path, together with wallows and the primitive three-toed print. Not far away, one or more of these beasts is listening, flicking its ears separately in the adaptation that accounts in part for its uncanny hearing, and making up its rudimentary mind whether or not to clear the air with a healthy charge.

The ridge is open, with thick trees and granite islands; a squirrel sways among strange star-shaped fruits of a sterculia. Andaranda on his short bent legs, a hyrax swinging from his waist, views all about him with a smile. His bare feet, impervious to burrs and stones, thump steadily against the earth, and his hands, too, are tough as stumps, as they must be in a life so close to bees and thorns and fire. The trail arrives at a water point, Halanogamai, which Mbulu or Mangati have fenced off with thorn brush to keep out wild animals. Enderlein attacks the fence without a word, hurling it into high piles for a bonfire, and the Hadza drag wood to the fire that has nothing to do with the thorn fence, the threat of which to their way of life they have not grasped. Maduru gets a thorn branch stuck to his back, and I pick him free. One day, emerging from beneath the Land Rover, I was picked free by Salibogo, and another day by Gimbe; no African would expect thanks for this basic courtesy, and Maduru did not pause to thank me now.

On the far side of the Sipunga, the track turns north, skirting the heads of narrow gorges; the gorges open out on a broad prospect of the Yaida Plain, pale in the desert sun of summer. All along the rim rise granite monoliths, and at one of these vast rocks known as Maseiba there lived until a few years ago an old Hadza named Seira and his wife Nyaiga. One day, says Maduru, Seira was out hunting hyrax, and had killed five with his bow, but the sixth fell into a dark crevice which hid a snake. Seira, three times bitten—Maduru slaps his arm, then chest, then side—ran home and applied snakebite dawa. Feeling better, he lay down to rest. But unlike most hunters, who avoid encumbrance, Seira had two wives, and Nyaiga was very jealous of the second wife, even though she lived at Gidabembe. Nyaiga rubbed arrow poison into Seira's bites and he shortly died.

The Hadza leave the elephant trail, circling west through windy glades toward high rocks bright with orange, blue-gray, and crusting gray-green lichens. Below, a cleft between two portals forms a window on the Yaida plain, and nestled in the cleft, entirely hidden from the world except from the spot on which we stand, is a small ledge shaded by a grove of three commiphora. The myrrh trees stand in heraldic triangle, and set against their scaly trunks are three shelters so well camouflaged by cut branches that the trees appear to grow out of a thicket. In seasons when the commiphora is in leaf, the shelters would not be visible at all.

We descend quietly, watched from hiding by the inhabitants. This place is Sangwe, Maduru whispers, and eight Hadza live here. They are very shy and hide behind the huts, though they have recognized Maduru, and been greeted. All three huts are roofed and lined with grass. The wall of one sustains the next, and the tight interiors are spare and orderly as new bird nests. As at Gidabembe, there is no scent of human waste and no notice taken of the seedy feces of baboons. Between the huts and the ledge rim where the cleft falls away into the canyon is a place scarcely large enough for the cooking fire, and beside the fire, on a kongoni hide, lies a strongly built young Hadza with a twisted eye and a stiff right hand bent back toward his wrist by the burnt hide. Healed flesh on his deformed left foot is a bare pink, but the crust on a hand-sized wound over his heel is oozing. This is Magawa, in whose wild eyes I see the choking struggle in the fire, and the thrashing on his rock of pain in the weeks afterward, under the far, unforgiving eye of the sun god, Haine.

Magawa says that he fled the clinic at Mbulu because he could not live so far from Sangwe, and like Mutu, he has no wish to go to Yaida Chini even though here he must remain a helpless cripple. Maduru decides to go to Yaida Chini in Magawa's place, and instead of remaining behind at Sangwe, he comes with us. The others watch Maduru go, and Magandula would say that in time they, too, will depart, leaving Magawa to the lions.

. . .

Nangai and Maduru know of a great rock with red paintings, which in this land may be thousands of years old; more recent drawings, usually abstract, are done in white and gray. Earlier this morning, off the trail, we found a large cave almost hidden in the thicket that had overgrown its mouth; Maduru had not known about this cave, which is occupied at present by bats and hornets but also contains an ancient hearth and vertical red stripes. The Hadza have no special curiosity about red markings, since every tree and boulder in this land which gives them life has its own portent and significations.

We descend the ridge, moving southeast along Sipunga. Maduru points out the holes of bees into which he has wedged stones. If the entrance to a hive must be enlarged to reach the honey, and if stones are handy, one or more may be stuck into the hole until the entrance is reduced again to the size approved by bees. "We put stones here," Salibogo says, "so that the honey will come back." Stones stuck in trees are one of the few signs of the presence of Hadza, who unlike the Mbulu and Mangati are invisible in their environment; they have no idea of wilderness, for they are part of it. At the foot of a ravine a bird comes to the trees with urgent trilling, then flies off again, pursued by Salibogo and Andaranda, who are trilling urgently themselves. This bird is the black-throated honey guide, which has evolved the astonishing habit of leading honey badger and man to the hives of bees and feasting upon the leavings of the raid; if no honey is left for the honey guide, Africans say, it will lead the next man to a snake or lion. But this bird is soon back again, still trilling, having left the Hadza far away under the hill.

Southeastward, under the soaring rock, we follow in the noble paths of elephant. Maduru points at an overhanging wall, like a wave of granite on the yellow sky: Darashagan. A hot climb brings us out at last onto a ledge under the overhang, well hidden by the tops of trees that rise from the slopes below; the ledge looks south down the whole length of the Yaida Valley. There is a hearth here, still in use, and on the wall behind the hearth, sheltered by the overhang, are strong paintings in a faded red of a buffalo and a giraffe. We stand before them in a line, in respectful silence. One day another man, all nerves and blood and hope just like ourselves, drew these emblems of existence with a sharpened bird bone spatula, a twist of fur, a feather, and others squatted here to watch, much as the Hadza are squatting now. The Mbulu and Barabaig have no tradition of rock painting, whereas the Bushmen, before they became fugitives, made paintings very similar to these. The only other red paintings in this country are found in the region of Kondoa-Irangi, in the land of the click-speaking Sandawe.

Andaranda makes a fire and broils hyrax and a guinea fowl. When we have eaten, he picks grewia leaves, and the Hadza trim the leaves and roll tobacco from their pouches. I try Nangai's uncultivated weed, and the Hadza giggle at my coughs. Of the drawings they say shyly, "How can we know?" Pressed, they ascribe them to the Old People or to Mungu (God), searching our faces in the hope of learning which one we prefer: our need to *understand* makes them uncomfortable. For people who must live from day to day, past and future have small relevance, and their grasp of it is fleeting; they live in the moment, a very precious gift that we have lost.

Lying back against these ancient rocks of Africa, I am content. The great stillness in these landscapes that once made me restless seeps into me day by day, and with it the unreasonable feeling that I have found what I was searching for without ever having discovered what it was. In the ash of the old hearth, ant lions have countersunk their traps and wait in the loose dust for their prey; far overhead a falcon—and today I do not really care whether it is a peregrine or lanner—sails out over the rim of rock and on across the valley. The day is beautiful, my belly full, and returning to the cave this afternoon will be returning home. For the first time, I am in Africa among Africans. We understand almost nothing of one another, yet we are sharing the same water flask, our fingers touching in the common bowl. At Halanogamai there is a spring, and at Darasha-gan are red rock paintings—that is all.


In a few swift days of a dry summer this ancient cave in central Africa, blackened by centuries of smoke, has become for me my own ancestral place where fifty millenniums ago, a creature not so different from myself hunched close to the first fire. The striped swallow that nests under the arch was here before man's upright troupes came through the silent baobabs, and so were the geckos, hornets, and small mice that go about their bright-eyed business undisturbed.

Giga and Gimbe mind the cave, which stays cool in the dry heat of the day, and one or the other is always by the fire, playing delicately on an mbira. Meals are at random in the African way, and we have no wish to give them order. We eat before going on a hunt and after we return, and on some days there are two meals and on others four or five. When least expected and most wanted, Gimbe will come with a basin of fresh water—karibu—and then he will stir our posho into his charred pot with his wood spoon and present this warming stuff with a fine stew of whatever wild meat is at hand. In the afternoons, we bathe in the river and stand on the cool banks to dry, and toward twilight almost every night we climb onto the top-pled monolith that forms the roof over the cave, and smoke, and watch the sun go down over Sipunga.

To the rock cast like a gravestone, the oldest woman, muttering, comes home each twilight with a bundle of sticks for her night fire. When, out of happiness, I greet her, she gives me the cold cheerless stare of ancient women—Why do you greet me, idiot? Can't you see the way that the world goes?—and totters past me to her hearth without a word. At darkness, in wind, three fires light the rock face, with leaping shadows of the three small human forms, clattering and cawing under the skeleton of their lone tree. But the dance of shadows dies as the fires dim, and the three panakwetepi, the "old children," fall silent. The eldest draws bat-colored rags about her, hunched and nodding, and subsides into a little heap of dim mortality. I wonder if she hears hyenas howling.

An Mbulu donkey gives its maniacal cry, and far away on the escarpment, probing slowly across the mountain darkness, shine the hard eyes of a truck, bringing in cheap trade goods for the duka. From the Seven Hearths, the Hadza see the outside world, but the world cannot see them. "This valley, this people—it is a tragedy we are watching!" Enderlein cries. "And it is a sign of what is happening everywhere in this country, in the whole world! Sometimes I really don't think it is bearable to watch it, I have not the heart for it, I will have to leave. And other times, especially when I am drunk, I can see myself as a spectator at the greatest comedy there ever was, the obliteration of mankind by our own hand."

When the air grows cold we come down off the rock. In the cave, Hadza are gathered at the fire, shoulder to shoulder like the swallows, clicking endlessly in their warm tongue, with big signs and little groans of emphasis and soft *n* and *anh* and *m* sounds, hands moving in and out among the embers, the scraping of a knife blade on a stone, a cough, a whiff of bangi, until finally the people of the Seven Hearths depart. The last man squatting, Magandula, crawls off to his sleep with a loud self-conscious sigh that tells the white men, stretched silent as two dead beneath the stars, that the worldly Magandula, although patient to a fault, has no place among such simple folk. Already Giga the fire tender is breathing his night breath that sounds like a man pulled down in flight; I watch his face, asleep, and feel a tingling at the temples. Giga has been in Africa forever, he is the prototypic model of a man, the clay, and one loves not Giga but this being who is mortal, a kind humorous fellow of great presence and no small intelligence who will die. And Gimbe, too, singing his songs and playing his sweet irimbako, and even the brash Magandula, donning his magic street shoes for his flight from the old ways: to perceive them in their sleep—Enderlein, too—is to perceive and to make peace with one's own self.

Toward dawn, Giga hurls faggots on the fire and rolls himself a fat and lumpy smoke and coughs and coughs and coughs to his heart's content, and one forgives him even this. Soon the cricket stops its singing, and after a silence there is birdsong, the bell note of the slate-colored boubou, the doves and turacos, a hornbill. At sun-up comes an electric screeching that signals the passage of swift petal-colored lovebirds.

The Hadza hunch close to their fires, getting warm; when the sun has heat in it, the day begins. Soon the akwetepi, the "little people," come past the cave, first boys with bows, then younger children seeking berries—"*Shai-yaamo!*" they call. And the answer is *Shai-yamo mtana*, to which they echo a soft *m-taa-na*. They pull berry branches down and strip them, laughing. At the fire, long-legged in shorts and boots, the restless white men sip their tea and listen, warming cold hands on their tin cups. In the next days we will go away without the game scout Magandula, who is muttering about poachers in this region, and asks if he might linger in the bush.

The last day at the cave is slow and peaceful. The hunters come down from the Seven Hearths to a discreet fire from where they can spy politely on the visitors; they carve and chew and soften and sight new arrow shafts, bracing them by inserting them between the toes, or cut pipe holes into new pieces of stone found in the river.

"*Dong-go-ko.*" One man sings softly of zebras and lions. "*Dong-go-ko gogosala . . .*"

Zebra, zebra, running fast . . .

The women are out gathering roots and tubers, and also the silken green nut of the baobab which, pounded on a stone and cooked a little, provides food for five months of the year. The still air of the hillside quakes with the pound of rock on rock, and in this place so distant from the world, the steady sound is an echo of the Stone Age. Sometimes the seeds are left inside the hull to make a baby's rattle, or a half shell may be kept to make a drinking cup. In the rains, the baobab gives shelter, and in drought, the water that it stores in its soft hollows, and always fiber thread and sometimes honey. Perhaps the greatest baobab were already full grown when man made red rock paintings at Darashagan. Today young baobab are killed by fires, set by the strangers who clear the country for their herds and gardens, and the tree where man was born is dying out in Hadza Land.

From a grove off in the western light, an arrow rises, piercing the sun poised on the dark massif of the Sipunga; the shaft glints, balances, and drops to earth. Soon the young hunters, returning homeward, come in single file between the trees, skins black against black silhouetted thorn. One has an mbira, and in wistful monotony, in hesitation step, the naked forms pass one by one with their small bows in a slow dance of childhood, the figures winding in and out among black thorn and tawny twilight grass, and vanishing once more as in a dream, like a band of the Old People, the small Gumba, who long ago went into hiding in the earth.

# *from* The Snow Leopard

**1978**

*Considered by many to be Matthiessen's best work of nonfiction,* The
Snow Leopard *describes a two-hundred-and-fifty-mile trek across the
Himalayas taken by Matthiessen and the wildlife biologist George
Schaller (called GS throughout), whom we first met in* The Tree
Where Man Was Born. *Matthiessen and Schaller, with a small
band of sherpas and porters, set out for the Crystal Mountain on the
Tibetan Plateau to study blue sheep and try to glimpse the legendary
snow leopard. The journey was far more than a field study: Matthiessen's wife Deborah Love (referred to in his text as D) had just died of
cancer, and for Matthiessen, a committed student (and later teacher)
of Zen, the trip was also one of reflection and spiritual self-
interrogation. In addition to his field research, Matthiessen hoped to
visit the remote Crystal or Shey Monastery and pay tribute to its resident Lama of Shey.* The Snow Leopard *begins with a quotation
from Rilke that could stand as an emblem of Matthiessen's work as a
whole: "That is at bottom the only courage that is demanded of us: to
have courage for the most strange, the most singular and the most
inexplicable that we may encounter. That mankind has in this sense
been cowardly has done life endless harm; the experiences that are
called visions, the whole so-called spirit-world, death, all those things
that are so closely akin to us, have by daily parrying been so crowded
out of life that the senses with which we could have grasped them are
atrophied. To say nothing of God."*

*The following excerpt, taken from "At Crystal Mountain," fuses
the scientific and spiritual elements of Matthiessen's journey and permits him to reflect upon the Buddhist teachings: "'Regard as one, this
life, the next life, and the life between,' wrote Milarepa. And some-*

*times I wonder into which life I have wandered, so still are the long nights here, and so cold."*

# At Crystal Mountain

*November 1*
This Black Pond Camp, though well below the Kang Pass, lies at an altitude of seventeen thousand feet, and an hour after the sun sinks behind the peaks, my wet boots have turned to blocks of ice. GS's thermometer registers −20° Centigrade (4° below zero Fahrenheit) and though I wear everything I have, I quake with cold all night. Dawn comes at last, but making hot water from a pot of ice is difficult at this altitude, and it is past nine before boots are thawed and we are under way.

The snow bowl is the head of an ice river that descends a deep canyon to Shey. In the canyon we meet Jang-bu and Phu-Tsering, on their way up to fetch some food and pots: Dawa, they say, is down again with acute snow blindness.

Sherpa tracks in the frozen shadows follow the glassy boulders of the stream edge, and somewhere along the way I slip, losing the hoopoe feather that adorned my cap. The river falls steeply, for Shey lies three thousand feet below Kang La, and in the deep snow, the going is so treacherous that the sherpas have made no path; each man flounders through the drifts as best he can. Eventually, from a high corner of the canyon, rough red-brown lumps of human habitation come in view. The monastery stands like a small fort on a bluff where another river flows in from the east; a mile below, the rivers vanish into a deep and dark ravine. Excepting the lower slopes of the mountainside behind the monastery, which is open to the south, most of this treeless waste lies under snow, broken here and there by calligraphic patterns of bare rock, in an atmosphere so wild and desolate as to overwhelm the small huddle of dwellings.

High to the west, a white pyramid sails on the sky—the Crystal Mountain. In summer, this monument of rock is a shrine for pilgrims from all over Dolpo and beyond, who come here to make a prescribed circle around the Crystal Mountain and attend a holy festival at Shey. What is stirring about this peak, in snow time, is its powerful shape, which even today, with no clouds passing, makes it appear to be forging through the blue. . . .

A gravel island under Shey is reached by crossing ice and stones of a shallow channel. At the island's lower end are prayer walls and a stone stockade for animals; farther on, small conduits divert a flow of river water to a group of prayer mills in the form of waterwheels, each one housed separately in its own stone shrine. The conduits are frozen and the wheels are still. On top of the small stupas are offerings of white quartz crystals, presumably taken from the Crystal Mountain in the summer, when the five wheels spin five ancient prayer drums, sending OM MANI PADME HUM down the cold canyon.

On the far side of a plank bridge, a path climbs the bank to two big red-and-white entrance stupas on the bluff: I go up slowly. Prayer flags snap thinly on the wind, and a wind-bell has a wooden wing in the shape of a half-moon that moves the clapper; over the glacial rumble on the river stones, the wistful ring on the light wind is the first sound that is heard here at Shey Gompa.

The cluster of a half-dozen stone houses is stained red, in sign that Shey is a monastery, not a village. Another group of five small houses sits higher up the mountain; above this hamlet, a band of blue sheep may be seen with the naked eye. Across the river to the north, stuck on a cliff face at the portals of the canyon, is a red hermitage. Otherwise, except for prayer walls and the stone corrals, there are only the mighty rock formations and dry treeless mountainside where snow has melted, and the snow and sky.

I move on slowly, dull in mind and body. Gazing back up the Black River toward the rampart of icy cornices, I understand that we have come over the Kanjirobas to the mountain deserts of the Tibetan Plateau: we have crossed the Himalaya from south to north. But not until I had to climb this short steep path from the wintry river to the bluffs did I realize how tired I was after thirty-five days of hard trekking. And here I am, on this first day of November, standing before the Crystal Monastery, with its strange stones and flags and bells under the snows.

The monastery temple with its attached houses forms a sort of open court facing the south. Two women and two infants, sitting in the sun, make no sign of welcome. Fearing Kham-pa brigands, the women had locked themselves into their houses a few days ago, when Jang-bu and GS first appeared, and plainly they are still suspicious of our seemingly inexplicable mission. The younger woman is weaving a rough cloth on an ancient loom. When I say, *"Namaste!"* she repeats it, as if trying the word out. Three scraggy *dzos* and an old black nanny goat excepted, these are the only sentient beings left at Shey, which its inhabitants call Somdo, or "Confluence," because of the meeting of rivers beneath its bluff—the Kangju, "Snow Waters" (the one I think of as Black River, because of the black pond at its head, and the black eagle, and the black patterns of its stones and ice in the dark canyon), and the Yeju, "Low Waters" (which I shall call White River, because it comes down from the eastern snows).

For cooking hut and storeroom, Jang-bu has appropriated the only unlocked dwelling. Like all the rest, it has a flat roof of clay and saplings piled on top with brushwood, a small wooden door into the single room, and a tiny window in the western wall to catch afternoon light. The solitary ray of light, as in a medieval painting, illumines the smoke-blackened posts that support the roof, which is so low that GS and I must bend half-over. The earth floor is bare, except for a clay oven built up in three points to hold a pot, with a hole near the floor to blow life into the smoky fire of dung or brushwood. . . .

The cooking hut is the sometime dwelling of the brother of the younger woman, Tasi Chanjun, whom the sherpas call Namu, meaning hostess. (Among Tibetans as among native Americans, it is often rude to address people by their formal name.) Her little boy, aged about four, is Karma Chambel, and her daughter, perhaps two, is Nyima Poti. Nyima means "sun" or "sunny"—Sunny Poti! The old woman's name is Sonam: her husband, Chang Rapke, and her daughter Karima Poti have gone away to winter in Saldang, and Sonam lives alone in the abandoned hamlet up the mountain. Namu says that before the snows there were forty people here, including twenty-odd monks and two lamas: all are gone across the mountains to Saldang, from where — is this a warning to outlandish men who come here without women? — her husband will return in a few days. Namu's husband has the key to the Crystal Monastery, or so she says, and will doubtless bring it with him when he comes to visit, in four or five days, or in twenty. Namu is perhaps thirty years old, and pretty in a sturdy way, and self-dependent. She speaks familiarly of B'od but not Nepal; even Ring-mo is a foreign land, far away across Kang La.

That the Lama is gone is very disappointing. Nevertheless, we are extremely happy to be here, all the more so since it often seemed that we would never arrive at all. Now we can wake up in the morning without having to put on wet boots, break camp, get people moving; and there is home to return to in the evening. There are no porters harassing our days, and we are sheltered, more or less, from evil weather. The high pass between Shey and the outside world lies in the snow peaks, ghostly now in the light of the cold stars. "God, I'm glad I'm not up there tonight," GS exclaims, as we emerge from the smoky hut, our bellies warm with lentil soup. We know how fortunate it was that the Kang Pass was crossed in this fine, windless weather, and wonder how long fair skies will hold, and if Tukten and Gyaltsen will appear. It is November now, and everything depends upon the snows.

### November 2

At almost fifteen thousand feet, Shey is as high as the Jang Pass. It is located in what has been described as Inner Dolpo, which is walled off from eastern Dolpo by a surrounding crescent of high peaks, and must be one of the highest inhabited areas on earth. Its people are of pure Tibetan stock, with a way of life that cannot differ much from that of the Ch'ang Tartars out of Central Asia who are thought to have been the original Tibetans, and their speech echoes the tongue of nomads who may have arrived two thousand years ago. Dolpo was formerly a part of western Tibet, and it is certain that some form of Buddhism came here early. Beyond the Karnali River, to the north and west, the Tibetan Plateau rises to Kailas, the holy "Mount Sumeru" or "Meru" of Hindus and Buddhists, home of Shiva and the Center of the world; from Mount Kailas, four great

rivers—the Karnali, the Indus, the Sutlej, and the Brahmaputra—
flow down in a great mandala to the Indian seas. . . .

On my way here, I entertained visions of myself in monkish garb
attending the Lama in his ancient mysteries, and getting to light the
butter lamps into the bargain; I suppose I had hoped he would be
my teacher. That the gompa is locked and the Lama gone away
might be read as a karmic reprimand to spiritual ambition, a silent
teaching to this ego that still insists upon itself, like the poor bleat of
a goat on the north wind.

Last night, the temperature sank to −13° Centigrade and a strong
east wind rattled my tent: this morning I move the tent into the
stockyard of an empty house. On the corral walls lie some excellent
stone carvings, one of them portraying Tara (in Tibetan, *Dölma*),
born of the compassionate tear of Avalokita (Chen-resigs) and the
embodiment of the Bodhisattva spirit. As the feminine aspect of
Chen-resigs, Dölma is the great "Protectress" of Tibet, and so I am
pleased to find her on my wall.

The temple is distinguished from the buildings that abut it on
both sides by the ceremonial raised entrance under a roofed porch
and the abundant ornaments upon the roof, which include prayer
flags, tritons, the great horns of an argali, and the gigantic antlers of
a Sikkim stag, a creature of northern Bhutan and southeastern
Tibet. (Since neither animal is supposed to occur here, GS is fascinated by the origins of these horns and antlers, especially since the
Sikkim stag is said to be extinct.)

Although the gompa is locked tight, the two large stupas on the
bluff over the river bridge give a clue to the iconography within.
Perhaps thirty feet high, they have the typical square red base and
red-garlanded white dome, with a tapering cone topped by a lunar
crown and solar disc. On the four sides of the base are crude clay
frescoes of symbolic creatures—elephants on the east face, horses
south, peacocks west, and on the north face the garuda, or mythical
hawk, here represented as a man with wings bearing what appears
to be the sun and moon. The garuda, like the swastikas inside the
stupa, is a pre-Buddhist symbol, and so is the yin-yang symbol on

the door, which is thought to antedate the early Taoism of three thousand years ago in China. . . .

Between these stupas and the monastery houses, heaped up into a platform five feet high, is a whole field of carved slabs, thousands upon thousands, by far the greatest assemblage of prayer stones that I have ever seen, before or since. OM MANI PADME HUM is the commonest inscription, but there are also wheels of life, carved Buddhas, and quotations from liturgical texts, heap upon heap. The stones vary in weight from ten pounds to several hundred; some are recent, while on others, the inscriptions are worn to shadow by the elements, and all of these conceal the masses more that lie beneath. In addition, a great wall of these stones nearly encircles the monastery and its adjoining houses as well as a group of smaller stupas on the northern side, and there are extensive prayer-stone walls on the river island and along the paths as well. The prayer stones at the bottom of these walls must be many centuries old. Though nobody seems to know who lived here when the first of them were made, the great accumulation of old stones in the Shey region supports the idea that the Crystal Mountain is a very ancient shrine of Tibetan Buddhism, and perhaps B'on before it. Samling Monastery, not far north of this mountain, is an old redoubt of B'on and the repository of B'on's most ancient texts, and I like to imagine that this archaic kingdom might be none other than the Kingdom of Sh'ang-Sh'ung that the B'on-pos claim as the home of their religion. That Sh'ang-Sh'ung is deemed "mythical" may be discounted: the Land of Dolpo is not found in the geographies, and it seems mythical even to such people as myself, who like to imagine they have been here.

This morning I bathe inside my sunny tent, and sort out gear. Dawa is still groaning with snow blindness, but Jang-bu and Phu-Tsering have crossed Black River to hunt scraps of low shrub juniper for firewood, and GS is up on this Somdo mountainside viewing his sheep; he returns half-frozen toward midmorning. After a quick meal of chapatis, we set off on a survey of other sheep populations in the region, heading eastward up the Saldang trail, which follows the north bank of the White River. Like the Saure and other east-west rivers in this season, this one is snowbound on the side that faces north, and across the water, we can see snow tracks of marmot, wandering outward in weird patterns from a burrow; perhaps the animals, sent underground too early by those blizzards of the late monsoon, had gone out foraging. But they are hibernated now, there is no fresh marmot sign, the land seems empty.

Snow clouds come up over the mountains, and the shining river turns to black, over black rocks. A lone black dzo nuzzles the stony earth. GS has picked up scat of a large carnivore and turns it in his hand, wondering aloud why fox sign, so abundant at Black Pond, is uncommon here at lower altitudes. "Too big for fox, I think. . . ."

As GS speaks, I scan the mountain slopes for bharal: on these rolling hills to the east of Somdo, we have not seen even one. Abruptly, he says, "Hold it! Freeze! Two snow leopard!" I see a pale shape slip behind a low rise patched with snow, as GS, agitated, mutters, "Tail's too short! Must have been foxes—!"

"No!" I say. "Much too big—!"

"Wolves!" he cries out. "Wolves!"

And there they are.

Moving away without haste up an open slope beyond the rise, the wolves bring the barren hills to life. Two on the slope to northward frisk and play, but soon they pause to look us over; their tameness is astonishing. Then they cut across the hill to join three others that are climbing a stone gully. The pack stops each little while to gaze at us, and through the telescope we rejoice in every shining hair: two silver wolves, and two of faded gold, and one that is the no-color of frost: this frost-colored wolf, a big male, seems to be leader. All have black tail tips and a delicate black fretting on the back. "That's why there's no sign of fox or leopard!" GS says, "and that's why the blue sheep stay near the river cliffs, away from this open country!" I ask if the wolves would hunt and kill the fox and leopard, and he says they would. For some reason, the wolves' appearance here has taken us by surprise; it is in Tibet that such mythic creatures belong. This is an Asian race of *Canis lupus*, the timber wolf, which both of us have seen in Alaska, and it is always an exciting animal: the empty hills where the pack has gone have come to life. In a snow patch are five sets of wolf tracks, and old wolf scats along the path contain brittle gray stuff and soft yellow hair—blue sheep and marmot.

Down the path comes an old woman who has walked alone from Saldang, over the Shey Pass to the east; we are as surprised by her appearance as she is by ours. The old woman has seen the five *jangu*, and two more, but seems less wary of the wolves than of big strangers.

We wonder about the solitary dzo, not more than a half-mile from the place where we had turned the wolves back toward the east. Later Namu says that wolves kill two or three dzos every year, and five or six sheep at a time in the corrals. She sets out upriver to fetch her dzo, and is back with the lone beast just before sundown.

### November 3

There is so much that enchants me in this spare, silent place that I move softly so as not to break a spell. Because the taking of life has been forbidden by the Lama of Shey, bharal and wolves alike draw near the monastery. On the hills and in the stone beds of the river are fossils from blue ancient days when all this soaring rock lay beneath the sea. And all about are the prayer stones, prayer flags, prayer wheels, and prayer mills in the torrent, calling on all the elements in nature to join in celebration of the One. What I hear from my tent is a delicate wind-bell and the river from the east, in this easterly wind that may bring a change in the weather. At daybreak, two great ravens come, their long toes scratching on the prayer walls.

The sun refracts from the white glaze of the mountains, chills the air. Old Sonam, who lives alone in the hamlet up the hill, was on the mountain before day, gathering the summer's dung to dry and store as cooking fuel; what I took for lumpish matter straightens on the sky as the sun rises, setting her gaunt silhouette afire.

Eleven sheep are visible on the Somdo slope above the monastery, six rams together and a group of ewes and young; though the bands begin to draw near to one another and sniff urine traces, there is no real sign of rut. From our lookout above Sonam's house, three more groups—six, fourteen, and twenty-six—can be seen on the westward slopes, across Black River.

Unable to hold the scope on the restless animals, GS calls out to me to shift the binoculars from the band of fourteen to the group of six sheep, directly across the river from our lookout. "Why are those sheep running?" he demands, and a moment later hollers, "Wolves!" All six sheep are springing for the cliffs, but a pair of wolves coming straight downhill are cutting off the rearmost animal as it bounds across a stretch of snow toward the ledges. In the hard light, the blue-gray creature seems far too swift to catch, yet the streaming wolves gain ground on the hard snow. Then they are whisking through the matted juniper and down over steepening rocks, and it appears that the bharal will be cut off and bowled over, down the mountain, but at the last moment it scoots free and gains a narrow ledge where no wolf can follow.

In the frozen air, the whole mountain is taut; the silence rings. The sheep's flanks quake, and the wolves are panting; otherwise, all is still, as if the arrangement of pale shapes held the world together. Then I breathe, and the mountain breathes, setting the world in motion once again.

Briefly, the wolves gaze about, then make their way up the mountainside in the unhurried gait that may carry them fifty miles in a single day. Two pack mates join them, and in high yak pasture the four pause to romp and roll in dung. Two of these were not among the five seen yesterday, and we recall that the old woman had seen seven. Then they trot onward, disappearing behind a ridge of snow. The band of fourteen sheep high on this ridge gives a brief run of alarm, then forms a line on a high point to stare down at the wolves and watch them go. Before long, all are browsing once again, including the six that were chased onto the precipice.

Turning to speak, we just shake our heads and grin. "It was worth walking five weeks just to see that," GS sighs at last. "That was the most exciting wolf hunt I ever saw." And a little later, exhilarated still, he wonders aloud if I remember "that rainy afternoon in the Serengeti when we watched wild dogs make a zebra kill in that strange storm light on the plain, and all those thousands of animals running?" I nod. I am still excited by the wolves seen so close yesterday, and to see them again, to watch them hunt blue sheep in such fashion, flying down across the cliffs within sight of our tents at Shey Gompa—what happiness!

### November 4

Descending from steep snowfields under Crystal Mountain is a series of ridges that terminate in buttresses or points where the mountain falls away into Black River; between these ridges, each one higher than the next as the path goes north, lie deep ravines. Winding in and out of these ravines, the path follows the contour around the outer points, which like all eminences in the region are marked by prayer flags and a wall of prayer stones. In an hour we are opposite the red hermitage, which sits high against the cliff across the gorge: three huge Himalayan griffons turn and turn on the cold updrafts from Black River Canyon. The path continues round the point and into the ravine, which is still in shadow, and sheeted with ice and snow on this north exposure; here the incline is so steep that any misstep might be fatal. At the head of the ravine, the trail crosses an icy stream and climbs up to the hermitage, which is perched on a ledge against bright cliffs of blue and red. A smaller hermitage, more isolated still, sits on the corner of a precipice still farther north. Such locations are traditional for spiritual pursuit in the Tibetan region, "proudly isolated on summits beaten by the wind, amidst wild landscapes, as if bidding defiance to invisible foes at the four corners of the horizon." [Alexandra David-Neel]

Tsakang itself consists of four stone structures plastered to the rock wall, like nests of swifts. One is a cell with a single narrow window slot that looks out on a world of snow and sky, pure white, pure blue; another has crooked doors and windows of carved wood. A tiny potato plot has been constructed on a ledge, and sliced potatoes lie drying on a stone. By the cliff wall are stacks of dung and juniper for winter fuel, and water issues from a cave, dripping sonorously onto slate conduits that conduct it to a copper caldron; in the cave a small stupa has been built in honor of the water.

This hermitage is a true gompa, which is not really a monastery but "a dwelling in the solitude," located wherever possible against a cliff that overlooks a lake or stream, and often inhabited by a solitary monk. Tsakang is bedecked with prayer flags, white and blue, and has an astonishing ornate balconied window painted in red and fire orange, blue, and turquoise; carved Buddha stones adorn its sunny walls.

The hermitage is situated so that nothing may be seen but snow peaks rising to a shining sky; even Shey is hidden by the slopes above the village. The effect is so hallucinatory that GS, disturbed, is stirred to protest at the hermit's life, and solitary meditation: "You have to have *something* coming in!" But the point of meditation is to let everything go: "When your mind is empty like a valley or a canyon, then you will know the power of the Way."

On a ledge, two bronze-skinned monks sit quietly, as if in wait. One is patching his wool boots, the other is curing a goat hide in a yellow mix of goat brains and rancid yak butter. Smiling, calm, they let our greetings wander; perhaps they live here under vows of silence. The boot-mender is a clear-faced youth, little more than twenty, while the other, curiously ageless, is a handsome cripple in strange rags of leather. When we say good-bye, the two figures bow slightly, smile again, and keep their silence.

A steep path climbs to the slope above the cliffs, where the only color is a lichen of unearthly yellow-green; all else is thorn and the shale of mountain desert. On the stones of a large stupa we eat discs of greasy dough that Phu-Tsering identifies as "pancakes"; on other days there are dry-dough chapatis, or "breads," made with green buckwheat flour, unleavened, unadorned—no matter. At supper in the cooking hut, the dull food is disheartening, but here in the mountain sun and wind, in the bright cold, whatever is at hand tastes pure and vital.

Leaving GS to observe the Tsakang sheep, I descend the trail again, to gather fuel. On my way I meet a wild-haired stranger, bound for the hermitage, it seems, since this trail leads nowhere else. Chanting, he comes up the mountain to the ridge point where I have paused to let him pass, and there slings down his basket, steps behind a boulder, squats, returns, and says aggressively, *"Timi kaha gani?"* (You where go?) "Shey Gompa," I say, and he repeats it: we both point at Somdo, to make sure. This wayfarer is clad in blackened sheepskins, with the usual assortment of beads and amulets, silver pouch, silver flint case, silver dagger. Demanding a smoke, he laughs loud in disbelief when I say that I have none, and raises his dagger toward my throat in demonstration of my fate, were he but given to low banditry. Without good-byes, we go our separate ways.

Farther down, where the wolves chased the sheep, lie mats of recumbent juniper, and I cull the tough brush for dead branches. The juniper is the only firewood available, though a stunted birch lives in the deep ravines, beyond the reach of man. With the line I carry in my rucksack, I tie up a big bundle of faggots, and humping it onto my back, descend the mountain, cross the river, and climb the bluff to Shey. The monastery is lively, for as it turns out, the man on the trail is a member of a Saldang group that has come in pursuit of eleven yaks: the beasts had summered here, taken a liking to the place, and returned spontaneously of their own accord. Several animals are visible on the hillside, and others have made their way down to the river islands, where there is more grass.

The visitors crowd into our cook hut to watch the sherpas unload the broken food baskets brought down from Kang La. These herders say that nine or ten wolves pass through Shey regularly on their hunting circuit, and that two or three snow leopards live along the river cliffs.

*November 5*
The snow stopped just at dark last evening, and soon the moon appeared, then stars. This morning the sky is clear: at dawn, the black and shaggy yaks stand motionless by the ice river.

For the first time since September, GS is entirely happy. Like myself, he is stunned by Shey, which has more than repaid the long, hard journey; he scribbles his data even while he eats. I keep thinking, How extraordinary!—knowing that this adjective is inadequate and somehow inaccurate, as well; it's not so much that what we have found here is extraordinary as that all has the immediate reality of that region of the mind where "mountains, wolves . . . snow and fire had realized their true being, or had their source." [Malcolm Lowry] And yet I grow uneasy every day, when dark clouds build in the north and south. At the Kang Pass and southward, it looks as if it is snowing. To waste time in worry that the snow will trap us makes me feel ashamed, all the more so since GS shows no concern. Yet this morning he said that the night view of those icy peaks over which we came was enough to scare him back into his sleeping bag, and of course he knows as well as I do that the monastery has no food to spare us, or not enough, at least, to get everyone through the winter.

In midafternoon, there comes a sudden hail. Soon the hail has turned to snow, and after dark, it is still snowing. Returning from Black Pond, Jang-bu reports that our track down from the Kang Pass has disappeared, and the Saldang people tell us that the trail to Samling, where we hoped to visit in the next few days, is blocked by drifts. As long as the Shey Pass to the east is open, one can cross over to Saldang in a single day, and these people speak of a lower route from Saldang across to Tarap and the Bheri River that usually is passable all winter. However, we have no permit for the Tarap region, nor any wish to spend a winter in the Tarap jail. GS speaks of "passing the Tarap police post at night," but it would be difficult to do this undetected by the dogs. Usually he refers obliquely to the problem, and then when I take it up, will say offhandedly, "Well, let's not dwell on it; let's just do our work, and see what happens."

## November 6

The nights at Shey are rigid, under rigid stars; the fall of a wolf pad on the frozen path might be heard up and down the canyon. But a hard wind comes before the dawn to rattle the tent canvas, and this morning it is clear again, and colder. At daybreak, the White River, just below, is sheathed in ice, with scarcely a murmur from the stream beneath.

The two ravens come to tritons on the gompa roof. *Gorawk, gorawk,* they croak, and this is the name given to them by the sherpas. Amidst the prayer flags and great horns of Tibetan argali, the gorawks greet first light with an odd musical double note—*a-ho*—that emerges as if by miracle from those ragged throats. Before sunrise every day, the great black birds are gone, like the last tatters of departing night.

The sun rising at the head of the White River brings a suffused glow to the tent canvas, and the robin accentor flits away across the frozen yard. At seven, there is breakfast in the cook hut—tea and porridge—and after breakfast on most days I watch sheep with GS, parting company with him after a while, when the sheep lie down, to go off on some expedition of my own. Often I scan the caves and ledges on the far side of Black River in the hope of leopard; I am alert for fossils, wolves, and birds. Sometimes I observe the sky and mountains, and sometimes I sit in meditation, doing my best to empty out my mind, to attain that state in which everything is "at rest, free, and immortal. . . . All things abided eternally as they were in their proper places . . . something infinite behind everything appeared." [Thomas Traheone] (No Buddhist said this, but a seventeenth-century Briton.) And soon all sounds, and all one sees and feels, take on imminence, an immanence, as if the Universe were coming to attention, a Universe of which one is the center, a Universe that is not the same and yet not different from oneself, even from a scientific point of view: within man as within mountains there are many parts of hydrogen and oxygen, of calcium, phosphorus, potassium, and other elements. "You never enjoy the world aright, till the Sea itself flows in your veins, till you are clothed with the heavens, and crowned with the stars: and perceive yourself to be the sole heir of the whole world, and more than so, because men are in it who are every one sole heirs as well as you." [Thomas Traheone]

I have a meditation place on Somdo mountain, a broken rock outcrop like an altar set into the hillside, protected from all but the south wind by shards of granite and dense thorn. In the full sun it is warm, and its rock crannies give shelter to small stunted plants that cling to this desert mountainside—dead red-brown stalks of a wild buckwheat (*Polygonum*), some shrubby cinquefoil, pale edelweiss, and everlasting, and even a few poor wisps of *Cannabis*. I arrange a rude rock seat as a lookout on the world, set out binoculars in case wild creatures should happen into view, then cross my legs and regulate my breath, until I scarcely breathe at all.

Now the mountains all around me take on life; the Crystal Mountain moves. Soon there comes the murmur of the torrent, from far away below under the ice: it seems impossible that I can hear this sound. Even in windlessness, the sound of rivers comes and goes and falls and rises, like the wind itself. An instinct comes to open outward by letting all life in, just as a flower fills with sun. To burst forth from this old husk and cast one's energy abroad, to fly. . . .

Although I am not conscious of emotion, the mind-opening brings a soft mist to my eyes. Then the mist passes, the cold wind clears my head, and body-mind comes and goes on the light air. A sun-filled Buddha. One day I shall meditate in falling snow.

I lower my gaze from the snow peaks to the glistening thorns, the snow patches, the lichens. Though I am blind to it, the Truth is near, in the reality of what I sit on—rocks. These hard rocks instruct my bones in what my brain could never grasp in the Heart Sutra, that "form is emptiness, and emptiness is form"—the Void, the emptiness of blue-black space, contained in everything. Sometimes when I meditate, the big rocks dance.

The secret of the mountains is that the mountains simply exist, as I do myself: the mountains exist simply, which I do not. The mountains have no "meaning," they *are* meaning; the mountains *are*. The sun is round. I ring with life, and the mountains ring, and when I can hear it, there is a ringing that we share. I understand all this, not in my mind but in my heart, knowing how meaningless it is to try to capture what cannot be expressed, knowing that mere words will remain when I read it all again, another day.

Toward four, the sun sets fires on the Crystal Mountain. I turn my collar up and put on gloves and go down to Somdo, where my tent has stored the last sun of the day. In the tent entrance, out of the wind, I drink hot tea and watch the darkness rise out of the earth. The sunset fills the deepening blues with holy rays and turns a twilight raven into the silver bird of night as it passes into the shadow of the mountain. Then the great hush falls, and cold descends. The temperature has already dropped well below freezing, and will drop twenty degrees more before the dawn.

At dark, I walk past lifeless houses to the cooking hut where Phu-Tsering will be baking a green loaf; the sherpas have erected two stone tables, and in the evenings, the hut is almost cozy, warmed by the dung and smoking juniper in the clay oven.

As usual, GS is there ahead of me, recording data. Eyes watering, we read and write by kerosene lamp. We are glad to see each other, but we rarely speak more than a few words during a simple supper, usually rice of a poor bitter kind, with tomato or soy sauce, salt and pepper, sometimes accompanied by thin lentil soup. After supper I watch the fire for a time, until smoke from the sparking juniper closes my eyes. Bidding goodnight, I bend through the low doorway and go out under the stars and pick my way around the frozen walls to my cold tent, there to remain for twelve hours or more until first light. I read until near asphyxiated by my small wick candle in its flask of kerosene, then lie still for a long time in the very heart of the earth silence, exhilarated and excited as a child. I have yet to use the large packet of *Cannabis* that I gathered at Yamarkhar and dried along the way, to see me through long lightless evenings on this journey: I am high enough.

"Regard as one, this life, the next life, and the life between," wrote Milarepa. And sometimes I wonder into which life I have wandered, so still are the long nights here, and so cold.

## November 7

High on the mountain, I come upon a herd of twenty-seven blue sheep that includes males and females of all ages; until today the Somdo rams formed their own herd.

At the sight of man, the bharal drift over a snow ridge toward the north. I trail this promising mixed party, hoping to make observations for GS, who is working near Tsakang. Eventually, the sheep lie down on a steep grassy slope that plunges toward the mouth of Black River Canyon, and I withdraw to a point where they cannot see me, letting them calm themselves before attempting to go closer.

For a long time I sit very still. To a nearby rock comes a black redstart, bobbing in spry agitation and flaring its rufous tail. Then choughs come squealing on the wind, lilting and dancing in a flock of fifty or more: the small black crows, in escadrilles, plummet from view, filling the silence with a rush of air.

In my parka I find a few wild walnuts from Rohagaon, and crack them open with a stone. From this point of mountain, I can see in four directions. Eastward, the White River comes down out of the snow—this is the direction of Saldang. To the south, the Black River canyon climbs into the Kanjirobas. To the west is the great pyramidal butte of Crystal Mountain, parting the wind that bears uneasy clouds down the blue sky. Northward, beyond Somdo mountain, on a hidden plateau above the canyons, lies the old B'on stronghold at Samling.

The Somdo herd has moved uphill, above fifteen thousand feet. Since the wind is from the south, bearing my scent, I traverse a half-mile to the east before starting to climb; by the time the climb is finished, the wind has shifted to the north, and I can wriggle to a point not one hundred yards away from the nearest animal.

To be right among the sheep like this is stirring. I lie belly down, out of the wind, and the whole warm mountain, breathing as I breathe, seems to take me in. All the sheep but two are lying down, and four big rams a little uphill from the rest face me without alarm. The sun glows in the coarse hairs of their blue coats as they chew their cud, carved faces sweeping back to the huge cracked horns. . . .

The lead female comes out of the hollow not ten yards up the hill, moving a little way eastward. Suddenly, she gets my scent and turns quickly to stare at my still form in the dust below. She does not move but simply stands, eyes round. In her tension, the black marks on her legs are fairly shivering; she is superb. Then the first ram comes to her, and he, too, scents me. In a jump, he whirls in my direction, and his tail shoots straight up in the air, and he stamps his right forefoot, venting a weird harsh high-pitched whinny—*chirr-r-rit*—more like a squirrel than any ungulate. (Later I described this carefully to GS—so far as we know, the first datum on the voice of the blue sheep.) Boldly this ram steps forward to investigate, and the rest follow, until the mountain blue is full of horned heads and sheep faces, sheep vibrations—I hold my breath as best I can. In nervousness, a few pretend to browse, and one male nips edgily at a yearling's rump, coming away with a silver tuft that shimmers in the sun. Unhurriedly, they move away, rounding the slope toward the east. Soon the heads of two females reappear, as if to make sure nothing is following. Then all are gone.

On the way down the mountain, I stop outside Old Sonam's yard in the upper village. In sooty rags and rough-spun boots, wearing the coral-colored beads of her lost girlhood, Sonam is sitting legs straight out in the dry dung, weaving a blanket on a crazy hand-loom rigged to rocks and sticks, bracing the whole with old twine soles pushed stiff against a stone. Her wool has a handsome and delicate pattern, for there is design in the eye of this old wild one. I admire her sudden grin, strong back, and grimy hide indifferent to the cold.

Once Sonam was an infant with red cheeks, like Sunny Poti. Now she works close in the last light, as cold descends under a faint half-moon. Soon night will come, and she will creep through her narrow door and eat a little barley; what does she dream of until daybreak, when she goes out on her endless quest for dung? Perhaps she knows better than to think at all, but goes simply about the business of survival, like the wolf; survival is her way of meditation. When I ask Jang-bu why Sonam lives alone all winter in the upper village when she might use an empty house near Namu, he seems astonished. "She has the habit of that place," he says.

*November 8*
Namu is setting mousetraps for GS, and he soon has a series of fluffy short-tailed mice, a set of voles, and a small shrew, collected on the mountainside. Besides sheep and wolves, there is sign of weasel, Tibetan hare, and fox, but all of these stay out of sight, like the hibernating marmots; except for one glimpse of the hare, we have had to be content, so far, with a few droppings. This is also true of an unknown grouse—very likely, the Tibetan partridge. There is a small company of mountain birds—eagles, griffons, lammergeiers, choughs, hill pigeons, finches, redstarts, accentors, and larks—and also the hardy skinks of the sunny slopes, and an assortment of ants, bees, grasshoppers, and spiders.

I wonder about the populations of small creatures that live just over the White River. For more than a month, they have been locked under heavy snow, and ordinarily they must spend about four more months each year in hibernation than individuals of their own species that live here on the sunny side of the same valley. It seems to me that the resulting adaptations (or lack of them) across millennia, in otherwise identical populations of the same species, would make a fascinating study, and GS agrees.

Yesterday, more yaks appeared, and a belled pony led by Ongdi, brother of Namu and the owner of our cooking hut, who has come here with his daughter-in-law and sons. No doubt Ongdi has got word in Saldang that one of his houses has been occupied by outlanders, here to collect dead mice and wolf shit, and thought to turn this unhealthy situation to his own advantage. Impressed, perhaps, by the stone tables set up by the Sherpas, this sharp-eyed, shifty, and forever smiling fellow demands five rupees a day for his poor hut, but agrees to settle for one rupee if a pound of cheap tea is thrown in. Ongdi covets everything we have, he is possessed by the fury of acquisition: later this month, his sister says, this insatiable trader is off on a bartering expedition across eastern Dolpo to Jamoson and the Kali Gandaki, and even, perhaps, as far as Kathmandu. He has been to Kathmandu before, and is much celebrated in these parts on that account. In exchange for biscuit tins, plastic containers, and other treasures that would have been left behind in any case, had Ongdi not come, Phu-Tsering acquires a good stock of potatoes and some yak butter. Last night, we had butter on potatoes baked in coals—the first butter since Pokhara, and the closest thing to *haute cuisine* in weeks.

Sunrise, illuminating my thin tent, transforms it from an old refuse bag of brown plastic to a strange womblike balloon. True, it remains a wretched tent, stained, raggedy, and sagging, yet I find I have grown fond of it, for it is home. Each day I sweep out the heavy dust that comes creeping, blowing, seeping from the bottomless supply of dry dung in the yard. One understands better the local indifference to cleanliness when one is shrouded with dust within moments of each washing: I am grained with filth.

By the prayer wall, in an early shaft of sun, Namu is gathering her dried yak chips, tossing them back over her shoulder into her wide-mouthed wicker basket; these chips are precious, and her brother Ongdi, when he leaves, will lug some with him over the east mountains to Saldang, where fuel is still more scarce than it is here. Yak dung burns with a hot, clear flame that is almost without smoke, and in these mountain deserts above tree line, it is worth its weight in almost anything.

This morning Ongdi's young son, Tema Tende, in his own unfathomable rhythm, is pounding stolidly on a hide drum, and the hollow sound resounds in the mountain air.

*BUM-bum-bum, BUM-BUM-BUM, bum.*

With his older son, Karma Dorje, and Karma Dorje's pretty child wife, Tende Samnug, Ongdi packs potatoes, meat, and barley on his yaks for trade in Saldang, together with a small crude chest of drawers. . . .

When Ongdi isn't looking, Tende Samnug slips me four potatoes as a gift: the gift is spontaneous and simple-hearted, and she stands there smiling in the pleasure of it, round-eyed and red-cheeked in the sun. Meanwhile Ongdi is entreating me to part with the only kerosene lantern that we have; should he return in a week or two, when our kerosene is gone, it shall be his. Karma Dorje, another smiler, is also begging me for something, and so we chatter back and forth in the greatest animation, although "Saldang" is the only word in the entire conversation that is comprehended by both sides.

*November 9*

From the path that leads beyond Tsakang, along the precipices of the Black River Canyon, there is a stirring prospect of the great cliffs and escarpments, marching northward toward the point where this Yeju-Kangju flows into the great Karnali River. The path is no more than a ledge in many places and, on the northward face of each ravine, is covered by glare ice and crusted snow. Even on the southward face, the path is narrow, and concentrating hard on every step, I come upon what looks like a big pug mark. Because it is faint, and because GS is too far ahead to summon back, and because until now we have found no trace of leopard, I keep quiet; the mark will be there still when we return. And just at this moment, looking up, I see that GS has paused on the path ahead. When I come up, he points at a distinct cat scrape and print. The print is faded, but at least we know that the snow leopard is here.

Mostly we spend the day apart, meeting over the clay oven for breakfast and supper, but whenever we act like social animals, the impulse has brought luck. A little farther on there is another scrape, and then another, and GS, looking ahead to where the path turns the cliff corner into the next ravine, says, "There ought to be a leopard scat out on that next point—it's just the sort of place they choose." And there it is, all but glowing in the path, right beneath the prayer stones of the stupa—the Jewel in the Heart of the Lotus, I think, unaccountably, and nod at my friend, impressed. "Isn't that something?" GS says. "To be so delighted with a pile of crap?" He gathers the dropping into one of the plastic bags that he keeps with him for this purpose and tucks it away into his rucksack with our lunch. Though the sign is probably a week old, we are already scanning the sunny ledges and open caves on both sides of the river that we have studied for so many days in vain.

On the ledge path we find two more scats and a half dozen scrapes, as well as melted cat prints in the snow on the north face of the ravines. Perhaps this creature is not resident but comes through on a hunting circuit, as the wolves do: the wolves have been missing now for near a week. On the other hand, this labyrinth of caves and ledges is fine haunt for leopard, out of the way of its enemy, the wolf, and handy to a herd of bharal that is resident on the ridge above and often wanders down close to these cliffs. Perhaps, in the days left to us, we shall never see the snow leopard but it seems certain that the leopard will see us.

Across the next ravine is the second hermitage, of earth red decorated in blue-gray and white. It lacks stacked brush or other sign of life, and its white prayer flags are worn to wisps by wind. In the cliffs nearby are smoke-roofed caves and the ruins of cells that must have sheltered anchorites of former times; perhaps their food was brought them from Tsakang. This small gompa, half-covering a walled-up cave, is tucked into an outer corner of a cliff that falls into Black Canyon, and like Tsakang it faces south, up the Black River.

Because the points of the Shey stupas are just visible, its situation is less hallucinatory than the pure blue-and-white prospect at Tsakang, but the sheer drop of a thousand feet into the gorge, the torrent's roar, the wind, and the high walls darkening the sky all around make its situation more disturbing. The hermitage lies on the last part of a pilgrim's path that climbs from Black River and circles round the Crystal Mountain, striking Black Canyon once again on the north side of this point and returning to Shey by way of Tsakang; but most of the path is lost beneath the snows.

Taking shelter on the sunny step, leaning back into the warmth of the wooden door, I eat a green disc of Phu-Tsering's buckwheat bread that looks and tastes like a lichened stone mandala from the prayer walls. Blue sheep have littered this small dooryard with their dung, a human hand has painted a sun and moon above the lintel, yet in this forlorn place, here at the edge of things, the stony bread, the dung and painted moon, the lonely tattering of flags worn to transparence by the wind seem as illusory as sanity itself. The deep muttering of boulders in Black River—why am I uneasy? To swallow the torrent, sun, and wind, to fill one's breath with the plenitude of being . . . and yet . . . I draw back from that sound, which seems to echo the dread rumble of the universe.

Today GS is stumbling on the ledges. He speculates about atmospheric ions that affect depression, as in the mistral winds of southern France (there are recent speculations that negative ions, which seem to be positive in their effect on animals and plants, may be somehow related to *prana*, the "life energy"), and we agree that one is clumsy when depressed, but he feels that his own stumbling is a sign of incipient sickness, a cold coming on or the like. Perhaps he is right, perhaps I imagine things, but earlier on this same ledge, as if impelled, my boots sought out the loose stones and snow-hidden ice, and I felt dull and heavy and afraid; there was a power in the air, a random menace. On the return, an oppression has lifted, I am light and quick. Things go better when my left foot is on the outside edge, as it is now, but this cannot account for the sudden limberness, the pleasure in skirting the same abyss that two hours ago filled me with dread. Not that I cease to pay attention; on the contrary, it is the precise bite and feel and sound of every step that fills me with life. Sun rays glance from snow pinnacles above and the black choughs dance in their escadrilles over the void, and dark and light interpenetrate the path, in the all-pervading presence of the Present.

## November 10

The high stone wall of the compound of this house separates my tent from the others. Therefore it is vulnerable to theft, which is not unheard of in these parts, and I keep a sharp eye on two wool traders, filthier than most, who came yesterday from Saldang, bearing no wool or other evidence of honest trade. The first I saw on my way home from the west side of the river, eating barleycorns in Namu's yard; the second paid an uninvited visit to my tent, poking his head straight through the flap to feast his eyes upon the contents—a larcenous overture if there ever was one, so thought I. The tent is so small that in effect one wears it, and the abrupt intrusion of another head—and a strange, wolfish, dirty head at that—put our faces much too close together for my liking. That this head was not withdrawn upon discovering that the tent was occupied was, I suppose, an evidence of innocence, but all the same I made sign to it, not cordially, that it take leave at once. At this point the head spoke for the first time. In English, very gently, it inquired, "I go?" I was astounded. Then it vanished, after offering a smile that transfigured what had seemed to me a sly, distempered face, not a charming smile but a smile truly blessed in its wholehearted acceptance— approval, even—of the world and all its ways.

I opened the tent flap to call after him, but did not know what to say; the man waved good-bye to me and my bad manners and vanished from the yard.

I soon discovered that the other wool trader, the one who was eating barleycorns in Namu's yard, has a fine smile, too, though this man lacks the seraphic air of his companion. At supper, I decided not to talk about these smiles in the face of GS's stern conviction, shared by Phu-Tsering, that the two were temple looters who would cheerfully make off with our last lentil. It was agreed that the wood door to the cooking hut should be locked, lest they steal poor Dawa blind in his thick sleep; tomorrow the sherpas would keep watch until this unsavory pair had slunk away.

Now it is morning, and all precautions have been foolish, since the wool traders departed at first light, up the Black River toward the Kang Pass. I am sorry about this, as I wished to make up for my lack of trust by wishing them Godspeed in a warm way. In truth, they are our benefactors, for if they cross over the Kang La, they will reopen the trail in the high snows for Tukten and Gyaltsen, who might arrive this very day at Ring-mo. Learning that two men had crossed the Kang Pass in recent days, the sherpas would feel inspired to do the same.

Namu takes tea with us this morning, bringing roast barleycorns, which give a welcome character to the gray porridge. She vouches for the traders, telling us that they had come through here last year from their home on the Bheri River. Formerly they traded into Bhot, or B'od, which she pronounces "Po." The Land of Po. Traditionally, the central provinces of U and Thang are known to Tibetans as "B'od," which has been translated as "native place," or "home": eastern Tibet is known as Khams, and western Tibet was composed formerly of small kingdoms such as Lo (Mustang) and Dol. I think of Tsurton-Wang-Gay—like Milarepa, a disciple of Marpa—who came from the Land of Dol; if, as may be, the ancient Dol and Dol Po are the same, then the oldest prayer stones deep in the stone field west of the gompa might have been carved in the days of the eleventh century when Tsurton-Wang-Gay walked these mountains, and Milarepa's skin was turning green due to subsistence on the nettles near his cave. Perhaps it was just such light-fingered fellows as our visitors from Saldang that Milarepa had in mind when he referred to "those lawless folk, the Yepo and Yemo of Dol."

This morning I go up on Somdo mountain to observe twelve rams that so far show no interest in the females; they remain on the horizon, under the snows. After two hours of hard climbing, I am higher than Black Pond, and the whole canyon of the Black River, ascending toward the Kang Pass, lies exposed to view. Beyond the Kang soars a resplendent wall of white that dominates the sky to the southwest; it is the great ice wall of Kanjiroba, a rampart of crystalline escarpments and white-winged cornices, well over twenty thousand feet in height. Here there is only a light air from the east, but the high wind on Kanjiroba is blowing clouds of a fine snow from points and pinnacles that turn into transparency against the blue.

Two black specks of life twitch on the whiteness. The wool traders are nearing the Black Pond and by early afternoon might reach the pass; perhaps they will sleep tonight at Cave Camp and be safe at Ring-mo late tomorrow. For some reason, the sight of the two figures on the waste brings to mind Ongdi the Trader, then the Kathmandu of my first visit in 1961, in winter, when the old bazaars were thronged with mountain folk come down to trade. That year, the refugee Tibetans were numerous in the Nepal Valley, bartering their precious religious objects in order to survive: most were indistinguishable from Bhotes like Ongdi, down out of the hills in beads and braids to trade their wool and salt for knives and tea. In the Asan Bazaar I found the green bronze Akshobhya Buddha that became the center of a small altar in D's last room; Akshobhya is the "Imperturbable," being that aspect of Sakyamuni's nature that resisted the temptation of the demons under the *bodhi* tree at Gaya. The Buddha was placed on a throne of pine bark, a red berry in his lap and over his head a bodhi tree made from a bunch of pearly everlasting, very like this everlasting here on the slopes of Shey.

These days are luminous, as in those far October days in Tichu-Rong. There is no wisp of cloud—clear, clear, clear, clear. Although the shade is very cold throughout the day, and wind persists, the sun is hot—imagine a striped and shiny lizard above fifteen thousand feet, in deep November! For the first time in my life, I apprehend the pure heat of our star, piercing the frigid atmospheres of so many million miles of outer space.

Rock, and snow peaks all around, the sky, and great birds and black rivers—what words are there to seize such ringing splendor? But again something arises in this ringing that is not quite bearable, a poised terror, as in the diamond ice that cracks the stone. The brain veers; the sun glints like a weapon. Then Black Canyon writhes and twists, and the Crystal Mountain looms as a castle of dread, and all the universe reverberates with horror. My head is the sorcerer's skull cap full of blood, and were I to turn, my eyes would see straight to the heart of chaos, the mutilation, bloody gore, and pain that is seen darkly in the bright eye of this lizard.

Then lunacy is gone, leaving an echo. The lizard is still there, one with its rock, flanks pulsing in the star heat that brings warmth to our common skin; eternity is not remote, it is here beside us.

My plan is to stalk the bharal rams from above and from the east, with the sun behind me; the light east wind will soon die out, as it does each morning in fair weather, giving way after a lull to a north wind that will not carry my scent. I climb to snow line at the east end of the ridge and wait for the wind to die.

Across the crest fly the Tibetan snow finches that until now I have only seen across the distance, blowing in flurries through the blue. The finches land among the rocks, accompanied by larks, then rise with faint tinklings as suddenly as they have come, circling the summit in the morning light in showers of white wings, and bounding away into the north.

In a shift of wind, it is so still that melt trickles can be heard from beneath the snow: the whole world rests. I work west along the ridge, peering down over mixed scree and snow until a strange outcrop of horn crescents comes in view. The bharal are wary, watching the lower mountain: the nearest horns are perhaps two hundred yards to westward and below. Crouching, I make my way in stealth to a rock clump within stoning distance of my quarry. There I indulge myself in a silent chortle of self-satisfaction, at which, in instant retribution, there falls upon my ears the hollow drumming of wild hooves upon the mountain.

The sheep move west and north around the summit, and I follow. This time I arrive safe at my vantage point, and keep stern watch as consenting males push, shove, lick, sniff, and mount upon their colleagues. But soon there comes a familiar *chirr-it, chirr-it, chirr-it*, so very like a scolding rodent that I search among the grass tufts for a marmot. More than one bharal is snorting in alarm, and in seconds the band is off again at a scattering gallop on the gravel, leaving me dumbfounded, for I am well hidden, and I have not stirred.

Perhaps I underestimate my smell.

A golden eagle, with shrill peeping, glides down along the snows almost at eye level; the deep voice that would better suit this noble bird would not carry very far in so much emptiness. Soon afterward, wild pigeons pass on snapping blue-gray wings—the Turkestan hill pigeon that replaces the snow pigeon here on the Tibetan Plateau. In the frozen air, pigeons and eagle are superb, but they do not console me for the loss of my sheep, which I track over the ridge to the northern buttes; there the fresh prints in the snow lead down an incline so steep and icy that neither man nor wolf would care to follow. But the sheep have led me to the only point in all this landscape from which one might see those two pale buildings, far away on a plateau to the north and east. This view is my first and last in my present incarnation of the old B'on monastery called Samling, for the deep gorge of Black Canyon is impassable, and the way over the mountains blocked by snow.

### November 11

In the east, at dark, bright Mars appears, and soon the full moon follows the sun's path, east to west across a blue-black sky. I am always restless in the time of the full moon, a common lunatic, and move about the frozen monastery, moon-watching. Rising over the White River, the moon illuminates the ghostly prayer flag blowing so softly on the roof of the still hut, and seems to kindle the stacked brushwood; on its altar stone my small clay Buddha stirs. The snow across the river glows, and the rocks and peaks, the serpentine black stream, the snows, sky, stars, the firmament—all ring like the bell of Dorje-Chang. *Now!* Here is the secret! *Now!*

At daybreak, when the blue-black turns to silver in the east, the moon sets with the darkness in the west. On frozen sun rays, fourteen pigeons come to pick about the yard, pale blue-gray birds with a broad white band across the tail that fills with light as they flutter down upon the rigid walls. Like all wild things at Crystal Mountain, the hill pigeons are tame, and do not fly as I draw near, but cock their gentle dovelike heads to see me better.

I climb the mountain with the sun, and find the mixed herd high up on the slope; I try angling toward them, then away again, zigzagging as I climb. For some reason, this seems to reassure them, for after watching me awhile, and perhaps concluding that I am not to be taken seriously, they go on about their business, which this morning is unusually dull. I keep on climbing. Far below, the torrent, freed from daybreak ice, carries gray scree down out of the mountains.

In hope of seeing the snow leopard, I have made a wind shelter and lookout on this mountain, just at snow line, that faces north over the Black Canyon all the way to the pale terraces below Samling. From here, the Tsakang mountainsides across Black River are in view, and the cliff caves, too, and the slopes between ravines, so that most of the blue sheep in this region may be seen should they be set upon by wolf or leopard. (GS estimates a population of one hundred seventy-five to two hundred animals on the mountainsides in the near vicinity of Shey.) Unlike the wolves, the leopard cannot eat everything at once, and may remain in the vicinity of its kill for several days. Therefore our best hope is to see the griffons gather, and the choughs and ravens, and the lammergeier.

The Himalayan griffon, buff and brown, is almost the size of the great lammergeier; its graceful turns against the peaks inspire the Tibetans, who, like the vanished Aryans of the Vedas, revere the wind and sky. Blue and white are the celestial colors of the B'on sky god, who is seen as an embodiment of space and light, and creatures of the upper air become B'on symbols—the griffon, the mythical garuda, and the dragon. For Buddhist Tibetans, prayer flags and wind-bells confide spiritual longings to the winds, and the red kites that dance on holidays over the old brown city of Kathmandu are of Tibetan origin as well. There is also a custom called "air burial," in which the body of the deceased is set out on a wild crag such as this one, to be rended and devoured by the wild beasts; when only the bones are left, these are broken and ground down to powder, then mixed into lumps of dough, to be set out again for passing birds. Thus all is returned into the elements, death into life.

Against the faces of the canyon, shadows of griffons turn. Perhaps the Somdo raptors think that this queer lump on the landscape— the motionless form of a man in meditation—is the defunct celebrant in an air burial, for a young eagle, plumage burnished a heraldic bronzy-black, draws near with its high peeping, and a lammergeier, approaching from behind, descends with a sudden rush of feathers, sweeping so close past my head that I feel the break of air. This whisper of the shroud gives me a start, and my sudden jump flares the dark bird, causing it to take four deep slow strokes—the only movement of the wings that I was ever to observe in this great sailor that sweeps up and down the Himalayan canyons, the cold air ringing in its golden head.

Dark, light, dark: a raptor, scimitar-winged, under the sun peak—I know, I know. In such a light, one might hope to see the shadow of that bird upon the sky.

The ground whirls with its own energy, not in an alarming way but in slow spiral, and at these altitudes, in this vast space and silence, that energy pours through me, joining my body with the sun until small silver breaths of cold, clear air, no longer mine, are lost in the mineral breathing of the mountain. A white down feather, sun-filled, dances before me on the wind: alighting nowhere, it balances on a shining thorn, goes spinning on. Between this white feather, sheep dung, light, and the fleeting aggregate of atoms that is "I," there is no particle of difference. There is a mountain opposite, but this "I" is opposite nothing, opposed to nothing.

I grow into these mountains like a moss. I am bewitched. The blinding snow peaks and the clarion air, the sound of earth and heaven in the silence, the requiem birds, the mythic beasts, the flags, great horns, and old carved stones, the rough-hewn Tartars in their braids and homespun boots, the silver ice in the black river, the Kang, the Crystal Mountain. Also, I love the common miracles—the murmur of my friends at evening, the clay fires of smudgy juniper, the coarse dull food, the hardship and simplicity, the contentment of doing one thing at a time: when I take my blue tin cup into my hand, that is all I do. We have had no news of modern times since late September, and will have none until December, and gradually my mind has cleared itself, and wind and sun pour through my head, as through a bell. Though we talk little here, I am never lonely; I am returned into myself.

Having got here at last, I do not wish to leave the Crystal Mountain, I am in pain about it, truly, so much so that I have to smile, or I might weep. I think of D and how she would smile, too. In another life—this isn't what I know, but how I feel—these mountains were my home; there is a rising of forgotten knowledge, like a spring from hidden aquifers under the earth. To glimpse one's own true nature is a kind of homegoing, to a place East of the Sun, West of the Moon—the homegoing that needs no home, like that waterfall on the upper Suli Gad that turns to mist before touching the earth and rises once again into the sky.

## November 12

Yesterday a circumambulating wolf left a whole circle of tracks around the prayer wall across the river, at the foot of the trail that climbs around the mountains to Tsakang, and this morning, on the trail itself, there are prints of leopard. As if seeking protection, the blue sheep feed close by the hermitage, where I go with Jang-bu to call on the Lama of Shey.

When we arrive, the Lama is inside chanting sutras, but his attendant sits outside, still cutting and sorting the small store of potatoes; he is an aspirant monk, or *trapa*, whose clear gaze makes him look much younger than he is. His name is Takla, he is twenty-two years old, and he comes from the great northern plain of Tibet.

On the sunny ledge, under the bright blue window of the gompa, we listen to the murmurs of the Lama and contemplate the prospect of the snows. Soon the mountains stir, then shift and vibrate—how vital these rocks seem, against blue sky! If only they would fly apart, consume us in a fire of white light. But I am not ready, and resist, in fear of losing my death grip on the world, on all that provides the illusion of security. The same fear—of loss of control, of "insanity," far worse than the fear of death—can occur with the hallucinogenic drugs: familiar things, losing the form assigned to them, begin to spin, and the center does not hold, because we search for it outside instead of in.

When the Lama appears, he seems glad of our visit, though we lack the gift of a *kata*, or ceremonial white scarf, that is customary on such occasions. He is an imposing man with the long hawk nose and carved cheekbones of a Plains Indian; his skin is a dark reddish copper, his teeth are white, his long black hair is tied up in a braid, and he wears an old leather jacket with brass buttons, patched with burlap homespun of strange colors. When talking, he sits with legs crossed, barefoot, but puts on ancient laceless shoes when he moves around; in the doorway behind him hangs a wolf skin that he wears about his waist, indoors, to warm his back.

Rising painfully, the Lama hobbles out upon a stone platform that overhangs the cliff and squats to urinate through a neat triangular hole, into the ravine; as if to enjoy this small shift in his view, he gazes cheerfully about him, his *tulku* pee drop sparkling in the sun upon the stone.

Presently we are led into the gompa, through small dark rooms full of barley, oil, red peppers, and the like, all given to Karma Tupjuk by his people. The lamasery owns farmland at Saldang, worked by sharecroppers who bring it half the produce, but most of its tea and yak butter and *tsampa* come as offerings. Karma Tupjuk mounts a log ladder to a room on the second floor that contains a brazier and some large copper pots and urns. He removes the top from a canister of water, laying it down on a pile of dung chips while rinsing his hands. Then he enters the little prayer room that looks out over the snows through its bright blue window. On the walls of the prayer room hang two fine *thankas*, or cloth paintings. . . . The walls all around are crowded with frescoes and religious paintings, and each corner is cluttered with old treasures, all but lost in musty darkness. Lighting incense, the Lama opens a small trunk and takes out sacramental cakes, which he presents in silence, with a smile.

## November 13

The last fortnight has been clear and warm, day after day, but early this morning there were wisps of cloud which could mean a change in weather. On these last mornings, just an hour after sunrise, sun and moon are in perfect equilibrium above the snows to east and west. High cirrus in the north, seen yesterday, foretold a drop in temperature: it is −11° Centigrade this morning. The wind on

Somdo mountain has a hard bite in it, and the lizards have withdrawn into the earth. . . .

I descend the mountain to the Saldang path, turn west toward Shey. Already the path lies in twilight shadow, but the rocks on which the blue sheep stand, not thirty yards above, are in full sun. And now these creatures give a wild sunset display, the early rut that I had waited for all day. Old males spring off their rocks to challenge other males, and chase them off, and young males do as much for the females and young, and even the females butt at one another. Unlike the true sheep, which forges straight ahead, the bharal, in its confrontations, rears up and runs on the hind legs before crashing down into the impact, as true goats do—just the sort of evidence that GS has come so far to find. The whole herd of thirty-one joins in the melee, and in their quick springs from rock to rock, the goat in them is plain. Then one kicks loose a large stone from the crest, scattering the animals below, and in an instant, the whole herd is still.

Gold-eyed horned heads peer down out of the Himalayan blue as, in the silence, a last pebble bounces down the slope and comes to rest just at my feet.

The bharal await me with the calm regard of ages.

Have you seen us now? Have you perceived us?

The sun is retreating up the mountain, and still the creatures stand transfixed on their monument of rock.

Quickly I walk into the monastery to tell GS he can study his *Pseudois* by poking his head out of his tent. But a note says that in the hope of photographing the snow leopard he will sleep tonight across the river near the Tsakang trail: with a creature as wary as this leopard, there is no place for two.

If all else fails, GS will send Jang-bu to Saldang to buy an old goat as leopard bait. I long to see the snow leopard, yet to glimpse it by camera flash, at night, crouched on a bait, is not to see it. If the snow leopard should manifest itself, then I am ready to see the snow leopard. If not, then somehow (and I don't understand this instinct, even now) I am not ready to perceive it, in the same way that I am not ready to resolve my *koan*; and in the not-seeing, I am content. I think I must be disappointed, having come so far, and yet I do not feel that way. I am disappointed, and also, I am not disappointed. That the snow leopard *is*, that it is here, that its frosty eyes watch us from the mountain—that is enough.

At supper the sherpas, in good spirits, include me as best they can in their conversation, but after a while I bury myself in these notes, so that they can talk comfortably among themselves. Usually this means listening to Tukten, who holds the others rapt for hours at a time with that deep soft voice of his, his guru's hands extended in a hypnotizing way over the flames. I love to watch our evil monk with his yellow Mongol eyes and feral ears, and it is rare that I look at him when he isn't watching me. One day I will ask this yellow-eyed Tukten if, in some other incarnation, he has not been a snow leopard, or an old blue sheep on the slopes of Shey; he would be at no loss for an answer. At supper, he regards me with that Bodhisattva smile that would shine impartially on rape or resurrection—this is the gaze that he shares with the wild animals.

### November 14
Crossing Black River, I climb the west slope trail, out of the night canyon, into the sun. In the matted juniper is a small busy bird, the Tibetan tit-warbler, blue-gray with a rufous cap, and an insistent call note, *t-sip*: what can it be insisting on, so near the winter? On this bright morning, under the old moon, leopard prints are fresh as petals on the trail. But perhaps two hundred yards short of the trip line to GS's camera, the tracks appear to end, as if the cat had jumped aside into the juniper; the two prints closer to the trip line had been made the day before. Beyond the next cairn, where the path rounds the ridge high above the river and enters the steep snow-covered ravine below Tsakang, more fresh tracks are visible in the snow, as if the snow leopard had cut across the ridge to avoid the trip line, and resumed the path higher up, in this next ravine. Close by one print is an imprint of lost ages, a fernlike fossil brachiopod in a broken stone.

From Tsakang comes the weird thump of a *damaru*, or prayer drum, sometimes constructed of two human skulls; this instrument and the *kangling* trumpet, carved from the human thigh bone, are used in Tantrism to deepen meditation, not through the encouragement of morbid thoughts but as reminders that our time on earth is fleeting. Or perhaps this is the hollow echo of the cavern water, dripping down into the copper canister; I cannot be sure. But the extraordinary sound brings the wild landscape to attention: somewhere on this mountainside the leopard listens.

High on the ridge above Tsakang, I see a blue spot where GS is tracking; I come up with him in the next hour. "It fooled me," he calls by way of greeting. "Turned up the valley just below the trip line, then over the ridge, not one hundred yards from where I was lying, and down onto the path again—typical." He shifts his binoculars to the Tsakang herd, which has now been joined by the smaller bands of the west slope. "I've lost the trail now, but that leopard is right here right this minute, watching us." His words are borne out by the sheep, which break into short skittish runs as the wind makes its midmorning shift, then flee the rock and thorn of this bare ridge, plunging across deep crusted snow with hollow booming blows, in flight to a point high up on the Crystal Mountain. Blue sheep do not run from man like that even when driven.

The snow leopard is a strong presence; its vertical pupils and small stilled breaths are no more than a snow cock's glide away. GS murmurs, "Unless it moves, we are not going to see it, not even on the snow—these creatures are really something." With our binoculars, we study the barren ridge face, foot by foot. Then he says, "You know something? We've seen so much, maybe it's better if there are some things that we *don't* see." He seems startled by his own remark, and I wonder if he means this as I take it—that we have been spared the desolation of success, the doubt: is this *really* what we came so far to see? . . .

Because his sheep, spooked by the leopard, have fled to the high snows, GS accompanies me on my last visit to Tsakang. There we are met by Jang-bu, who has come as an interpreter, and by Tukten, who alone among the sherpas has curiosity enough to cross the river and climb up to Tsakang of his own accord. Even that "gay and lovable fellow," as GS once said of Phu-Tsering, "hasn't the slightest curiosity about what I am doing; he'll stand behind me for two hours while I'm looking and taking notes and not ask a single question."

Once again, the Lama of Shey lets us wait on the stone terrace, but this time—for we are here by invitation—the aspirant monk Takla has prepared sun-dried green yak cheese in a coarse powder, with tsampa and buttered tea, called *so-cha*, served in blue china cups in the mountain sun. The sharp green cheese and bitter tea, flavored with salt and rancid yak butter, give character to the tsampa, and in the cool air, this hermit's meal is very very good.

Takla lays out red-striped carpeting for us to sit upon, and eventually the Lama comes, wrapped in his wolf skin. Jang-bu seems wary in the Lama's presence, whereas Tukten is calm and easy and at the same time deferential; for the first time since I have known him, indoors or out, he doffs his raffish cap, revealing a monk's tonsure of close-cropped hair. Tukten does most of the translation as we show the Lama pictures from our books and talk animatedly for several hours. Lama Tupjuk asks about Tibetan lamas in America, and I tell him about Chögyam Trungpa, Rinpoche (*rinpoche*, or "precious one," signifies a high lama), of his own Karma-pa sect, who left Tibet at the age of thirteen and now teaches in Vermont and Colorado. . . .

Horns high, flanks taut, the blue sheep have begun a slow descent off the Crystal Mountain, in a beautiful curved line etched on the snow. The leopard is gone—perhaps they saw it go. Through binoculars, now and again, a ram can be seen to rear up wildly as if dancing on the snow, then run forward on hind legs and descend again, to crash its horns against those of a rival.

In the high sun, snows shift and flow, bathing the mind in diamond light. Tupjuk Rinpoche speaks now of the snow leopard, which he has seen often from his ledge, and has watched carefully, to judge from the accuracy of all his observations: he knows that it cries most frequently in mating time, in spring, and which caves and ledges it inhabits, and how it makes its scrape and defecation.

Before we leave, I show him the plum pit inscribed with the sutra to Chen-resigs that was given me by Soen Roshi, and promise to send him my wicker camp stool from the tea stall on the Yamdi

River. The Lama gives me a white prayer flag—*lung-p'ar*, he calls it, "wind pictures"—printed with both script and images from the old wood blocks at Shey; among the Buddhist symbols is an image of Nurpu Khonday Pung-jun, the great god of mountains and rivers, who was here, says the Lama, long before the B'on-pos and the Buddhists: presumably this was the god who was vanquished by Drutob Senge Yeshe and his hundred and eight snow leopards. Nurpu is now a Protector of the Dharma, and his image on flags such as this one is often placed on bridges and the cairns in the high passes, as an aid to travelers. The Lama folds it with greatest concentration, and presents it with the blessing of his smile.

The Lama of the Crystal Monastery appears to be a very happy man, and yet I wonder how he feels about his isolation in the silences of Tsakang, which he has not left in eight years now and, because of his legs, may never leave again. Since Jang-bu seems uncomfortable with the Lama or with himself or perhaps with us, I tell him not to inquire on this point if it seems to him impertinent, but after a moment Jang-bu does so. And this holy man of great directness and simplicity, big white teeth shining, laughs out loud in an infectious way at Jang-bu's question. Indicating his twisted legs without a trace of self-pity or bitterness, as if they belonged to all of us, he casts his arms wide to the sky and the snow mountains, the high sun and dancing sheep, and cries, "Of course I am happy here! It's wonderful! *Especially* when I have no choice!"

In its wholehearted acceptance of *what is*, this is just what Soen Roshi* might have said: I feel as if he had struck me in the chest. I thank him, bow, go softly down the mountain: under my parka, the folded prayer flag glows. Butter tea and wind pictures, the Crystal Mountain, and blue sheep dancing on the snow—it's quite enough!

Have you seen the snow leopard?

No! Isn't that wonderful?

## November 15

All morning the moon hangs frozen on the sky, and the wind-bell rings unheard on the hard east wind. The robin accentor has per-

---

*One of Matthiessen's early Zen teachers in Japan.

ished, or fled south across the mountains, since it no longer turns up in my yard. To the cook hut, in the bitter cold, comes Namu with a blanket wrapped around her head, to take a cup of tea: ordinarily, her wild black hair blows free. The days are shorter now. The sun is gone by midafternoon, when this primordial woman fills the mountain dusk with her wild cries, calling her black dzo, scaring off wolves.

I climb early to the northwest ridge of Somdo mountain, from where I can watch all the trails, scan all the valleys of the western slopes, beyond Black River: if the snow leopard is abroad, then I may see it, and if it makes a kill, I shall see birds. GS has crossed the river early to look for more fresh sign: he tries not to let the leopard interfere with his study of blue sheep, but the great cats have a strong hold on him, and the snow leopard is the least known of them all. It is wonderful how the presence of this creature draws the whole landscape to a point, from the glint of light on the old horns of a sheep to the ring of a pebble on the frozen ground. . . .

Near my lookout, I find a place to meditate, out of the wind, a hollow on the ridge where snow has melted. My brain soon clears in the cold mountain air, and I feel better. Wind, blowing grasses, sun: the dying grass, the notes of southbound birds in the mountain sky are no more fleeting than the rock itself, no more so and no less—all is the same. The mountain withdraws into its stillness, my body dissolves into the sunlight, tears fall that have nothing to do with "I." What it is that brings them on, I do not know.

In other days, I understood mountains differently, seeing in them something that abides. Even when approached respectfully (to challenge peaks as mountaineers do is another matter) they appalled me with their "permanence," with that awful and irrefutable *rock*-ness that seemed to intensify my sense of my own transience. Perhaps this dread of transience explains our greed for the few gobbets of raw experience in modern life, why violence is libidinous, why lust devours us, why soldiers choose not to forget their days of horror: we cling to such extreme moments, in which we seem to die, yet are reborn. In sexual abandon as in danger we are impelled, however briefly, into that vital present in which we do not stand apart from life, we *are* life, our being fills us; in ecstasy with another being, loneliness falls away into eternity. But in other days, such union was attainable through simple awe.

My foot slips on a narrow ledge: in that split second, as needles of fear pierce heart and temples, eternity intersects with present time. Thought and action are not different, and stone, air, ice, sun, fear, and self are one. What is exhilarating is to extend this acute awareness into ordinary moments, in the moment-by-moment experiencing of the lammergeier and the wolf, which, finding themselves at the center of things, have no need for any secret of true being. In this very breath that we take now lies the secret that all great teachers try to tell us, what one lama refers to as "the precision and openness and intelligence of the present." The purpose of meditation practice is not enlightenment; it is to pay attention even at unextraordinary times, to be of the present, nothing-but-the-present, to bear this mindfulness of *now* into each event of ordinary life. To be anywhere else is "to paint eyeballs on chaos." [Dogen] When I watch blue sheep, I must watch blue sheep, not be thinking about sex, danger, or the present, for this present—even while I think of it—is gone.

## November 16

The snow leopard has been hunting in the night, for part of the Tsakang herd has fled off toward the north, taking shelter in the yard of Dölma-jang, and the rest have crossed the ridges to the west; from Somdo, a calligraphic track up Crystal Mountain can be seen that disappears at the white rim, into blue sky. Having dispersed the Tsakang herds, the leopard crossed over the Black River—or perhaps a second leopard has arrived—for here on Somdo, the big herd is also scattered, with males and females reverting to their separate bands. As we climb the broad mountainsides above the village, a lone band of nine male animals is in sight.

Not a thousand feet above our tents at Shey, on the path that I walked yesterday, a leopard has made its scrape right in my boot print, as if in sign that I am not to leave. The leopard may still be present on this slope, for the rams are skittish. Even so, the rut is near, activity is constant, and GS scribbles in his notebook. "Oh, there's a penis-lick!" he cries. "A beauty!" The onanism is mingled here and there with fighting, especially among the older rams, which rear repeatedly on their hind legs; remarkably, another rears at the same instant, and the two run forward like trained partners, coming down together with a crash of heads. For most creatures, such an encounter would be fatal, but bharal are equipped with some two inches of parietal bone between the horns, together with a cushion of air space in the sinuses, thick woolly head hair, and strong necks to absorb the shock, and the horns themselves, on the impact side, are very thick and heavy. Why nature should devote so many centuries—thousands, probably—to the natural selection of these characters that favor head-on collisions over brains is a good question, although speaking for myself in these searching days, less brains and a good head-on collision might be just the answer.

Watching blue sheep in the sun and windlessness is pleasant, and reminds us that this pleasantness must end. We discuss logistics briefly, and also the implications of our journey, and our great good fortune. Last night at supper, GS remarked that this was one of the best trips he had ever made, "tough enough so that we feel we have really accomplished something, but not so tough that it wiped us out entirely." I feel the same. . . .

GS feels that our journey has had the quality of adventure because we depend entirely on ourselves; that this is an old-fashioned expedition in the sense that we are completely out of touch with our own world, with our own century, for that matter—no vehicles, no doctor, and no radio, far less airdrops or support teams or other such accoutrements of the modern "expedition." "This is the way I like it," GS says. "You haven't got the whole goddamned society backing you up, you're on your own: you have to take responsibility for your mistakes, you can't blame the organization. And inevitably, you make mistakes—you just hope they aren't too serious." I like it, too, for the same reasons, and also because the penalty for error makes me mindful as I walk among these mountains, heeding the echo of my step on the frozen earth.

At midmorning, when the blue sheep have settled for their rest, we walk a long eastward traverse, then west again, hoping to jump the leopard from a gully. On the stony ground, the few prints are indistinct, with nothing fresh enough to indicate where the creature might be lying. If this is the Tsakang cat, then it is hungry, and there is a chance that it will kill tonight. Since it will stay close enough to guard its kill from the lammergeiers and griffons, this is my last hope of seeing it.

With the herds scattered, it appears unlikely that full rut will get under way in the next fortnight; if the leopard is gone, it is not apt to return again in the next week. And so I have put aside my doubts about departing here the day after tomorrow, and have asked Tukten to obtain stores and a few utensils from Phu-Tsering for the outward journey.

### November 17

GS continues up the valley to the herd near snow line, while I return slowly down the ridges, wishing to spend most of this last day on the home mountain. At each stupa on the canyon points, the prayer stones are lit by fire-colored lichens; in the shine of thorn and old carved stones, the print of leopard and thick scent of juniper, I am filled with longing. I turn to look back at Tsakang, at the precipices and deep shadows of Black Canyon, at the dark mountain that presides over Samling, which I shall never see. Above the snowfields to the west, the Crystal Mountain thrusts bare rock into the blue; to the south is the sinuous black torrent that comes down from Kang La, the Pass of Snows. And there on the low cliff above the rivers, silhouetted on the snow, is the village that its own people call Somdo, white prayer flags flying black on the morning sun.

I climb to my old lookout, happy and sad in the dim instinct that these mountains are my home. But "only the Awakened Ones remember their many births and deaths," [Bhagavad Gita] and I can hear no whisperings of other lives. Doubtless I have "home" confused with childhood, and Shey with its flags and beasts and snowy fastnesses with some Dark Ages place of forgotten fairy tales, where the atmosphere of myth made life heroic.

In the longing that starts one on the path is a kind of homesickness, and some way, on this journey, I have started home. Homegoing is the purpose of my practice, of my mountain meditation and my daybreak chanting, of my *koan*: All the peaks are covered with snow—why is this one bare? To resolve that illogical question would mean to burst apart, let fall all preconceptions and supports. But I am not ready to let go, and so I shall not resolve my koan, or see the snow leopard, that is to say, *perceive* it. I shall not see it because I am not ready.

I meditate for the last time on this mountain that is bare, though others all around are white with snow. Like the bare peak of the koan, this one is not different from myself. I know this mountain because I am this mountain, I can feel it breathing at this moment, as its grass tops stray against the snows. If the snow leopard should leap from the rock above and manifest itself before me—S-A-A-O!—then in that moment of pure fright, *out of my wits*, I might truly perceive it, and be free.

# *from* **Sand Rivers**

**1981**

"The last safari into the last wilderness" was the way a trip into Tanzania's huge Selous Game Reserve was described to Matthiessen in
1979. The expedition was sponsored by a young British member of
Parliament named Tom Arnold and led by the former warden of the
park, the irascible Brian Nicholson. Tanzania at the time was under
enormous economic strain, partly from an oil crisis and partly from a
long-standing war with neighboring Ugandan strongman Idi Amin.
Moreover, both Ugandan and Tanzanian troops had taken to
butchering wild animals for food and profit. According to one estimate, "more than six thousand buffalo had recently been slaughtered, mostly by machine gun fire and often from the back of speeding
trucks." Given this climate in east Africa, Matthiessen writes, "the
last safari into the last wilderness did not seem such a fanciful
description after all."

The southern wilderness of the Selous Game Reserve, one of
Africa's largest, was a place most tourists never reached; its remoteness,
while intriguing, also meant that its wildlife was difficult to study. In
the following selection, Matthiessen and Nicholson set off into the
trackless South Selous on foot, following game trails and fording
rivers. "This is the heart of the Selous," Nicholson told him at the outset, "and you and I will be the first into most of the country that we're
going to cross." The only people as familiar with the Selous, indeed,
were the poachers themselves, many of whom Nicholson had arrested,
put in jail, and then recruited to help in his work protecting the
reserve. The original edition of Sand Rivers includes Hugo von Law-
ick's stunning photographs—battling hippos, backlit songbirds,

*stampeding buffalo—which match Matthiessen's prose for both sensitivity and crashing energy.*

## Foot Safari

**On an early African morning,** we set off for the south, wading across the Mbarangandu not far above its confluence with the Luwegu. Climbing the ridges between rivers, we shall follow the game trails for about eight miles, then descend to the Luwegu and continue south for perhaps three days before turning east to explore a high plateau with its own extensive swamp or pan. From the plateau, we shall descend a tributary river that comes down off the west escarpment of the plateau and turns northeast, arriving eventually at the Mbarangandu. There is no good map of this region, and neither the plateau nor the river has a name; as for the pan, Brian Nicholson is the only white man who has ever seen it. Excepting Ionides and Alan Rees, the warden of the western Selous, he is the only white who has ever walked through the vast southern reaches of the Reserve. "This is the heart of the Selous," Brian told me, "and you and I will be the first into most of the country that we're going to cross." If the water has subsided enough in the next fortnight to permit Land Rovers to come upriver, bringing supplies, we shall explore still further south, up the Mbarangandu; otherwise we shall head back downriver, returning to Mkangira in about ten days.

All but the Nicholson family, still asleep at camp, and David Paterson, who is sick with fever, have come to see us off, and Maria and Hugo wade across the river with us under the armed escort of Bakiri Mnungu. When Hugo tells our porters not to notice his camera, there is an outburst of laughter over the fact that Africans, too, are to be photographed, and one porter's sweet squeal is so infectious that in a moment all of us are hooting senselessly, to let off the nervous energy of the departure. Bakiri Mnungu makes the young Ngindo laugh harder and harder, watching the white man as he does so, and Renatus takes such delight in this convivial moment that he is literally falling about on the white sand. Even Nicholson is grinning. Then he says gruffly, *"Haya tayari, basi twende!"* "Let's go!" Looking worried now, Renatus calls good-bye to his friend Abdallah, the young porter with the infectious laugh, and Abdallah calls back, *"Mungu aki penda, tuta onana!"* "If God pleases I shall see you again!"

At this place the river is edged by high elephant grass where big animals might be hidden, and as we pass into it and our friends disappear, the laughing young porters fall silent in an instant, as if entering the unknown. For the next hour, as the sun rises and the file of men climbs to the open woodland of the ridge, there is no sound but the tentative duets of barbets and boubous, and the soft whisper of our passage through dry grass.

In crossing the Mbarangandu, leaving behind the tracks and Land Rovers, the tin-roofed game post, the green tents of our camp at Mkangira, we have also left behind all roads, all sign of man, and in doing so, we seem to have entered a new Africa, or rather, "the Old Africa," as Brian calls it: behind the heat and the still trees resounds the ringing that I hear when I am watched by something I cannot see. "You're getting the feel of it now," he mutters, peering about him, for he, too, has sensed the power and waiting in the air. "Only people to come this way in years, I reckon; I don't think the bloody poachers have got this far." Years ago, he had laid out a track for patrolling this part of the Mbarangandu, but all that was left was the pathway made by the round wrinkled pads of elephants, in the silent years without sound or smell of man when the huge gray apparitions had followed the abandoned road. The shadow of the road is only visible to the eyes of Goa, and soon it vanishes in the sun and dust.

As tracker and gunbearer, Goa is in the lead, a rifle over his small shoulder with the butt extended toward Brian Nicholson. The gun is a heavy-bore .458 of Belgian make, an "elephant gun," very useful for stopping large charging animals. Goa holds his free hand far out in front of him, as if extending it to be kissed, fingers pointed down as if to dowse the ground before him for the slightest sign or sound or scent of danger, he moves so lightly that he seems to rise ever so slightly off the ground, at the same time, craning his head as if to see over tall grasses that, much of the time, are well above his head.

There are six porters, young Ngindo who were recruited from Ngarambe village, just outside the eastern boundary at Kingupira, and behind the porters, making sure that none falls by the wayside, is the young Giriama camp assistant named Kazungu, who will serve as cook. Kazungu did not wish to accompany this foot safari because he thought he would have to carry a load upon his head, like these unsophisticated young Tanzanians; as late as yesterday, he was complaining of an excruciating pain in his right foot, screwing up his lively face for emphasis. But when informed that he would only have to carry his own gear, together with a panga for cutting firewood and brush, he was happy enough to come along; in fact, as I discovered later, he kept an enthusiastic journal of the safari which he and his friend, the Taita mechanic John Matano, translated from Swahili into English were kind enough to let me use:

> We began our safari at the junction of two rivers, the Luwegu and Mbarangandu, and the date that I left was 2nd September 1979. We were eight of us and two Europeans, one as our guide, whose name was Bwana Niki, and the other a book writer from America whose name is Mister Peter. And I was the tenth one, as the cook. One of us was an askari of the bush [the game scout, Goa] so we had no doubt with wild animals. We walked for a number of kilometers until we came to the Luwegu.

The porters take turns carrying the old-fashioned tent that Brian wished to bring along, despite my feeling that we did not need it. Since I am carrying nothing but binoculars and notebooks, I feel slightly ashamed, whereas Brian is not sheepish in the least. "If I had to carry one of those loads in this sort of heat," he admits cheerfully, "I wouldn't last out the first hour. I've never carried a thing on trek in forty years, and I never shall." What I was hearing wasn't laziness—Nicholson is anything but lazy—but a principle left over from the reign of Ionides who liked to say, "I never do anything that can be done for me by somebody else." Brian is proud that all his old safaris were elaborate—far more elaborate, as he says, than this one. "Always had my own tent, of course, with tent fly and camp table and chair, and my gunbearer and cook and a hell of a lot of porters. Sometimes I'd be out five months at a time, so I needed a lot of equipment, but also it was important to be comfortable. Took along whatever I wanted, as a matter of fact. I had one man who just carried books, another who carried a coin chest for buying food in the settlements; the rest carried my personal gear and the food for all the others. On short safaris through settled areas, I had fifteen porters; on long ones through the bush, I would have forty. But once the food started to go, I couldn't have all those people sitting around eating up what was left, so I'd send them back in lots of six; they couldn't be sent off in ones and twos, not in *this* country."

On the ridge between the rivers, the file moves rapidly, in antlike silence, as if in flight from the accumulating heat. Since leaving the Mbarangandu, we have encountered no animals at all, only the pale rump of a kongoni, vanishing like a ghostly face into high grass. Other animals have come and gone—we see a rhino scrape, the elegant prints of greater kudu, old droppings of elephant and buffalo—but as the day grows, so does the sense of emptiness in the still woodland, which is not a closed canopy but open to the sun, and everywhere overgrown with high bronze grass. "All dead, dry stuff," Nicholson mutters. "No good to animals at all. In my time, the whole Reserve would be burned over every year, two at the most; I had over four hundred game scouts who spent most of their time out in the field, and burning was their main job." He murmurs to Goa in Swahili, then stalks on, and Goa steps off the elephant path and sets fire to the tinder grass, which ignites with a hollow rush of the dry air. The fire leaps up with a hungry crackling, and a dark pall of smoke rises in our wake as we move southward.

This thin, tall man walking ahead of me in his big floppy hat, old shirt and shorts, and worn red sneakers looks more like old Ionides must have looked than the conventional idea of the East African professional hunter, or the crisp old-style warden in regimental khaki: I like this "Mister Meat" for his lack of vanity. In his angular, stoop-shouldered gait, he keeps up a long easy pace, remaining close to the swift, effortless Goa, yet every little while he turns and casts a hard, bald eye back along the line, noticing quickly when the porters fail to keep close ranks in river thickets and karongas, or when one or more tends to fall too far behind. "*Wanakuja?*" he calls. "Are they coming?" And with the barrel tips of the shotgun that he carries he moves a thorn branch off the thin trail, anticipating the bare feet of the young porters. His concern is professional—foot injuries will cripple our safari—but it isn't unfeeling, whatever he might have one believe.

Ahead, three young bull elephants are standing beneath a large and dark muyombo tree, which at this season, in anticipation of the rains, is covered with a red canopy of seed pods. Getting our scent, the elephants move away in no great haste as we come down into a grassy open glade. The blue acanth flowers of day ground give way to blue commelina and lavender morning glory, and there are meadow springs and frogs and singing scrub robins. "At this season, most *miombo* is pretty dry from one end of Africa to the other, but here in the Selous it's so well-watered that these little paradises occur everywhere in the dry woods," Nicholson says, as the porters set down their loads beneath a tree. "That's why we didn't bother to bring water bottles." But Goa is out putting the torch to the dry grass all around, and over this paradise black smoke is rising; within minutes, the racquet-tailed rollers appear, filling the crackling heat with strident cries as they hawk the insects that whir up before the flames.

We head southwest across the river bends to the Luwegu. Unlike the Mbarangandu, the Luwegu still carries a swift flood of brown-gray water that in most places fills the river bed from one side to the other. This high water, unusual at this time of the year, must account in part for the scarcity of animals along the margins, since there is more water than they need in the pools and springs back in the woods. Where we come out on the banks of the Luwegu we see no elephant at all, only a large crocodile which lies out on a bar along the bank, its jaws transfixed in the strangled gape with which these animals confront their universe. In the mile between bends of the river two large herds of hippopotami are visible; it seems likely that there are too many, that one of these long, slow years there will come a great dying-off of the huge water pigs, to bring their numbers back into balance with the wild pastures that they have pushed further and further from the banks. According to Brian, such dying-off occurs in the Selous about once every seven years, in separate places; he remembers it once in the Ruaha, and another time on the Kilombero. But today they steam and puff and honk in great contentment, though two get at each other every little while in a great blare and thrash, to banish the monotony of river life.

Everywhere as we walk upriver the animals are starting to appear; it seems to be true, as Brian claims, that here in the Selous the animals are not especially active early in the day, as they are elsewhere, and do not move about until midmorning, though *why* this might be true is not clear. Among the small animals that cross our path are ground squirrels and the green monitor lizards, small relatives of the great Komodo "dragons" of the East Indies, and a black-tipped mongoose, scampering along the bank, that is red as fire; the banded and pygmy mongoose are common in the Selous but this is the first of this weasel-like species I have seen. Impala are numerous and remarkably tame, and a band of waterbuck under a tamarind beside the river lets man walk up within a few yards before prancing off in a pretty canter into the woods; further north these animals would take off at a dead run at the sight of vehicles, which ordinarily disturb them less than a man on foot. Wart hog and wildebeest are also rather tame, though not confiding. Under a big tree by the corner of the river, from where the Mahoko Mountains can be seen off to the west, stands a placid group of elephants; not until we move a little uphill to the east of them, to let the breeze carry down our scent, do they give way. Kazungu described the scene in his journal:

> We saw elephants where we wanted to pass. We went upwind of them to give them our smell, and this make me understand that no matter how dangerous an animal is, if he is not familiar with a smell, he will run.
> We went up and down the hills and met some different animals.

Behind the elephants is a large grove of borassus palms, with their graceful swellings high up on the pale boles; from each palm, or so it seems, a pair of huge griffons violently depart, their heavy wing beats buffeting the clack of wind-tossed fronds. At this season, the borassus carries strings of fruit like orange coconuts, which are sought out by the elephants; here and there in the dry hills, far from the nearest palms, lie piles of dried gray borassus kernels, digested and deposited, from which the last loose dung has blown away. The mangolike kernels remind Brian of the elephant habit of gorging on the fallen fruits of the marula tree. "Used to ferment in their stomachs, make them drunk or sleepy; they'd just lie down on their sides and snore. Ever hear an elephant snore? Oh, you can hear that a *hell* of a long way!"

Keeping the porters close, we push through thickets to a shady grove beside the river. This first day we shall quit early, while the sun is high, to give the Africans a chance to dry the strings of dark red meat jerked from the buffalo killed yesterday near Mkangira; the biltong will be their main food for the journey. Goa and Kazungu string a line between high bushes on the bank to hang the meat, which is brought up in big handfuls by the porters; once dry, the biltong is very hard and tough and may be slung around amongst the luggage.

Abdallah spreads green canvas in the shade, and the sahibs lie down upon it to take tea. Since Brian's red sneakers are blistering his toes, the decision to stop early is a good one; also, the Ngindo are not trained porters and will collapse quickly in this heat—it must be 100°F or more—unless they are given a day or two to get broken in. The remarkable Abdallah of the squint eye and sweet laugh is now doing headstands in the sun—actually jumping on his elbows in a small circle on the thorny ground—but two of his companions are laid out like corpses. One of these is Kalambo, who wears huge blue boxer's shorts with a white stripe that extend below his knobby knees, and the other is a heavy boy with the name David who wears a bright red shirt. Then there is Amede—short for Muhammed— who walks with the sway of a giraffe, and Shamu, whose face is wide-eyed, innocent, faintly alarmed, like the face of a small antelope; his small size and slight body, his expression, make him look too young to be carrying loads that might bend his bones, but on closer inspection I see that Shamu is a full-grown man who has retained a childlike air of innocence. Most of the time he sits quietly to one side, smiling delightedly at the witty sallies of his friends.

Finally there is Mata, small-faced as a vervet and given to harsh yapping barks; Mata likes to walk apart from the file of porters, and once or twice he dared walk on ahead when Goa and Brian had paused to light their fires. Bwana Niki had murmured something in Swahili which brought a bad look to Mata's face; he seemed to consider a spry remark, but then thought better of it.

"You'll have trouble with that one," Rick Bonham had said, but the Warden knew better. "Once you put a bit of distance between them and the camp, and they have to depend on you for their protection, they're quite anxious to please," Brian had said, and he was right; after the first encounter with the elephants Mata fell back into line, and gave no more trouble after that first day. "Oh, there are exceptions to the rule of course," Nicholson reflected later. "Once had to kick a porter in the balls and give him a good clout to go with it. No choice, really." When he says these things, old Mister Meat fixes me with that bald eye and gives a faint clack of his false teeth, and I can't make out whether he intends this as a literal account of makeshift discipline in the bush, or if he is teasing my "American" notions about Africans, or whether he is feeling nostalgic about the grand old days when Ionides could have a whole Ngindo village flogged and get away with it. But as it turned out, he meant just what he said: the offending porter, Brian told me later, "was using blackmail in a very remote place, threatening to dump all the loads and abscond with his fellow porters unless I doubled the agreed pay. He was a huge man, who could have torn me apart easily if I hadn't disabled him."

By early afternoon the clouds have gone, and the day is dry and hot. Drinking gratefully from the brown river, I realize how rare now are the places left in Africa where one can drink the water without risking bilharzia or worse; in the Selous, one can sip with impunity from pools and puddles and even from big footprints in the mud. Later I find a safe bathing place behind a silvered log, and lie back for a long time in the warm flood, watching the western sky turn red behind a gigantic baobab across the river. Behind me in the forest, an elephant's stomach rumbles—or perhaps the elephant is pondering my scent, for Brian says that what is usually called stomach-rumbling in elephants is actually a low growl of apprehension and perhaps warning. Trumpeter hornbills gather in the mahoganies over my head, and I am attended by a small dragon-fly, fire red in hue, that might have flown out of the sunset. I am extremely content to be here, yet I do not look forward to the evening; Brian and I have got on well enough, all things considered, but other people have always been around to smooth over the rough edges. I don't know this man as yet. We have been thrown together by fate, not by affinity, and doubtless he regards our enforced companionship as warily as I do.

When I get back to camp the Warden is lying on his cot before his tent, head raised on his elbow, watching me come. I am not surprised that he and I have been having the same thoughts, or when he says, coming straight out with it, "You know, Peter, when this idea came up that you and I should go off together on a long foot safari, I was dead set against it. As late as Kingupira, I was telling Tom Arnold, Absolutely not! You can't just go bashing off into the bush with some fella you've never set eyes on; had to have a look at you first." Especially, I thought, after having read my book on Africa—and once again, Brian anticipates me. Although we have been together for two weeks, he mentions the book for the first time, and actually says, "I thoroughly enjoyed it." Together we laugh about that first night in Dar. "Didn't know *how* to act!" Brian said. "Didn't know what was wanted of me, really."

Not only his words but his whole manner confirm what I thought I had already noticed, that he has left his mask behind at the main camp in Mkangira. He seems happy and relaxed, eager to talk, and the talk is almost entirely free of that cynicism and intolerance that I thought would cause trouble between us. Over our simple supper of beans and rice, he speaks with real affection and respect of some of the Africans on his old staff, such as a scout named James Abdallah who as a youth had been conscripted to help haul that steam engine up there to Madaba. "Terrible work. After three months, I think, James ran away and hid out in the forest."

In those early days, Brian says, he spent most of his time on elephant control, which was often a bit risky. "I lost a very good man once to an elephant, one of my head game scouts, like old Saidi— you might think of a head game scout as a sort of regimental sergeant-major. Today they call them game assistants: I suppose they think it's less demeaning to be an assistant than to be a scout! But anyway, this other Saidi—Saidi Nasora Kibanda—was a first-class shot, which is very rare among Africans; he was also a superb hunter, and very knowledgeable, one of my best men. One day about 1965 Kibanda was out with a trainee on elephant control, and the trainee wounded an elephant which Kibanda had him follow up. I'll never really know what happened; when these things occur, the survivor always puts things in the best light for himself. But apparently the elephant attacked, and the trainee ran, and for some reason, Kibanda failed to stop that elephant, although they were in open country and it should have been a routine shot. That elephant destroyed him." Brian paused as if granting Kibanda a moment of silence. "Old Kibanda was a hell of a good fellow, and his death came as a hell of a shock to me, I don't mind telling you— that man was my right arm. Very loyal, very intelligent—a very nice man altogether."

Brian clears his throat, frowning a little. "I suppose I lost one or two game scouts every year, out on control work, but I can't think what could have happened to Kibanda. These large-bore precision weapons stop an elephant pretty easily, although most Africans have a hard time believing it; perhaps that's why they don't aim properly. Usually the animal will come at you with his head low, and you shoot at the forehead, above the eyes, to hit the brain; if the head is raised, of course, you shoot just at the base of it. Either way he goes right over, no problem at all.

"Of course there are times when nothing seems to go right, and probably it was one of those times that caught up with poor old Kibanda. I had a day like that myself. I was stationed on Mahenge at the time. We had been asked to deal with three bull elephants that were getting into the shambas, then becoming aggressive with whoever tried to drive them out, and running around knocking over houses, too. The people had these flimsy sort of *kilindos*, or huts-on-poles, that they would put up to keep watch on the crops;

when elephants came, they would try to drive them off by beating on tins and the like. One day there was an old woman in one of these huts, and when three bulls turned up in the gardens, she started beating on her tins, and the elephants came for her, knocked over the hut, and trampled her and tore her to pieces—made a real mess of her.

"When I arrived and finally had them located, I had to stalk them through very high grass, over my head, and when I came up with them, they were all together in a kind of opening they had beaten down in the high grass under a sausage tree. Two were broadside to me, one completely screening the other, and the third was looking off in another direction. When you shoot an elephant in the brain, it always sits back on its haunches, and I reckoned that the near one, falling back that way, would give me a fair shot at the one behind it. Then my gunbearer would give me the other gun, and I'd have two barrels to use on the third animal.

"Well, the first part of the plan worked well enough; the first sat backward, I dropped the second, and grabbed the other gun. But the third animal was already taking off, and I got off two quick shots aimed at the pelvis, because a pelvis shot will cripple an elephant and stop him so that you can finish him off properly. However, I had shot too fast, and he kept going. Because I wasn't absolutely sure the second elephant was dead, I told the gunbearer to load up the first gun, showed him just where he should point the barrel, and then I took off after number three. He was only about sixty yards away, and badly hurt, but my third shot didn't drop him, I still don't know why, just set him running again, and a fourth shot intended for the pelvis didn't stop him either; all it did was turn him right around. I realized that the gun was empty and I had no more cartridges, hadn't thought I'd need them, you see, and I did the only thing I *could* do: I ran like hell back down the path that the elephant had made through the tall grass. After about five yards, I tripped and fell, and he was on me.

"This elephant was badly hurt, and his trunk was full of blood, spraying all over me, but he couldn't smell me, you see, and after he missed me with his tusks, he somehow lost me, and I was able to roll away. Luckily, he decided to take off again, and I ran back to my gunbearer. I didn't have Goa at that time; this man was only a trainee who never did make it as a gunbearer, and when he saw me all covered with blood, he panicked; he thought the elephant had got me, and because I was running, he imagined it was still hot after me, and so he departed in the opposite direction. When I caught up with him, I gave him a hell of a clout to calm him down, and grabbed a handful of cartridges out of his pouch and went back and finished off that elephant. That was the closest call I ever had with a wild animal."

A half-moon rests on the borassus fronds over our heads, and a tiny bat detaches itself, flits to and fro, and returns into the black frond silhouette. We lie peacefully upon our cots and watch the stars. From the forest comes the hideous squalling of frightened baboons trying to bluff a leopard, or so we suppose, since there is plentiful leopard sign around the camp.

In the moonlight the bull hippos of the herd move in close to the bank to bellow at our fire; in trying to frighten us away, they panic one another and porpoise heavily away over the shallows, causing great waves that carry all the way across the river and slap onto the mud of the far bank. Man does not belong here, and the hippopotami cannot seem to accept us; we have disrupted their whole sense of how the night time world unfolds in the Old Africa. They do not go ashore to feed but remain out there just beyond the fire light, keeping watch on the intruders and banishing our sleep with outraged bellows.

A light unseasonal rain that fell last night is attributed by the Warden to the bush fires that in these months are set all across Africa in the miombo belt, from southern Tanzania and northern Mozambique to the coastal forests of Zaire and Angola. The morning is heavy and humid after the rain, and two of the porters, complaining of headaches, are given aspirin. Behind their round dark aching heads, a flight of egrets passes down the early river.

During the night, a small leopard made off with one of Kazungu's sneakers, which on this foot safari have replaced the green Welling-tons he was wearing for a while as a precaution against cobras. As the only staff member with shoes (although Goa uses rubber sandals that make a faint *snick-snick* as he goes along) Kazungu is understandably upset, but the cat prints are clear in the damp sand, and he soon locates the spat-out sneaker a short distance back in the thickets.

This morning we abandon the Luwegu in order to cross the ridges toward the east and explore an unnamed sand river that comes down off a high plateau. On the north end of that plateau, high above the dry savanna woodlands all around, is the large pan that the Warden remembers as "crawling with elephant" and other animals. He is eager to revisit the nameless plateau and its pan, which he discovered in his last years in the Selous.

An hour is needed to cross the flat river plain of the Luwegu, on the east side of which a pair of Bohor reedbuck start up from high grass along the wood. The going is mostly very fast, but because of large animals we travel no more than a few miles in an hour. Buffalo tracks and buffalo manure are copious, and so are the attendant flies that do not sting but alight damply on the eyes and mouth. Then we are in thickets and karongas once again, and Goa squatting to see beneath the bushes, craning, listening, picking out the big and silent shapes that watch us pass, must move circuitously and with more care. Brian, too, is wary and alert, kicking apart a fresh elephant mound, then stooping without breaking stride to judge the proximity of its maker by the degree of warmth that rises to his fingers.

In a sand river—and he thinks this is the one that has no name—we meet a cow elephant with half-grown calf. The cow goes off into the thicket to our left and the calf dawdles, then blunders toward the right, starting to bawl. Unaccountably, Brian and Goa move between the animals, and a moment later the cow, no longer visible, is bellowing from a short distance away; reverberations from the thicket make it clear that other agitated pachyderms are behind her. Goa turns quickly, taking the shotgun and giving Brian his own Game Department rifle. ("He knows I am more skillful with it," Brian explained later, "so he doesn't mind.") The porters rush forward in a covey to take up positions behind the guns. After a mild demonstration charge that brings the guns up, the cow wheels and goes trumpeting off with the others; probably it was not that dawdler that had concerned her but a much younger one too low down in the bush for us to see.

A mile away, vultures spiral upward from a kill, and we have gone less than a few hundred yards when Goa's deep and urgent voice says, "Simba!" Two lionesses, then two more, shoot out from beneath an enormous tree fallen into the river perhaps thirty yards away; they are followed by a big growling male with a fine mane which accelerates as it sees the file of men, its big paws scattering hot sand. The lion bounds across the river bed and up the bank. The whole bend of the river stinks of lion, and there are print patterns of the litter of small cubs, which must be lying hidden just close by. Brian says, "I seriously doubt if these lions have ever seen a man before; even the poachers stick to the main rivers. Yet look at how fast they shot away! What makes them run off like that? Quite interesting, really. If we'd come up on them in a Land Rover, chances are that these wild lion would be just as tame as those lion in the parks. It's the cars that fool them; they can't seem to identify men in cars. If you're up in a tree, a lion will recognize you straight away, even though that's not the way he's accustomed to seeing you."

A lone African hare crosses our path in its age-old silence, and in the thicket, banded mongoose skirl and squabble, in furor over some edible find. Every little while we pass the dung-spattered double scar on the dry ground that marks a rhino scrape; although we have seen many fresh scrapes in the past few days, the great primordial beast itself has remained hidden. Soon the porters take their rest in a grove of the sand river, which twists and turns back and forth across our course toward the south, and Goa and Kazungu dig down in the dry sand until the hole fills with the clear water that will be used for morning tea and porridge.

In the early afternoon, blue water glints in the eastern distance; at this time of year, when all but the main rivers have gone dry, this can only be the Mbarangandu, which we had not expected to see until tomorrow. If the two rivers are so close—not much more than twelve miles—then we are further north than we imagined, which means that we have struck almost due east, instead of east by south as we intended; we have no compass, and throughout the morning the sun that would have given us a bearing has been hidden in the fire-shrouded sky. We turn due south. I am glad of the miscalculation, which brought us to this place at the right moment: we have hardly seen the glint of river when Goa points out two rhinoceros, a mile away down a long slope of the savanna; one fades quickly into the high grass but the other lingers a few moments, turning broadside, before barging off into the bush.

I yip with pleasure, and Goa is delighted. To Brian he says, "The only thing we must show him is leopard!" Goa has a sudden fine full smile that sends wrinkles back on his tight hide across the high cheekbones to the small tight ears: the old hunter looks like a hominid designed for passing through bush quickly and quietly, catching nothing on the thorns. Never watching the ground for vines and holes and sharp grass-hidden stones but seeming to drift over the earth, he scans the terrain with those yellowed eyes that see so much, on all sides and far away.

Old elephant paths of other seasons cross the rolling hills of high bronze grass, but there is no sign of animals whatever except for two pretty klipspringer, tawny and gray, which prance along the black granite rim of a low escarpment; from this black rock, in the white sun, so very hot that it bakes our feet, a dark thing flutters up like a great moth—the freckled nightjar, which makes its home on the black outcroppings of stone.

Here and there on these black platforms, emerging like low domes out of the grass, lie shards of quartz, agate, chert, and other stones, apparently brought here to be worked by stone tool cultures, for many are distinctly flaked, with the characteristic hump that betrays the method; occasionally I pause long enough to stuff one or two of these ancient tools into my pockets, including round tortoise cores flaked all the way around the edge, like those Hugo and I had found on the ridges north of Mkangira. The heat of the tools, and the feel of their great age, is somehow satisfying and profoundly reassuring, as if we had passed into another age, as if those Stone

Age men had paused here yesterday, taking the sun god's name in vain as they cursed their sharp, obdurate stones, scowling in the heat.

Cutting across a series of wide bends, still heading south, we come down to the river. Two waterbuck, two wart hog, and two buffalo wait on the bar, like creatures left behind by Noah's Ark; the buffalo refuse to give ground at our approach, although we shout. We have circled wide and now stand in the shallow water, trying to ease them up into the thicket so that we may proceed along the sand. "Don't want to make them think they're trapped," says Brian. We can go no closer to the lowering brutes, which have backed up with their spattered rumps against the bank. Before the wrong move can be made, the buffalo wheel suddenly and plunge off up the bank into the thicket, agitating a group of elephants that we had not seen.

In the shade of a big butterfly-leafed piliostigma we stretch out on the cool sand, and I listen to the young Africans behind me; they are still excited by our encounters with the *tembo* and the *simba*, and describe to each other in dramatic tones and with nervous squeals how Mzee Goa and the Bwana Mkubwa (for they are too young to have known Brian as Bwana Niki and refer to him as Head Bwana, the "Big Bwana") raised their *bunduki* to protect our lives.

While Kazungu busies himself over his pots, Goa walks inland and sets fire to the bush, then wades across the shallow Mbarangandu and fires the high grass on the far bank; in a few minutes, the clear African day beside the river is despoiled by a crackling roar and columns of black smoke, which stings the eyes, and stinks, and dirties the sky. A pair of hawks are circling a tree where the accumulated grass and deadwood is feeding fire that booms and reverberates as it moves away; perhaps their nestlings have been singed of their feathers, and even now nod just a little, blackening in death.

Brian, sensing my disgust, insists once more that early-season burning is essential to wildlife management in the Selous. There are moderate rains in the months of December, less in January; the heavy rain that renews the vegetation is concentrated between late February and early May, when twenty-five to thirty inches may fall here in the south and twice that amount in the Kilombero region and the west. The two rainy seasons tend to merge into one long one, in which the grass grows very high, coarse, and unpalatable, and smothers the wild pasture for the remainder of the year; the use of fire as much as the removal of the inhabitants is responsible for the fact that the game population of the Selous is many times greater than it was when the first Europeans came into this country.

No doubt Brian is right in terms of game management; it is the necessity of all this "management" that I resist. One day I ask him if any of these fires ever occur accidentally, through lightning or other random events, and he says that he thinks it very unlikely; even if they did, they would not travel far. This poses a question that neither of us can answer: since it is thought that this "dry forest" is a recent habitat type, created, perhaps, by the fires of those early hunters who left their flaked tools on almost every high place and granite outcrop in this landscape, and spread and maintained by human activity ever since, how it is that such creatures as Lichtenstein's hartebeest are endemic to the miombo, since they must have evolved many thousands of years before mankind had fire at all?

As we talk, Brian makes an odd drumming with his fingers on a log, two soft beats followed by two hard, and noticing that I notice, he says, "*Mgalumtwe.* That's the local dialect for 'A man has been eaten.' They drum this message on a hollowed-out log with a bit of hide stretched over one end: *M-ga-LUM-TWE!* The villagers come to the call of the drums, armed with spears and bows and arrows. Some times they harass the lion but they rarely kill it; it just goes off, more dangerous than before. That man-eater might be raiding in an area of a hundred square miles, which makes it very difficult to come up with, especially when you're traveling on foot. It might take two people in two nights in the same place, then disappear entirely for two weeks, presumably taking animals instead. Often man-eating is seasonal, during the rains; in the dry season, when animals are concentrated near the water points, these lion seem to prefer animals, returning to human beings in the rains when the animals scatter. But man-eating was certainly most prevalent where game was scarce because of human development; the lion that were unable to catch what was left—especially lion that were old or crippled—turned to human beings. I remember one I shot, still on the man whom it had killed outside his hut and dragged into the bamboo. That lion was in terrible condition, half-starved really, due to porcupine quills and an infection in its throat that kept it from swallowing. It could only take little bits at a time, which was why it was still feeding on that man when I arrived.

"But most man-eaters I saw were in good condition, and they were wary. Baits rarely worked on them, they were too clever. You had to wait until the next person was taken, doing your best to persuade the villagers not to drive it off the kill but to let it gorge itself. After that, it wouldn't go too far before it fell into a heavy sleep, and I'd have a chance to reach the place before it woke up again and moved away. Tracking it, you'd find places where it had lain down and then got up again, until it found the place where things felt right. Usually that was in deep thicket, and sometimes all you could see when you crept up was a patch of hide. Finally you had to shoot at that and hope the bullet would disable it. Otherwise, you might have it right on top of you."

One problem was the superstition among villagers that a man-eater must be a *mtu-ana-geuka-simba*, literally, "a man-turned-into-a-lion," a witch with whom it was dreadfully dangerous to interfere. This superstition was often shared by the local game scout stationed in that village or sent out to dispatch the lion—including the mighty Nonga Pelekamoyo or Take Your Heart, uncle of old Saidi (and also uncle of Rashidi Kawawa, Tanzania's first Prime Minister after Independence, and currently Minister of Defense). This two-hundred-pound Ngoni—the one who had set fire to all the Ngindo settlements on Brian's first tour through the region of Ngarambe—was sleeping in a bamboo stockade in a village beset by a man-eater when the lion burst straight through the bamboo in order to get at him. Miraculously the lion seized, not Nonga, but the wooden bed that the villagers had provided for their savior. The lion actually dragged the bed clean out of the stockade, and Nonga Pelekamoyo, managing to roll off, escaped unharmed. But afterward Nonga refused to consider any further dealings with this *mtu-ana-geuka-simba*, and turned the whole case over to Bwana Nyama.

Brian reckons he has killed about fifty lions, of which perhaps nineteen or twenty were man-eaters; the rest were stock-raiders, which usually got that habit from feeding on dead cattle after a drought or plague. Asked if fear had ever been a problem, he thinks a moment, as if such an idea had never occurred to him before. Frowning, he says, "One is bound to be tensed up, of course, but if it was *really* fear, you wouldn't bloody well do it, especially after you've put a bullet in some dangerous creature only to have him go thrashing off into the thicket. Then you've got to start all over again, and it's a lot worse than before." He shook his head, and changed the subject. "I recall one lioness over here on the Mbarangandu that jumped out and scattered the porters, then came towards me. I knew she was not a man-eater, in a place so remote from human habitation; I thought she must have cubs, so I didn't shoot, just held the rifle on her, backing up slowly. She kept on coming, keeping the same fifteen yards between us, snarling and thrashing her tail. And then, when she figured that her cubs were safe, she turned suddenly and bolted for the long grass. Quite interesting, really.

"In the north," Brian says, "man-eaters are rarely a problem, but here in the south they still occur regularly. Not so many in the settled areas anymore, because the lions themselves are dying out, and there is still enough game around to feed those that are left. But two or three people have been taken along that foot path"—and he pointed south—"between Liwale and Mahenge. Except for that porter at Kichwa Cha Pembe, I've never lost any of my people to a lion, but you have to be careful."

By nightfall the humidity has lifted, and the flying clouds part on a cold full moon. All around the horizon, as the wind chases them, the flames of Goa's fires leap and fall in the black tracery of trees like a demonic breathing from within the earth.

Dark clouds and wind. At dusk, under the eastern bluffs where an elephant is throwing trunkfuls of fine dust into the air, a ghostly puff of light explodes, another, then another. I cannot see the elephant, only the dust that rises out of the shadow into the sunlight withdrawing up the hill. At dark a hyena whoops and another answers, for the clan is gathering, but their ululations are soon lost in a vast staccato racket, an unearthly din that sweeps in rhythmic waves up

and down the river bars, rising and falling like the breath of earth —
then silence, a shocked ringing silence, as if the night hunters have
all turned to hear this noise. Somewhere out there on the strand, I
think, a frog has been taken by a heron; my mind's eye sees the long
bill glint in the dim starlight, the pallor of the sticky kicking legs,
the gulp and shudder of the feathered throat. The frog's squeak
pierces the racket of its neighbors, which go mute. But soon an
unwary one, perhaps newly emerged from its niche under the bank,
tries out its overwhelming need to sing out in ratcheting chirp;
another answers, then millions hurl their voices at the stars. The
world resounds until the frogs' own ears are ringing, until all identity is lost in a bug-eyed cosmic ecstasy of frog song. In an hour or
two, as the night deepens, the singing impulse dies, leaving the
singers limp, perhaps dimly bewildered; remembering danger, they
push slowly at the earth with long damp toes and fingers, edging
backward into their clefts and crannies, pale chins pulsing.

Toward midnight I am awakened by a bellow, a single long ago-
nized groan; a buffalo has cried out, then fallen silent. Perhaps
something is killing it, perhaps a lion's jaws have closed over its
muzzle, but I hear no lion, now or later. At daybreak a bird call
strange to me rings out three times and then is gone, a bird I shall
never identify, not on this safari or in this life. As a tropic sun rolls
up onto the red cliffs across the river, setting fire to a high, solitary
tree, the moon still shines through the winged piliostigma leaves
behind the tent.


A cold clear morning. Well before daybreak, voices murmur and
human figures move about, building up the fire to keep warm. A
smell of carrion hangs heavy on the air, but the leopard, heard
again last night, has not visited the buffalo, nor did the lions follow
up our circling vultures. As for hyena, none have been heard since
we left the Mbarangandu, nor are there hyena tracks in the sand
river.

The sun-dried meat is packed into the loads; every man must
help to carry it, since they mean to take it all. In the cold sunrise,
the porters are quickly ready. As we depart, a stream of parrots in

careening flight recaptures the sausage tree across the river; the fleeting human presence will lose significance with the last figure that passes out of sight in the dawn trees.

We are headed north again, into burned country, and the spurts of green grass in the black dust are sign that these fires preceded those we made on the way south; if this is the eastern edge of the large burn that we struck in the first days of our safari, then we are closer than we think to the Luwegu. In the bright grass the animals are everywhere, making outlandish sounds as we approach; the kongoni emit their nasal puffing snort, the zebra yap and whine like dogs, the impala make that peculiar sneezing bark. But the two buffalo that canter across our path are silent, the early red sun in the palm fronds glistening on their upraised nostrils, on the thick boss of the horns, the guard hairs down their spines, the flat bovine planes of their hind quarters.

As the edge of the plain, between thickets and karongas, Goa rounds a high bush and stops short; without turning around he hands the rifle back, as Brian and I stop short behind him.

In a growth of thin saplings, at extreme close quarters, stands a rhinoceros with a small calf at her side. The immense and ancient animal remains motionless and silent, even when the unwarned porters, coming up behind, gasp audibly and scatter backward to the nearest trees. Goa, Brian, and I are also in retreat, backing off carefully and quietly, without quick motion: I am dead certain that the rhino is going to charge, it is only a matter of reaction time and selection of one dimly seen shadow, for we are much too deep into her space, too close to the small calf, to get away with it. But almost immediately a feeling comes, a knowing, rather, that the moment of danger, if it ever existed, is already past, and I stop where I am, in pure breathless awe of this protean life form, six hundred thousand centuries on earth.

In the morning sun, reflecting the soft light of shining leaves, this huge gray creature carved of stone is a thing magnificent, the ugliest and most beautiful life imaginable, and her sheep-sized calf, which stands backed up into her flank, staring with fierce intensity in the wrong direction, is of a truly marvelous young foolishness.

Brian's voice comes softly, "Better back up, before she makes up her mind to rush at us," but I sense that he, too, knows that the danger has evaporated, and I linger a little longer where I am. There is no sound. Though her ears are high, the rhinoceros makes no move at all, there is no twitch of her loose hide, no swell or raising of the ribs, which are outlined in darker gray on the barrel flanks, as if holding her breath might render her invisible. The tiny eyes are hidden in the bags of skin, and though her head is high, extended toward us, the great hump of the shoulders rises higher still, higher even than the tips of those coarse dusty horns that are worth more than their weight in gold in the Levant. Just once, the big ears give a twitch; otherwise she remains motionless, as the two oxpeckers attending her squall uneasily, and a zebra yaps nervously back in the trees.

Then heavy blows of canvas wings dissolve the spell: an unseen griffon in the palm above flees the clacking fronds and, flying straight into the sun, goes up in fire. I rejoin the others. As we watch, the serene great beast settles backward inelegantly on her hind quarters, then lies down in the filtered shade to resume her rest, her young beside her.

We walk along a little way before I find my voice. "That was worth the whole safari," I say at last.

Brian nods. "Had to shoot one once that tossed a porter into a thorn bush and wouldn't give up, kept trying to get at him. But by and large, the rhino down in this part of the country have never given me much trouble." He turns his head and looks back at me over his shoulder. "Still, that's a lot closer than you want to get, especially with a gang of porters. If this was Tsavo—!" He rolls his eyes toward heaven. In an easing of the nerves, we burst out laughing, and the Africans, awe-struck until this moment, laugh as well: *kali* ("hot-tempered," dangerous) or not, a rhinoceros with new calf ten yards away was serious business!

Yet seeing the innocent beast lie down again, it was clear how simple it would be to shoot this near-blind creature that keeps so close to its home thickets, that has no enemies except this upright, evil-smelling shadow, so recent in its ancient world, against which it has evolved no defense. Its rough prong of compacted hair would be hacked off with a panga and shoved into a gunny sack as the triumphant voice of man moved onward, leaving behind in the African silence the dead weight of the carcass, the end-product of millions of browsing, sun-filled mornings, as the dependent calf emerges from the thicket, and stands by dumbly to await the lion.

# *from* Indian Country

1984

*While Matthiessen's more celebrated work* In the Spirit of Crazy Horse *focuses largely on the history of the exploitation of western native American tribes, particularly the Lakota,* Indian Country *reminds readers that tribes in the Southeast were ravaged by settlers—and those who followed—as well. An early chapter, "The Long River," set in the same country that serves as the setting for the three novels of Matthiessen's Watson trilogy, chronicles the troubled history of the Miccosukee Seminoles, who had fought the U.S. Army to a standstill in the Everglades.*

*The following selection, taken from the chapter "Lost Eloheh Land," tells of the Tennessee Valley Authority's notorious Tellico Dam, which uselessly choked off the Little Tennessee River over the protests of environmental and Cherokee activists. As elsewhere in his work about Indian people, Matthiessen uses a contemporary political struggle to lay bare centuries of bad blood between Indians and obdurate government agencies. "Why were the great historical values of this river, not to speak of its sacred importance to the Indians, given virtually no mention in the national debate on the Tellico Dam?" he writes. "For it seems clear that if the public had been fairly informed as to the true nature of what was being perpetrated at Tellico, the public servants could not have got away with it."*

## Lost Eloheh Land

**In the late nineteenth century,** a remnant band of Cherokee—descendants of those who had hidden in the Great Smokies in the

1830s when the rest of the tribe was "removed" on the Trail of Tears to Oklahoma—came down from the North Carolina mountains to a ceremonial place overlooking the valley of the Cherokee River. There an old prophet, climbing onto a high stump and gazing out over the traditional heartland of his people, received a vision of a dreadful day still several generations in the future when this valley would be flooded over, and the faces of countless buried ancestors would glimmer upward through the unnatural waters as through a floor of glass. Tearful and frightened, the old man told his people that they must resist the projects of the white men, "who didn't know what they were doing"; when the river no longer ran free through the sacred valley, the Ani Yunwiyah—"the Principal People"—would be destroyed forever as a tribe. The recent damming of the Cherokee River, now known as the Little Tennessee, fulfills this prophecy and affirms an older one that anticipated the white man's disturbance of the earth's natural balance, with calamitous consequences for mankind.

Although the Tennessee Valley Authority's Tellico Dam project had been repudiated for a decade in Congress and the courts as uneconomical, unlawful, and unnecessary, it finally achieved through procedural tricks and political blackmail what it had never been able to win in a fair hearing. In June 1979, a last-minute amendment insinuated into an energy and water appropriations bill authorized the TVA to complete the Tellico Dam "notwithstanding the Endangered Species Act or any other law"; this high-handed and very dangerous precedent is thought to be the first such rider ever to put an unfinished project beyond legal restraint. On September 25, President Carter, expressing "regret," failed to veto H.R. No. 4388, and on November 29, when the flood gates were lowered, a small perch called the snail darter, whose only known natural habitat was the last free-flowing stretch of the Little Tennessee River, became the earth's first living creature ever delivered willfully into oblivion.

Though only one of the many urgent reasons why the Tellico Dam should never have been started, this little fish was taken up by the news media to the virtual exclusion of more fundamental issues such as the transgression of Cherokee sacred ground. Even defenders of the darter became troubled by the trivialized controversy as set out by the dam's advocates and parroted in newspapers and on TV: did the perpetuation of a "useless" three-inch "minnow" justify the waste and critical energy loss of a nearly completed $110 million hydroelectric dam? As I discovered in early November 1979, when I went down to the Little Tennessee River to have a look at the historic valley before it disappeared, this presentation of the case was false from beginning to end.*

The TVA and its longtime supporters, led by local politicians and developers, big business, and big labor—all the old familiar well-fed faces—claimed that Tellico Lake was needed for recreation, improved navigation, and flood control; that much of the shoreline of the lake would be used for industrial development, providing jobs in this depressed pocket of western Appalachia; and that the dam would make a vital contribution to hydroelectric energy production in the region. In fact, twenty-four major dams and lakes already exist within sixty miles of Tellico, and most of them have large areas of undeveloped shores. The recreation, navigation, and flood control claims have no merit whatever, and as for the energy contribution, this dam contains no generator of any kind: its token contribution of twenty-three megawatts (out of a current TVA regional capacity of twenty-seven thousand) will be produced by a diversion canal through the nearly adjoining Fort Loudoun Dam on the Tennessee River.

How many Americans, I wonder, are even aware that the Tellico is a small dam in a thirty-eight-thousand-acre project and that most of that "wasted" $110 million was actually spent on speculative acquisition and road development of twenty-two thousand acres that were never intended to be flooded? Land appreciation of the proposed lakeside properties has long ago offset the $22 million in materials and labor (exactly one-fifth of the figure used for public

---

*Statements by traditional Cherokee people in what follows are taken mostly from affidavits supplied by their attorney, Ben Bridgers, of Sylva, North Carolina; Jimmie Durham's statements were provided by Mr. Durham himself. Environmental background material was furnished by the environmental attorney Zygmunt Plater, and the local residents Roy Warren and Janet Thiessen offered much incidental information.

consumption) that is the true cost of the dam and its embankments. And often these properties were taken by right of eminent domain with little or no concern for the rights of the legal owners. In a typical case, the TVA condemned the ninety-acre farm of an elderly widow, Mrs. Nell McCall, even though less than two acres were to be flooded. ("I offered to give them that for nothing," Mrs. McCall said, "but they said everybody had to go.") Under the circumstances, the 341 families evicted from their hard-won homesteads to make room for speculators in lakeside lots may be forgiven for calling the whole ruthless enterprise "a land grab."

In the Depression, when the Tellico was first conceived, the claims made for it by the TVA may have seemed valid: after all, the TVA had been set up to help the threadbare regional economy. Since then, it has ossified into a huge autonomous bureaucracy, influenced by special interest groups and "pork-barrel claques" tied to federal agencies. Grown immense at the bulging pork barrel of highway, dam, and waterway construction, it requires increasingly vast projects and appropriations merely to justify its girth—hence, the oppressive grid of steel and concrete that has locked up the rivers of this region into a chain of stagnant ponds descending from the mountains all the way west to the Mississippi.

The Tellico, which proposed to throttle the last wild stretch of the Little Tennessee, seemed like one dam too many even to the U.S. Congress, where it had been debated annually for the past fifteen years. Throughout this period, the proposed dam was protested by the Cherokee, who went unheard. TVA—or someone in Tennessee—wanted this dam badly, and the state's politicians, notably Senator Howard Baker, were encouraged to persist far beyond the call of duty. Funds for the dam were finally appropriated in 1966, but construction, started the next year, was halted in 1971 by a coalition of local people and environmentalists, who were able to demonstrate in court that the project flouted the National Environmental Policy Act. Thus, the shortcomings of Tellico were obvious well before the summer day in 1973 when an ichthyologist named David Etnier discovered a small, pretty, banded perch, unknown to science, at Coytee Springs, the historic site where British troops in 1756 made their first treaty with the Indians.

Biologists concluded that the original range of *Percina tanasi*—which needs a clear, cool flow of water to oxygenate its clean, pebble-bottom spawning beds—included most of the Tennessee River drainage; it was only after the TVA had killed twenty-five hundred miles of river that this species was apparently confined to the Little Tennessee. A volunteer lawyer, Zygmunt Plater, who has fought for six years against the Tellico, recalls the meeting when the Valley farmers agreed to file a suit on behalf of the darter under the Endangered Species Act of 1973: "I lived on this river all my life and I never heard of it," said Asa McCall (who died during the struggle, and whose widow, Nell, now seventy-five, was one of the last hold-outs against TVA seizure). "But if this little fish can help us lick this thing, then I'm all for it."

Almost overnight, this obscure perch (together with a reticent Maine weed called the furbish lousewort) became a kind of wry national joke. The joke was hammered by Tellico's proponents, who saw that the public would soon lose sympathy for a "useless minnow," and eventually this ridiculed small creature, used originally as a delaying action, was doing the cause a lot more harm than good, despite all efforts to point out its role as an indicator of human and economic values. It was also claimed that the fish had been transferred successfully into nearby streams: the truth was that two of the three transplanted populations had died out, and the third was threatened by the acid spills and other pollutants in the Hiwassee River.

Meanwhile the TVA had acquired a new board of directors, and with it a strange ambivalence in its own attitudes. In a letter to Secretary of the Interior Cecil Andrus, in April 1978, TVA Chairman David Freeman conceded that "contrary to TVA position, forming a permanent lake is not vital to the Tellico Project and may not even be the option with the greatest public benefits." Subsequently, a 258-page TVA document, "Alternatives for Completing the Tellico Project," acknowledged that income from the valuable farmland to be flooded would probably exceed the "projected benefits" of the new lake by nearly a million dollars per annum;* that four-teen million dollars in additional construction would be needed before the dam could pass safety requirements; that annual dam maintenance would substantially exceed its income; that local job opportunities created by the dam were outnumbered by those that would be lost; and that aside from the Endangered Species Act, the dam was in legal difficulties on numerous counts, including the Historic Preservation Act, the Environmental Policy Act, the Rivers and Harbors Act, the Clean Water Act, the Fish and Wildlife Coordination Act, and the Executive Order on Floodplain Management, none of which the TVA had complied with. ("TVA does not argue the law," says Ben Bridgers, attorney for the Cherokee. "They argue that they are *above* the law.")

Even the TVA, in short, had now concluded that its dam made no practical sense at all. From other points of view—moral, aesthetic, and environmental—it was what the Philadelphia *Inquirer* called "an abomination of irresponsibility . . . a towering symbol of almost everything that is rotten in the District of Columbia." A beautiful river known affectionately throughout the state as the "Little T" has been stopped up like a clogged pork barrel to create a muddy artificial lake, and silted beneath this superfluous lake will lie not only the drowned homesteads of hundreds of defenseless people but also sixteen thousand acres of some of the richest river-bottom farmland in the United States, and an historical treasure perhaps as important as all these other losses put together: the hundreds of archaeological sites in the Little Tennessee Valley include not only ancient mounds but the buried ruins of the Seven Towns that two centuries ago were the sacred center of the Cherokee Nation. (Most Eastern Cherokee now live on the Qualla Boundary reservation in the Blue Ridge Mountains, just across the North Carolina border, but the Little Tennessee remains the spiritual homeland.) A report prepared for the TVA by Interior Department archaeologists—dated

---

*TVA's candor about "projected benefits" would be more impressive in the absence of a congressional study made by the General Accounting Office in 1977, which concluded not only that the dam was uneconomic but that all but about one percent of TVA's dam benefit claims were unreliable.

May 24, 1979, but mysteriously withheld until after the final Tellico appropriations were signed into law by President Carter on September 25—ascribes "world-wide significance" to these sites, declaring that "the physical records of American prehistory present in Tellico cannot be matched in any other area this size in the continent."*

Why were the great historical values of this river, not to speak of its sacred importance to the Indians, given virtually no mention in the national debate on the Tellico Dam? For it seems clear that if the public had been fairly informed as to the true nature of what was being perpetrated at Tellico, the public servants could not have got away with it.

I had not expected that the place would be so lovely. In the sad, soft light of early November, the muted fire colors of the fall, moss-green faces of the rock walls at the river bends were reflected like memories of other centuries in the clear, swift water rolling down from the blue ridges of the Great Smoky Mountains, to the east. The day was filled with drifting leaves, the rich mineral smell of humus, a wistful resonance that echoed in the autumn calls of birds. "You don't have to be a Cherokee to feel the spiritual power here," murmured Roy Warren, a local environmentalist and amateur archaeologist who had fought for years against the loss of "the Little T," and who had kindly volunteered to share his knowledge. Warren had met me at Fort Loudoun, site of the first British outpost west of the Appalachians, and from where we stood, just upriver from the mouth of the stream known to the Indians as "Tellico," we could see the tattered cornfield that marks the buried town known as Tuskegee, birthplace of Sequoyah, the great Cherokee teacher whose name has been commemorated in a national park as well as a mighty tree. The Indians planted corn, beans, peas, potatoes, pumpkins, cabbages, melons, and tobacco. Gerhard de Brahm, the surveyor-general who built Fort Loudoun in 1756, recognized the superb quality of the topsoil in this "American Canaan," which he deemed "equal to

---

*Cultural Resources of the Tellico Project (TV-50461A), Department of the Interior, Interagency Archeological Services.

manure itself"; yet the white men had to be restrained by the Indians from building their fort right on top of the rich gardens.

In the eighteenth century, the domain of the powerful Ani Yunwiyah—the largest Indian nation in the South—extended into what are now eight states, and protected the beleaguered British of the Middle Atlantic states from French-led Indians to westward (the safety of the colonists "does under God depend on the friendship of the Cherokees," according to a declaration of the Carolina General Assembly in 1730). Yet four years after it was built, Fort Loudoun was destroyed by an embittered Ostenaco, who had once sent warriors to help George Washington and the Virginia Militia in the Big Sandy Expedition against the Shawnee; the Fort's only survivor was saved by Chief Attakullakulla, who had been painted by Hogarth in London in 1730 (Ostenaco himself was painted at a later date by Sir Joshua Reynolds) and who would say before his death, "I pity the white people, but the white people do not pity me." By the time Independence was declared, in 1776, the Cherokee and the colonists were mortal enemies, and the following year, the proud "Principal People" were defeated. Even so, Old Tassel refused the white men's demand for all land north of the Cherokee River, which would have put the white man's farms within sight of Chota:

> It is surprising that when we enter into treaties with our fathers the white people, their whole cry is more land. . . . It has seemed a formality with them to demand what they know we dare not refuse. . . . Much has been said of the want of what you term "Civilization" among the Indians. Many proposals have been made to us to adopt your laws, your religion, your manners, and your customs. . . . We should be better pleased with beholding the good effects of these doctrines in your own practices than in hearing you talk about them."*

A rabble of "American" settlers was already coveting the Valley, and pieces of its land began to go. In 1814, still trying hard to accommodate and even emulate the white men, the Cherokee set Andrew

---

*Alberta and Carson Brewer, "Valley So Wild: A Folk History" (Knoxville: East Tennessee Historical Society, 1975).

Jackson on the road to the White House by turning the tide in the Battle of Horseshoe Bend against the Creek, an act of friendship which was promptly repaid by a final rush upon their lands in Tennessee. In 1828, gold was discovered on Cherokee lands in Georgia, and the following year President Jackson recommended that his old allies—most of them Christians—be sent away to Indian Territory west of the Mississippi, where a number of displaced Indians had gone as early as 1817. The Removal Act passed by a single vote in 1830; it was fought by such distinguished Americans as Henry Clay, Daniel Boone, and Daniel Webster, and was also repudiated by Chief Supreme Court Justice John Marshall. (But Marshall did Indians a fatal disservice by declaring them "domestic dependent nations" of the American republic, and this at a time when many of these nations were still uncontacted, far less conquered; this opinion by a great jurist "friendly" to the Indians has been cited ever since as an argument against Indian claims to sovereignty.) The Cherokee were banished to present-day Oklahoma, together with the Choctaw, Chickasaw, and Seminole, as well as their old enemies the Creek, and the cost of the Removal was deducted from the $4.5 million awarded them in compensation for the loss of most of the southeastern United States. "Their calamities were of ancient date, and they knew them to be irremediable," de Tocqueville wrote of the passing bands of stoic, ragged Choctaw. The exodus culminated in 1838, when almost all the Cherokee remaining were rounded up by General Winfield Scott and "removed" westward: this was the infamous Trail of Tears, which at least four thousand Indians did not survive. "The Cherokee Removal was the cruelest work I ever saw," said one of Scott's own soldiers.

Driving farther up the Valley, we left the main road and crossed old fields, now condemned, that according to Warren had been farmed by the same family ever since the Cherokee were driven out. (The Indians' rights to their own land have been ignored since their first land claims in 1820.) A sharp-shinned hawk darted back and forth, once, twice, three times, over the hedgerows, in apparent pursuit of small foraging parties of titmice and chickadees, and a marsh hawk tilted at slow speed over the dun and wheat and gold of the river bottom. On high ground overlooking the broad valley, where sparrows flicked and twitched through the yellowed leaves, stood huge red and black oaks that had served as shade trees for a farmstead that had come and gone, leaving an emptiness in the old grove that was somehow deepened by the autumn clamor of the jays and crows. The farmstead overlooked the sites of Tommotley (Hewed-Timber Town) and Toqua, named for a great mythic fish which inhabits the river at this place. Toqua was a Mound-Builder site before the coming of the Cherokee, and throughout the Valley the buried evidence of Stone Age man and the mysterious Mound-Builders—some of the sites are thought to be eight thousand years old—is scarcely touched, despite the crude and hasty digs that the threat of flooding has inspired. In 1967, archaeologists of the University of Tennessee were invited by the TVA to investigate these sites as well as others, which they did on an emergency "salvage" basis, using TVA's backhoes and bulldozers. Though later work was more responsible, the early "digs" were crude and greedy. "It was infuriating," said Roy Warren, an amateur archaeologist who located the old gate of Fort Loudoun about six years ago. "Those so-called archaeologists went ripping into one of the most beautiful Indian mounds in the whole country, and when they were finished, there was nothing but a pile of dirt crisscrossed with ditches." He showed me ugly photographs that he had taken of the damage done at Toqua and the other villages, the exposed skeletons in the broken graves, the ornaments, pottery, axe heads, and other artifacts that lay hidden in such profusion here beneath our feet, the gangs of unsupervised looters—or "grave poachers," as the Indians call them—who descended on the place: 634 graves were excavated at the Toqua site alone. "It was quite a while before TVA got around to putting in that fence," Warren said, pointing at a rectangular enclosure with a sign that read "Archeological Site—Property of the U.S. Government." For some reason, the bureaucrats had kept the patch inside the wire carefully mowed, and the spot of caged lawn looked lonely in the autumnal colors of the valley, like an unused cemetery for dogs. "Yessir," Warren said, disgusted still. "That's what these people call the Chota Mound. It isn't Chota and it isn't a mound, not anymore."

As he spoke, he turned his head toward the sound of a fast-moving car: a white van was howling down upon us with undue speed, considering the fact that we were parked in a dead-end turnoff. "They're pouncing on us even before we *do* anything!" Roy complained, mildly amused. As the van wheeled to a halt, I could see that the uniformed guard inside was holding a microphone to his mouth, as if summoning assistance; recognizing Warren, he relaxed his vigilance only slightly. "Back again, huh?" he said. "We never give up," Warren said affably. The guard, heavyset with slicked black hair, in crisp khaki and a bright white T-shirt, looked me over; he asked Warren my identity, which he wrote down. Aggravated by the way he did this, I made a show of reading his badge and taking down *his* identity, then inquired if this wasn't public land. "Feder'l land!" he said. "That's not public?" I asked. He eyed me narrowly, to show me he had me spotted as a troublemaker, and certainly, he was equipped for trouble: besides the handgun on his hip, he had an Ithaca .37 riot gun mounted upright beside him and a carbine rifle ready on the back seat. "What are you guarding?" I inquired, jerking my chin at all the shooting irons. "Berl grounds," he said, "'n' loot-ers." Warren sighed. "Won't need to guard them much longer, I guess," he said pleasantly. "OK if we look around a little?"

We continued eastward up the Valley, on the new road along the wood edge bulldozed up out of the "borra pits" and bulwarked by stone riprap wall; when all this bottomland is flooded, this road will be the lakeside drive for the new shorefront owners on Tellico Lake. The fallow bottomlands were set about with gentle wooded hills, in the last oak reds and sweet-gum purples and hickory yellows of the autumn, and here and there a gold leaf-burst of sassafras, in one of the loveliest prospects of river and mountains I have ever seen. In this broad and harmonious bend on the south side of what was once known as the Cherokee River were the sites of Tennasee, or Old Town, for which the state was named, and Chota, the Council Town, the secular and ceremonial center of the Cherokee Nation. Like Toqua, Tanasi and Chota had been grievously assaulted by the emergency archaeology demanded by the TVA: when Roy Warren had first come here, four years earlier, the old lady whose family had lived here since the nineteenth century burst into tears as she described to him the desecrations that had taken place. Warren pointed out a three-acre riprapped elevation that is soon to be an island: "They bulldozed that thing up and named it Chota," he said, "as a consolation to the Indians."

Here at Chota in 1797, the future French king Louis Philippe fell off his horse in the furor of an Indian ball game, and later slept in the place of honor between the chief's grandmother and great-aunt; Warren pointed out the flat where it is thought the ball field was located. And here at Chota, just two weeks ago, the Cherokee and a number of white sympathizers, undeterred by nails strewn across the access road and some sticks of dynamite—apparently planted by those local people whose property near the new lake has soared in value—had held a cheerful rally by the river. That day, Roy Warren had made friends from the Cherokee reservation on the Qualla Boundary, fifty miles eastward in the North Carolina mountains, where the remnant Cherokee had hidden when their kinsmen were rounded up and driven off to Oklahoma.

At Chota, the river flowed between grassy meadow banks and beautiful white rock, and Warren searched the sandy riffles, hoping to show me one of the big fish that have made this the finest brown trout stream in the East. "There's trout in here up to thirty pounds," he told me, "and the fishermen bring a million dollars every year to local business; nobody talks much about the trout, but they're going to go, too." There were still two ancient Indian fish traps in this part of the river, stone walls that supported weirs of sticks, with a wicker basket net at the point of the V where the walls met, downstream. But today the clear river ran too deep, too swift, and like the doomed trout, the ancient fish traps remained hidden.

Roy Warren waved an arm at the empty woods and the blue mountains rising beyond. "They even claimed they wanted to 'improve navigation'! What're they gonna do, run up a barge load of garbage for the possums?!"

The easternmost of the Seven Towns (seven is a sacred number to the Cherokee) was Tseetaco, "Good Fishing Place," located between two hills, for at this place the Valley had already begun to narrow, and the strange steep ridges known to the Cherokee as "the Enemy Mountains"—home of the dread ogress known as Spear-

Finger—loomed high over the river in the northeast. At Tseetaco, in 1788, in the course of the last resistance to white encroachment, a Cherokee war party surprised and killed a detachment of militia raiding the Indian orchards, in what became known as the Battle of the Peaches. Warren wonders if Tseetaco might not have been the oldest and the largest town of all: in just one and one-half acres of excavated ground, he said, there was evidence of 234 burials. As at the other sites, the Indian remains, together with ceremonial artifacts of burial, were made off with by the white people, despite the distress and protest of the Cherokee, and he suspected that most of them wound up in labeled boxes in the McClung Museum at the University of Tennessee. Some 1,140 Indian remains are known to have been taken, and Indian requests for reinterment have been ignored, whereas the graves in the white cemeteries in the Valley have been carefully relocated elsewhere. The Indians, profoundly upset by the disturbance of sacred burial grounds and ancestral spirits, would prefer that the graves were damaged by the rising water rather than have the bones picked over by the curious fingers of the white man; nevertheless, they dread the artificial flood, which they perceive as an unnatural inversion that forces man out of harmony with his surroundings. "If the homeland of our fathers is covered with this water," an old medicine man named Lloyd Sequoyah has said, "it will cover the medicine and spiritual strength of our people because this is the place from which the Cherokee people came. When this is destroyed, the Cherokee people cease to exist. . . . Then all of the peoples of the earth cease to exist."

A few miles above Tseetaco is Chilhowee Dam, named for another Cherokee town submerged above it. Warren asked if I wished to see this dam, and I said no. On the way back down the Valley, in the sharp shadow lines of autumn dusk, we passed the parked van of the guard. "Next time we see you," Roy Warren called out to him, "I guess we'll be riding in a boat."


How amazing it seemed that in this state, where the economy is based in tourism and agriculture, its congressmen would sacrifice a lovely, historic valley in the face of so much well-informed opinion that for more than a decade has dismissed Tellico as a bad idea. Yet in 1978, Senator Howard Baker, sensing that hard times had diverted public sympathy from that pesky "minnow" to all those "wasted" megawatts and millions, cosponsored a Cabinet-level review committee (including the Secretaries of Interior, Agriculture, and Army) whose first business was to decide if Tellico should be exempted from the provisions of the Endangered Species Act. To his dismay, this imposing group agreed unanimously that Tellico was economically unsound (as the Chairman of the Council of Economic Advisers, Charles L. Schultze, pointed out, the total projected benefits of the dam amounted to less than the cost of completing the damned thing, let alone building it) and therefore did not deserve exemption: after more than a decade of court and congressional hearings, the Tellico pork barrel was sealed. But on June 18, 1979, in a nearly empty House, Baker's confederate, Republican Representative John Duncan, flouting House Rule No. 21 that forbids using appropriations bills to change existing laws, used a whole bag of procedural tricks to sneak an unseen, unread, undescribed, and undebated amendment past his unsuspecting colleagues in just forty-three seconds. One of the victims, Representative Paul McCloskey (Democrat from California), warned the House that its integrity had been undermined, that the public would condemn Congress for adopting without reading "an amendment of this degree of controversy."

On its first test, the amendment was repudiated by the Senate, but on September 10, Senator Baker made last-minute deals with (let us name these heroes) Senators Danforth, Dole, Domenici, Gravel, and Wallop, to win by just four votes, declaring untruthfully to the end that the dam represented vital energy and that the future of the transplanted darter was assured. Baker may have suspected that President Carter, in his eagerness for re-election, did not have character enough to veto a whole "energy" bill merely to eliminate a dishonest amendment, although Secretary Andrus urged the veto ("I hate to see the snail darter get credit for stopping a project that was ill-conceived and uneconomic in the first place"); if so, his instinct was correct: "with regret" the President signed into law an amendment designed to frustrate the will of the American people as expressed in Congress and the courts. (The day after President Carter signed the fatal amendment, he telephoned the environmental lawyer Zygmunt Plater from the presidential airplane, asking Plater, in effect, to tell him that what he had done was for the best. "He seemed to be whimpering for forgiveness," recalls Plater, who told the President that no conservationist in the country could conceivably support what he had done.) In cynical ambition — to embarrass Carter, to assist a crony, or perhaps just to please those local politicians who had invested in lakeview properties back home — Baker had sabotaged the unanimous findings of the responsible review committee sponsored by himself, thereby damaging not only the integrity of Congress but the long-term welfare of the nation that he claimed, every four years, to be fit to lead.

The day after Carter's cave-in, the TVA rushed in its machines to complete the dam. But on October 12, the Eastern Cherokee, citing the American Indian Religious Freedom Act of 1978, appealed to the U.S. District Court in Knoxville for an injunction against the flooding, pending a hearing on their claim that the Duncan Amendment was unconstitutional: the destruction of their spiritual homeland, which many still visited regularly, they said, would deny religious rights that were guaranteed by the free-exercise clause of the First Amendment.

The TVA attorneys, calling the Cherokee appeal "unfair," pretended that the religious issue had been brought up too late, even though the Indians (who had no constitutional right to sue until the federal government acquired ownership of the land) have been protesting the wholesale desecration of their sacred burial grounds and ceremonial sites since 1967. The TVA made much of the fact that Ross Swimmer, Chief of the Cherokee Nation in Oklahoma, expressing gratitude to the TVA for having located Chota for the Indians, had belittled the idea that Chota was a sacred site; his view was repudiated by the traditional Ketooah Band on his own reservation, who strongly support the position of the Eastern Cherokee. Chief Swimmer, a well-to-do bank president and tribal attorney (and protégé of the larcenous "principal chief," W. W. Keeler), had recently declared himself a Republican candidate for Senator from Oklahoma, an ambition in which, interestingly enough, he had the pledged support of Senator Howard Baker of Tennessee.

On the morning of the day that I visited Chota, the Cherokee appeal for a temporary injunction against the flooding was turned down by the U.S. District Court in Knoxville on the grounds that ownership of the property involved was a prior condition of a First Amendment claim. Subsequently it was dismissed by the Sixth Circuit Court of Appeals in Cincinnati, and by Justices Stewart and Brennan of the Supreme Court, who simply scribbled on the appeal the word "Denied." The judiciary, it appeared, was weary of the fight, and anxious to bury the whole smelly mess as soon as possible. As the Cherokee's lawyer told me, "We've been overwhelmed by the past, not by the merits of the case; all we're asking for is a chance to appeal the merits. The judges are reading their newspapers, not the Constitution." In questions of First Amendment rights, the government must demonstrate a "compelling state interest" before a Constitutional protection can be overruled; "compelling state interest" scarcely describes the ambiguous situation acknowledged in the TVA's own big book of "Alternatives."

On November 3, a bright blue mountain day, I drove eastward up the Pigeon River into the Great Smoky Mountains; in the fall breeze, the red dogwood leaves and berries seemed to flutter in the cold sun-sparkle of the stream. Crossing the North Carolina line, I arrived soon afterward at the town of Cherokee, where I was met by a pretty young woman named Myrtle Driver. Ms. Driver, who helps the elderly people of the community as an interpreter in their dealings with white people and who served as a tribal interpreter in court depositions having to do with the Tellico Dam, led me to an out-of-the-way community back in the mountains known to the Indians as Raven's Ford, called commonly "Big Cove," where I hoped to talk to two elderly medicine people, Ammoneeta and his brother Lloyd Sequoyah, about the Cherokee's continued interest in the valley. But Ammoneeta was in the hospital and Lloyd could not be found; instead we visited Myrtle's father, a traditional healer named Charlie Johnson, who said that when his great-great-grand-mother visited Chota as a little girl, crossing the mountains on a walk that required several days, there were a few old Indians living there still. "That place was sacred to us," he said, "and it was also the capital of our nation, the way you people think of Washington, D.C." Not until these years of struggle to save the sacred valley, Myrtle said, had she realized how much her heritage still meant to her. In the words of Jimmie Durham, a Western Cherokee who had testified against the dam in 1978, in a Congressional hearing,

Is there a human being who does not revere his homeland, even though he may not return? . . . In our own history, we teach that we were created there, which is truer than anthropological truth because it was there that we were given our vision as the Cherokee people. . . . In the language of my people . . . there is a word for land: Eloheh. This same word also means history, culture, and religion. We cannot separate our place on earth from our lives on the earth nor from our vision nor our meaning as a people. We are taught from childhood that the animals and even the trees and plants that we share a place with are our brothers and sisters. So when we speak of land, we are not speaking of property, territory, or even a piece of ground upon which our houses sit and our crops are grown. We are speaking of something truly sacred.

Myrtle's aunt, Emmaline Sequoyah Driver, who lives deeper in the mountains, up the Straight Fork of the Oconaluftee, had made a recent pilgrimage to the sacred Eloheh Land, where she had visited the place where the old seer "made his last prophecy" upon the stump: she is a full-blood Cherokee who prefers to speak in her own tongue, and so is her brother Ammoneeta, who had lived for five years in an abandoned cabin at Chota and still makes regular journeys there to gather medicinal herbs, chant *idi-gawe-sti*, or sacred incantations, and perform the going-to-water purification (the bather dips seven times into the flowing river, facing the rising sun). "We have always been told that the Valley was the Center, that's where we began," Myrtle Driver said. "We don't have to live there. Just knowing it is there makes us feel better."

Like her brothers, Emmaline Driver had given a deposition against the dam on religious grounds, but now she shrugged. "White people mostly don't care what we think, we're just Indians. They say, Sorry, we can't help you," the old lady said.

"No, they *won't* help you, just *because* you're an Indian!" Myrtle Driver exclaimed, relating the trouble she had had in getting anyone to pay attention after her brother had been shot by a white man. "Had to have his leg amputated. Wouldn't give us a court hearing until I said I was friends with the U.S. marshal over in Asheville, and when they *had* the hearing, they wouldn't let us know the day, so because my brother wasn't there, they threw his case out!" I nodded unhappily: from travels among Indians elsewhere in the country, I knew there was nothing unusual about this sort of justice.

The Eastern Cherokee of the Qualla Boundary are among the few Indian peoples east of the Mississippi still living in their original homeland, but these mountains were not the "Center" of their nation. "In talking to these elders," Myrtle said later, "it seems that a lot of our words and traditions and legends began down there at Chota: this place up here in the mountains came much later. Seems like that place is the source of almost all the myths of the Cherokee people. Like Dakwa, the big fish—that's Toqua—well, the snail darter became 'a big fish' to the Cherokee people when it stopped the flooding. TVA tried to say we weren't aware of that place—it isn't true. In our own family, people always went over there. That chief out in Oklahoma, Ross Swimmer, he sold us out, and he ought to be hung; he actually *thanked* the TVA for letting us know where our own place was!" The Indians are under no illusion about the real purpose of the Tellico, which in the words of an old man named Goliath George, is there to "fatten someone's hip pocket"; and this, too, he says, fulfills a prophecy, for "Tellico" is the white man's distortion of the Cherokee *ade la eqwa*, or "big money." "Even if they didn't respect us living Indians, they should at least respect our dead Indians," Goliath George said in an affidavit. "Since I have heard about this dam, I have been on my knees about these things many times."

The next day, I telephoned Lewis Gwin, a TVA spokesman for the Tellico, who said that no definite date had been set for the closing of the dam; the last crops in the Valley, grown under lease, had not been harvested, and there were still a few people, including Mrs. McCall, who had not moved out of their homes as they were told. Mr. Gwin seemed anxious to point out that the present Board of Directors was not originally responsible for this project, and had sponsored the candid "Alternatives" report in order that Congress might make the proper choice. True, Congress had decided against the dam three times, but once Congress had ordered the TVA to proceed "notwithstanding the Endangered Species Act or any other law," the TVA had no choice—"Our hands are tied," Mr. Gwin told me. As for the Cherokee appeal, he acknowledged that they had protested the dam for fifteen years, but he could not comment on the validity of their claim while the case was in litigation.

After talking to Gwin, I drove over to Tellico on the highway that crosses the huge old Atomic Energy Commission (now the Nuclear Regulatory Commission) reservation in Oak Ridge. Off to the west, I could see the huge strip-mine scars along the high slopes of the Cumberlands, commemorating the days when this country had been stripped of its virgin forests. When the day of gigantic hydroelectric and nuclear power schemes arrived, the poverty-stricken people of Appalachia said very little; dependent on the timber and coal companies, then big government, they were evicted from their homes over and over to clear the way for dams and lakes and AEC reservations.

In this sinister forest, unsettling signs directed the authorized traveler to such destinations as the Weapons (Y-12) and Gas Diffusion (K-24) Plants; other signs read "Bear Creek Road—Closed to Public"; "Experimental Area—Trespassers Will Be Prosecuted"; "No Swimming or Fishing"; "Water Unfit for Human Consumption." Here and there, bright yellow warnings read "Radiation Hazard—Keep Out." Although it was Sunday, a line of military tanks clanked down the highway, escorted by the pervasive security vehicles, and both tanks and police seemed to intensify an oppressive atmosphere of man at war with his own habitat, of a blind few imposing their will upon the many. However, public relations are still important: the TVA's nuclear reactor in Chattanooga has been made part of the "American heritage" by being named after the great Sequoyah,* and in this region big green signs do their best to persuade the casual observer that the TVA's Tellico Project is "Building a Better Environment."

Where the highway crosses the huge Fort Loudoun Dam across the Tennessee River, one can see the small Tellico Dam where it blocks the mouth of the Little T downriver: the lakes behind these dams will be less than a half mile apart, and largely devoid of the local recreationists for whom they were constructed, to judge from the sterile emptiness of Fort Loudoun Lake on a sunny, warm, and windless Sunday morning. Finding the Tellico heavily fenced against the taxpayers, with a gate that brandished warning signs as well as chains, I drove down to a parking lot under the Fort Loudoun Dam, then walked downriver, passing without difficulty through a fence in the river woods and moving inland through the fields at the mouth of the Little T to the long embankment for impounding water that leads out to the dam itself. Climbing the embankment, I could see far up into sun-misted distances of the lovely valley; in the softened autumn light of the river bottom, a lonely farmer was working on Sunday to harvest the last crop from this "American Canaan" that has fed man bountifully for perhaps three thousand years. The sight of that lone, hastening figure, working against time and greed and folly, brought on a wave of melancholy and profound anger.

At both ends of the embankment stood large herds of huge yellow earth-moving machines. Because it was Sunday, these dinosaurs were still, but at the sight of a loose citizen, a security vehicle came in a great hurry down the road. "Ain't supposed to *be* in here!" the guard exclaimed, instructing me to get into the back. I could truthfully say that I had seen no signs to that effect down by the river, and he seemed happy to accept my alibi. "They knock 'em all down!" he said, perplexed. "Can't keep a sign up for two days!" He drove me out to the chained gate where another guard in big black

---

*In 1981, the Sequoyah Plant led the nation with 238 potentially dangerous "incidents"; it operated only 11 percent of the year. TVA's controversial Clinch River nuclear breeder reactor in the same region is named for Colonel Douglas Clinch, who led a detachment of Tennessee Cavalry to "chastise" the Seminole in 1813.

shades, thumbs hooked into his holster belt, awaited us: this one's manner suggested that I was getting off too easy. When I asked him why the Tellico needed so much security, he said they had had a bomb threat just four days ago. Both guards blamed the destruction of the signs on "environmentalists," probably "them ones that had planted that dynamite up there at the Chota Mound two weeks ago, and strewn them nails on the road while they were at it."

The first guard, going off duty, was kind enough to offer me a lift back down to the "T." He was an older man, born up the Little T in the region of the Indian villages, and he admitted that the dam was a poor idea, but like most Americans, he had come to accept the version of the controversy drilled into all of us by the news media, and felt that not to finish the job now would be an unacceptable waste of money. Anyway, he said, there were no snail darters left in the Little T; they had all been transplanted out of Coytee Springs and other places. The old man pointed at the mud gray Tennessee. "Hell," he said, "they's a big sandy bar down here on the T, they doin' better there than they *ever* done up the Little T! Why, right out here where we're lookin' at, they's so many of them darters, the fishermen been dippin' 'em right with the minnas, usin' 'em for bait!"

He granted that the Cherokee had a case. "Hell, they's Injuns buried all over the place up here, and U.T. [the University of Tennessee] has people all over, diggin' up graves." He shook his head in disapproval, then jerked his head in the direction of what I took to be a certain grave he knew in some town on the far side of the river. "I don't blame them Cherokees for bein' so upset. Anybody tried to dig up *my* son, I mean, I'd *do* sump'n about it!" I nodded. How would a white community react if more than a thousand of its forebears had been excavated without ceremony and heaped up in a museum basement?

The following week, official vehicles descended upon the last hold-outs in the Valley, Mrs. Nell McCall and Thomas Moser, who were evicted from their homes by federal marshals. Mrs. McCall had been promised that her belongings would be spared, including her mother's china, but when she returned that afternoon, her house had been burned down, china and all. Mr. Moser's house, also destroyed, was the house where he was born. In the words of

Mrs. McCall's daughter, in a letter sent me a few days after the eviction, "The 'horrors' that happened on November 13 are not easily forgotten or forgiven."

On the morning of November 29, without waiting for the Indians' court hearing, the TVA closed the Tellico Dam, and the clear waters of the Little T backed up behind it; in a few weeks, the darter's spawning beds would be silted over. The twenty-fifth artificial lake within sixty miles rose to flood the Seven Towns, as the Cherokee (supported now by the ACLU and the National Council of Churches) kept on fighting for a hearing in the courts. The Indians believe that wave action from the rising water will erode the ancestral graves that escaped the backhoes of the archaeologists; they also believe that the Little T will return into its bed and that the sacred valley will restore itself if the dam is opened by court order in the next few years.

Having made four desperate appeals to the White House in the final months without receiving so much as an acknowledgment, the Eastern Cherokee had abandoned any hope of honest dealing with the TVA, for reasons made plain in a letter from John Crowe, Principal Chief of the Eastern Cherokee, to Chairman Freeman:

> The Cherokee people are well aware of the fact that white graves in the Tellico project area were removed and reinterred with all due respect to the law and religious beliefs. They are also aware that TVA did not treat their ancestors with the same respect and regards for religious beliefs but chose to sack up their bones and toss them into a basement at the University of Tennessee.
>
> TVA is guilty of the most flagrant racial and religious discrimination by its actions and this has been made clear by your refusal to honor our request. I cannot find words strong enough to convey my contempt for the lack of honor to be found among TVA and federal officials.

The Tellico Dam is a transgression against whites as well as Indians; much that is vital to our national well-being will be lost forever under the dead waters of Big Money Lake. Let them dynamite the dam and drain the Valley. Let the concrete ruin stand as a monument, not to short-sightedness and greed but to the wise redress of a national calamity; as a symbol and a deterrent, the ruin would more than justify the wasted money. A beautiful river can be restored, invaluable farmland and historic sites can be recovered without undue damage, and perhaps one day the farmers, too, will have their day in court. Only a small pretty gleam of river life called the snail darter will be gone, like the old way of the Cherokee before it.

A Cherokee has said, "We want our universe, our Eloheh Land, with all of its fish and all of its life to continue. And we are sure that this *cannot* be against the interests and wishes of the American people." If the Cherokee River is not restored, the "strong water" will be transformed into *ama huli wotshi,* or "dead water," the floor of glass of the old prophecy through which the faces of the ancestors will appear, like pale dead leaves seen dimly through black ice.

*In November 1980, the snail darter was "rediscovered" about eighty miles south of the dam site; since then, it has turned up at three other locations (in Alabama and Georgia as well as Tennessee) and is no longer considered an endangered species.*

*Three years after its gates were closed, the TVA itself acknowledges that the Tellico Dam Project is a failure. Not a single industry has located there, and much of the land around the lake is on the market. Yet previous owners of this land are denied the right to buy back their property, about half of which was transferred in November 1982 to a "nonprofit development agency," composed, predictably, of Tennessee politicians and local bankers, presumably for future speculation. "I'm not a defender of the Tellico," former Chairman David Freeman says today, taking refuge behind the Congressional order to complete it. "I don't think there's any way the Cherokee are ever going to feel good about the Tellico project. It's flooded out their ancestral homelands. . . . Every displaced landowner is going to be bitter the rest of his life."*

*Ammoneeta Sequoyah once observed that with the destruction of Eloheh Land the life of the Cherokee people and his own would come to an end. Both Ammoneeta and his brother Lloyd died in 1981, the last Cherokee medicine men to be born into their ancient tradition.*

# *from* Men's Lives

1986

*For all his world travel, Matthiessen remains well-rooted in the tiny Long Island hamlet of Sagaponack, where he has lived for the last four decades. During his early years as a writer, Matthiessen wrote only from late fall to early spring; other seasons were spent working as a commercial fisherman and running a charter fishing boat out of Montauk. In* Men's Lives *he pays homage to a local community facing pressures similar to those faced by the wild lands and animals he explored abroad. Here, small-scale commercial fishermen are confronted both by depleted stocks of striped bass—victims of pollution and overfishing—and legislation backed by "powerful sportsmen's organizations," who want the remaining fish reserved for their own clients. Commercial fishermen were, in effect, becoming an endangered species themselves. "Among South Fork fisheries, the one most imperiled by bass legislation is ocean haul-seining, which no longer exists anywhere else in the United States except on the Outer Banks of North Carolina," Matthiessen writes in his preface. "Because their fishery will be the first to disappear, Long Island's ocean haul-seiners are the main subject of this book. In haul-seining, a net-filled dory is launched through the open surf, an enterprise that, on a rough Atlantic day, demands nerve and experience as well as skill. Without the striped bass, haul-seining is unlikely to survive, and the end of this fishery will mean the end of a surfboat tradition that began when the Atlantic coast was still the American frontier."*

*In the following excerpts, from chapters throughout the book, Matthiessen tells the story of several generations of fishing families— many of whom he knew and worked with during his own fishing career—and of the difficulty of wresting a living from the inshore waters.*

**Two humpback whales,** the first I have seen in a decade, roll softly on the surface, like black shining rocks in the silver ocean. Great whales were once so common off the coast at this far east end of Long Island that shore whaling was an industry, but I have seen them from the shore only a few times in my life, and, feeling elated, walk with them along the beach a little way. They move slowly to the east, off the narrow strip of sand that separates Georgica Pond from the Atlantic.

The wind is out of the northwest, and the day is cold, but already the sea breathes its sweet stink of regeneration. The great animals spout thinly in the cold clear light, and the wind fans the spume to mist on the huge horizon.

A few years ago, on another day of spring, a Sagaponack neighbor brought a fish into my yard that had turned up in the nets early that morning. For several years I had hauled seine with the beach crews, and this farmer-fisherman had done so for much longer, and neither of us had ever seen this beautiful silver fish, ten pounds or better, that he held before him with both hands in instinctive ceremony.

I turned toward the house to fetch my book of fishes, then turned back, grinning. It was not the arrangement of the fins that told me what it was but a pang of intuition. Perhaps this rare fish from the cold Atlantic was on its way to the ancient mouth of the Connecticut River, which fifteen thousand years ago (before the melting glaciers raised the level of the seas, separating Long Island from the southern New England coast) was located at what is now Plum Gut, off the North Fork of this great fish-tailed island. Like the great whales, the Atlantic salmon—once so abundant in the fresh clear rivers that the Massachusetts colonists were forbidden to feed it to indentured servants more than once a week—had been reduced to these wandering survivors, to be wondered at in the cold spring sun like emblems of a New World prematurely old.

This book is witness to the lives of the commercial fishermen of the South Fork of Long Island. The inshore fisheries with which it will concern itself fall into five divisions—netting, trapping, dragging, shellfishing, and setting pots. A full-time fisherman, or bayman, might participate in most of these activities in a single year. Those with large work boats of thirty-foot or better may devote themselves to dragging all year long, adapting their boats in certain seasons to lobstering, or setting cod trawls, or long-lining for tilefish, swordfish, tuna. Because a big boat with high fuel costs and overhead must be kept working, such men rarely fish inshore, and are not baymen. However, many baymen crew on draggers in the wintertime, and many draggermen return to the bay as they grow older.

Full-time baymen—there are scarcely one hundred left on the South Fork—must also be competent boatmen, net men, carpenters, and mechanics, and most could make good money at a trade, but they value independence over security, preferring to work on their own schedule, responsible only to their own families. Protective of their freedom to the point of stubbornness, wishing only to be left alone, they have never asked for and never received direct subsidies from town or county, state or federal government. Being self-employed, they receive none of the modern social supports such as unemployment insurance and sickness compensation, and because their income is uncertain and irregular, they can rarely obtain bank loans and mortgages. Yet every year they find themselves taxed harder for boats and trailers, trucks and gasoline, shellfish digging and fish shipping licenses, docking license, scallop opening license, permits to take certain species (shellfish, lobster, striped bass). Nearly a dozen taxes, permits, and licenses plague every bayman ready to engage in the various fisheries according to seasonal availability and market demand, as the inshore fisherman must do if he is to earn his living all year round.

Meanwhile his livelihood is threatened by powerful sportsmen's organizations seeking to limit the commercial harvest of so-called game fish, in particular the striped bass, a species that, for most commercial men of the South Fork, represents the difference between bare survival and a decent living. For the past half-century, the sportsmen's crusades to reserve this fish for their own use were defeated by the bass itself, which seemed to grow more plentiful each year. Then, in the seventies, the species suffered a serious decline, apparently the result of cumulative pollution of its main spawning grounds in the tributaries of the Chesapeake Bay. In New York State in 1983 the anglers' organizations, supported by federal agencies, succeeded in promoting legislation that drastically curtailed the striped bass harvest by commercial fishermen and threatened the very survival of their way of life.

Among South Fork fisheries, the one most imperiled by bass legislation is ocean haul-seining, which no longer exists anywhere else in the United States except on the Outer Banks of North Carolina. Because their fishery will be the first to disappear, Long Island's ocean haul-seiners are the main subject of this book. In haul-seining, a net-filled dory is launched through the open surf, an enterprise that, on a rough Atlantic day, demands nerve and experience as well as skill. Without the striped bass, haul-seining is unlikely to survive, and the end of this fishery will mean the end of a surfboat tradition that began when the Atlantic coast was still the American frontier.

Most of the surfmen come from the main fishing clans, which descend from the farmer-fishermen and the offshore whalers of centuries ago. In recent decades, most fishing families have been forced to sell off land that had been in the family for generations. Those who are left subsist in the last poor corners of a community in which they were once the leading citizens. Meanwhile their townsmen, prospering on the bland resort economy, have mainly lost a historical sense of the ocean character of the South Fork that attracted so many wealthy visitors in the first place. Few of the few who are even aware that a fishing community still exists enjoy the continuity with the past represented by boat-filled backyards in the oak woods of Amagansett and the Springs, by sharpies and scallop dredges, flag buoys and fish traps, by a dory in black silhouette on the huge empty sky off the ocean beach.

Here within sight of the blue shadow of New England's industrial seaboard ten miles to the north, moving at daybreak on back roads, the fishermen go their traditional way down to the sea. They are tough, resourceful, self-respecting, and also (some say) hidebound and cranky, too independent to organize for their own survival. Yet even their critics must acknowledge a gritty spirit that was once more highly valued in this country than it is today. Because their children can no longer afford to live where their families have harvested the sea and land for three hundred years, these South Fork baymen—old-time Americans who still speak with the Kentish and Dorset inflections of Elizabethan England—may soon become rare relics from the past, like the Atlantic right whales, a cow and calf, that in the winter of 1984–85 have been appearing here and there off the ocean beach.

On December 4, 1984, finishing the first draft of these journals, I walked down to the ocean for a breath of air. The day was cold, with a northwest wind shivering the rainwater where ice was broken in the puddles. Rising and falling in flight along the dunes, a flock of gulls picked up the last ambient light from the red embers in the west. The silent birds, undulating on the wind, shone bone white against massed somber grays, low over the ocean; the cloud bank looked ominous, like waiting winter.

From the beach landing, in this moody sky and twilight, I saw something awash in the white foam, perhaps a quarter-mile down to the eastward. The low heavy thing, curved round upon itself, did not look like driftwood; I thought at first that it must be a human body. Uneasy, I walked east a little way, then hurried ahead; the thing was not driftwood, not a body, but a great clean skull of a finback whale, dark bronze with sea water and minerals. The beautiful form, crouched like some ancient armored creature in the wash, seemed to await me. No one else was on the beach, which was clean of tracks. There was only the last cold fire of dusk, the white birds fleeing toward the darkness, the frosty foam whirling around the skull, seeking to regather it into the deeps.

By the time I returned with a truck and chain, it was nearly night. The sea was higher, and the skull was settling like some enormous crab into the wash; I could not get close enough without sinking the truck down to the axles. I took careful bearings on the skull's location, and a good thing, too, because four hours later, when the tide had turned, the massive skull had sunk away into the sands, all but what looked like a small dark rock in the moon white shallows. I dug this out enough to secure a hawser, then ran this rope above the tide line, as a lead to the skull's location the next morning. But fearing that an onshore wind or storm might bury it forever, I went down at dead low tide that night, under the moon, and dug the skull clear and worked it up out of its pit, using truck and chain. Nearly six feet across, the skull was water-logged and heavy, five hundred pounds or better. Not until one in the morning—spending more time digging out my truck than freeing the bone—did I hitch it high enough onto the beach to feel confident that the tide already coming in would not rebury it. By morning there was onshore wind, with a chop already making up from the southwest, but the whale skull was still waiting at the water's edge. Bud Topping came down with his tractor and we took it home. When Milt Miller, who was raised by the old whalers, had a look at it a few weeks later, he said it was the biggest skull he ever saw.

With windy weather, as Indian summer turned to fall, the scallops became scarce in shallow water. We turned to heavy labor with the dredges, dumping the west loads of eelgrass and codium, or Sputnik weed,* onto the culling board. The load was never twice the same. The elegant scallops, snapping their shells, were occasionally accompanied by an unwary flounder, together with an indiscriminate assortment of crabs, horsefoots, sand worms, glass shrimp, sea horses, sponges, whelks, stones, bottles, sneakers, dead shells, and—not uncommonly—a small clump of wild oysters.

Later that autumn, when the scallops thinned out inside the harbors, we went prospecting for virgin scallop beds as far away as Napeague, Montauk Lake, and Gardiners Island, putting in at Promised Land for our supplies. One day of late October, as we scalloped off the western shore of Gardiners Island, a cold front came in toward midday, with a stiff wind out of the northwest. Though heavily crusted with quarterdecks, or boat shells, the scallops on this rocky bottom were plentiful, and we were hurrying to complete our twenty-

---

*Codium was introduced accidentally in Greenport harbor in the twenties or thirties apparently from Japan, and is now widespread on the East End; it is called Sputnik weed because it seemed (and looked) as if it might have dropped from outer space.

bushel boat limit and head home when the one-cylinder motor on my old boat conked out and would not revive. Hoisting the Vop's patched gaff-rigged sail, we beat upwind toward the mainland.

Already a hard gale was blowing; despite her deep keel, the boat was banging into white-capped waves. Halfway across the channel the pine mast broke off at the deck, and mast, boom, and canvas crashed upon our heads. Not saying much, we sorted out the mess as the wind carried us back toward Gardiners Island. (Years ago, an old-timer named Puff Dominy broke down off Lion Head Rock and drifted back east to Gardiners on this same course. Told to throw over the anchor, his retarded crewman cried, "No twing! No twing!" Impatient and uncomprehending. Puff hollered, "Let 'er go, goddamn it, 'twing' or no 'twing'!" Thrown overboard with no "string" attached, Puff's anchor disappeared forever, but "twing or no twing" has survived in local lore.)

Nearing the island, we threw over an anchor, but by the time the grapnel finally took hold, the Vop was scarcely two hundred yards offshore in Bostwick Bay, buffered by wind and seas in the growing weather. It was midafternoon of a swift day of late autumn, and a cold sun was sinking fast, with no boat in sight, nothing but white-caps and wind-blown gulls and long black ragged strings of cormorants beating across the wind toward the southwest. Not only was the boat wide open, but the hatch covers of the fish holds forming her deck were only three inches lower than the gunwales, which provided no shelter from the wind. On this north end of Gardiners Island, never inhabited, the view from the sea was as wild as it was three centuries before when the Algonkian people known as Montauks escorted Lion Gardiner to his New World home.

In 1676, by the Dongan Patent, Gardiners Island—roughly seven by three miles, or about thirty-three hundred acres—had been deemed a manor, and it is, in fact, the last of the old English manors to remain in the same New World family to the present day. In the 1690s, Captain William Kidd, a minister's son and retired sea captain pressed into service as a privateer by a syndicate that included the English governor of Massachusetts, was arrested in Boston and sent to England. There he was hanged for disputed reasons, among them, it is said, the protection of the reputations of those who had benefited from his voyages, including the hard-living "Lord John" Gardiner, son of the incumbent Lord of the Manor, David Lion Gardiner, who had first welcomed Kidd to Gardiners Island. Captain Kidd's only known treasure of gold dust, gold coin, jewelry, and the like, retrieved from the pond behind the beach in Cherry Harbor off which we had been scalloping when the boat broke down, was turned over to the authorities by Lord John, who escaped unpunished. In 1728 the manor was commandeered for three days by real pirates, causing the family to look for safer lodgings in East Hampton Village. Since then, Gardiners Island has been occupied intermittently by the Gardiner family, which has often leased it to other people.

In the 1950s the island was still inhabited by an estimated five hundred pairs of ospreys, by far the largest colony of these striking fish hawks in North America and perhaps the world. High cliffs to the eastward (a source of clay for the early settlers) slope gradually to low fields in the west, with broad lowlands, salt marsh, ponds, and sand spits, north and south. Where we were anchored was the windward shore of the northern sand pit, in Bostwick ("Bostic" to the fishermen) Bay, where a bad August storm of 1879 had overturned a lobster boat out of New London, drowning two crewmen. Another storm in 1892 parted this sand spit, creating an islet out at the north point where a lighthouse had been built in 1855;* the shoddily constructed building, weakened by storms, collapsed two years later, and the light was abandoned. During the Spanish-American War, a round structure called Fort Tyler was built upon this shored-up islet, part of a whole string of forts on Plum, Gull, and Fishers Islands designed to protect Long Island Sound from unfriendly gunboats.† Since its abandonment in 1924, Fort Tyler has been much diminished by erosion and bombing practice, and is usually referred to as "the ruin."

---

*Lighthouses were installed on Little Gull Island in 1806 and on Plum Island in 1827; both of these lights are still in operation, though no longer manned.

†The construction of this problematic chain, out of date so long before its own completion, eliminated an obscure species of mouse called the Gull Island vole, but an uncommon bird called the roseate tern still nests in the crumbling ruin of the gun emplacements on Gull Island, which is now owned and administered by the American Museum of Natural History.

. . .

Twilight had come, and a sharp autumn cold. To the north the old fort, in dark and gloomy silhouette on a cold sunset, rode like a ship in the running silver tide against the lightless islands and the far black line of the New England hills where the last light faded in the sky. Our young wives would not worry about us until after nightfall, so no help could be expected until next day.

Eight miles to the northeast lay Fishers Island, the easternmost point of Suffolk County, where I had spent most of my first fifteen summers;* five miles to the southwest lay Three Mile Harbor in East Hampton, where I visited first in 1942. Now it was 1953, I was in my midtwenties, and had moved permanently to the South Fork. Thus I had lived in Suffolk County all my life, on or about the edges of these waters; this wild and lonely place where our small boat washed up and down on the high chop lay at the very heart of my home country.

On this cold rough October evening, hunched knee to knee in a cramped anchor cuddy, we ate raw scallops from the upright burlap bags that hunched like refugees on deck, and listened to the waves slap on the hull; if the anchor dragged during the night, our small wood boat would wash ashore on Gardiners Island. It was already gunning season, and we wanted no night dealings with Charlie Raynor, the caretaker and dangerous enemy of enterprising young gunners such as ourselves who would sneak ashore at the south end while out coot shooting around Cartwright Shoals and be reasonably sure of snagging a few pheasants along the airstrip. Raynor's reputation as a man who would shoot first and talk afterward saved him a lot of trouble on the job. Especially in the hunting season, he made no distinctions between castaways and trespassers, and anyway he lived too far off to be of help.

At daylight the cold wind from the northeast had not diminished, and there were no signs of boats or sail. All Gardiners Bay was

*It is sometimes said that Fishers Island was named after a certain Vischer, who served the Dutch navigator Adriaen Block as a cartographer, but more likely it refers to an isle of fishers, or fishing Indians, who called the island Munnatawket (very likely these Indians were the seagoing Montauks).

tossed in a white chop, crossed by the strings of cormorants, the hurrying scoters and solitary loons, the wind-tailed gulls, hard wings reflecting a wild light that pierced the metallic clouds.

Toward midmorning a Coast Guard plane came over; when we waved our arms, the plane went away, and still there were no boats on the rough horizons.

In early afternoon a black fishing boat appeared. Its hardy skipper was Fanny Gardiner Collins of Three Mile Harbor, a member of the island clan and avid fisherwoman who knew much more about Gardiners Island and its waters than her wealthy kinsmen. Fanny took us in tow and hauled us back to Three Mile Harbor.

In November, when the scallops became scarce, I helped out now and then on a small haul-seine rig led by Jimmy Reutershan, who came from a local "up-street" family of nonfishermen, and had John Cole and Pete Scott as his steady crew. The rig consisted of Jimmy's Land Rover, small dory, and small seine, and it stuck pretty close to a stretch of beach near the old Georgica Coast Guard Station.* On those bright cold autumn days, with sharp sand blowing, the silver ocean, sparkling and clear, seemed empty; we were beginners, and we made one dry haul after another, standing around the limp and forlorn bag as if puzzling out an oracle. On one such morning Jimmy drew an ancient black banana from the seat box on the Land Rover and offered it upright, with his wry tough smile, to his weary crew. "Have a banana," Jimmy said, "lightly flecked with brown."

For the next two days, the surface of the sea was calm, but big rollers came in from a distant ocean storm, and no dory could go off through the surf. On Sunday, November 6—the last day that small bass could be taken legally for local sale—the Havens crew went down before daylight to the easternmost set, known as Umbrella

*Like most of the beach lifeboat stations—there were twenty-eight on the Long Island shore in 1929—Georgica had been closed down after World War Two, when depth finders, radar, and loran became standard equipment on oceanic vessels and kept them from going aground in snow or fog.

Stand, where a beach pavilion had once stood in Montauk's hey-day. It was a beautiful clear windless morning, with autumn warmth in the early sun out of the ocean, and a deep red color in the beach plums on the cliffs, but the smooth rollers were too big for the dory, and the fishermen sat in their trucks and watched the surfcasters, shoulder to shoulder, drag big bluefish flopping from the sea. "Week ago today," Benny Havens said, "right here, we had the biggest haul of bass we made this year. Know what it was? Maybe eight boxes! And them fellas there"—he pointed at a knot of surfcasters—"them ones that's throwin back their bluefish cause they ain't no money in 'em, they come over and told us we was destroyin the striped bass, it was goin extinct, just like the buffalo!"

"Just like the buffalo!" Billy Havens said, disgusted. He described the time, back in the seventies, when they had taken the rig south right after the bass season to haul seine at Cape Hatteras, North Carolina. "All the crews from up here went that first time, and we took over the whole stretch of beach; didn't know we was doin it, you know, but we put them local boys right out of business. We done so good that the fella that run the packin house come down and told us that he wasn't goin to take no more of our fish. Them Rebels had told him that if he did, they was going to burn that packin house right to the ground, so we went home. But another year just this one crew went, us two and Lindy and Pete Kromer and our cousin John. And they kind of took to us at first, cause we helped 'em out, you know, and showed 'em things. But then we got 1,245 boxes in one set, and I guess that kind of changed their atti-tude."

Billy whistled, as if exhausted by the memory. "We was thirty-six hours nonstop on that one haul. A lot of them fish was eighty pounds or better, had to be, it took a man on both ends to heave 'em up into the truck. And they was full of roe; the roe was just runnin out of all them fish, I got sick of the smell of it. Them fish must be goin up into *all* them rivers! That is the home of bass down there, the home of bass! We landed two thousand boxes in three days. And not long after that them Rebels got the federal government to outlaw haul-seine rigs from out of state in the goddamn Carolina fishery."

We waited a couple of hours, watching the ocean, in the hope that the seas might diminish when the tide turned. "Had a lighter boat, now," William Havens said, pointing at a narrow break in the wave pattern, "we could go off right in that little place there, scoot right through quick." Though William does not complain except in a joking manner, one of his crewmen told me that he had been depressed all year by the poor fishing. The crew has made about one half of last year's earnings, which were already the lowest in recent memory. Both bass and weakfish have been scarce this autumn, and a few days before the crews were notified not to ship any more bluefish to the market.

Any day now, the small bass would start to show up in the nets, and no one knew just what would happen. William shook his head. "Brent Bennett told me yesterday that them small bass are just strikin into his gill nets around Gardiners, but they ain't goin to be no good to nobody."

Doug Kuntz, who has fished with the Havens crew for many years, repeated Stuart Vorpahl's observation that the baymen were "walking around like dead men." Speaking quietly, Doug said, "It's true. The fishermen seem to have lost their spirit, all but Calvin; that guy is amazing. He just fishes hard day after day, just looks straight ahead, never lets it bother him, no matter what. Until two years ago, this crew was high hook on the beach, nobody near us, but it's Calvin now, and even Calvin's getting wired.

"It's not just the lack of fish, it's all the pressure. The sportsmen and tourists crowding them off the beach, and the cost of living. Used to be that the farmers and fishermen were this whole town; now the town doesn't care about 'em anymore, all they care about is the goddamn resort economy. Benny has had to tell his kids that they're going to have to find some other way to make a living, or else there's no way they can even afford to live here. That's a hell of a sad thing to have to say in a fishing family. Because the Havenses and the Lesters are the main fishing families left, and Benny thinks that in ten years they'll all be finished."

On Monday, November 7, the day the bass law went into effect, Pete Kromer's crew seined fifty-eight hundred pounds of large bass at Hither Plains, one of the best hauls recorded in these failing years, and the Havens crew had thirty-three hundred pounds not far to the eastward, at Umbrella Stand. These landings did not include the undersize bass scattered among big flopping cows of forty pounds or better. The Havenses had five hundred pounds on Tuesday, November 8, and nine hundred and eighty pounds the following day, and this first—and last—good week of the bass season was spiced by the Election Day defeat of the bass bill's sponsor, Patrick Halpin.

Most of the crews culled their large bass out of piles of giant bluefish. With thousands upon thousands of attendant gulls, the blues were ranging everywhere along the beach, and the surfcasters caught as many as they wanted. I had a twelve- and a fifteen-pounder on Election Day, and took one still larger in a few minutes on the beach the following afternoon. In the market, the price on bluefish fell to ten cents a pound. As William Havens said, it was painful to see so many tons of bluefish dumped back into the surf when so many people in the country had to go hungry. "Ain't that somethin, now, bein a fisherman and not wantin to catch such a good fish?" Although some blues, freed fast enough, survived the shock and beating of the nets, this species is much more volatile and less well-armored than the bass, which is designed for rocks and surf, and many of those returned into the water washed up again farther down the beach.

Inevitably the sportsmen's magazines decried the callousness and waste of this "dirty fishery." Yet all American fisheries are dirty because so many edible species go to waste as trash fish—too bony or ugly to attract overprivileged consumers. Countless tons of fine protein are destroyed each year that would be precious anywhere else on earth, including Europe, and the waste is much more damaging to the commercial men than it is to the sportsmen, who rarely show much righteous indignation when dogfish and daylights and sea robins die in the nets.

Jens and Francis's crew was the only one that had not had at least one good catch of bass, and on Thursday morning it was first to arrive on the Montauk set in front of Gurney's Inn, where Calvin had had good fishing all that week. ("We're not competin," Danny

King says, "but if one guy catches fish in one spot for a couple of days, another crew will say, 'Well, they're not goin to have that set tomorrow morning, *we're* gonna be there.' ") Autumn fogs under the crescent moon of the night before had been a sign of a change in weather, and by dawn the wind had shifted to the eastward. The crews hurried to make a haul before the sea became too rough to set.

No crew that morning had more than a few bass in the nets, and Francis was discouraged. "No matter where we go," he said, "we can't seem to get it right." He started to pick blues from the net, wandered away, then picked briefly somewhere else, as if too disheartened to work systematically. There was no hurry anyway, since with blues everywhere, and the longshore current accumulating with the east wind, none of the crews would make a second set. He called to the younger men to save a few blues for local sale, to pay for gas, but they continued skittering the fish in the general direction of the sea, and Francis shrugged. "They're just sick and tired of having these things chew hell out of the net, sick of having to ice 'em and pack 'em up and ship 'em and not get nothin for it but more net-mendin. In all my life I never seen so many big bluefish, not as late as this, and looks like we're stuck with 'em, too, long as the ocean stays so warm."

Down the beach to the eastward another crew was finishing a haul, and driving past I recognized the man standing in the truck bed, on the ocean sky, as Lindy Havens. He had a gray mustache and long gray sideburns, but otherwise he was the same tall, rangy, and good-looking man with big hands and big ears who had once vowed to throw his congressman into the surf.

As I approached, Lindy's glance looked dim and guarded, without the humor I remembered, and when I said, "Don't guess you know me," he turned back to the winch, saying, "Don't guess I do." But when another man yelled across the wind, "Where *you* been, bub? Ain't seen *you* around in years!" Lindy turned back for a better look. Reminded of that disastrous haul back in 1954, when all those fish had poured out of Ted's bunt, he nodded somberly. "I remember that day, all right. Don't forget a thing like that. I seen one other bunch like that, fishin with Bill around 'sixty-eight, only that day we saved most of 'em, must have landed pretty close to four hundred boxes. They ain't beat *that* yet, not around here. And even that was nothin like we seen in 'seventy-three, down in Carolina—thirty-eight truckloads! Thought we'd never get off the beach, it was a nightmare! Caught too many, that's what we done. Didn't mean to, but we caught too many. With all them fish, there was no price on 'em, and that one haul, more than anything else, got outside crews kept out of Carolina. All we done was teach them fellas how to fish. They never had no waders and no winches, not even a bag in the goddamn net! Used to run down into the water, try to gaff those fish up on the beach!"

The other crewman, Milton (Minny) George, was observing me carefully, trying to place where he had seen me a quarter-century before. Finally he said, "Didn't you work one year over there t'the seine house at Promised Land?" When I shook my head, he said, "Could swear I seen you there. Ain't you the one had that old double-ender, that one still had the bark on the double hull?" Pleased to run into someone who recalled the *Vop-Vop*, I told him that sometimes while out scalloping, she had put into Promised Land for fuel. "*Thought* that was you," Minny said, very pleased, too; he is celebrated among the fishermen for his strong memory, and so is his mother, who was born around the turn of the century and still loves to eat bunkers ("Sweet but bony," as one fisherman says. "Takes quite a while to pick 'em bones out. That's why we say, when a feller is late, Where *you* been, bub? Home eatin bunkers?")

Another veteran, Don Eames, Sr., was on the far wing with Pete Kromer, who had bought Ted Lester's rig back in the sixties; this crew was the most experienced on the beach. A man loading the net looked familiar, too, and when Minny spoke to him, I recognized Lindy's old partner, Dominick Grace. Dom-Dom had lost some teeth and looked his age, but he yelled at Lindy as peevishly as ever as the bunt came into the surf— "Goddamn it, Lindy, pull her in, don't you see the other side? You're runnin 'at goddamn winch too slow again!" Minny George winked gleefully, and I laughed. Lindy and Dom had always hollered at each other, and as in the old days, the abuse served to ease the suspense of bunting up, and was ignored. But the bag held another haul of useless bluefish; there were seven or eight bass altogether. "That weather's got to change, clear out them bluefish, fore we do any good at all," Minny said.

December 2 was a cold clear windless morning, with bright stars. For the first time this autumn, the temperature had fallen below freezing. With the last stretch of bad weather in late November, Jens Lester, Pete Kromer, and Danny King had left the beach; the Havens and Calvin Lester crews were the last ones left. At Brent's Store in Amagansett, Walter Bennett turned up at 6:00 A.M. for coffee, and Calvin, rolling up with the dory a few minutes later, told him that they would be heading west for Flying Point, in Water Mill, where a few medium bass had appeared the week before.

At William Havens's house, on Abraham's Path, Ann Havens was bandaging her husband's thumb, splayed to the bone while shucking chowder clams the previous day. "Told him to go to the doctor, but he wouldn't; just like a little boy!" Mrs. Havens was angered by the editorial in the *Long Island Fisherman*, which expressed disdain for haul-seining as a "dirty fishery." "Them people always get everythin wrong! Had a picture of *our* crew there, longside a picture of Calvin's dogfish on the beach! Anyways, why don't they know it don't do no good to throw most of them fish back? It ain't the haul-seiners' fault nobody wants 'em! Last week my men here shipped three hundred and nine pounds of bluefish. Know what we got back, after payin the shippin? Eleven-fifty! Eleven dollars and fifty cents for three hundred and nine pounds of good *bluefish*! Does that seem fair to you?"

I shook my head, feeling outraged myself. In a local restaurant that week, a friend had ordered bluefish, paying precisely eleven-fifty for less than a half pound, or more than seven hundred times as much as the men who caught it were receiving. The Havenses knew that those bluefish that brought them three pennies a pound did not go to waste, that the markets and restaurants did fine while the men who supplied the fish went into debt, and this knowledge intensified their sense of futility and bitterness. Already the dragger-men were anticipating the same treatment; they were getting a good price for early whiting, but within a few weeks, when the whiting came in thick, the price would drop quickly to three cents a pound, which would scarcely be enough to pay for fuel.

We went down to Napeague just as the sun came up on a calm wintry sea. In this season whales are sometimes seen from shore, and the white flash of diving gannets, harassing the fish schools heading south, but this morning the sea was entirely empty, a gray waste extending without a mark to the horizon. The clouds of bait had disappeared, and the bird legions; the rush of storm seas had subsided to a soft whisper in the shining shallows. On the tide line were thin windrows of dead sand fleas, killed by the first frost of coming winter. (Whiting are sometimes gathered on the beach as "frost fish" because they chase bait into the shallows and are trans-fixed by the frozen air.)

The quiet men stared out at the dead ocean; its very emptiness seemed somehow ominous. The autumn storms had carved the beach away, making it narrow and difficult to work. The rain-soaked sand no longer drained well or packed down, and in the half-frozen mush, the trucks were balky. "Don't know if we should set at all, with all them dogfish," William said after a while, still gazing off into the empty distance. "Goddamn dogs! You get a mess of them things gilled from one end of your net to the other, take you all day to get it straightened out!" Most fish move offshore as the sun rises, and Benny thought they ought to wait a little before set-ting, despite the risk that any bass would move off, too. Over the CB radio from Flying Point came word that Calvin's crew, for fear of dogs, was also waiting. For the past two weeks, the dogfish had plagued the draggers and net fishermen up and down the coast.

"Hell," Billy Havens said, in sudden restlessness. "This season's over. Let's make our set and get it done with, get off this damn beach." He backed the dory trailer down toward the water's edge, and Ben climbed up into the boat and started up the motor; Doug Kuntz, still half-asleep, would set the net. Through the cab window, Billy hollered, "Ready?" He backed the trailer fast into the water, then slammed on the brake, and the dory shot off the roller, coasting easily through the surf, and moved rapidly offshore as Doug tossed over a big coil of line that made a loud slap on the surface.

The dory turned away toward the southeastward. Soon it was silhouetted on the sun. Young Fred Havens hitched the line to William's truck, then got into Ben's old Dodge with Billy and headed eastward to where the dory would come ashore. "How come they tossed that whole coil into the water?" William complained. "No sense in that; could have left most of it ashore. And they turned off east too soon . . ." He stopped fretting and shook his head. "Getting nervous, I guess. Everybody on the beach is nervous, noticed that? Guess we don't know what's to become of us. That one crew Old Bill had, I guess we was together near to fifteen years, and I don't recall no snappin and snarlin, not like this." When I reared back a little raising my eyebrows, William grinned. "Well, we done some yellin, buntin up, I guess, to let off steam. Remember Ted jumpin around like a jack rabbit when the bunt come in? Seems to me we had more fun in them years. The crews always helped each other out—now you can't count on it." He grumbled about this CB radio that had recently come into use; one time he had spotted fish and sent word back to Benny's truck, only to have another crew come flying in and make the set ahead of them. "Other day here, one gang got loaded up with dogs, and we helped pick 'em out, thought nothin about it; next day was us got loaded up, and they come along, looked at the mess that we was in, and took off to westward."

William laughed, remembering a day that Ted's old Model A had gotten sanded here at Napeague, and before he could dig it out again, his brother Bill had come along and took the set. "Course Ted got pretty good at that hisself, but that day he was hollerin some, yes, yes. Well, Bill went right ahead. He got one fish!" William shook his head. "Don't think I could do that—just ain't worth it. But there's a couple of 'em would do that yet today."

William climbed onto the truck bed as Doug Kuntz came back down the beach and took the jack line to the water's edge to tie on. Asked if he would be a fisherman if he had it to do all over again, William said quickly and bitterly, "Not if I knew how it was goin to be in these last years." He shrugged, looping the sandy rope around the winch and taking a strain. "Hell, I don't know, Pete. Probably too stupid to do anythin different."

All of the longtime fishermen say this in one way or another, and one way or another they believe it. But it's also a way of declaring something that, most of the time, they are too shy to say out loud: that they are fishermen because their fathers and their grandfathers were fishermen, it's "in their blood," there's nothing to be done about it; that this is not only their livelihood but their way of life— this is where they belong—and that they will stay on the water as long as they can put food on the family table. This year, for the first time in their long memory, their independence has been seriously threatened by a law rammed through by well-organized outsiders who have lined up all the bureaucrats and politicians, who have no true sense of this ocean land or its fish and sea and weather, or any real need for the extra money that they make on striped bass. "My brother Orie," William was saying, "that lives over there by Hampton Bays, he's the only one had the brains to get out of fishin, but he never done no better'n the rest of us."

A green pickup came along the beach from Amagansett, and William said, "Here's Richard. That fella had him a mess the other evenin." The night after Richard had wrenched his back as a volunteer fireman, the rusted-out axle on his trailer had given way, dropping his boat on the road. Stuart Vorpahl and Tom Field had given him a hand, and Stuart had jerry-rigged a new axle, but this one, too, had busted under the heavy boat, and the men did not get home until two in the morning.

Wearing thin street pants and street shoes, Richard looked stiff as he got out; he held on to the truck door as he watched the haul. Any other day he would be shouting at the other fishermen, teasing them in his rough cheerful way, but today he kept apart and remained silent. He was behind two payments on his house, and his small dragger, the *Rainbow,* was for sale.

Doug Kuntz was dealing with driftwood snarled up in the net, and I took the line down to the water to tie on. My hands remembered how to do it, but when I lifted one hand in signal to William to take up on the winch, Richard hollered, "You forgot how to tie on there, bub? Got to face the ocean, the way I do!" He was grinning, but he moved carefully, and his eyes looked red and tired. "Works better this way," he said, showing me his style, then looked uncertain as my own hitch, working just fine, bobbed past his street shoes. "For me, anyway," Richard said.

We watched the bunt just coming in to the soft breakers. There was no sign of fish at all, and the men were quiet. "Rough life, ain't it? What we gonna do this winter?" Richard threw his head and shoulders back and jerked his chin at me, just as Ted used to do when posing a question for which there was no answer. He cleared his throat. "Know something, Pete? This is the first time I been broke in twenty-eight years!" He said this in a bewildered way, as if still unable to believe it. "Always had a couple thousand dollars in the bank, a little money in my pocket; now I'm down to nothin and can't pay my bills!" He tried to laugh, as if this was just ridiculous, but others were as desperate as he was. Someone had said that Danny King had two bank accounts, one of which held twenty-eight dollars and the other seventeen. "Well, he's the president of the Baymen's Association," another said. "Guess we can't *all* be rich."

Now Donnie Eames had come up in his truck, and Richard called, "What's the matter with you fellas? Never hauled?" Donnie said that most of Calvin's crew had wanted to wait a little while before going off, for fear of dogfish, and that Calvin had yanked the dory off the beach and headed home. "He's been so wired up and nervous this past week, with nothin goin for us, nobody can talk to him!"

"Well, how come *you* ain't nervous?" Richard demanded. "Everybody else is!"

"Not me. I was takin it out on my wife, y'know, practically had a divorce! Everybody on the beach been doin that, snappin at each other right over the radio. And then I figured there ain't nothin I can do about no weather and no goddamn fish and no goddamn money and that goddamn law, nothin at all, I just got to take her one day at a time."

"Shit!" Richard said. "You got your bills paid, ain't you? Guess *I* could take her one day at a time, I had my bills paid. Somebody show me five hundred pounds of them short bass, I'd know what to do with them, by Jesus!"

"You ain't the only one." Donnie glanced at me. "Them people are makin criminals out of us," he remarked bitterly. ("Might as well go to jail, get somethin to eat," says Wally Bennett. "Give us somethin to do for the next five years.")

Now Jens Lester had arrived, and J. P. Fenelon came up in an old beach wagon, driving Bill Lester, who had come to see the last haul of the year. Cap'n Bill greeted me out of the window: "Don't like this cold weather much no more, do you?" Bill said he had fixed some caviar from a sturgeon taken recently by a Shinnecock dragger but otherwise had not been doing much. "Got eighteen pounds out of it, but kind of fatty, y'know. There's only so much you can do with it."

Someone had seen a striped bass in the bunt, and Richard, favoring his bad back, walked down slowly toward the water. "It's a great life if you don't weaken, ain't that right, Pete? Maybe you and me better get together, write up my story." He managed a short laugh, and Donnie Eames laughed, too. "He's got stories, all right! Can't even write his own name hardly, Richard can't, and here's he's talking about writin books! Open up *that* book, find nothing but X's in there!" Donnie yelled with laughter, we all laughed, Richard, too. "People ain't gonna go for *that* shit, Richard!" The laughter died as the bag came up into the shallows.

"Have a daylight," Donnie muttered, stepping up onto the boat-sized bag and treading on the sliding creatures, balanced like a tightrope walker; the anger in the gesture was disturbing. The bag was solid full of dabs, two tons or more of worthless daylights, mixed in with a few skates and squid, a sculpin, some short bass: there were only eleven medium bass, less than one hundred pounds in all, that could be marketed under the new law. There was also the last bluefish of the autumn, and with it the first whiting of the winter. Ben Havens opened the puckering string, and the pile of brown fish poured away into the shallows.

The season was over and the long winter had begun, and Ben and Billy loaded the net in silence. Asked what they would do this winter, Billy Havens said, "Go on the draggers. With scallops the way they are, we got no choice." Ben Havens nodded, as Jens and Richard and Donnie and Old Bill walked up the beach to their cars.

At a Baymen's Association meeting in late April, Donnie Eames announced that he was giving up fishing for a caretaker's job at the Amagansett School, and no one doubted that there would be others. "I was just beatin my head against the wall," he told me a week later on the Flag Set at Amagansett, where he was making his last haul as a regular on Calvin Lester's crew. "Calvin's still kinda stiff about it, but when you have young kids you got to have some kind of security." He shook his head. "That decision was the hardest of my life."

I asked Calvin's son Danny, who was helping load the net, if he intended to be a fisherman, and without hesitation this twelve-year-old boy said, "No." He shook his head firmly. "No," Danny Lester said again. "Won't be nothing to fish for." And Donnie Eames said, "Kind of sad to hear that from a Posey, ain't it? When I was his age, the one thing that I wanted to do, that was go fishin."

On Sunday afternoon, May 12, Lindy Havens and Eddie Trufanoff went out on Gardiners Bay in Lindy's sharpie to try out Lindy's new outboard motor and perhaps pick out some locations for his gill-nets. Lindy wore knee boots, and E.T. wore the heavy black waders he had used on the beach the previous spring. A southeast wind was blowing, and the day was cold, but in the lee of Hedges Bank, between Cedar Point and Sammis Beach, where the Northwest Woods overlooks the water, the bay was calm.

Lindy must have been teasing E.T. as usual, for the two were heard shouting and laughing by people in the housing development above. The motor, which had apparently cut out, now started up again, and a few moments later, a man standing on the stair that leads down to the rocky beach heard the sharpie suddenly accelerate. Glancing over, he saw both men floundering in the boat's wake.

The man on shore was casually acquainted with Ed Trufanoff, and reported that E.T. had gone over first, since he saw his reddish head twenty or more yards farther back in the boat's wake than

Lindy's dark one. Though Lindy was a veteran boatman, it appeared that he had lost his balance and gone over the side when he spun the boat hard to retrieve the other man. Since the two were less than two hundred yards offshore, the onlooker considered swimming out to help them—he told me he had once been a lifeguard—but he knew from recent experience, out clamming, that he would go numb in this cold water once he was in over his waist and would never reach them.

The man with the dark hair was treading high in the water with his shoulders out, dodging the sharpie, which was making tight circles. A few seconds later, when the witness ran to telephone for help, Lindy seemed to be making his way toward E.T., who was flailing desperately without making a sound. Glancing back just once, the witness thought he saw them both, but he wonders now if what he thought was E.T.'s head, low in the water, was actually a pot buoy, and if E.T. went under before Lindy reached him. Perhaps Lindy never got there at all, for when the witness got back to the stair less than three minutes later, both heads were gone. (Later Lindy's old friend Dominick Grace would ask him mildly, Why didn't you go in after them? Dom-Dom nodded his head understandingly when the man explained.)

During those three minutes, a second witness who had come to the cliff edge saw one man—almost certainly Lindy—waving his arms and crying out for help. Then the bay was still but for the empty sharpie, which spun in tight circles until she ran aground, an hour later.

Apparently the balky motor had been started up in gear and at full throttle, kicking the skiff out from beneath the upright Eddie. Apparently E.T. knew how to swim, but even a strong swimmer would have trouble staying afloat in heavy waders, which are difficult to take off in deep water. He appears to have surfaced only briefly, whereas Lindy seems to have been in good control. Perhaps Lindy hollered when he felt himself growing paralyzed in the cold May water, and very likely his heart stopped, since if his lungs had filled in drowning, it seems unlikely that he would have floated. Yet he went under at least briefly, since both men on the cliff edge say he disappeared. By the time his body was recovered about twenty-five minutes after the accident (by a private boat out of Three Mile Harbor that answered a "May Day" emergency call on its ship-to-shore radio), the southeast wind had drifted him several hundred yards to the northwest, off Tom Lester's fish trap.

"Salt water and drinkin just don't mix," said a bayman on the Dory Rescue Squad, which tried to coordinate the search for E.T.'s body. The police divers worked mainly in the offshore stretch where the drifting body was recovered, despite the first witness's strong feeling, relayed over the baymen's radio, that Trufanoff must still be on the bottom at the inshore spot right off the cliff stair where he disappeared. "I clam there all the time, and there's no current, not inshore," the unhappy man told me a few days later, still upset by the thought that there was some way he might have helped. "I feel sure he's right there now. I liked E.T.; you couldn't help but like him. He didn't have anything much to say but he was always smiling. It gives me a funny feeling about going clamming, knowing he's out there." Eddie Trufanoff's body washed up on Sammis Beach two Sundays later.


A memorial service for Sidney Lindbergh Havens, one of the best fishermen on the East End, was held in a funeral home on Newtown Lane in the late morning of May 16, an hour which permitted most baymen to attend. There were copious flowers and floral wreaths, some in the shapes of fish and anchors, and the room was crowded. The Amagansett Fire Department, of which Lindy was a member, carried his flag-draped casket to the Oakwood Cemetery, where he was buried toward midday of a soft spring morning. Three old friends from the haul-seine crews, Don Eames, Sr., Pete Kromer, and Milt Miller, were among his pall-bearers, and Milt was chewing on his lip as the casket was lowered into the Bonac earth.

Leaving the cemetery, Milt put his arm around my shoulder, and we walked along a little. "Kind of a sad day," I said. "Old Lindy had a lot of spirit." But Milt had grieved and made his peace with his friend's death and was on his way back to the bay, which is just what Lindy would have wanted. He nodded politely at my glum remark before cocking his head to look at me with that wry squint. "Well, I don't guess *none* of us are goin to get away with it, now are we, Pete? Try as we might." I laughed quietly, and he laughed, too, shaking his head. It was what Lindy might have said at Milt Miller's funeral, and we both felt better.

# *from* African Silences

1991

*Between the trips to Africa that provided the material for* The Tree
Where Man Was Born *and* Sand Rivers, *Matthiessen joined the pri-
matologist Gilbert Boese for a wildlife survey of Senegal, Gambia,
and Ivory Coast. Eight years later, in 1986, he returned to Central
Africa with the Kenyan ecologist David Western to investigate the
health and numbers of the forest elephant, whose ivory was starting to
appear on the black market. Crossing equatorial Africa in a small
Cessna airplane, the two visited the last northern group of the rare
white rhinoceros in the northern Congo, the gorilla forests of the
Congo Basin, and the Ituri Forest, where they camped in the forest
and went hunting with the Mbuti Pygmies, one of the world's last
bands of hunter-gatherers.*

*As in* The Snow Leopard *and in* The Tree Where Man Was
Born, *each of these expeditions features rare animals that provide the
narrative with a sense of mystery beyond the stated scientific objec-
tives, as in the sudden appearance of the "wild black face" of a silver-
backed gorilla from behind a tree. In the following passages, taken
from the chapters "Of Peacocks and Gorillas" and "Pygmies
and Pygmy Elephants," the eventual survival of these threatened
animals—symbols of their diminishing rain forests—is of central
concern.*

## Of Peacocks and Gorillas: Zaire (1978)

**Leaving Nairobi, the plane** turns northwest across Kikuyu Land and
the Rift escarpment, heading up the great Rift Valley between the

Mau Range and the Aberdares. As it crosses Lake Naivasha, I peer down upon the bright white heads of fish eagles and a shimmering white string of pelicans; off the white soda shores of Lake Nakuru is a large pink crescent made by thousands upon thousands of flamingos. Then we are crossing the equator, droning northwestward over the Kakamega Forest, the easternmost outpost of the equatorial rain forests that extend all the way into West Africa. Off to the north rises Mount Elgon, on the Uganda border, as a great migratory flight of European storks passes south beneath the plane, on their way, perhaps, to winter range in the Serengeti.

The high winds of the new monsoon, blowing out of Chad and the Sudan, have shrouded the rich farmlands of Uganda in a haze of dust. The sun looms, disappears again, behind bruised clouds that are thickened by the smoke of fires in this burning land. The rebel forces of Yoweri Museveni might bring peace and stability to this bloodied country—in early January of 1986 still under the control of the violent soldiery of the beleaguered Milton Obote, who is now known to have presided over the tribal slaughter of even more thousands of his countrymen than did his predecessor, Idi Amin. (Even among African countries, Uganda seems unusually beset by bloody-minded tyrants, who were already ruling when the first explorers came up the Nile; in the days of Henry Morton Stanley, the despotic ruler was a man named Mwanga, for whom Idi Amin named his son.) The long red roads are strangely empty of all vehicles, for the countryside below, so green and peaceful in appearance, is in a state of utter anarchy and fear, with all communications broken down and the hated, vengeful army of the latest tyrant in retreat across the land, looting and killing.

The broad morass of lakes and swamps called Lake Kyoga, with its primitive island villages, is utterly roadless and indeterminate in configuration, like some labyrinthine swamp of ancient myth; there are no landmarks for calculating a precise heading, and the monsoon wind carries us just far enough off course so that we pass east of the Victoria Nile, which we had intended to follow down as far as Murchison Falls. By the time we correct our course, we must backtrack across the Albert Nile to the Victoria, following white water rapids to the extraordinary chute where the torrent hurtles through a narrow chasm and plunges into the broad hippo pool below. Twenty-five years ago, when I first came here, hitchhiking south from the Sudan into East Africa, this park (renamed Kabalega but now Murchison again) was famous all over the world for its legions of great-tusked elephants and other animals. Today most of the animals are gone, cut down by the automatic guns of marauding armies, including the Tanzanian forces that helped to depose Idi Amin. In February of 1961, this pool was fairly awash with hippopotami; now there is not a single hippo to be seen. The park's twelve thousand elephants are now three hundred. We see none. The only animals in view are a few kob antelope that scatter wildly at the coming of the plane. The booming white falls of the Victoria Nile, descending from Lake Kyoga, thunder undiminished in an empty and silent land.

From Murchison Falls, we take our final bearing for Garamba. The day is late, the skies in all directions dark with haze and smoke, as we set out across northeastern Zaire. Air charts of Zaire are out of date, therefore misleading, and Jonah, frustrated, must resort to my small relief map for his navigation. On this large-scale map, in the poor light, we confuse the town of Arua, on the Uganda side, with Aru in Zaire, so that none of the scarce roads and landmarks seem to fit, and the light fails nearly an hour earlier than expected as the sun sinks behind a dark shroud of smoke and desert haze off to the west. We are now disoriented, with only a very rough idea of our location. Small clusters of huts below, in the old fields and broken forest of rough hill country, are already dimming in the shadow of the night, and suddenly we know without discussion that we will not arrive this evening at Garamba, that even a forced landing in rough country is much better than finding ourselves in the pitch dark with no place to come down. (Not all pilots, as he told me later, feel confident about landing in the bush, and some tend to hesitate until the light is so far gone that *any* landing becomes very dangerous.)

The dirt roads are narrow and deeply rutted, and we must choose quickly among rough shrubby fields. Jonah banks for a quick approach, and slows the plane to stalling speed. Because coarse high grass hides the ground, and the field is small, he is forced to touch down quickly. Nose high, we settle into the stiff grass. The plane strikes the bricklike laterite with a hard bounce and hurtles through bushes with a fearful whacking of stiff branches against metal. Missing the hidden termite hills and ditches, it suffers no worse than a few dents in the tail planes.

To make such a wild landing without mishap is exhilarating, and I congratulate Jonah on his skill, grateful to be wherever the hell we are still in one piece. All we have to do, I say to cheer him, is refuel the wing tanks, lay out our bedrolls, and be off again at dawn. But this is the first time in thirteen years as a bush pilot that Jonah has been lost at nightfall and forced down, and though he is calm, with scarcely a blond hair out of place, he is not happy. As a man who neither drinks nor smokes and is before all orderly and neat, he takes pride in his preparations and efficiency, and he has not yet figured out where things went wrong. "Getting off again, Peter, may be quite another matter," he says stiffly, descending from the plane and staring about him, hands on hips.

From every direction, Africans come streaming across the country; we had seen some running toward the scene even before the airplane touched down. Within minutes, they surround the plane in a wide circle, and a few come forward, offering long, limp, cool, callused hands. They touch the wings, then turn to look at us again, eyes shining. Everyone is scared and friendly—the children run away each time we move, women smile and curtsy. "It is like an apparition to them," one young man tells me gently, in poor French, thereby separating himself discreetly from these hill peasants who have never seen an airplane before.

Many of these Bantu folk of the northeastern region known as Haut-Zaïre (Upper Zaire) have some French or Swahili, and so we are able to converse freely, and a good thing, too. The first group of several dozen shy onlookers has swelled quickly to a noisy crowd of hundreds—at least seven or eight hundred, by the end—all of them growing more and more excited in that volatile African way that can lead very quickly to irredeemable gestures, and sometimes violence. Politely but firmly, our well-wishers warn us to move away into the dark, to let the people calm themselves a little. We are told that we have landed near the village of Dibwa, and soon the village headman, who is drunk, asserts his authority by demanding to see identification. An ad hoc committee, heads together, draws our passport numbers on a scrap of paper amidst random officious shouts and cries of suspicion and bewilderment.

In 1903, when the first Baptist missionaries penetrated this huge region west of the Nile—said to have been the last region without whites in the whole Dark continent—it was known to other Africans as "the Land of the Flesh-Eaters," due to the rampant cannibalism of its inhabitants, and the reputation of these local Azande people (of northeast Zaire, southwest Sudan, and southeast Chad) has not improved much since that time. After the Belgian Congo achieved independence (became Zaire in 1960), there began a six-year struggle for power, and Haute-Zaïre was pillaged by waves of undisciplined soldiery, guerrilla bands—the Simba rebels—and South African and Rhodesian mercenaries. Because of this recent memory of bloodshed and famine, and because Zaire is surrounded by unstable, often hostile African states, the Zairois are highly suspicious of unidentified white foreigners. But as in most Africans, their excitability is offset by a great courtesy and gentleness, and we were treated well by almost everyone in this remote community.

Now it is dark, but the people do not disperse. Increasingly it becomes clear that we will not be permitted to sleep here at the plane, that we are, in fact, to be taken into custody. "After all," my confidant explains, when I protest, "our people are very simple, they do not know why you have come here suddenly like this, or what you will do during the night." I look over at Jonah, who is getting the same message in Swahili. Having no choice, we agree to be escorted to the nearest hut, a quarter-mile away, where in a yard swept bare as a defense against night snakes, granary rodents, and mosquitoes, a fire is built and well-made chairs of wood and hide provided.

"We *have* to keep you here, we *have* to report you!" the headman explains, somewhat mollified now that we have decided to come peaceably. We sit surrounded by admirers, who wish to hear our story over and over. Soon we are shown inside the hut, where cane mats have been spread for us on the earth floor. "This is not what you are used to," one man suggests shyly, not quite sure of this, and eager to inquire about our customs. Two men ask to borrow my flashlight and have yet to bring it back when, still in good spirits, I close my eyes.


Toward midnight we were woken up and led outside. Someone had run across the country to fetch some sort of district secretary, and we gathered once more at the fire. Once again we produced our passports and told our story, which was duly recorded. The secretary had walked here from six miles away to gather this information. "I have done it for the security and welfare of my people," he informed us.

Another herald had been sent by bicycle to the town of Aru, almost twenty miles away, to notify the district commissioner, who arrived in a van with his aides and soldiery about one-thirty in the morning. This time a gendarme in green uniform banged into the hut, shouting abusively, shoving Jonah, and loosening his belt, as if in eagerness to whip us along faster. Outside, the calm, cold-faced commissioner had already been seated, and the foreigners were led to two chairs placed directly in front of him. Once again we showed our passports and accounted for ourselves, but this time the passports were not given back. Though we said we wished to stay nearby, to watch the plane, the commissioner informed us that a soldier would be assigned to guard it, and that we were to be taken back to Aru.

Under armed escort, we were marched across the fields toward the road. Without my flashlight, I could not see the hard-baked ground; I made a fatal misstep at the edge of a ditch, and tore my ankle. I fell to the hard earth with a mighty curse, aware that at the very outset of this trip, which would involve a lot of forest walking, I had resprained an ankle already injured in cross-country skiing. The pain was so violent that I did not notice the safari ants that everyone else was slapping: I simply hobbled ahead while I still could, gasping in anger and shock. Not until I was inside the van, seated opposite a sullen African with a machine pistol and another with two carbines, did I feel the *siafu* attacking me under my pants. I dealt with them all the way down the rough road to Aru.

Beside me, Jonah seemed as stunned as I, and we did not speak. Jolting along in the dead of night, with no idea what was coming next, there was little to say. With each new development, our predicament seemed to be worsening. We had no clearance for landing in this region, only at Kinshasa, where we were scheduled to arrive a few weeks later, and Zaire, with its reputation for violence and corruption (it is sometimes referred to as a "kleptocracy"), was no place to have one's papers not in order. Also, an investigation might identify me as the author of an article about a previous visit, a few years before, in which I was sharply critical of Zaire's puppet dictator—reason enough in this feverish climate to be arrested as an enemy of the state, if not a suspected mercenary or spy.

Twenty-five years ago to the very month, scarcely a hundred miles east of this place, on the Sudan border, I had also been in custody, under much worse circumstances (the murder of Zaire's prime minister, Patrice Lumumba, in January of 1961, had inflamed Africa, turning Sudanese friends into fierce enemies), and I had no wish to repeat any such experience.

In Aru, to our great astonishment we were not locked up—we could go nowhere, after all, without passports or airplane—but were dropped off almost casually at the quarters of a British pilot for the United Nations' High Commission for Refugees, which is kept very busy in this part of the world. Our host, routed out at 3:00 A.M., kindly showed us where we might lie down, observing in passing that Zaire was paranoid these days about "mercenaries," which has been a dread word in this country since the anarchy and massacres of the 1960s. Rumors had implicated Zairois soldiers when seven French white water boatmen who had entered the country without permission disappeared on the Zaire River a few months ago. The government revealed that they had perished in the rapids, though their boats were found intact and right side up, and the one body that turned up had been beheaded.

The pilot was flying to Nairobi at daylight, now two hours away, and Jonah, fearing that our friends at Garamba might radio an alarm when we failed to appear, sent off a message to his neighbor Philip Leakey to notify his wife that we were fine.

At 8:00 A.M., the pilot's Ugandan assistant drove us around to the district commissioner's house to inquire about our passports. We were referred to the chief of immigration, who referred us to the chief of police, who said he had reported our arrival to his superiors in the regional capital at Bunia and could not return our passports without their permission. Surely Bunia would decide to check our identities at Kinshasa, and, since it was Saturday, it now appeared that we might be detained here through the weekend.

Meanwhile, the authorities had no objection if Dr. Western brought his airplane to Aru; they assumed that he would not vanish, leaving me and his passport behind. As Jonah wished to take off with an empty plane, the obliging police chief returned with him to Dibwa, where the people were ordered to chop brush, knock down termite hills, and fill up ditches while the plane's extra fuel and other cargo were unloaded for ground transport to the strip at Aru. As it turned out, the pair who had absconded with my flashlight the night before had used it to off-load all they could find in the unlocked cargo pod under the fuselage, including three jerry cans of fuel, a computer printer destined for Garamba, and a duffel containing all my clothes and personal belongings. The duffel, minus some of its original contents—toilet kit, malaria pills, spare flashlight, sneakers, sweater, hat, and every pair of socks and underwear—was retrieved eventually, but the fuel and the printer were gone for good.

Jonah made a skillful downhill takeoff and followed the road into Aru. By the time he arrived there, word had come to let us go. (Apparently Bunia had learned from Kinshasa that our visit was expected by the minister of national parks.) By early afternoon, we were in the air again, and headed north.

Nagero, on the Dungu River, forms the southern boundary of Garamba National Park. At its small airstrip, we were met by Alison (Kes) Smith, a pretty woman in her thirties with dark red hair. Dr.

Smith, born in England and now a Kenyan citizen, is the biologist on the Garamba Northern White Rhino Project, which is funded by various conservation groups and private donors. Her husband, Fraser Smith, is in charge of restoring to good operating order the logistical system of Garamba, which was the first of Zaire's parks, established by the colonial authorities in 1938. Accompanied by their infant daughter, the Smiths escorted us in the afternoon to the flat rocks by the hippo pool where they had been married just a year before in a roaring and blaring serenade from these hundred hippos. The silver limbs of the dead tree across the Dungu were decked with a winged red inflorescence made by companies of carmine bee-eaters, which, with their blue heads, cobalt rumps, and long streaming tails, are among the most splendid of African birds. With them were some smaller, only slightly less spectacular red-throated bee-eaters, and by its nest on a high tree sat a thickset white bird, the palm-nut vulture. Already we were far enough west so that endemic bird species of East and West Africa were overlapping; I had last seen this peculiar bird in Senegal.

Fraser Smith had constructed a small house on the banks of the Dungu, and the household presently included a large dog (a second dog had been taken by a crocodile), two cats, and a banded mongoose, which had enjoyed the run of the camp before taking up a habit of attacking people; its victims included its mistress, severely bitten twice. Since Dr. Smith had mentioned its bad character, I was unpleasantly surprised to see the snout and beady eyes of this large weasel relative appear beneath the wood stockade of the outdoor shower into which I had limped just before dusk. There was no mistaking the intent of its opened mouth, which was to bite me as speedily as possible, and sure enough it whisked into the shower and nipped my heel before I could take defensive action.

As anyone knows who recalls Kipling's Rikki-tikki-tavi, a mongoose is much too quick for any cobra, let alone a crippled man in a cramped shower slippery with soap. With my inflamed and swollen ankle, I was already a bit rickety on the wet uneven bricks, and this evil-tempered viverrid, renewing its attack, had me at enormous disadvantage. Jonah and Fraser were away from camp, refueling the airplane, so I called to Dr. Smith, more or less calmly, that she could find her mongoose near the shower. She had meant to take "Goose" for a walk, she said, and commenced to call it. The mongoose ignored her, darting in and out of sight under the stockade. I flicked hot water at it and made frightful growling noises, all to no avail; it backed out of view, came in swiftly from another angle, and sank its teeth into my toe, eliciting a sharp cry of vexation. "Is Goose biting you?" his mistress called. "So sorry!" It seemed that she was nursing her baby, but would come and fetch the mongoose in a minute.

For the nonce, I seized up a steel bucket and banged it down in front of my tormentor. This drove him back a little but did not deter him. Hopping mad, he dug furiously at the sandy earth—what field biologists call displacement activity, in which strong emotions are vented inappropriately. My toe was bleeding, my ankle hurt, and I, too, was full of strong emotion. Though loath to execute a household pet by bashing its brains out with my bucket, I was considering this last resort when it darted out of sight, made a flanking maneuver, and shot in again from yet another angle, affixing itself to the top of my left foot with a terrific bite. There it remained until I kicked it free, emitting a wild oath of rage and pain.

Perhaps afraid for her pet's life, my hostess appeared almost at once, joining me in the shower without warning. On the soapy floor, her legs flew out from under her, and she landed on her bottom, careening into the stockade as the mongoose disappeared beneath. Looking up, soaked by the shower, she found herself confronted by the nudity of her amazed guest, covered a bit late by the bucket. "Sorry," she said, starting to laugh, and I laughed, too. "I have no secrets," I said, groping for a towel. "Just remove that mongoose." I pointed sternly at my bloody foot. And with suspicious speed, or so it seemed to me—as if, in this camp, an emergency mongoose-bite repair kit was ever at the ready—Dr. Smith was back at the shower door with bandages and disinfectants. "Sorry," she said. "Better take care of that. Might turn septic quickly in this climate."

The mongoose episode occurred exactly twenty-four hours after the forced landing at Dibwa, and considering all that had taken place so early in our journey, I felt the need of a stiff whiskey, in which Kes joined me. I asked her first of all to explain her nickname (it's from "Kesenyonye," or "Live in Peace," a name given her by Maasai tribesmen when she and her first husband, Chris Hillman, who was working on an eland study, lived in Maasai Land south of the Ngong Hills) and, second, for details of the white rhino project—specifically, why she felt so strongly that such a large international effort should be expended in a probably doomed attempt to save the last seventeen animals of the northern race, when the very similar southern race is well protected, and the species as a whole not currently in danger.

Among all land mammals on earth, white (from the German *weit*, or wide-mouthed) rhinos are second only to elephants in size. Dr. Smith pointed out that the southern white rhino (the originally described race, *Cerathotherium simum simum*) was already endangered by the turn of the century and virtually exterminated in the 1920s by South African hunters; it was reduced to a remnant hundred animals before its protection was seriously begun. This number has now been increased to approximately three thousand, most of them in South Africa's national parks; white rhinos have also been reintroduced in Botswana, Zimbabwe, and Mozambique (though it seems unlikely that the Mozambique animals have survived that country's wars). This recovery lends at least faint hope for the recovery of the northern race, which is worth saving not only for itself but as a symbol of the conservation effort. (By spring 1989, the population has increased to twenty-two animals.)

The northern white rhinoceros was originally found in far northwest Uganda and northeast Zaire, the southern savannas of Sudan and Chad, and the Central African Republic, throughout suitable habitat north of the rain forest and west of the River Nile. In 1938, when Garamba was established, several hundred rhino were located by surveys, which until recent years have all been made on foot. By 1961, when I first saw these huge placid animals in the small park at Nimule, in the Sudan, an estimated one thousand to thirteen hundred white rhino were living in Garamba. Not long thereafter, the Simba rebels, protesting the murder of Lumumba and the ascendance of a pro-European regime, took control of most of Haute-

Zaïre, including the Garamba Park. In the next few years the Simbas slaughtered 90 percent of the white rhinos solely for their horn, the proceeds from which were used for the purchase of more weapons. In 1969, parks control was restored, but by 1977, when the rhino's numbers had increased to about five hundred, lack of government funding and logistical breakdown had removed all protection from the park's animals, which were now attacked more or less at will by organized poaching gangs from Uganda and Sudan, armed with automatic weapons from both countries' wars. By 1981, just thirty-six animals remained, and a survey two years later would locate less than twenty. The Garamba population has not increased in the years since, and everywhere else the northern race has probably been exterminated. The few lone animals that may still wander the empty eastern reaches of the Central African Republic will die without contributing to the population, since any meaningful increase in this remnant group would have to be achieved quickly, before the gene pool and breeding potential are further reduced by scattering, accident, or senility.

As the one certain defense against poaching, removal of these animals to a safer area has been considered, but there is no other safe, suitable habitat in Zaire, whose president-for-life Mobutu Sese Seko has decreed that these "Zairian" rhinos shall not leave his country. Instead he has promised help to the rhino project that has not been forthcoming. For the several months prior to our visit, Garamba's faithful guards and rangers had not been paid; they grew gardens by their huts in order to survive.

The Garamba rhinos might conceivably be protected in a small fenced area, but there are no funds for such confinement, which would introduce a whole new set of problems. As a last resort, they could be transferred to a zoo. Mark Stanley Price, a young biologist we spoke with in Nairobi, was involved in a successful program to restore a captive population of the white Arabian oryx to the Oman deserts. On the evidence of successful zoo propagation of the southern white rhino—there are now two hundred in world zoos—he does not doubt that these northern animals could also be raised successfully in captivity and thereby "saved." But reintroduction—a far more lengthy, expensive, and complicated process than mere release—is quite another matter. Even if a safe and suitable habitat still awaited them, the slow-breeding animals are huge and difficult to manage, and the ultimate irony might be that new veterinary regulations or new laws against international transport of wild animals might forbid the return of the saved species to its own environment.

Kes Smith, whose own plane was out of commission, was anxious to go on an air survey of Caramba, which she had been unable to make in several months. In the early morning, before breakfast, we flew north with Jonah across a vast plain of savanna grassland, already browning in the dry season, interspersed with shining, languid rivers. In the grassland stand large isolated trees—mostly the sausage tree, *Kigelia*. The more permanent watercourses are enclosed by gallery forest—sometimes called "finger forest," because it penetrates deep into the savanna in long fingerlike extensions of the rain forest that lies farther to the south. The rich green strands, which shelter many forest animals and birds, are set off by lovely lavender leaves of the combretum liana that here and there climbs to the canopy.

In comparison with the East African savanna, which has many medium-sized animals, including zebra and antelopes, both large and small, this northern grassland has very few, a discrepancy mainly attributable to climate. Equatorial East Africa has two rainy seasons of about three months each, with corresponding dry seasons in which herbivores can crop back the new grasses, whereas in this northern savanna, with its mixed woodland, a single long rainy season produces and sustains a high, rank, thick-stemmed grass ten to fifteen feet tall. Such grass cannot support herds of small herbivores, being not only unpalatable but too coarse to be managed except by large browsers with big guts; there are no zebra, and the few antelope species resort to flood-plain grasses and burned ground.

Human beings and domestic animals, or the lack of them, are also factors. In East Africa, the pastoralists, with their diet of blood and milk, can encourage calving in the rainy season and still have milk throughout the dry, whereas in this region, calves born in the long rains are weaned off long before the dry season, which is harsh and long. Thus, the Sudanic pastoralists such as the Nuer and the Dinka must eke out their milk diet with sorghum and millet and savanna game, or "bush meat." Farther west, in these woodland savannas, the presence of tsetse is inimical to livestock, and the use of bush meat is much heavier, with a corresponding wildlife decline. Especially in West Africa, where the savanna belt between rain forest and the near-desert known as the Sahel is very narrow, and the human population very high, the need for animal protein has all but eliminated the wild animals.

On the flood plain are fair numbers of antelope—tiang, kob, and waterbuck—together with buffalo and warthog and a few small herds of elephant. The Congo giraffe is also here though we do not see it. Kob and buffalo are by far the most common animals, and large black herds of buffalo may be seen along most of the many streams that flow south to the Garamba River.

The northern region of the park, which adjoins the meaningless Lantoto Park in Sudan, is rocky and hilly country, with only a small animal population, vulnerable to poachers. Unlike elephants, which are wide-ranging, rhinos are sedentary and are very easily tracked and killed, and the horn can be bashed off with a stone in a few minutes. Ivory poaching, on the other hand, is always risky and considerably more difficult and requires an efficient organization, since time is required to remove the tusks from a fresh carcass, and tusks are heavy to transport through roadless country. But the park rangers have not been provided with the means to patrol this remote area, with its poor roads, rivers, and precarious log bridges, and such animal protection as exists is concentrated on a thirty-two-square-mile area in this southern third of the park, entirely composed of savanna and slow watercourses. This region contains almost all the remaining rhinos, but even here they are threatened: a captured poacher recently admitted having killed two rhinos in 1983 and another two in 1984, effectively eliminating, all by himself, any increase that the animals might have made.

In an hour's flying, we count ourselves lucky to spot three white rhinos, a lone male and a cow with calf; seeing our plane, the calf moved closer to its mother, which raised her head toward the sky but did not run. The huge, calm, pale gray creatures with their primordial horned heads might have been standing on the plains of the Oligocene seventy million years ago, when they first evolved. Except for a lion rolling on its dusty mound, they were the only creatures at Garamba that did not flee at the airplane's approach. Kob scattered widely through the tall coarse grass, and the buffalo herds, panicking one another, rocked along aimlessly in all directions, and the big bush elephants of the savanna, wariest of all, hurried along through the high grass in their stiff-legged, ear-flapping run.

## Pygmies and Pygmy Elephants: The Congo Basin (1986)

**The Mbuti were** once famous elephant hunters, popularly supposed to run under an elephant and drive spears into it from beneath. "They had to work close, using jabbing spears, but I doubt if they did that very often," John Hart says.* "They're the ultimate opportunists; they would bring it down any way they could." Elephant hunting died out in the early seventies, with the decline of the elephant itself, and the only Mbuti who go after them today are those who serve poachers as gun bearers and trackers. . . .

The hunters return in late afternoon with four blue duiker, not enough to feed our growing camp. There are twenty-six huts at Ekare, most of them occupied; there must be sixty people here in all. Sibani the Leper, one of several Pygmies more yellow in skin color than brown, can no longer tend his net due to sore feet, but he has a big bright yellow-green-and-black monitor lizard that he shot with his bow and arrow. With glee, he describes the fury of the finish: "I jumped right into the water with my pants on!" At supper I accept his offer of fresh lizard meat, only to be told, once I had started, that I could not have antelope as well, since mixing the two might jinx tomorrow's hunt. . . .

Slowly, as the evening passes, the men begin to sing, keeping

*The American biologists John and Terese Hart had conducted the first study of the elusive forest relative of the giraffe, called the okapi, found only in this region of Zaire.

time with fire-hardened sticks and an old plastic oil container as a drum. The simple harmonies, rising and falling away like strong quiet fire, are intensified by choruses and clapping and the counterpoint of solo voices, in an effect intensely subtle and sophisticated, despite the repetition of the simple lyrics. "Let us all sing this song"—or, better, put ourselves into this song, be one with this song. Or "I didn't eat; other people ate." Or "The food we put out for the Ancestors got eaten by the dogs." For often there is humorous intent, especially in the love songs: "If you can't climb the buo tree [a tall, straight-trunked relative of the elm without lower limbs], forget my daughter." There are also hunting songs, and honey songs and dances, especially in August, when the brachystegia trees come into blossom and honey becomes the most sought-after item of diet. "Go out with your lover and spend the day beneath the honey tree" is a song of explicit and joyful sexuality, with vivid gestures of a honey-eyed arm thrusting in and out of the hive.

All songs are implicitly sacred. "The forest gives us this song," the people say, meaning, "The forest *is* this song."

Another night, a man named Gabi dances slowly with a bow, tapping the bowstring with a stick, using his mouth at one end of the string to achieve resonance. Later he dances as Dekoude the Trickster, a masked green figure bound head to toe in leaves who gets people lost in the deep forest. Soon the girls and women rise to dance, in an intricate pattern in and out of a half hoop of stiff liana that one of their number, seated on the ground, raises and lowers on the waves of music. Before each culminating leap, each woman holds her hand out over the ground and sings, "Before I am given another child, this one must be as tall as this!" Each time this is said, the women laugh loudly at the men.

The best dancer and best singer in the camp is Atoka's sister Musilanji, who is lighthearted and bursting with life. According to John, she is much in demand among the truckers and other Bantu in the villages, and, not being possessed of a grudging character that might permit her to say no, she has contracted syphilis along the way. As a strong and beautiful solo voice in both the women's group and men's, Musilanji sings with all her heart, and later, after everyone has crawled into their huts, she laughs with the same all-out spirit at the dirty jokes of old Sibani, laughing until she rolls upon the ground, gasping for breath, laughing until she hurts and squeals for mercy, her passionate abandon so infectious that, stretched out in our leaf hut across the circle, unable to understand a single word, I laugh hard, too.

Before daybreak, the cries of forest animals awake the camp, and the din intensifies, with staccato arm claps, as the men make ready to set off on the hunt. Over the breakfast fire, Kenge* says, "It is all joy, it is making the *mangese* of the forest happy," and his sister-in-law Asha nods agreement. Kenge, a handsome, serious man, now gives a speech, reminding the hunters that they must no longer kill okapi or elephant, that any outsider found in the forest with a snare must be arrested, that nets are all right because the People come and go and do not harm the forest life.

There is something chastened about Kenge, who is no longer the lighthearted young hunter to whom Colin Turnbull's book was dedicated a quarter-century ago. He is now an elder, and he takes himself seriously, and is taken seriously, for everyone knows that his picture appeared in a book. In camp, though he laughs at us with all the others, he sits in a chair with his arms folded, talking mostly to Asha, who cooks for the whites, and keeping himself subtly aloof, as if, at ease in neither world, he was fated to mediate between the groups. "Kenge knows he is somebody," says John Hart sympathetically, "but he doesn't quite know who."

Atoka is all nerved up for the hunt. With great finesse and delicacy, and sounds to match, he mimes the approach, the rush at the net, the finish of the big yellow-backed duiker he intends to kill. His arms and pointed fingers dart in imitation of the antelope's quick legs and sharp hooves, he claps his arm with a loud hollow report to alert the others that his duiker has been netted, he squats, he leaps, grabbing one leg of the animal and twisting it over on its back, screeching in triumph even as he demonstrates how the others will come running with their spears.

*A Mbuti guide.

Dodging driver ants, Rick Peterson and I cross the Ekare on a dead tree and follow the path into the forest, where we come upon a small unattended fire that one of the hunters had gone out earlier to prepare. Here Atoka drops his net and summons the Ancestors to witness this offering of precious fire to the forest and the purification of the hunters in its smoke; if the forest is contented, all will go well in the hunt. One by one the hunters come, squat down, let the smoke bathe them. Tambo holds a leaf over the smoke, then rubs his chest with it. The men smoke *bangi*, "to give them strength and get them ready," says Atoka. We rise and go.

Moving off the path into the forest, the hunters are quiet and keep signals to a minimum; in the thick cover, each man seems to know just where to go. Already some are stringing out their nets, unwinding the long coils from their shoulders as they run deftly through the understory, then returning along the line to raise the net and hang it firmly on shrub branches and saplings, taking pains to see that the bottom edge is firm against the earth. Atoka's net, overlapping others at each end, is three to four feet high, seventy-five yards long, and by no means the longest. With twelve hunters, the entire set will be a half-kilometer around, enclosing about twenty acres in a semicircle.

Atoka's net overlaps that of Asumani, who nods as we go by. "*Merci*" is a word he has learned to say, and he tries it out quietly in greeting. Already the women are appearing, following around outside the nets to the narrow entrance. A signal comes, they enter and fan out, whooping and calling, each one headed for her husband's sector.

We wait just inside the net, on a log that overlooks a forest gorge. It is Atoka's turn for a poor spot, close to one end; he does not expect much. We listen to a great blue turaco, green pigeons, an unknown cuckoo; a scrub robin flits briefly into view, cocking its head in the thrush manner. Off in the distance, a great tree topples of its own accord—a crack of thunder and an avalanche of matter as a hundred and fifty feet of timber, dragging down vines and lianas, snapping limbs and saplings, tears a long slash in the canopy and thumps the waiting earth. A wave of silence follows, like a forest echo.

The silence is broken by a loud arm clap, for game has been seen near the nets. From the shouts that follow, Atoka learns that a big red duiker, *nge*, has pierced Gabi's net.

Quickly we rise and make another set, not far away. This time an nge is entangled. There comes a wild yell from the west, two nets away, and we follow Atoka on a dead run through the trees toward the strange sheeplike bleats of this forest antelope that the hunters imitate so skillfully. The men there ahead of us at Mayai's net have seized the legs of what turns out to be a Peter's red duiker, a species I have never seen. The mesh is freed roughly from its long head and neck as it flops and thrashes, staring up at us with strange blue-filmed night eyes. Without ceremony, Asumani hacks its throat, and at the rush of blood, everyone laughs. Though the forest has given them this food, the hunters are no more reverent toward it than they are to their camp dogs; this irreverence, rare among tradi-tional peoples, seems curious in the light of the earlier propitiation of the forest. "*Ekoki*," they say to us, and "*malamu*." Both words mean "good."

Returning to fetch Atoka's net, we pass the deaf man, Poos-Poos, who has the narrow shoulders of a woman and often wears his *kik-wembe* tied around his neck, the way a Pygmy woman wears it near the road. Poos-Poos is grieving. A *seke*—a white-bellied duiker—approached his net, then ran away. But later, when the men have gathered after an unsuccessful set, Poos-Poos cheers everyone with a very comic imitation of his drunken self leaving the truck-stop bar, trying to find his way back to the forest, putting twigs in his eyes, butting his head into the tree trunks. The hunters laugh, and laugh still harder when they see that Rick and I are laughing, too. They feel protective about Poos-Poos, who cannot articulate, and often emits weird hoots, shrill cackles; Mayai accounts for him by tapping his ear and then his temple, to indicate why Poos-Poos is incomplete, and when he does this, Poos-Poos, his soft brown eyes wide and round as a lemur's, smiles an enchanted smile, as if blessing us all.

Yet Poos-Poos, able in every chore, has his own net and spear and travels as an equal with the hunters except in rainstorms, when he loses his bearings and has to be led by the hand. He is very kind and popular with the small children, and he is alert, as he has to be, to keep up with the rest in an existence so dependent on good hearing. Poos-Poos is chronically in a high state of tension, and his strange face, slightly askew, is scarred by grievous marks of concentration, pinching his forehead, that are lacking in his lighthearted companions. Perhaps he is not retarded as I had imagined, but on the contrary, atremble with trapped intelligence, wild with frustration.

Slipping through the forest, the hunters see bees moving back and forth, and the hunt is suspended while they search without success for the hive. We cross a pretty tributary brook known as Ekare's Daughter. An elephant has crossed ahead of us, and okapi sign is everywhere. Then the set is made, we wait again, watching a bird party of leafloves and greenbuls that glean the understory foliage, in shafts of sun. Another nge and also a blue duiker, *mboloko*, are taken, to great whoops of triumph that drown out the hoots and yelling of the beaters.

In the next set, a blue duiker escapes, nothing is caught. Rain comes. The Mbuti seek out a big tree with heavy lianas, which thicken the canopy above with their own leaves, providing shelter. With his hands idle, Atoka is restless. "This is the work of the Forest," he says. "We hunt, we wait, we get up and go again." So far today he has caught nothing, but he knows that in the partition of the antelopes his family will be given meat. "The first thing we learn is *kosalisa*—to take care of others. We Mbuti do no one any harm. If I sleep hungry, you sleep hungry; if I get something from the forest, you will have it, too."

In the next surround, a heavy animal wheels and crashes away through the thickets just in front of us, and a woman who has seen the creature comes running down the line of nets shouting, "*Moimbo!*" This is the yellow-back, largest of all duikers, up to a hundred and forty pounds. But the rarely caught moimbo slips past the line of nets and flees; only a blue duiker is caught. Another blue duiker, on the final hunt, comes to Atoka but pierces his net in an explosive jump at the last second. Atoka does not complain or appear disheartened, and on the way home he remains behind to gather up wood for the fires. This evening we will eat antelope with the others.

The following day three animals are caught. One is a moimbo and another is a water chevrotain, not an antelope at all but a relation of the primitive tusked deer of Asia. The moimbo was speared by old Pita, and Atoka, with wild snorts and cries, acts out each second of its final moments, to show how the big yellow-back, pierced between the ribs, twisted frantically on Pita's spear, heart pumping.

Even dressed out and cut in pieces, the moimbo was too big to fit in Pita's old wife's basket, and Tambo's young wife, asked to help carry the meat, threw a tantrum in the forest, relieving the tensions that build up in an Mbuti camp. She worked herself into a frenzy, screeching and rolling on the ground to ensure attention, hurling wild insults at the people in general and her husband in particular. Gentle Tambo, one of the few unexuberant Mbuti, tries to ignore her like everybody else, but after a half-hour, when her drama threatened to disrupt the hunt, he felt obliged to come and beat her. Returning to camp, she started in again, accounting for her behavior with a tearful and aggrieved oration that the people heard out with intense discomfort, after which she took shelter in another hut, among one of the households which, while not rejected, seem subtly excluded from the group that leads the hunting and the singing. (The small family in the hut beside my own, I notice, rarely join in the jokes and banter, which for all I know may be at their expense.) A long, tense silence was broken by some ribald observation that collapsed the whole circle of huts in grateful laughter, after which camp life proceeded in the same gay and offhand way as it had before.

On the first of February we left Ekare, walking straight south to Epulu, about fifteen kilometers away. At the Bougpa spring, black colobus monkeys were making their deep rolling racket; near Lelo two big red colobus, long tails hanging like question marks, sprang into the bare limbs of a high tree to watch us pass. Kenge, who helps Terry Hart with her botanical collections, identified various fruits and medicines along the way, including an orange shelf fungus used by the Mbuti to cure diarrhea. He pointed out odd termite nests like huge gray mushrooms in the tree roots, and the orange paste spat out by fruit bats, and a place where the forest hid the People from the successive waves of soldiers, rebels, and mercenaries who pillaged and murdered in this region in the first years after independence.

On the night of our return there was an *elima*, or girl's initiation ceremony, and the sound of drums and chanting came from the Mbuti camp along the road east of Epulu. Later we heard shouting from the Babila village that could only mean trouble, and next morning the local gendarme turned up in his crisp green beret and green uniform with red shoulder tabs and made a complaint to Terry Hart, who was talking with me on a terrace overlooking the river. Kenge had got drunk and stirred up trouble, and his family had led in a drunken brawl that had ended with the destruction of a Bantu house, and Atoka and the spirited Asha had been jailed, the gendarme said. He suggested that their American friends pay for the damages, having brought them back out of the forest where they belonged. The Harts were mistaken in treating the Pygmies like real people, he continued; they should simply be given food and a few rags to wear. As for Atoka, he should be "tortured," said this new African, by which he meant—to judge from prior episodes—beaten bloody with clubs, since there was no other way for him to repay his debts. It turned out that the victim had provoked Atoka by denouncing the Mbuti as "*nyama*," or "wild animals," an opinion in which the gendarme fully concurred. The Pygmies had to be treated like the animals they were, he assured Terese Hart, who winced but said nothing. We stared away over the striking rocks that emerge in the dry season from the Epulu River, which winds southwest to the Ituri, the Nepoko, the Aruwimi, and a final confluence with the great Congo west of Kisangani.

# *from* In the Spirit of Crazy Horse

1983, 1991

*The introduction to Matthiessen's most controversial book begins: "On June 26, 1975, in the late morning, two FBI agents, Jack Coler and Ron Williams, drove onto Indian land near Oglala, South Dakota, a small village on the Pine Ridge Reservation. Here a shoot out occurred in which both agents and an Indian man were killed. Although large numbers of FBI agents, Bureau of Indian Affairs (BIA) police, state troopers, sheriff's deputies, and vigilantes surrounded the property within an hour of the first shots, the numerous Indians involved in the shoot-out escaped into the hills. The death of the agents inspired the biggest manhunt in FBI history." The investigation concluded with the indictment of four men, three of whom were later released or acquitted. One, Leonard Peltier, was convicted on two counts of murder. Peltier, from the FBI's point of view, was an ideal catch; he was the leader of the group and a member of a radical civil rights organization that, despite its often aggressive encounters with white authority, was admired by supporters for asserting a forceful Indian identity. Distrust of the U.S. government, of course, has been widespread among Indians for centuries, and many natives suspected the FBI had been infiltrating AIM for years, perhaps, as Matthiessen suggests, to make it easier for corporate mining interests to open up the uranium beds of western South Dakota for industrial extraction. Peltier's conviction came about despite the fact that, as Matthiessen writes, even his prosecutors would dismiss as worthless the testimony of the only person ever to claim to have witnessed his participation in the killings. The witness herself later repudiated her testimony, saying it had been extracted under severe FBI duress. Not long after this book's initial publication in 1983, Matthiessen and* *the Viking Press were sued for libel by an FBI agent and by William Janklow, the former (and present) governor of South Dakota, in what was effectively a joint suit totaling $49 million. Six years later, when a federal appeals court threw the case out for good, Matthiessen's book, republished in 1991, had become a symbol of victory over government censorship. Despite the victory, First Amendment rights of free speech had been chilled by this harassment, which cost the publisher's insurers some $3 million in legal fees, and no book like it has appeared since. More than an account of this notorious case, however, In the Spirit of Crazy Horse is a broad condemnation of U.S. government relations with our native people in a three-hundred-year history of bad blood. Whatever the nature and degree of Peltier's participation at Oglala, Matthiessen writes, his ruthless persecution had less to do with his actions than with underlying issues of history, racism, and economics, in particular Indian sovereignty claims and growing opposition to massive energy development on treaty lands and the dwindling reservations.*

*The following excerpt, from the chapter entitled "Red and Blue Days," provides a summary of the case, as Matthiessen interviews those connected with Peltier several years after his conviction, including John Trudell, a national spokesman for AIM, and Bob Robideau and Dino Butler. Robideau and Butler had been with Peltier at the Pine Ridge shooting; both were tried and acquitted. Peltier, who escaped to Canada but was later extradited on the basis of depositions that the government itself now admits were false, was sentenced to two terms of life imprisonment. He remains in Leavenworth Penitentiary, despite protest against his conviction from all over the world.*

**Bob Robideau,** in vest and cowboy boots, long black hair blowing, moved restlessly from group to group, settling nowhere; finally he squatted on his heels against the cabin side, gazing out over the river woods of White Clay Creek. Sensing something, I intruded on his privacy, asking him what his feelings were, being back here on Jumping Bull land on June 26. Bob gave me a brief wary look, then let a silence hang on this stupid question, which he recognized as an effort to smoke him out. After a time, he said shortly, "I don't feel no different. Why?"

After many days together, in California as well as South Dakota, this man and I understood each other pretty well. For Leonard's sake, as long as there was hope of a new trial, he had to be careful about what he told me, and trust to my good sense in what I wrote; once that trust was established, he had been as candid as he could be under the circumstances, which had changed considerably with the appearance of the FOIA documents. The Defense Committee and the attorneys felt that the time had come to tell the truth about Oglala, or at least most of it, and Bob (and Leonard and Dino, too) had been speaking much more openly about the shoot-out than he had fourteen months before, on that cold April day when we first visited this property.

"I was on security the night before," Butler had told me in Vancouver. "It was a very long night with a lot of rain, and I was tired, so I slept late; I remember the young girls were cooking pancakes. Norman Brown came and woke us when he heard the shots, and he ran up ahead of me. By the time I got going, and came up out of the woods, the Long Visitors were already on their way out, and I told them which way to go; they were hurrying toward the road, maybe a mile across that field, and the way they were moving, even with the kids, that distance could not have taken them more than ten minutes. Later they said that a car came along right away and picked them up, and that just down the road toward Pine Ridge, there was a big van parked, and someone was handing out weapons to white lawmen. So that was already happening within fifteen minutes after they left the compound!

"By the time I got up there, Adams and the BIA cops had already arrived, and the two Normans were shooting in their direction. There was a lot of automatic fire coming from the cars, and Norman Brown got pinned down by the outhouse; I could hear the bullets whack into the wood. Norman hollered at me that they had him trapped, so I let off a clip to keep their heads down while he ran for it; I was shooting an M-1 .30-06 with a top clip that day.

"At that time, them agents could still have got away without any trouble." Saying this, Dino had seemed vaguely regretful that they had not done so. When I mentioned the reported cross fire that might have held them there, the trial evidence that one or more people were shooting at them from around June Little's cabin, he shook his head. "There was no one shooting at them from June's cabin. All those shell casings over there were old ones, used for target shooting a few days before. So the agents could have gone back out that way, but they didn't. And the reason they didn't was because they thought that people were coming in there quick to back them up."

When I repeated this account to Robideau, he nodded in confirmation. He was silent a moment, as if making a decision, then spoke out quickly in a flat even tone, as if he wished to get something over with as quickly as possible. "Leonard was down there by that big elm near where them junked cars used to be. He never moved from that place during the shoot-out. I was up there by that old car past the green shack. Dino was over by that woodpile, Joe and Norman Charles were near him, and another guy and another guy whose names are not going to be mentioned, they were here and here—hell, there were Indians all over. What we couldn't understand was why them two men stayed right where they were, down in that field; they couldn't have picked a worse position in the first place. The least they could have done was backed them cars down into the woods—that would have been easy. Or at least run for those corrals, where they had a little cover. They didn't even *try* to take cover; the most they did was kneel down alongside their car. The rest of the time they just stood there, right out in the open. Of course, we was quite a ways away,* but even so, it's just amazing that they lasted as long as they did.

"I remember that one of 'em was trying to get into the car for some reason, probably the radio; by that time, I had taken that .44 from Joe, and when I let off a clip of five, that agent raised his rifle and let go at me."

I didn't ask him who had fired the first shot. By his own account and those of others, he had not been up there when it happened,

---

*It was approximately 150 yards from the cabins—and also from Peltier's position—to the agents' cars.

and knowing this man's instinctive discretion, I felt it was conceivable that he had never asked and did not know; if he *did* know, and the truth would have helped Leonard, he would have told me. Not counting Poor Bear, the only known firsthand account was still Mike Anderson's rooftop story, but in the light of Anderson's earlier versions (in September 1975, in Wichita, and February 1, 1977, in Rapid City; what he told the grand jury in July 1975 is still unknown), there was no good reason to believe it.

On the other hand, the evidence suggests—to me, at least—that Coler and Williams had indeed been chasing one or more vehicles, and that whether or not those being pursued stopped at the Y-fork above the junked cars (not wishing apparently to lead the FBI cars either down toward the camp or up into the compound), the agents pulled up in that vulnerable place down in the pasture because they heard a warning shot or came under fire; if there is another persuasive explanation of the location and position of their cars, I cannot find it. (According to one report, the two cars had been pulled up in a defensive V, with the agents between them, using the engine blocks for protection; this isn't true, according to Robideau, who says the two cars were one behind the other, headed almost in the same direction.) Not that this means much in terms of Peltier's guilt or innocence, since even if it could be shown (it never was) that the red-and-white van was the vehicle in question, and that Peltier was driving it again just before noon—or even that Peltier emerged from the car and started shooting—no connection has ever been established between this event and the executions of the agents perhaps fifteen minutes later.

In the absence of any contradictory account from the defense—from the start, there has been total silence on this subject—it seems probable that the Indians started the shooting. *Why* they did so, of course, is another matter; no onus is necessarily attached to the first shot. Perhaps the beginning of the fatal episode was trivial ("Maybe those guys in the truck got themselves chased because they flipped those two agents a bird," one Indian girl says, elevating a finger. "That's all it would have taken, the way things were"), but whatever the details, there seems to be no doubt that the agents repeatedly invaded hostile territory, sparking an impulse to drive off these hated intruders who had already been warned away at least once before. I imagine a wind of anger and a yell, a warning shot. When Coler and Williams stopped short in the pasture, someone may have fired in grim fun, not yet deadly serious, and instead of retreating, the agents fired back, without even improving their exposed position. And by the time they realized that the situation was out of control, that the backup cars—if they heard them come—had already retreated, long-haired figures were running here and there along the rim, shooting down at them from more vantage points than they could cover. In a few wild minutes, Coler had received that shocking wound, and Williams could not or would not desert him—the details, the degree of bravery, the precise order of events are lost. But a tension that had been gathering on Pine Ridge for almost a century burst like the lightning in the huge black skies of the summer thunderstorm the night before, and three men died.

With both agents wounded and one down, Robideau says, he ran down the slope to the edge of the tree line where Peltier was stationed and suggested that they take the two as hostages; cars were already arriving on Highway 18, they would soon be surrounded, and some sort of bargaining power was needed if they were going to survive the day. When Peltier agreed, Robideau went back up to fetch Butler, after which the three made their way down through the thick woods, then northward in the cover of the neck of trees, not far from the agents' cars; unable to see any sign of the agents ("Their heads never showed above the windows") but covered by the Indian guns on the rim above, they began to make their way toward the cars, taking advantage of the scattered cover of small trees.

Bob gazed at me like a poker player raising his eyes over his cards. It was now he said, that a red truck "came down the road fast from somewhere up around this cabin. At the cars, it slowed down, maybe even stopped, though I never heard anyone get out; we couldn't see, because the truck was on the far side of them cars, but we heard the shots. Then the truck took off again up the hill, got the hell out of there."

Taken aback by this unexpected story, I stared at him; he didn't flinch. I asked why the defense attorneys had not revealed this, since S.A. Gary Adams's report of the red pickup that fled the area at 12:18 seemed to confirm it. "We discussed it," Robideau said calmly. "But there was no way to prove it, not without getting them others into trouble, and anyway, it was decided that it was better to keep us out of the area of the cars entirely, not only because of aiding and abetting [even minor involvement in the commission of a crime could invite prosecution on this charge] but because it might have been too hard for a jury to believe what really happened."

When I grunted, still a little dazed, Bob said, "You see?"

How had that truck escaped through the BIA roadblock?

"Hell, there was people passing through them roadblocks all day long. They didn't really have 'em set up right, and we think that's because them agents jumped the gun before the rest of 'em were ready."

I supposed aloud that Williams must have thrown his gun down (Price had said he was wounded in his gun arm) before stripping off his shirt without unbuttoning it and trying to tie a tourniquet on Coler; perhaps he had waved that white shirt first in sign of surrender. Robideau shrugged. "I never seen no sign of surrender," he said. "But of course that could have happened while we was down there in the woods; maybe that's why we never seen their heads show in the windows of the car when we were creeping up there, trying to get the drop on them. If I had known they had surrendered, I would have hollered for a cease-fire; we would have taken them prisoners, taken them hostage, like I said."

Asked what the group would have done with two hostages who were probably bleeding to death, and who certainly could not have been taken along on an escape, Robideau gazed at me, unblinking. "I don't know," he said, after a while.

Trying to ease a sudden tension, I suggested that for a jury there would be a big difference between wounding the agents in a long-range exchange of fire and going down there to finish off the helpless men. What I wanted to hear, I guess, was some sort of moral disapproval of the "execution," because try as I would to understand the event in historical and sociological perspective, it was still horrifying in terms of the live victims ("a voice yelling for help, sounds like a scream. This voice was vague and appeared to be quite a long way off"). I could not get Ron Williams's last minutes out of my mind—that panic, apparently intensified by the sight and sound of his maimed partner, which was so painfully evident on those radio transmissions ("Come on, guys! Come on, guys!"), the knives of terror in heart and temple as the depthless hole of the rifle muzzle rose before him, as his hand flew up before his face in the shocked realization that he was about to be killed *right now* by another man as crazed and frantic as himself. The long black hair, the sweating forehead, the wild eye squinched by the rifle stock—NO!—as Jack Coler, mercifully unaware (the experts say) of what was happening, sat slumped against the car, the light already fading from his eyes as the barrel of this gun or another turned toward him. As it had so many times before, this recurrent scene or something like it fled through my mind in that long moment while Robideau and I considered each other.

But Bob had no intention of claiming innocence for himself or for his partners; as in Dino's case, his wonder that the agents had not fled while there was time had carried an overtone of vague regret, but he was not going to let either of us off the hook by making excuses. In fact, he looked at me as if I were just obstinate; from the Indians' viewpoint—and increasingly from my own—any talk of innocence or guilt was beside the point. All the Indians who were here that day were warriors, and the nameless figures in the red truck were no more guilty than he and Dino and Leonard, because no Indian that day was guilty; the only thing that might have been questioned was the judgment of those men, and Robideau refused to question even that. "None of us was innocent," he said finally, referring to the three who were finally prosecuted. "We fired on the agents and we hit the agents: we participated. But we didn't kill them."

According to one veteran police reporter, Bob Robideau has "the eyes of a killer; I been around guys like this for a long time and I know the eyes of a killer when I see 'em." Perhaps what he is referring to is a kind of lidded ex-con look that reveals nothing; once Bob relaxes, his eyes open wide in disconcerting youthfulness. He has a good sense of humor and laughs at himself often, never attempting the mildest excuse for messing up in the course of his youthful burglaries, and taking complete responsibility for such fiascos as the badly fitted tailpipe that caused the near-fatal explosion on the Kansas Turnpike. He gives an impression of bare honesty even when, to protect others, he is not telling the truth; that you suspect he may be lying does not bother him, since he knows that you know that he has no choice. It is not "the eyes of a killer" that one sees but a certain deadliness of intent that makes one wonder if his cousin Leonard is only referring to Robideau's thin build when he calls him "Razor."

("Bob's got his faults, we all do," Leonard says, "but there's one thing we learned about him after all these years: if he says he'll do something, he's gonna do it. He speaks right out, he's very blunt, and he doesn't worry at all what the person thinks about him, but he's not someone who speaks rashly. Everybody that's met Bob through the years all like him; I've never run into anyone who said, I don't like that guy, I don't like his attitudes. The same goes for Dino. They're quite a lot alike in many ways. They're both very quiet and sincere, and they're both dedicated to the people's struggle. With them, it's not a romantic thing, the way it is with a lot of people, and they're still gonna be there when the going gets rough.")

After a pause, I asked if those men in the truck had finished off the agents so that there would be no witnesses, no one left to point a finger at the Indians who had participated in the shoot-out. Robideau shook his head. "I don't think they did it to eliminate witnesses. I think they just did it out of years of pent-up frustration and rage about not being able to do anything about the hopeless kind of lives that they were leading on this reservation." For the first time since I had known him, Bob Robideau, in a very controlled way, was upset and angry; his body was restless, and his voice had taken on a subtle thickness. "I've never killed anybody in my life," he said, "and I hope I never have to, because I hate the idea. But if I have to, I can do it, and I could have done it that day. We were just sick of being pushed around; we didn't care about them agents. They were shooting at us, and we shot back."

· · ·

We went down the hill from the Little house, on the pasture road toward the corrals which the agents had descended that day to the place they died. A great blue heron lifted on slow summer wings out of White Clay Creek, and the noisy killdeer cried—*kee-dee, kee-dee*—from the fields near the Pumpkinseed cabin on the far side of the trees.

The old corrals were sagging with disuse. "Everything's grown up quite a bit," Bob said, inspecting the narrow neck of woods that he and Leonard and Dino used as cover in trying to sneak up behind the agents. Then he walked out, as he had six years before, to the foot of the steepening slope below the cabin where the white-over-tan Colorado car and the green Rambler had sat in the dead heat of midday summer. From this low place, all the two agents could have seen was the silvered wood of the root cellars in the long grass of the ridge line, and the dark doorway of the leaning out-house on the bluff, and the shivering dark leaves of the trees that shaded the Jumping Bulls' white cabin, and the silhouettes of long-haired figures running down the hot pale sky of the Dakotas.

Everywhere, wild roses were in bloom. "Lots of sage here now," Bob said. "We had it pretty well picked clean when we was here, had to go all the way to Lone Man's for it." Near the Y-crossing between the green shack and the woods stands a big elm with a depression all around the base of the trunk where Peltier had lain during the shoot-out; not far downhill from this tree, inside the wood edge, is another large elm—very likely the one climbed by Eastman and Waring when they first saw the Colorado car. On this tree is tacked a weathered blue tin sign, #13—EXQUISITE, that advertised some unknown long-gone product.

Asked where the red pickup truck had come from, Bob glanced at me, then shrugged his shoulders. "There you go with them questions again," he said. I pressed him a little: had he seen it earlier? "Could have been up around the houses. I wasn't too aware of what was going on up there; from the time I come up from the camp, I was concentrating on them two guys down in the pasture. And I stayed pretty much over there on the south end, by the green shack; I never went among the houses until after them agents were dead.

Anyway, the first time I saw that truck was when it started coming down the hill. Those other people up on the hill—so far as I know, they never saw who was in the truck because it cut back up the hill way over this side of the Jumping Bulls' and then went out."

When the red truck had gone, the three men crossed the pasture to the agents' cars. A shotgun was leaning against the rear bumper, and there was a rifle on the ground. "I didn't really look at them two bodies, but I noticed they was laying right beside each other by the left-side rear wheel of the car. While Dino and Leonard was searching 'em for weapons, I was gathering up whatever I could find. On the green car, in front, the radio was still going strong, and we could hear what was coming down on us. I figured we would have to leave here quick, and that we better know just what the FBIs were up to. I don't think I even asked Dino and Leonard; I just loaded the guns in the backseat and got in that car and drove straight ahead up over this hill and down toward our camp, flat tires and all. By that time there was a lot of cars arriving on the highway, and them guys up there was running around, trying to cover all sides; probably they never noticed me drive off. Draper was already down at camp, and I assigned him to listening to the radio while I headed back on up the hill to tell Leonard and Dino that there was law coming at us from all over, that we better get out while we still had a chance. Not that I really thought we had a chance."

Butler, Robideau, and Peltier were still down at the cars when Joanna LeDeaux entered the property. "I first seen her up there by that woodpile," Bob remembered, "and she started coming down the hill past them old root cellars; she got down maybe fifty feet before we waved her off. We were headed that way"—he pointed—"toward the Y-fork and our camp, so she kind of angles down across the slope to meet us. I guess maybe that was when I was moving that green car on its flat tires. Anyway, I seen Leonard get angry. Leonard don't get excited too often, but when he does, you can see it from a long way off."

(In his own account of the silence after the killing, when he and his partners had approached the bodies, Leonard had grunted, his face colorless. "I felt we were all dead," he said somberly. "I was feeling crazy because there were still women and children up there in June's cabin. When Joe come down there to the cars, I said to him, I think they're gonna kill everyone here. That's when I told him, This is the day to be a warrior, but all I could think of was, We gotta get *outa* here, or we're dead, too. So I was running back and forth, making sure that everybody was moving out; we knew what was coming. And all of a sudden I look up and see this *white* woman!" In a long pause, he shook his head, as if still stunned. "*Shock!* Where in hell did *she* come from! I had known her, you know, before she moved over to Porcupine a few weeks earlier; she was living right close to us for a while in Russ Loud Hawk's old house when we were living at Ted Lame's, and we became friends. I went over to investigate when she arrived, check out who she was, and I . . . stuck around." Leonard grinned, a little sheepish, then shrugged his shoulders. "I was going around with Jean Day, too—I was just . . . *happy!* But that day of the shoot-out, I got pretty excited—I did. I couldn't take it in—what was she *doing* there? Here was this white woman up there on the hill screaming, Stop! Stop! Stop *what?* What the hell's she talking about? I mean, this was a while after they were killed. Joe was back up there, and I hollered to him, Get her *out* of here! I wasn't trying to hurt her or nothing, she knows that, it was just shock. It was no use trying to explain to her what really happened, because it wouldn't do no good; no matter *how* it happened, they were going to kill us, and we all knew it.")

"When I got back up to the compound," Robideau said, "I seen this woman over by the cabins, and I went on over. She was asking if anyone on either side needed medical attention because there was an ambulance out on the road. Leonard was all hyper after what had happened, same way I was, and he calls over, *No!*—kind of rough, you know—No, nobody needs medical attention! And he told someone to get her out of there. But I guess she had looked over the edge of the hill on her way in, and she wanted to go down there and see if them agents needed medical assistance. She started to insist, and he got mad, yelling, Nobody down there needs medical assistance, because they are dead! What we need here now is ammunition! And that was the truth; our bullets were almost gone."

("Joanna said she wanted to help get the women and children out," Butler remembers. "All the women and children in the cabins had gone, so I took her down to our camp in the woods because I was worried about Nilak and the kids. I hollered around, but there was no sign of them; I guess that was when Nilak was off exploring for an escape route. So I sent Joanna back while I did some reconnoitering on my own. Leonard was angry that she was in there in the first place; I guess he figured that this white woman was the last thing we needed at a time like that.")

Nobody tried to explain to LeDeaux that they had not killed the agents, Robideau said; she had seen them down there at the cars, and even if they had felt like accounting for themselves, they did not really expect to be believed. However, he told her that everyone was upset and that she should not take Leonard's anger personally. "She understood that, but she was pretty upset, too, and I had to cool things out a little. I said, Look, it's OK, but there's nothing you can do, so just get out of here. Some of them Oglala women didn't like her so much—there was some kind of a personality problem—but she never said one word to the feds about who she had seen in there, or what, even though she spent eight months in jail.

"Leonard was still very distracted, and when he saw I was carrying one of the agents' revolvers, he asked me to try it out, although I told him it wouldn't carry very far unless I fired it up in the air. After we looked the situation over, we headed back down to the camp, leaving Joe and Norman Charles behind to keep an eye on everything until we got organized. Then Mike and Norman Brown come in, and Wishie took off up the hill to tell Joe and Norman Charles we were ready to go. Leonard still had this idea that we were going to make a run for it in the van; I think that was part of the same crazy state of mind that made him yell like that at Joanna LeDeaux."

I mentioned the account of S.A. Dean Hughes, in which the Indian who was hit was apparently wearing a white shirt; this seemed to confirm what some people had said, that Joe Stuntz had never put on that FBI jacket in which the agents said they found him. Yet the FOIA documents include reports from at least three people who saw him wearing it before he died. One of these people, accompanied by a deputy sheriff, had "gone up on a butte to observe the firefight":

> About 2:30 P.M. he saw an Indian in a green jacket killed. The Indian in the jacket and another man in a white T-shirt were shooting toward an area where he knows that Bureau of Indian Affairs officers were located at the time. The man in the green jacket was firing what he believes was an automatic weapon. When he was struck, this man dropped immediately to the ground. . . . The man in the white T-shirt dropped his own weapon, picked up the automatic weapon, and left the scene. He said he understands the FBI recovered a shoulder weapon by the dead Indian but said this is not the weapon the man was actually using.

On July 3, an unnamed Indian who lived near the Jumping Bull property informed the agents that he had been mending fence on the morning of June 26 when he heard "quite a lot of shots," both shotgun and rifle or pistol; when he left to go check on his family, "he could hear a voice yelling for help, sounds like a scream. This voice was vague and appeared to be quite a long way off, coming from the direction of the gunshot sounds." Subsequently he led some (unidentified) lawmen to "a hill . . . across from the shooting scene where he could see a man in a white T-shirt and another in a dark-colored coat standing by a green shack. Both of these men were shooting at something. As he watched, he saw the man in the dark-colored coat go down. He is not sure whether the second man was shot or if he knelt down to check on the man on the ground."

"Joe put that jacket on," Bob said. "Him and Norman Charles come down after the shooting. Norman found that rifle clip they took off him the day before, and Joe took that jacket."

("I seen Joe when he pulled it out of the trunk and I looked at him when he put it on, and he gave me a smile," Leonard remembers. "I didn't think nothing about it at the time; all I could think of was, We got to get *out* of here! And you have to know Joe: he wasn't smiling because he picked up the jacket, he was *always* smiling. You look at Joe, and he'll smile at you—that's the way he was, especially with me, because I was always joking with him, wisecracking." Remembering Joe Stuntz, Leonard smiled himself. "You would have loved him if you could have gotten any words out of him. Joe was a very gentle guy." Asked why they had taken the agents' guns and why they had never gotten rid of them, Leonard stopped smiling. "We took them because we didn't have real weapons," he said, "and it never occurred to us to get rid of them because it never occurred to us that we might be taken alive.")

It was Norman Charles who was wearing a white shirt that day, and who probably dove down when he was shot at, making BIA Officer Gerald Hill think he had hit him. The Indians do not believe that Hill killed Joe; they believe he was killed by S.A. Gerard Waring, drilled through the forehead by the only man in Hughes's squad with a sniper scope, and that the FBI gave Hill credit for the kill—he boasted of it to Gary Adams—because, from a public-relations point of view, it looked better to have that Indian killed by an Indian.

We walked along the grassy slopes west of the old fields on the plateau which have not been planted since the elder Jumping Bulls moved away; along this bluff the Long Visitors had fled, and Jimmy Zimmerman, hands high, had first been spotted from the highway. Off to the northeast was a high white butte, called Onogazi, or "Last Stand," according to Sam Moves Camp, who came down the hill to join us: Onogazi had been the refuge of Red Cloud's people, who retreated up there, fearing the worst, after news came of the massacre at Wounded Knee.

We were going back to Pine Ridge [from Wounded Knee], because we thought there was peace back home; but it was not so. While we were gone, there was a fight around the Agency, and our people had all gone away.... We crossed White Clay Creek and ... soon we could hear many guns going off. So we struck west, following a ridge to where the fight was. It was close to the Mission, and there are many bullets in the Mission yet....

While we were over at the Mission Fight, they had fled to the O-ona-gazhee and were camped on top of it where the women and children would be safe from soldiers. . . . Afraid-of-His-Horses came over from Pine Ridge to make peace with Red Cloud, who was with us there.

Our party wanted to go out and fight anyway, but Red Cloud made a speech to us something like this: "Brothers, this is a very hard winter. The women and children are starving and freezing. If this were summer, I would say to keep on fighting to the end. But we cannot do this. We must think of the women and children and that it is very bad for them. So we must make peace and I will see that nobody is hurt by the soldiers."

The people agreed to this, for it was true. So we broke camp next day and went down from the O-ona-gazhee to Pine Ridge, and many, many Lakotas were already there. . . .

I did not know then how much was ended. When I look back now from this high hill of my old age, I can still see the butchered women and children lying heaped and scattered all along the crooked gulch as plain as when I saw them with eyes still young. And I can see that something else died there in the bloody mud, and was buried in the blizzard. A people's dream died there. It was a beautiful dream.

And I, to whom so great a vision was given in my youth,—you see me now a pitiful old man who has done nothing, for the nation's hoop is broken and scattered. There is no center any longer, and the sacred tree is dead. [Black Elk]

At a grassy knoll just at the wood edge, the slope falls off steeply to the cottonwood flats along the creek. "Here's where I left that car," Robideau said over his shoulder, and kept on going down into the woods. In the cool shade of the big cottonwoods, in long fresh grass, he uncovered the old hearths where Dino's tipi and the cooking fire had been located. Sam Moves Camp offered us a handful of wild currants and showed me a plant called "kidney tea," good for the stomach; wild grape and poison ivy grew where sunlight pierced the heavy leaves of summer. By the creek bank was the stone circle where the small sweat lodge had stood; the skeletal lodge frame of cottonwood saplings, splayed and sagging, had been almost reclaimed by underbrush and humus. Across the creek, the wood margin was narrow, letting in sunlight from the fields that ascended gradually toward the school road.

Along the creek the pale clay mud was crisscrossed by the sharp prints of raccoons, and near the water was a tree gnawed long ago by beaver. I told Sam about the big footsteps in the creek heard on the night before the shoot-out by Jean Bordeaux and Jimmy Zimmerman and Norman Brown, and he nodded, saying, "That was a sign, a warning."

"There is your Big Man standing there, ever waiting, ever present, like the coming of a new day," Pete Catches had told me two years earlier, here on Pine Ridge. "He is both spirit *and* real being"— he had slapped the iron of his cot for emphasis—"but he can also glide through the forest, like a moose with big antlers, as if the trees weren't there. At Little Eagle, all those people came, and they went out with rifles and long scopes, and they couldn't see him, but all those other people at the bonfire, he came up close to them, they smelled him, heard him breathing; and when they tried to get too close, he went away. He didn't harm no one; I know him as my brother. I wanted to live over there at Little Eagle, go out by myself where he was last seen, and come in contact with him. I want him to touch me, just a touch, a blessing, something I could bring home to my sons and grandchildren, that I was there, that I approached him, and he touched me.

"It doesn't matter what you call him; he has many names. I call him Brother, Ci-e, and that's what the Old People would call him, too. We know that he was here with us for a long time; we are fortunate to see him in our generation. We may not see him again for many many generations. But he will come back, just when the next Ice Age comes into being."

On our return, Bob paused at the top of the hill, hands in hip pockets, and gazed around the Jumping Bull land, as if there were something he could not quite remember. Then he shrugged his shoulders and walked on. "At the Black Hills Survival Gathering last summer, we seen some of them people who were here that day. They just nodded to us, and kept on moving—didn't want to stop and talk about old times. Nobody talks about it much, even me and Dino, and that's probably best—only particular incidents, if there was something funny about it that we didn't understand. Maybe it's distasteful to us, or maybe because there is no *need* to talk. We were there, we seen it, we done what we had to do—why talk about it?"

When the work was finished, the women changed into fresh clothes, and everyone went over to the gravesite, which lies a few miles down the road on Wallace Little's property, overlooking the Little ranch in the valley below. From here there is no sign at all of the "bunkers" discovered by the FBI investigators in early June 1975. ("The Black Elk family had a burial up there along about that time," June Little says, shrugging contemptuously, "and that fresh grave was probably what them feds was looking at.") As the mourners gathered, a fast-food wagon pulled in among the cars to sell the Indians a few sticks of water ice in the dry heat; the glistening confection came in patriotic colors, a hard chemical red-white-and-blue.

The previous day, a fence had been erected, setting off the AIM warriors' graves from those of the Little family. Roslynn Jumping Bull said that the remains of Little Joe and Anna Mae would probably be moved to the Jumping Bull land, where the community felt that they belonged. "We'll have to talk to the medicine men first, of course, because it has to be done right," she said; the medicine man Billy Good Voice Elk, who had buried Anna Mae and assisted at Joe's burial as well, would be here today. A good-natured person who likes to laugh, Mrs. Jumping Bull regrets all her angry words when the place was ruined and her family harassed by the U.S. government after Oglala, and like almost everyone in this community, she feels grateful to the young AIM Indians who stood up for the local people on that day.

"Joe was a real good person," Jean Bordeaux sighed, "the same way Anna Mae was a good person, and Tina Trudell; they gave everything to everyone and never asked questions, never complained, as if taking care of other people was what they were there for. It's funny how people like that are always the ones to get killed."

Bare to the waist, his feather-tipped braids bound with ribbons of red and blue—the red of the day and the blue of *skan*, the sky—

Steve Robideau welcomed the people, and Billy Good Voice Elk gave a ceremonial invocation in Lakota. With three other Lakota singers, long black hair blowing against the white bluffs of the Badlands, the medicine man commenced a sad high chanting song to the hard pound of the Plains drum, while Robideau made the ritual purification, taking the sacred pipe from its rack before the ceremonial fire and lifting it to the blue sky in the four directions. In the midday sun, in the good scent of dried cow dung and fresh grass, the transparent flame of the small fire made the green earth around it dance and shimmer, as a meadowlark sent its sliver of sweet song down the south wind. The wind quickened the red, black, white, and yellow flags at the corners of the graves, and the green flag that honored the earth Mother: the red flag represents the east, and the sun rising, and the spirit of day; the black flag is west, land of big mountains and dark weather and the sacred rain, of evening and darkness and the spirit of death; the yellow is south, the warm soft winds, the warmth that brings growth and harvest; and the white is north, the home of the giant Waziya, whose icy breath brings cold and death, and the purifying snows that turn the autumn browns to green again when the land awakens in the spring.

> O You, sacred power of the place where the sun goes down, where we shall journey when that day comes to us. . . .

> Hee-ay-hay-ee, Tunkashila, Wakan Tanka, Grandfather, Great Spirit! Give to our people your red and blue days, that they may walk the sacred path in a *wakan* manner!

> O You, Grandmother and Mother Earth from which we have come, You are *wakan*, nourishing all things, and with You we are all relations. [Adapted from *The Sacred Pipe*, Joseph E. Brown, ed.]

Robideau spoke of the sacrifices made by Joe and Anna Mae, and also by Dallas Thundershield and Bobby Garcia, who had paid with their lives for trying to help Leonard, and also by the family of John Trudell. He offered the latest news of Leonard and Dino, who sent greetings from prison,* and told of the fight against uranium contamination of their land and life by the Dine nation in the U.S. and the Dene in Canada, of the Six Nations people and many others now struggling for sovereignty, and of the support that Indian peoples of the Americas were receiving in the tribunals and world courts of Europe; and he spoke of the patience needed by reborn Indians such as himself, who were "lost in the cities and want to come back home."

John Trudell also talked about those Indians who had wandered away from their people's traditions and from the healing spirit and power of the earth. Moving restlessly, lifting his hands, he exhorted the gathering to give up the greed of the white man's way that had corrupted them, and return to the spirit of sharing and self-sacrifice that Joe and Anna Mae had died for. He warned the people of the ten years of trouble that were sure to come, trouble of the kind that their grandparents had known, because "this government is our enemy. It is owned by the moneymakers, and they don't care about us, and that is the reality. They want to assassinate us; they did it to our ancient ones, and they are doing it again today by different methods. If we are to continue to survive, to endure, we must keep our spirit connection to our people who came before us; in this earth is where our power lies.

"The next generation, their spirit will be more strongly connected to the earth than ours. Many of us were lost out there; we made many mistakes, we became dependent on the white-man poisons, alcohol and chemicals, and it weakened our spirit power. But our little ones, they will have their power with them. This is what we want the young ones to understand; we do not engage with the U.S. government over ownership of land, because 'owning' land is white-man talk and white-man values; we engage with the U.S. government over the natural creation. We are a part of the natural world, and the white Americans are the enemies of the natural world."

Across from me in the circle of silent Indians stood a white woman named Candy Hamilton, a friend of Anna Mae and, for a

---

*In March 1982 Dino Butler was sentenced to four years in Canada's prisons; it is believed that Oregon will seek his extradition sometime in 1983.

time, a permanent WKLDOC aide on the reservation, where she has good friends; Candy had come all the way from North Carolina for this occasion, and as Trudell spoke of the white enemies, I wondered what she might be thinking. Earlier I had mentioned to Bob Robideau how disturbing it was to feel oneself—as I did at times—part of an unwanted and despised group, not just a stranger but an intruder, a *wasicu*, even an "enemy," and we had agreed that if all white people were exposed to this experience, race problems in America might diminish quickly. "White people just can't handle being disliked," Bob said, and burst out laughing.

Nilak Butler, dressed in a long skirt, was offering a message from Dino, which concluded:

June 26, 1975, was the day I became a red man. It was the day that truth was born in my mind and heart, uniting me with my spirit and the spirits of all our ancestors. It was the day I learned about life without death. There was no fear in me for the first time in my life, and I knew I could never die, for the fear of death no longer limited my perception of life, which is everlasting. That is what my brother Joseph taught me that day, and I know he has not been lost in the past but awaits me in the future.

I know that I can continue on no matter what burden I must carry. I will always stand with honor and dignity in the dust of my ancestors upon Mother Earth amongst my people—all people. I shall never be defeated by our enemy—that is my freedom. That is what Annie Mae taught me.

We must always fight for what we believe in. We must never tire in our fight. It does not really matter how we fight, what matters is what we are fighting for. It is our right to live: that is our first right. That is why we fight for our unborn, for it is through them that our nations live on. If we have to shed blood for them—the unborn—it is only right. As it was right on June 26, 1975.

Despite her rough talk and fierce squint, Nilak is gentle, easily moved; though her voice never faltered, she was flushed with emotion as she finished reading and strode away from the sacred fire with her head high. She is "a brave-hearted woman," as the Lakota say, and a generous one. "I wish I could do some of Leonard's time for him," says Nilak wistfully, "I really do. And a lot of people feel that way, because he really stood up for us that day."

Cecelia Jumping Bull, now nearly eighty, came to the fire in a blue shawl and print dress and black laced shoes. Standing straight and still, the old lady spoke strongly to her people in their native tongue, which not all of them understood; her words were translated by Melvin Blacksmith, who told me later, "I am Grandma's son in the Indian way." Mrs. Jumping Bull thanked everyone for coming from so far to honor Little Joe and Anna Mae. "Six years ago, these boys lived on my land. I used to talk to them every day, especially their leader, Leonard, warning them that they must be very careful." The old lady described her return from Gordon, Nebraska, on that summer evening just six years before, how young girls at the roadblock up the way toward home had told her and Grandpa that their house had been shot up, and how, arriving at the ruined house, they had found a big crowd of armed white men "standing around the body of Little Joe in three circles like you are standing now. I became angry. My thoughts went back to World War Two, when my son got killed for America, got killed for these people who ruined my house and killed this boy. When the ambulance came to take him away, I told them he had died for his people, and they treated me roughly. . . . I have a right to be proud because I took care of these boys. I'm getting old now, and when I am gone, I hope that the people here today, and the AIM people, will bury me, and honor me." In this way, the old woman talked for a long time in the soft harmonies of her language, standing stone-still without once shifting her feet, hands folded on her breast as she gazed outward toward the high white monument of Onogazi, on the southern rampart of the Badlands.

In another quadrant of the circle, Bob Robideau stood beside the mother of his son. We met each other's gaze without expression. Although respected here, he had not spoken to the gathering, and somehow I felt certain he would not.

Earlier that afternoon, he had nodded toward a high ravine in the white hills to the northeast, where dark green pines, black in the summer sun, rose to a point on the blue Dakota sky. "That's where old Noah Wounded's cabin was. Back up in there, maybe an hour's walk. When I come in, Leonard was sitting there with the old man, and he says, Noah wants a picture of a buffalo; can you do it? Because Leonard knows I've been drawing since I was five. So I looked at that old man a minute. Then I said I could, and he gives me an old raggedy piece of paper and a broke-up pencil, and I made the picture. Old Noah's dead now; I often wonder what he did with it." Bob paused to consider his words carefully, making absolutely certain that I understood. "You see, I didn't do that buffalo picture just because he *wanted* it. I did it because I realized that that buffalo was very significant to that old man in some old-time way."

# ALSO BY PETER MATTHIESSEN

## AFRICAN SILENCES

A powerful and sobering account of the cataclysmic depredation of the African landscape and its wildlife. Through Peter Matthiessen's eyes we see elephants, white rhinos, gorillas, and other endangered creatures of the wild, we share the drama of his journeys, and, along the way, we learn of the human lives oppressed by bankrupt political regimes and economies.

Current Events/Travel/0-679-73102-4

## FAR TORTUGA

"*Far Tortuga* is a singular experience, a series of moments captured whole and rendered with a clarity that quickens the blood. . . . From its opening moment . . . the reader senses that the narrative itself is the recapitulation of a cosmic process, as though the author had sought to link his storytelling with the eye of creation."                —*The New York Times Book Review*

Literature/0-394-75667-3

## KILLING MISTER WATSON

*Killing Mister Watson* is a fictional masterpiece, the first novel of the Watson trilogy, written at the peak of Peter Matthiessen's powers as a novelist. Drawn from fragments of historical fact, it brilliantly depicts the fortunes and misfortunes of Edgar J. Watson, a real-life entrepreneur and outlaw who appeared in the lawless Florida Everglades around the turn of the century.

Fiction/Literature/0-679-73405-8

## LOST MAN'S RIVER

In the second volume of the Watson trilogy, Lucius Watson tries to discover the truth of his father's life and death while braving the threats of moonshiners, poachers, and renegades in the Florida Everglades. Beautifully composed and filled with the eerie splendor of an endangered world and the voices of its people, *Lost Man's River* is a drama of fathers and sons, land and rapacity, murder, honor, and revenge.

Fiction/Literature/0-679-73564-X